The Claims of Kinfolk

The John Hope Franklin Series in African American History and Culture

WALDO E. MARTIN JR. AND PATRICIA SULLIVAN, EDITORS

The Claims

of Kinfolk

African American
Property and
Community in the
Nineteenth-Century
South

Dylan C. Penningroth

The University of North Carolina Press

Chapel Hill and London

Designed by April Leidig-Higgins
Set in New Baskerville by Copperline Book Services

The paper in this book meets the guidelines for
permanence and durability of the Committee on
Production Guidelines for Book Longevity of the
Council on Library Resources.

Library of Congress Cataloging-in-Publication Data
Penningroth, Dylan C.
The claims of kinfolk: African American property
and community in the nineteenth-century South /
Dylan C. Penningroth.
p. cm.—(The John Hope Franklin series in African
American history and culture)
Includes bibliographical references and index.
ISBN 0-8078-2797-5 (cloth: alk. paper)
ISBN 0-8078-5476-x (pbk.: alk. paper)
1. African Americans—Southern States—
Economic conditions—19th century. 2. African
Americans—Southern States—Social conditions
—19th century. 3. African Americans—Land
tenure—Southern States—History—19th century. 4. Slaves—Southern States—Economic
conditions—19th century. 5. Slaves—Southern
States—Family relationships—History—19th
century. 6. Property—Southern States—History—
19th century. 7. Southern States—Economic
conditions—19th century. 8. Southern States—
Social conditions—19th century. 9. Slaves—
Emanicpation—Ghana—History—19th century.
10. Property—Ghana—History—19th century.
I. Title. II. Series.
E185.8 .P39 2003
333.33'5'08996073075—dc21   2003000212

cloth   07 06 05 04 03 5 4 3 2 1
paper   07 06 05 04 03 5 4 3 2 1

Portions of this work appeared, in somewhat different form, in Dylan Penningroth, "Slavery, Freedom, and Social Claims to Property," *Journal of
American History* 84, no. 2 (Sept. 1997): 405–35
(reprinted by permission).

To my family,
who showed me
what it is all about,
and the memory of
my uncle Craig

Contents

Illustrations, Maps, and Figure

. . . .

MAPS

FIGURE

Kinship and the Slaves' Economy
from Slavery to Freedom

• •

My name is Pompey Bacon. I was born in Liberty County, Georgia, I am 70 years of age I am farming and the claimant in this case." With this statement Bacon, a former slave of plantation owner Thomas Mallard, claimed compensation for property he had owned as a slave, property Union soldiers had taken for "forage" on a raid during the Civil War. With him on this late summer day in 1873 were Bacon's wife, Bellu, his older brother, Joseph, and three other freedpeople from farms near the one he worked; all intended to serve as his witnesses.[1] Except for Mrs. Bacon, each had a petition before the Southern Claims Commission. Under oath, Bacon unfolded his story of the raid in response to a long list of standardized questions read by Virgil Hillyer, a special commissioner of the federal commission.

During the siege of Savannah in December 1864, Judson Kilpatrick's cavalry, part of General William T. Sherman's army, was ordered to forage supplies. Most white people had fled the countryside near Savannah, with Sherman's westerners hard on their heels. The troops arrived at Thomas Mallard's plantation just after harvest, when mornings turned the earth "white with frost." Liberty County was a rich agricultural area, and 1864 had been a good year for food crops. Hogs were "in good flesh" in December, when the business of butchering and salting began in earnest. Pompey Bacon remembered that the marauding Union soldiers "said they never got provision until they got to Liberty Co. among the colored people." Bacon gladly welcomed them; he later told the claims agent that "after the Union Army came into the county I did all I could in the way of cooking and feeding the poor soldiers. One poor fellow came to me almost naked. I gave him my own hat, clothed and fed him." Bacon reported that such generosity "was a common thing at that time for the Colored people to do; we thought of nothing then but our own freedom and those who made us free." Bacon's brother Joseph, who had watched cavalrymen feed his bountiful 1864 crop to their worn-out horses, told Hillyer that "it seemed to us as if the 'Lord has blessed the earth on purpose to help our deliverer.' "[2]

But the foraging parties turned deliverance into a plague of confiscation. A claimant recalled that the soldiers descended "like a hungry wolf & thick as sand-flies" on the grand mansions and slave cabins alike. The "poor soldiers" who freed Pompey Bacon also stripped him of nearly everything he owned. "The soldiers did not say anything," Bacon recalled of the men who crowded into his yard, "only [that] they were in need of the property & would have it." They stuffed his corn into sacks made out of his bed sheets and his wife's underclothing. They took his wagon and shot down his hogs in his yard and carried them off slung across his horse. "We all rushed there to see what was done," said another ex-slave who witnessed the raid on the Mallard plantation, "& we were so scared we went in gangs." All across Liberty County black people rushed to and fro watching gangs of soldiers take property from their friends and relatives, then from their own homes. Kilpatrick's men "were all over the plantation," an ex-slave from the nearby Winn plantation concluded; "every nigger[']s house was full of them."[3]

Some slaves found an officer in the crowd and made a futile protest. "'Massa' you going to take all, & leave me nothing to live on," pleaded Samuel Elliott. The soldier replied: "We are obliged to, we come to set you free, & we must have something to eat, but you must go to '*Uncle Sam*.' Uncle Sam's pockets drag on the ground." Soldiers told Paris James that "they had the law to take meat & bread &c wherever they saw it." James complained and got a receipt from an officer, but other troopers tore it up in his face and went on taking what they wanted. Where the army went the laws of property were suspended or ignored. James recalled the soldiers telling the slaves that "wherever we saw them & wherever their horses made their track that was free ground & that they had to eat as they went along." After three weeks Kilpatrick's cavalry marched away, but then, said Bacon, "the rebels came in and took every little thing the Yankees left." Bacon found himself "naked as

FORAGERS "STARTING OUT" IN THE MORNING.

Union general Judson Kilpatrick's operations in Georgia. During the last year of the Civil War, *Harper's* published numerous accounts of foraging by Union and Confederate soldiers. This drawing appeared in the April 1, 1865, issue (*Harper's Illustrated Weekly*, April 1, 1865, p. 204).

FORAGERS RETURNING TO CAMP AT NIGHT.

General Kilpatrick's men returning to camp. This drawing suggests that not all confiscated items were "army supplies" and hints that such property circulated among the troops and perhaps among local whites (from *Harper's Illustrated Weekly*, April 1, 1865, p. 204).

a bird" after two huge and barely disciplined armies had rampaged through the plantations and villages of Liberty County. He and many other slaves entered freedom ruined as property owners.[4]

Across the South, Union troops not only devoured slaves' property, they also smashed a long-standing system of compromises between masters and slaves that had enabled slaves to own property. Some masters offered to accommodate "to their little matters of property," thinking that this would entice their slaves to join them as they "refugeed" deeper into the Confederacy.[5] But when the Union army drew near, slaves fled the plantations, with or without their property. At a government-run "contraband" camp near Washington, D.C., one master was allowed behind Union lines to talk privately with slaves who had run away from his plantation. "He argued with them and plead with them," a bystander remembered, "saying 'Havent you had your pig? and dident I let you go to meeting? and now will you let your poor master go back alone?'" But the contrabands "did not want to talk with their master at all," and in the end, "he did not convince one of them."[6] Few people gave up the chance for freedom, whatever their privileges as slaves.

However, although freedom outweighed property for most slaves, property still mattered to them. "Many have been laying up their money for months, preparing to leave their masters," noticed observers in Tennessee.[7] And when slaves ran for freedom, they tried to carry along their property, often at great risk. An officer who helped liberate "contrabands" in western Missouri in 1861–62 testified in 1863 that he "was often troubled, when in a hurry to get them away from localities" filled with Confederate "guerrillas, by their desire to get away what little property they had around them."[8] To army officers caught in the crashing chaos of battle it was "almost provoking to see the way in which they [the slaves] cling to their blankets, feather beds, chickens, pigs, and such like. But this is to be expected—these things represent the net result of all their labors up to this time."[9] A few brave people tried to make the soldiers stop their foraging. "Well, my wife was a very fractious woman," remembered Alabamian Jackson Daniel, somewhat ruefully, "and when she saw them taking her meal, she objected to it and they talked about slaying of her, see, I just told her to hush and say nothing and it would be best for us."[10] Freedom may have outweighed property in the minds of slaves, but African Americans knew that they would need property all the more after they were free.

But many of the people who fled the plantations lost whatever property they managed to carry with them at the gates of the contraband camps.[11] Witnesses from posts throughout the Tennessee District and elsewhere reported that "contrabands" were bringing in horses, mules, wagons, cotton, oxen, and other property, and that the army confiscated and used these items.[12] And once slaves were inside army lines, Union soldiers continued to plunder their property. "From the moment the contraband lands within our lines and gets any money he is the victim of fraud and robbery," testified D. B. Nichols, the superintendent of a camp at Washington, D.C. The army quickly put the freedpeople to work, but "[t]he money is got away from them one way or another and they generally bring none [of their pay] back. They work hard but their wages are all taken for board, cooking utensils &c."[13]

Moreover, these camps would not replace the things slaves left behind. The camps were supposed to provide rations for the freedpeople, but sometimes rations were never delivered. Edward Pierce, an officer in South Carolina, thought it was ironic for the army to strip slaves of their property, throw them onto charity, and then lose their rations in the bureaucracy. "It required no *red tape* to take the corn" from the slaves, he pointed out, "but it requires red tape to distribute rations" to the freedpeople.[14] Soon, some contrabands began asking for armed escorts to fetch property that they had "left . . . on the m[ainland]" in their hurry to get away.[15] With nothing more than emergency food and clothing forthcoming from the Union government, the contrabands were largely thrown back onto their own resources and the charity of other black people.[16]

Thus, for many of those who had grown up in slavery, the long-awaited day of jubilee mixed joy with disappointment. "I was pleased enough at the taking of the town," remembered Benjamin S. Turner, who watched Union troops liberate Selma, Alabama, "and rejoiced until they took everything I had, and then I got mad."[17]

By 1873, when Pompey Bacon had his hearing in Riceboro, ex-slaves had been waiting nine years for the government to compensate them for the property they had lost. During the Union raids, many had asked officers for vouchers, clearly intending to request reimbursement once they had an opportunity. The opportunity they had waited for came in 1871, when agents of the new Southern Claims Commission fanned out across the South to hear claims from Unionist southerners who had lost "stores or supplies . . . taken or furnished for the use of the [Union] army" during the Civil War.[18] But the commission originally sought to compensate white Unionist southerners. Few northerners thought that slaves had been disloyal, but even fewer imagined that slaves could have owned property. Indeed, General William T. Sherman, whose foragers had "raised hell" for Pompey Bacon and countless other southerners, believed that "[t]he clothing & effects of a negro are the property of the master."[19]

Yet Pompey Bacon and nearly five hundred other former slaves came forward, filed claims, and were awarded compensation for property they had owned while they were slaves. In their testimony about cows, corn, wagons, and other possessions, former slaves spoke about much more than simply the amounts and types of property they had owned. They revealed a complicated world of social relationships among African Americans, relationships that overlapped but were largely apart from those they had with whites and the formal institutions of the South. Part of the reason slaves "cl[u]ng to their blankets . . . chickens, pigs, and such like" was that these things were tangled in the same threads that tied the slaves to each other.

This book is about family, community, and property among African Americans: what they meant, how they were made, and how they changed between the last decades of slavery and the early years of freedom. It tries to explain how people who were legally considered to *be* property were able to earn and *own* property; it analyzes the social networks in which black people were involved and the compromises they struck over the years with masters, neighboring whites, government agents, and especially with other black people.

Between 1800 and 1880, an extralegal economy took shape in the South and was challenged and eventually molded anew. That system of property ownership and trade scarcely registered on the statute books but it went on in yards, cities, and back roads across the South; it was part of the fabric of southern society. While white people tolerated and often joined in it, black families and communities provided the muscle, the watchful eyes, and the social pressures that made the system work. In turn, property ownership and the special efforts it demanded from slaves put an unmistakable dynamism into their social ties, stretching and bending the lines of blood and marriage. Throughout the 1800s, black people were constantly negotiating with one another over family and community—who belonged, and what it meant to belong.

THE WORLD OF SLAVE PROPERTY ownership and independent economic activity was barely visible to scholars until fairly recently. In the last twenty years, historians have studied property accumulation by slaves, documenting its existence across the Caribbean, Brazil, and parts of the U.S. South. In these places, they argue, a significant "informal economy" existed within the more formal institution of slavery, one that allowed slaves to accumulate, own, and trade property among themselves and with white people.[20]

But what did it mean for slaves to own property? Were slaves "entrepreneurs," as a recent newspaper article put it?[21] Or did their holding of property reflect traditional African beliefs and values, a piece of African culture that survived the stormy Middle Passage? Since southern laws were against them, did they really "own" anything? It is hard to appreciate the implications of slaves owning property because the "slaves' economy" is still seen as a special case, confined to the narrow band of coastal South Carolina and Georgia known as the Low Country, where a unique combination of widespread slaveowner absenteeism and a labor system organized by "tasks" came together to create "particularly favorable conditions" for an informal economy. Even there, scholars insist, the informal economy was tiny compared with what South American and Caribbean slaves had.[22]

Historians have interpreted both the slaves' economy and the history of black families and communities using two long-standing themes in African American history—the "dialectic" of accommodation and resistance and the debate over cultural "survivals" and acculturation, themes that are sometimes fused into a framework of "cultural adaptation and resistance."[23] Under the searing heat of slavery and other forms of racial oppression, they show, African Americans created institutions and practices—families, religion, and, in some places, an informal economy—that helped them resist their oppression and carve out "a measure of autonomy."[24] Masters tolerated, even encouraged, these things because it suited their interests.[25] Within this semiautonomous space that masters left them, slaves drew on their family and community relationships for help in acquiring and accumulating property. Independent economic activity fostered a sense of pride, "communal solidarity, and personal responsibility" that helped blacks resist the oppression of slavery and foreshadowed their responses to emancipation.[26] For African Americans, it is argued, there were few distinctions between family and community;[27] the slave quarter was, as one recent study argues, "virtually one extended family."[28] Some scholars, convinced that concepts of ownership were "alien" to supposedly communal African societies, argue that the slaves' economy was part of the acculturation process by which Africans became African Americans.[29] Property ownership brought black culture closer to the individualism and nuclear family structure of European Americans, values and practices that better prepared blacks for the new modalities of freedom than did the old "community" of the slave quarters.

Framing "the black community" and the "slaves' economy" within the master-slave relationship reveals one complex world of struggle under slavery, but it also shifts attention away from viewing black people's lives on their own terms.[30] Moreover, the acculturation view of slaves' economic behavior rests on four questionable but not uncommon assumptions: that all Africans had the same clear system of values about property in the 1700s; that this system was "communal" rather than individualistic; that slaves brought it through the Middle Passage; and that, over time, their values shifted toward the more American ethos of acquisitive individualism. Studies of many dif-

ferent parts of Africa from the seventeenth through the twentieth centuries
suggest that American historians should be careful in using a single character-
ization of "traditional Africa" as a baseline for sketching changes in cultural
values among African Americans.[31] There is another drawback to concentrating on white-black relations: it makes it hard to look clearly at relations
between blacks.[32] There is no reason to think that the black community in
the 1800s was any more harmonious than the white community, or any more
"egalitarian" than it is today. And yet our understandings of nineteenth-
century black life are grounded in just such assumptions.[33] Developed in
part to explore how slaves helped shape their own lives, the resistance framework's focus on conflict between the races, especially the master-slave relationship, tends to obscure or even romanticize the experiences of black people, whose understanding of economic and social life involved far more
than their relations with white people. Understanding black life in the 1800s
may mean looking outside the assumptions and interpretive frameworks of
American history altogether. African Studies, for example, can enrich the
way we think about African American history, not only through arguments
about cultural "survivals" but also through carefully limited comparisons
and new intellectual frameworks.

Africa had thriving systems of slavery for a thousand years, from at least
the 800s until the late 1800s. During the roughly four hundred years of the
Atlantic slave trade, some twelve million people stepped onto European slave
ships, while millions more stayed behind as slaves within Africa, most of them
women and girls. From the 1600s to the early 1800s, there were as many slaves
in Africa as there were in the New World. After about 1850, Africa's slave
population actually outnumbered North America's.[34] From the perspective
of world history, slavery in Africa was not unusual; slavery has flourished on
every inhabited continent, and it is still alive today.[35] And yet slavery in many
African societies was different from the plantation slavery of the New World.

Unlike American historians, who agree that slavery was defined in terms
of property rights and designed to produce commodities, most African historians argue that slavery was defined as the absence of kin.[36] In many parts
of Africa, kinship was central to people's lives because, among other things,
it defined crucial parts of their identities and rights. It was also flexible
enough to take in a wide range of relationships, from mothers and brothers
to distant grand-nephews and people with no blood ties at all, such as slaves.
Slavery stripped away a person's kin ties and fastened them onto his or her
new master's lineage (that is to say, extended families, who counted their
membership either matrilineally or patrilineally). Lineages wanted slaves

for two reasons: first, because slaves would work, and second, because, unlike the free-born, who had uncles and parents to claim them, a slave child belonged completely to the lineage that owned his or her parents.[37] As a result, while many slaves were captured during wars and taken far away from their families, others lived out their servitude very near where they were born. For them, kinlessness was not so much a literal fact as a socially accepted way to denote an extremely unequal relationship. Slaves could live near their blood relatives and yet be outside their arms of protection, cut off from all the rights of family membership. The economics and ideology of kinship didn't necessarily make slavery "milder" in Africa than in the Americas, but they did make it different. Thus, although Fantes and African Americans were both black, they were very different people living different lives. That is why the first chapter of this book is about southern Ghana. The point here is not to follow black culture from Africa to America but rather to compare two stories that unfolded at about the same time. It is exactly because these two groups of black folk were different that they make a historically important comparison.

If we read Pompey Bacon's words through the prism of African Studies, everything—the black family, the slave community, their relations with white people, even property—looks different. In many parts of Africa, being one of the family is not necessarily a fixed fact of birth or marriage; often it is something to be talked about, argued over, or hidden away. As much as people pride themselves on belonging, on knowing who their relatives are, family is often about useful indeterminacy. And because it was possible to be both a slave and a member of the family at the same time, a close look at slavery in Africa opens up a way to see power, property, and conflict in a place where it is usually hard for a historian to see much of anything— inside people's homes. In other words, the claims of kinfolk involved both people's use of social networks to claim property and the often powerful claims that social networks exerted on people. Finally, because the end of slavery in Africa came hand in hand with colonial rule, it brought questions and conflicts between African and European legal systems, much like those that Pompey Bacon faced at his hearing. In both the Gold Coast and the U.S. South, emancipation meant more than freeing slaves. It also meant taking widely recognized but unwritten rules about property, marriage, work, and family and adapting them to the framework of Anglo-American law. For these reasons, this book draws insights from scholarship on Africa and applies them to the study of African American history. Studying how slaves acquired, held, traded, borrowed, and talked about property opens new possibilities for African and African American history, both because it illuminates the struggles between masters and slaves and because it reveals how slaves negotiated over power and resources among themselves.

STUDYING THE LIVES of slaves has sometimes been difficult to do because there are very few places where one can read their words directly. Yet evidence of the ownership of property by slaves is everywhere—from antislavery narratives by fugitive slaves to travelers' accounts from England and the North, from the docket books of county courts in the 1820s to the case files of a federal compensation commission in the 1870s. Strikingly, when white southerners happened to mention their dealings with enslaved property owners, they did it matter-of-factly, almost without comment. This book brings forward three kinds of testimony about property, relatively underused by historians, recorded directly from slaves and former slaves in Ghana and the U.S. South.

The records of the Southern Claims Commission, held at the National Archives in Washington, D.C., contain testimony from thousands of claimants and witnesses, providing evidence about property ownership among slaves across the South and the practices, understandings, and kin ties that made such ownership possible. Of the more than 22,000 claims filed before the commission, about 5,000 of the "allowed claims" (those that won some amount of compensation) have been preserved with their testimony. Nearly 500 of these were filed by former slaves. This book concentrates on roughly half of those, mostly from Mississippi, Alabama, upcountry South Carolina, and Georgia.[38] The claims records say little about the huge chunks of the South where Union armies did not go foraging, and claimants probably downplayed aspects of property that would not help in winning compensation, such as disputes over ownership. But other sources corroborate and deepen the analysis, including fugitive slave narratives, travelers' accounts, the memoirs of former masters, and archaeologists' reports. While these sources do not concentrate on property in the way that the Southern Claims records do, they are peppered with information about property and kinship during slavery.

Military courts, county courts, and colonial courts left behind rich records of life after slavery. I have read more than 600 court cases from the National Archives of Ghana at Accra; the National Archives of the United States; and county archives in Virginia, North Carolina, and Mississippi.[39] Each case has anywhere from one paragraph to several pages of testimony. Of course, as rich as these records are, they do not tell everything we might want to know about life after slavery. For one thing, the courts that wrote them had very limited jurisdictions. Litigants in disputes may have minimized or neglected certain facts in their testimony before the courts, or emphasized others. Other people avoided going to court in the first place. Still, these court cases give voice to many of Fantes' and African Americans' concerns about property and kinship, permitting us to hear their words directly and broadening our understanding of what it was like to drop the chains of slavery.

The chapters that follow mine these sources for testimony by slaves and former slaves. Chapter 1 is a case study of southern Gold Coast, West Africa (today's Ghana), from the 1860s to the 1920s. Underlying my approach to African American history are perspectives from African history and anthropology, and this chapter makes them explicit. Chapters 2 and 3 explore kinship and property during slavery in the United States, reconstructing the networks of black-black social relationships that enabled slaves to accumulate property, moving outward to explore the meaning of ownership, and analyzing how those relationships made it possible for slaves to assert property claims that even their masters respected. Chapters 4, 5, and 6 explore what it meant for African Americans when, in the years following emancipation, the law finally recognized their families and their right to own property.

The book tells two stories. One is about property. It focuses on the limits of law alone to define what property was, who owned it, and even what ownership meant. By investigating the role of social relationships in creating property and making ownership possible, this story illuminates how people experienced property in their daily lives, how white and black rural people's understandings of property contrasted with legal principles, and what happened when the two systems of understanding collided. As historians of colonialism in Africa have shown, such collisions rarely wiped out the old systems; instead, they added layers of complexity to the always-changing relationship between state and society. The other story is about family and community. Many of us know an aunt or cousin who is not "really" related but who helped raise us when we were little, who shows up at family reunions, who talks, acts, and is considered one of the family. Drawing on the insights of African Studies, this book argues that if social ties helped "make" property, property was one of the things that "made" social ties. As a result, while the ending of slavery marked a new chapter in the master-slave relationship, it also touched off negotiations and even conflicts over the claims of kinfolk, over how black people were going to relate to each other in the new world of freedom.

There is an old American tradition of seizing on black people's disputes with each other in order to put down blacks as a people.[40] Any book that analyzes social change and conflict among African Americans can end up being used against African Americans. Social statistics from the nineteenth century are hard to come by, but it is safe to say that black people argued, cursed, loved, and nursed one another about as much as whites did. Always, there was the stifling blanket of white supremacy, and the soul-provoking tedium of grinding out a living in a society that was designed to keep African Americans "in their place." That struggle between whites and blacks is a key part of this story. But to make it the center of the analysis would make this a different book.

Studying negotiations over kinship, labor, and property among African Americans makes possible a richer understanding of slavery, and of the changes that freedom brought. Combining concepts advanced in recent scholarship on the Americas, the Caribbean, and Africa, this book proposes a new framework for analyzing the connection between people's social relationships and their interests in property. Rather than assess American blacks' claims to property as examples of cultural change or resistance, this book concentrates on those informal understandings and practices themselves: how they were created, how they worked, and how they changed between 1800 and 1880. A whole world of social relationships and negotiations lay behind the fact that slaves owned property. That world begins to come into focus if, instead of asking, "Whose corn was it?" we pose the more fruitful question, "How did people know whose corn it was?"

chapter one

One of the Family?

*Abolition and Social Claims to Property in
the Gold Coast, West Africa, 1868–1930*

. . . .

O n a hot December day in 1874, one year after Pompey Bacon's hearing before the Southern Claims Commission and exactly twelve years after the soldiers set him free, slavery officially ended in the West African city-states of Fante. Only a keen observer, though, could have marked the day as anything special, for there was no exodus, no angry revolts, no flooding of freedom lawsuits into the courts. Just as in many other parts of Africa, thousands of slaves greeted the official, legal end of slavery by staying right where they were.[1] From the perspective of American history, where freedom is defined in terms of individual autonomy, this fact raises difficult questions. Why didn't enslaved Africans quit and strike out on their own when Britain proclaimed that slavery was over?

Many historians and anthropologists agree that slavery in Africa was (and often still is) defined as an absence of kin. Slaves were viewed as kinless outsiders who were gradually assimilated into society by being absorbed into the family that owned them. During that process of kin incorporation, slaves were subject to forced labor and an array of social handicaps until they or their children finally became full-fledged members of the family. So it went, in principle. Yet, however slavery was defined, people experienced slavery in

SLAVERY-
ABSENCE
OF
KIN

many different ways, and, in practice, the kin incorporation commonly associated with slavery was not automatic. Some slaves became assimilated in their own lifetimes, while for others assimilation came only to their children or grandchildren, and many seemed destined to remain outsiders forever. During the seventeenth, eighteenth, and nineteenth centuries, African states expelled millions of slaves across the Atlantic and Sahara, rather than absorb them. Pompey Bacon was descended from one of those kinless outsiders. Millions of other slaves stayed in Africa and were incorporated into kin groups very slowly, or not at all.[2]

Slavery in Africa knit together claims of ownership with claims of kinship, two of the most mundane yet pervasive realities of everyday life. And though colonialism and independence mostly stamped out slavery, they did not unravel the knot of kinship and property that slavery depended on. Over the past 150 years, people have used a variety of processes to make their claims, including both the formal laws associated with Europeans and the "customary" processes associated with "tribes" and lineage groups.[3] Today, though slavery is gone, rights to resources are still bound up with social relationships, especially relations of kinship. Indeed, in Ghana today, "slave origins" are still used to exclude certain people from family property and other kin-based rights.[4] Such evidence suggests that, if we want to know what slavery and emancipation meant in Africa, the answers may not lie in waves of mass migration or national emergencies but in the small-scale negotiations that went on every day within ordinary households and communities.

This chapter plumbs those small-scale negotiations to investigate emancipation in southern Ghana: how it affected the meaning of property, how it created new definitions for slavery and buried old ones, and how it redefined what it meant to be one of the family. It focuses on cases in the colonial courts (now held in Accra at the National Archives of Ghana) from the 1860s through the 1920s, cases that pitted Akan people trying to make their way out of slavery against the Akan families who owned them. In their testimony about disputed inheritances, trespass, and other property "wrongs," Fantes (an Akan group) revealed a whole landscape of assumptions about property, slavery, and family—a landscape that was rumbling beneath their feet even as they spoke. Fantes thought of slaves simultaneously as economic assets and as junior kin—inferior members of the family. For that reason, the official ending of slavery in 1874 touched off negotiations and even infighting within nearly every household in the country, activity that often centered on property.

Why include the story of Gold Coast emancipation in a book that is mainly about African Americans? After all, the Gold Coast had a very different economy, cultural background, and political structure from Alabama or Georgia. One reason is that the Gold Coast and the American South faced remarkably similar circumstances at about the same time. Both regions had age-old traditions of slavery, which ended only when an outside power came in. Both faced a new regime of formal law, permeated with British legal traditions and administered by men who were outsiders to the region. Never in his life did the judicial assessor at the Cape Coast High Court meet a Southern Claims Commissioner, but both men shared many basic assumptions about property, family, and the role of law in society. Both men, moreover, were part of massive efforts during the mid-1800s to remake the ideas and legal systems of societies they viewed as backward and primitive. From their first days on the job, the two men would have confronted people who thought about property less in terms of individual, exclusive ownership than in terms of social relationships. While formal institutions and law carried weight in these postemancipation struggles, they did so in ways that were decisively shaped by informal understandings and ongoing negotiations. Thus, as ex-slaves sought to widen their claims of ownership, as their old masters scrambled to shore up their traditional powers, and as federal and British colonial officials tried to extend the reach of formal institutions, everyone had to adjust their conceptions of what property was and what slavery had been, and what it had meant to be one of the family.

The second reason for including Gold Coast in this book is to look outside the assumptions and interpretive frameworks of American history. What happened in Africa in these years did not make much difference in the lives of black southerners; many parts of African cultures lived on in the 1870s in the Americas, but those carryovers had arrived at least a hundred years earlier. Instead of suggesting cultural "survivals," beginning our story here, during the "slow death" of slavery in Africa, makes clear the perspectives on family, community, and property that frame this book as a whole.[5] As paradoxical as it seems in the American context, instead of walking away from the institutions that had given force to their bondage—family, property, and tradition—ex-slaves tried to participate more fully in them, and thus reshape those institutions in their own interests.[6] The ending of slavery in Fante helped transform both kinship and property because Akan slavery was rooted in the idea of claiming kin *as* property.

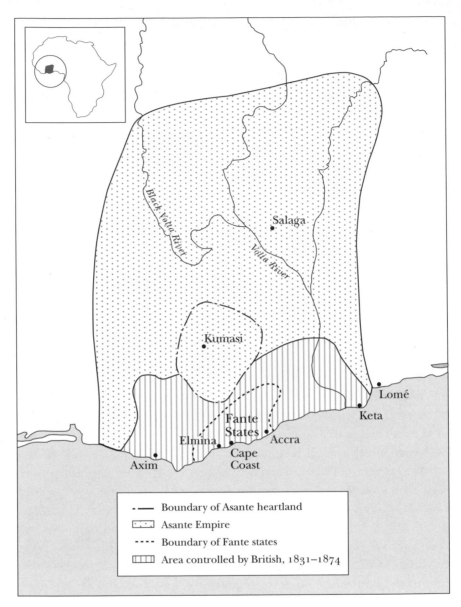

The Fante Region, Gold Coast, West Africa, mid-1800s

THE TOWNS OF Cape Coast and Elmina sat on the southward-facing Atlantic coast of West Africa, in what is now Ghana. Most residents of these towns spoke Fante, one of the Akan languages, and had long-standing cultural and political ties to the rich and powerful empire of Asante, just to the north. In those days, a person coming from offshore would see wide, bright beaches ribboned before a low treeline. If it was near dawn, there would be dozens of long, narrow fishing boats slicing through the heavy surf, each with a crew of paddlers, tools, nets, and its sides painted with the symbols of its *asafo* company. Inland from the "shrubby" lowlands near the coastal towns, the land turned to forest, dotted with the reddish upturned soil of small farms.[7] Beginning in 1481, the Fante towns also carried on a thriving trade with Portuguese, Dutch, French, and British commercial firms. Like so many nations along the coast of West Africa, the Fante permitted these European firms to build a string of stone forts, or "castles," along the shore. These forts encouraged and protected the business interests of both the Fante and the Europeans; they turned this region of fishing villages into a vital hub for global commerce. For more than four hundred years, the Fante acted as cultural and commercial brokers between their European trading partners on the coast and their sometime allies, the Asante.

The Fante region was a mixing bowl in the 1800s; its people came from many different backgrounds, spoke different languages, and swore allegiance to different sovereigns. Of the 15,000 people who lived in Elmina in 1830, most were free citizens of the Fante states and their slaves, but there was also an Asante community of about a thousand, led by a diplomatic "resident" who was appointed from Kumase, the capital of Asante. City streets thronged with Ga and Ewe people from towns farther east, with Jamaicans, Krus from Liberia, and various Muslim peoples, who the British ignorantly lumped together under the catch-all term "Hausas."[8] A tiny group of white people and people of mixed African and European descent staffed the government buildings and ran businesses in the towns.[9] During Britain's 1873–74 war against the Asante, the Cape Coast fort, only a few miles down the beach from Elmina, housed white British soldiers on its middle floor and black West Indian soldiers below.[10] Missionaries from Switzerland and England began building Christian churches and schools in the 1830s and occasionally got themselves tangled up in quasi-diplomatic mediation between the Asante, the Fante, and the Europeans. Ambitious Fante merchants began sending children to the missionary schools, and by the 1860s a distinct and visible Akan group emerged: western-educated, employed in a burgeoning colonial economy, and intensely connected to the culture and politics of Fante.[11]

Two views of Cape Coast Castle from along the rocky shore (top) and from town (from *Gold Coast: Photographs of Scenery, Natives, Buildings and Industries, 1901*, and *Gold Coast General Views, 1887*, respectively, courtesy of the Foreign and Commonwealth Office Library, London).

"Carriers going along beach (between Saltpond & Accra)," 1901. This photograph depicts one important use of enslaved people in Fante in the eighteenth and nineteenth centuries. Its 1901 date suggests that the colonial economy still depended partly on porters even after 1874, when slavery was legally abolished (from *Gold Coast: Photographs of Scenery, Natives, Buildings and Industries, 1901*, courtesy of the Foreign and Commonwealth Office Library, London).

Slavery played an important role in the economy of the Fante and Asante regions. Like Natchez, Charleston, and Richmond, these coastal towns of Cape Coast and Elmina contained wealthy groups and many slaves, but the grandees of the Fante region earned their riches as market brokers rather than as plantation owners. In the 1700s the Atlantic slave trade poured incredible wealth through Fante and helped turn Asante into the famous "kingdom of gold" we know today. After Britain outlawed the slave trade in 1807, the towns switched to trading raw and manufactured goods such as gold, cloth, and, later, palm oil. The new law said nothing about slavery itself, and so until the late 1800s, much of the new, so-called legitimate commerce among the coastal states, Asante, and the northern states was carried on the heads and shoulders of slave porters.[12] Although in the 1810s and 1820s some Afro-Europeans tried to start large-scale coffee and cotton plantations with as many as two hundred slaves,[13] the Fante region never became a plantation slave society.

Still, slaves and slavery affected nearly every part of Fante society. It is likely that slaves made up a hefty share of the region's population of about 500,000 during the early 1800s, though a much smaller proportion than those of the Caribbean, Brazil, and the Low Country United States.[14] If the experience of its neighbor, Asante, is any indication, the proportion of slaves in the coastal region's population probably swelled between 1810 and 1820. It was in those years that Britain began enforcing a ban on slave trading in the Atlantic, cutting off the stream of slaves out of West Africa.[15]

Instead of working in cotton fields for overseers, Gold Coast slaves were farmers, fishermen, and artisans; others worked as "professional canoemen and carriers, brokers or middlemen, including gold-takers, itinerant traders or peddlers and 'servants' in the European castles and forts."[16] Most slaves in Fante and Asante lived in small units at a family farm or urban business. As in many other regions of precolonial Africa, large numbers of Fante and Asante people from different social classes had slaves. Nobles and commoners, women and men, even slaves relied on slaves to do many different kinds of work. It was not unusual for free men to marry enslaved women, partly because the men could control them and their labor much more than they could control freeborn wives, whose families could protect them. It is likely that free women also benefited from such marriages, because the labor of enslaved "junior wives" released many free wives from working in fields and house, and enabled some free wives to set up as traders.[17] Slaves were part of life for a wide range of people.

Like slaves, property in Fante was enmeshed in networks of social ties. Testimony in cases from the colonial courts suggests that by the mid-1800s, most property in Fante, including slaves, was subject to claims of ownership from many different people. Property could belong either to individuals, to the state, or to lineages. Like black American farmers in the 1900s who doggedly fought to keep "heirs' property" in the family, these lineages could block the sale of land that they considered family property, and anyone who wanted to sell or grant rights usually found it prudent to consult with at least someone from the lineage that owned the land. Even the putative owners of land often did not have an unencumbered right to dispose of it. In one case, a landowner who had allowed a woman to live on his land "sent and asked" her to let another person live on it. Even though the land was his and the woman was merely an occupant at his discretion, she "refused and said she would wait till she was advised by her relations."[18] People tended to be careful about handling land because the right to be consulted was itself an indication of ownership, and some land cases hinged on whether settlers had consulted the correct people. Being a chief or lineage head did not lessen

"Grinding Corn." A rare view inside a southern Akan home. There is no way to
know these women's status. However, this was the kind of work most slaves in
Fante did: tedious, daily, and tightly linked to "domestic" places and needs (from
Gold Coast General Views, 1887, courtesy of the Foreign and Commonwealth Office
Library, London)

the need to take account of multiple claims on property. For example, one
group of people went to court to block the head of their lineage from selling land because it was "family land." "By the custom of the country," they argued in court, "it was necessary to let the family know of it."[19] This family did
not necessarily frown on selling the land. Property was not owned commu-
nally, and land sales were not unknown in precolonial Gold Coast. Rather,
the issue at stake was the family's right to be consulted before any decision
was made about its property. Even a family member's ability to give seemingly outright gifts was contingent on his satisfying various competing claims,
and the gifts could be changed or even taken back later if some relatives insisted that they should have been consulted and were not. An outsider's perspective is instructive: a Jamaican immigrant who married a woman from
Cape Coast found to his chagrin that he did not have exclusive rights over
his own house and farm. His mother-in-law claimed it, and, he complained
to the court, "it seems as though on that account every member of her family thinks he may do what he likes on the land."[20]

Part of the reason property was so complicated and contingent in nineteenth-century Akan society was the ubiquitous presence of slavery. A per-

son's right to claim property usually depended on where she stood in her kin group, and according to the prevailing ideology, slaves had no kin. Even though some enslaved people never left the region or ethnic group in which they were born,[21] slaves had to give up their own kin identities and were viewed as having been absorbed into the lineage group that owned them. These presumptions about slavery and kinship had an enormous influence on nearly everyone's claims to property. Defining slaves as metaphoric "orphans" gave masters sweeping rights over everything the slaves possessed: their belongings, their muscles, and their children. Slavery, with its presumptive absence of kin, stripped slaves of their claims to family property and reassigned those claims to masters. By the same token, masters and their relatives recognized and acknowledged their slaves in daily life as members of the family. Polite people rarely talked about where these assimilated outsiders had come from, a reluctance captured in the maxim: "*Obi nkyerɛ obi ase*" (no one reveals the origins of another). In the 1700s, the *Asantehene* (king of Asante) even enshrined this maxim as law.[22] But during moments when property and kin group leadership were at stake, long-hidden slave roots were often dragged out into a cold, brutal light. In 1869, for example, one woman lamented, "After the [funeral] custom Defendant took all my brother's property, slaves and pawns and when I asked him what right he had to take them away, he told me that I am a daughter of one of [his] slaves."[23]

Testimony in colonial court cases suggests that slavery stirred up ambiguities and complications within the formal laws of property, both British and Akan. During the decades before abolition, formal legal and political institutions treated slaves as a limited, somewhat ambiguous category of property. Although Britain banned slave trading in 1807, it was perfectly legal to own slaves in Britain's African colonies for almost the rest of the century, until 1874. However, because slaves could not legally be sold under British law after 1807—now and then a British Court would prosecute people for "slave dealing"—they lacked one of the key ingredients of property. In some ways, Akan law through the early 1800s also viewed slaves as property, as indicated by the thousands of slaves sold into the Atlantic slave trade. The practice of pawning offers more evidence. People in the Fante region who needed money, land, and labor to get through a crisis sometimes got it by placing their relatives in pawn, a form of servitude that was supposedly temporary and different from slavery.[24] Even in ordinary times, for those who could not afford to own slaves outright, pawning was a way to get more workers or raise cash. Yet pawns and slaves were different from a goat or a bag of yams; they were more than just property. In principle (though often not in practice), pawns were not actually sold but merely placed in someone's house as "collateral," and they could be redeemed at any time.[25] Even slaves, who *were* sold, were supposed to be absorbed into their masters' families. Both Akan and British laws recognized that people could be property, but they also set limits that greatly complicated that notion.

Not even the law could provide a conclusive definition of property, because legal jurisdiction was so complicated in Gold Coast. For more than 300 years, European courts and laws governed property roughly within cannon-shot of the fortified "castles." These courts did not pretend that they had any jurisdiction beyond that, either to ban slavery (illegal in British territory since 1834) or anything else.[26] For the vast majority of Fante people, property was governed by African laws, which kept pace with the baroque pageant of West African politics. In the 1820s, however, Britain began to carve out a larger presence, and, as its jurisdiction grew, increasing numbers of Africans came before its courts. The British decided that, rather than eliminate chiefs and precolonial legal systems, Africans should be governed according to their own customs and laws, so long as they could "mould th[ose] customs . . . to the general principles of British law."[27] They formalized this pattern in an 1844 "Bond" with the Fante chiefs. In essence, British officials tried to create a double judicial system, with separate rules for "natives" and "Europeans."

Several things prevented this tidy ideal of separate legal systems from becoming reality. Intermarriage between Europeans and Africans and between Africans of different nations raised sticky questions about which set of laws and customs should determine inheritance. Hauling Africans into court for violating the laws against "slave-dealing" meant imposing an ostensibly "foreign" law onto "native customs." And, increasingly, educated Euro-Africans like John Mensah Sarbah sat on juries and served as lawyers before British judges; their complex interests and cultural perspectives began to mold a new set of rules, which eventually became known as "customary law."[28] By the 1850s the Fante region's two judicial systems, officially separate, were in practice becoming more and more interdependent and even mixed.[29] Officially, the British courts had jurisdiction only over British citizens and dealt only in English law, but in practice they also judged many Africans and Afro-Europeans, and British judges often based their decisions on what they knew about the laws of African societies. In 1853, when Britain established a new supreme court system for the Gold Coast, it institutionalized this mixed legal system by providing for a "native assessor" (usually a chief) to sit beside the British justices as an expert on African "customary law."[30] This was a legal atmosphere ripe with possibilities for people determined enough to go to a court or savvy enough to become an "expert." Britain built its trading-post empire on a distinction between British and native institutions—the political ancestor to the indirect rule of full colonialism. That distinction made legal definitions of property extremely complicated, contingent on which of two legal systems—officially separate but hopelessly mixed together—did the defining.

If slavery shaped the meaning of property, it also left deep marks on kinship. Slavery deprived people of the family identities with which they were born and stripped them of all rights to their blood relatives' labor and property. At the same time, slavery also gave slaves a new kin identity, one that came with its own obligations and rights. Once purchased and brought to live in a household, slaves were viewed as members of their masters' families: inferior, but with potentially strong claims. Slaves and pawns were able to inherit among themselves.[31] More important, by the logic of kin incorporation, slaves could also inherit the property of their masters' families. If a slave wife converted to Christianity she might insist that she was the only "real" wife and claim all the household property when her husband died.[32] Some slaves even became the heads of their masters' lineages, so that people like Adjuah Abamba wound up having to sue their own family slaves to recover what they felt was their own royal stool (a lineage's leading political office). The "d[e]f[endan]t was placed on the stool," Abamba testified, because "there was no grown up person in the [master's] family, and defts Mother having been bought as a slave and he [the defendant] was born in the house."[33] Whether succession to a family stool changed a slave's status was a matter of dispute, especially in the years after emancipation. "Slaves are often headmen," explained witness Quow Quotah, but "[t]he fact of a slave being made a head man does not alter his status he does not become free." Of a slave who had inherited a stool near his own home, Quotah said, "I do not know whether he was a proper chief."[34] For many slaves it was enough, for now, simply to be a chief, "proper" or not. Thus, in Fante, not all slaves equated freedom with breaking away from the people who owned them. In fact, slaves often had an interest in affirming and acknowledging their slave status, precisely because that status gave them a kin link to a rich family and a claim to its property.

During the decades before abolition, then, the understandings and practices of slavery profoundly shaped the meaning of both kinship and property in Fante. Property was often tangled in a network of kin ties, and one's rights to property frequently depended on where one stood in one's kin group. Slavery broke, reassigned, and invented kin ties and thus lay near the very heart of the processes that defined kinship and property for all Akan people, not just the slaves.

THE MID-1800s was a time of dramatic changes for the people of the Fante region. First, along with many other parts of West Africa, southern Gold Coast's economy boomed from the 1860s to the 1900s, surging on the "legitimate commerce" that put coffee, soap (from palm oil), and chocolate (from cocoa) on nearly every shelf in Europe.[35] The central market in Cape Coast attracted more than 2,000 people on weekdays—mostly women and girls— trading everything from "Manchester cloth" to "native fish" and vegetables.[36] New government buildings went up beside the old forts, and while European and African elites moved into stately two-story residences, the towns' swelling poor populations crowded into thatched-roof houses or went homeless altogether.[37] By 1891, there were 11,600 people in Cape Coast, twice as many as at midcentury.[38] And most of the land around the coastal towns was claimed by royal stools or prominent families.[39] As a result, the demand for land in coastal towns throughout West Africa intensified in the 1860s and 1870s, making land transfers more frequent and more likely to be contested.[40] Second, during the 1850s and 1860s Britain's trading-post empire blossomed into colonial rule, and British magistrates began to extend their jurisdiction beyond their centuries-old boundaries near the European-held forts. Britain invaded Asante in 1873–74, burned Kumasi, and formally declared itself ruler of the entire Fante region in 1874. The new Gold Coast Colony established a system of district commissioners and supreme courts in 1876.[41] Village chiefs and heads of families continued to mediate disputes, but people increasingly had the option to take their problems to the colonial courts. At the same time, growing connections between people of different ethnic groups—often through marriage—brought together a whole range of different assumptions about family and property.[42]

Third, late in 1874, as its first official act, the newly established Gold Coast Colony passed an ordinance abolishing slavery. This ordinance, like those for Britain's colonies in Nigeria, abolished only slavery's legal status and was not accompanied by any forceful effort to set slaves free. The new law tried to surgically excise slavery and pawnship without disturbing any other dependent relationships in its new colony. "[I]t is not intended," the ordinance read, "to offer inducement to any persons to leave any master in whose ser-

"Commerical Strasse, Cape Coast Castle, Westafrika." By the early 1900s, the colonial government had moved out of Cape Coast, but new buildings, sewers, and streets combined to make the town's land and houses economically valuable (courtesy African Postcard Collection, Manuscripts and Archives, Yale University Library).

vice they may be desirous of remaining, or to forsake the krooms [home-steads] where they have been accustomed to inhabit, and that it is intended to permit the family and tribal relations to continue in all respects according as used and wont, except only that of slavery and such customs as arise therefrom and are thereon necessarily dependent."[43] Like their American counterparts, British officials worried that a sudden emancipation would throw their African colonies into economic chaos, creating thousands of homeless, lazy freedpeople and draining money from the British treasury. These officials designed abolition policies they believed would keep slaves "in place while at the same time diminishing slavery as a viable institution."[44] They were relieved to see that their 1874 Abolition Ordinance did not spark a revolt or mass migration among slaves. Most of the thousands of enslaved people in southern Gold Coast stayed where they were and did not even take advantage of the newly established court system to sue for their freedom.[45] Many Britons and some wealthy Afro-Europeans interpreted this quiet as a sign that Africa's "domestic slavery" was so mild that it did not really amount to slavery at all.[46]

Taken together, these developments loosed a flood of contentious lawsuits and searching intellectual debates over property and family.[47] Importantly, many of the property disputes that followed emancipation pitted slaves

"Colonial Hospital, Cape Coast (Residence of Sir Garnet Wolseley when administrator of the Gold Coast in 1874." The 1874 Abolition Ordinance was promulgated
from this building in Cape Coast. Wolseley was responsible for enforcing its provisions (from *Photographs of Sir William Maxwell's Tour of the Hinterland of the Gold
Coast, 1897*, courtesy of the Foreign and Commonwealth Office Library, London).

against masters and former slaves against former slaveowners and their descendants. British governors had long assumed that slavery played some role
in virtually "any [court] case in which property is concerned."[48] One official
interpreted the 1874 abolition law as "releasing slaves from the obligation of
service to their master," without "destroy[ing] their rights against him and
his estate."[49] By affirming that slaves had a "right . . . as against his master, to
private property,"[50] colonial officers permitted slaves to carry their visions of
Akan slavery—and its kin-incorporation ideology—right into colonial courts.
Kinship and property, the same two institutions that had long formed the
basis of Akan slavery, now held out the promise of freedom. Although most
disputes probably never reached the colonial courts, the cases that did get
there between 1874 and the 1920s offer glimpses into the often fierce struggles between ex-masters and ex-slaves over who owned what—and whom.
The long arguments over family identity and property ownership were part
of a widespread, momentous, and yet shadowed battle over the meaning of
freedom.

The legal system that Britain set up in the Gold Coast Colony in the 1870s

"District Commissioner's residence, Akusi, Volta River." District commissioners held courts in buildings like this one in Akuse, a town east of Cape Coast. The laundry on the railing suggests that such courts sometimes doubled as living quarters (from *Photographs of Sir William Maxwell's Tour of the Hinterland of the Gold Coast, 1897*, courtesy of the Foreign and Commonwealth Office Library, London).

complemented and interlaced older processes and understandings of property from the time before abolition. Analysis of a sample of thirty-eight cases in various colonial courts in which one of the litigants or his or her ancestors was allegedly enslaved to the other litigant discloses that most ex-slaves precipitated disputes by doing something "wrong" outside of court, leaving ex-masters to pursue the matter in court. Twenty-five of such identifiable master-slave disputes were brought to court by ex-masters or their descendants. Ex-slaves probably were reluctant to confront their former masters in the courts, although that did not stop them from vigorously contesting claims to property. Rather than walk directly into a chiefly or colonial court, slaves tended to bring on a crisis by deliberately overstepping (or neglecting) the bounds of their social ties and their accompanying rights to resources.[51] Any such dispute threw into question rights that had been enjoyed for years and that often linked many people through a complex system of acknowledgments and permission.

Property disputes between ex-masters and ex-slaves began to change the meaning of kinship. Before 1874, masters had confidently gone to British courts to claim runaway slaves as property;[52] after 1874, they were more

The Supreme Court building in Cape Coast. Enslaved people who wanted to challenge masters' claims to property had to come to this forbidding fortress for a trial (from *Gold Coast General Views, 1887*, courtesy of the Foreign and Commonwealth Office Library, London).

likely to claim property *from* their former slaves, often in ways that drew upon the long-standing notion that a slave was one of the family. In court, some masters affirmed kin ties, speaking of their former slaves as their children and claiming that these so-called children did not really own the property they occupied. Quacoe Abban sued a man named Sago for falsely claiming ownership of a house and land near Cape Coast. Because Sago was the nephew of one of Abban's pawns, Abban claimed him as "a slave born in the house." Sago "was my slave and lived in the house after the abolition of slavery," Abban testified. "I considered him as my son and we lived together in this house." But Sago retorted that he had never been Abban's slave and that the house belonged to him, not Abban. Sago admitted that his uncle had "pawned himself," but he insisted that his uncle never went to live on Abban's land. "He continued to live in his own house. . . . I am living there now and Abban wants me to go out."[53] By describing Sago as "my son" and as "a slave born in the house," Abban argued that both Sago and the house in which Sago lived belonged to him: a double claim of ownership.

Other ex-masters sailed right into the winds of change: they grabbed hold of potentially vulnerable pieces of property by cutting their ties with their former slaves. After 1874, some ex-masters began to argue that if emancipation had ended masters' rights over their slaves, it must also have ended slaves' rights to family property. Quamina Attah, whose ancestor had owned an ancestor of Quamina Sam, went to court to evict Sam and his household. "Since abolition of slavery I notified defendants to quit the land," Attah testified. "This action [was] brought because they would not leave the land."[54] The government's own assistant secretary for native affairs, a member of an old Afro-European slaveowning family, found himself in the delicious position of writing official memoranda on "the Vestiges of Domestic Slavery" while simultaneously fighting a court case that hinged on that very same issue. Not surprisingly, he told his superiors that slaves could not inherit family property: "If slavery is illegal the slave cannot legally be absorbed and therefore cannot become a member of the family."[55] For former slaveowners and their descendants, the end of slavery was an opportunity to clarify (or perhaps redraw) the boundaries of their families, often at the expense of old family slaves.

For their part, some ex-slaves believed that emancipation had *not* cut them off from their masters' families and that they still had rights to family property. Many ex-slaves chose to build ties to the families that used to own them, even if it meant affirming their slave origins. By exercising some right that the master did not think they possessed, pawns and slaves challenged masters to acknowledge the implications of slaves' kin membership. "I permitted him to build a house," complained one ex-master, "and I showed him a part of the land where he might work for his living. I gave these to him that he might remain on the property." Now this former slave "does not permit me to take any vegetables from the land. [H]e has taken the whole of the land and has turned me out of it."[56] This was probably unusual, but no exaggeration: even after abolition, the principle of slavery as kin incorporation was still a potent weapon for ex-slaves to claim property. Another slave, Kobina Kwansah, took advantage of the abolition ordinance to switch his kin affiliation: he left the family of his master and rejoined his birth family —and took the stool and part of his master's family property with him. Kwansah's former master, J. D. Taylor, protested that emancipation gave ex-slaves nothing more than the right to "go free, but in this they want to take the master's own family property which their grandmothers met in the family house along with them and change the tribal name to be their own. . . . And this I object [to] entirely. They are no more slaves to me and my family and have no right to take my tribal stool and all the properties in connection."[57] Slaves may have had certain rights to property that they "met" as they joined the "family house," but ex-masters like Taylor argued that emancipation terminated those property rights at the same moment that it broke the family bond between slave and master. From the viewpoint of slaveowners, slaves were part of the family only in a carefully limited sense, and only so long as they were slaves. With land prices climbing in towns like Cape Coast, ex-slaves and ex-masters alike found it convenient to ignore the old maxim *obi nkyerɛ obi ase*. Disputes over property in the years after "legal status abolition" helped change the meaning of kinship in Fante society because many former slaves asserted rights to property owned by their masters and based those claims on the old dictum that a slave was one of the family.

Colonial officials, who believed that the typical "native slave" was "regarded as a member of the family,"[58] inadvertently strengthened the links among slavery, property, and family by urging slaves and slaveowners to settle their disputes "as a family" matter.[59] In passing judgments on property, colonial courts often relied on testimony about slave origins, even though slavery itself had been outlawed. Between the 1870s and the 1900s, many people appeared in court armed with complicated genealogies to prove that they, and not their opponents, were the legitimate successors to family property. In his dispute with a descendant of one of his family's slaves, J. D. Taylor sent an elaborate genealogy to the secretary of native affairs to prove his "ancestral right" to a certain stool, lands, and house.[60] Litigants accused of slave ancestry countered with accusations of their own, laying out alternative genealogies that pointed out their opponent's own slave ancestry.[61] Guided by the native assessors, colonial courts tended to look away from other kinds of evidence to focus on these competing genealogies and the nature of the relationship between the plaintiff and the defendant. In January 1883, more than eight years after slavery had officially ended, the High Court of Cape Coast paused halfway through a case of land and house and decided to confine the issue "to whether [the defendants] were slaves or not."[62] This decision was a symptom of the growing attention that both ordinary people and British judges were paying to issues of slave descent. Membership in the family had long been a prerequisite for inheriting many kinds of property, but in the 1870s and 1880s, as new laws began to codify "native customs" such as slavery and lineage descent, the boundaries of family took on a theoretical rigidity, and participation in certain family ceremonies, in turn, began to be used in British courts as proof of family membership.

Genealogy became a battleground. Many people argued their property claims by trying to establish distinct lines of descent, with slave and legitimate branches. Some people claimed it was easy to tell slaves apart. "I would have known if they were slaves," said plaintiff Quow Attah. "If Ordayain was a slave I would have known."[63] And nearly everyone paid close attention to accusations of slave ancestry. A defendant charged with murder argued that he had every right to shoot because the victim "called me son of a slave woman." "If death ensued it was from him he caused."[64] But often it was far from obvious who had and who had not been a slave, especially if the allegation was based on some distant ancestor. Confident statements such as Attah's belied how difficult it was to squeeze the shifting, leaky realities of the past into an airtight theoretical category called "the slave," let alone using this image of slavery as evidence in a courtroom.

How did one know a slave? Litigants and their witnesses had many different answers. British judges tended to ask questions about treatment: feeding, whippings, and especially whether people were paid for their work. "I thought that I was a slave," testified Abinah Mensah under cross-examination by the court, "because when I went for water or firewood I was not paid."[65] The litigants themselves asked other sorts of questions to determine slave ancestry. "Is it not customary that when a slave is purchased to change his name?" asked Abinabah Mansah of one witness. "And if so what was the name given to my aunt if she were a slave as has been alleged by defendant?"[66] African litigants also pointed to body markings, such as a shaved head, as evidence of slave ancestry and argued about whether customary law had reserved particular patterns of head-shaving for slaves. "Coesey did not leave any lock on her head," said one witness. "It was that she was a slave."[67] Such testimony in property disputes about the customs of slavery had the power to remap family boundaries, casting whole branches of descendants out of their kin groups and taking away their claims to family property.

A complex interplay of secrecy and openness about ancestry—especially slave ancestry—had long been part of politics and property claims in Fante and elsewhere in Africa. People skillfully deployed the power of spoken (and unspoken) words on a landscape rich with social significance. In the 1860s, standing in someone's yard and calling him "son of a slave woman" was grounds for a lawsuit in village council or colonial court; it could even get you killed, because having slave ancestry was enough to disqualify a person from inheriting property or becoming a chief.[68] As disputes moved into colonial courts, concerns about ancestral knowledge and slave origins went with them. Asked why he was suing a man who had called him a "Negro," Eccra Qwacoe replied: "Because it implied I was a slave."[69] One subchief wound up in court for sending back his *Omanhene*'s (chief's) messengers with the words: "Tell the man who sent [you] that he has no jurisdiction over me," and "that his grandmother was a slave."[70] Knowledge about ancestry was gender specific. When litigants told the court where they had learned facts about ancestry, the informants usually turned out to be women. "The land has belonged to defdts ancestors," testified one witness, "I learned this from my grandmother. She was defdts gdmother [grandmother?]."[71] A defendant named Samuel Watts went on the offensive in his land suit by describing relationships from before he was born. "I was born in 1818," he admitted, but "I was informed by my mother and her relations of the position of the plaintiff's family particularly that of the woman Abinabah Coesey."[72] Watts went on: "At that time old people did not like to show that some members of their families were slaves, and this was kept very private. . . . My mother did not wish to make it appear that Coesey [her cousin] was [also] her slave." Nevertheless, after emancipation, when Coesey attempted to claim a share of the family property, the polite silence ended and Watts sued her on the grounds of slave ancestry. The presence of slaves in people's family histories had long been sensitive matters, hushed but rarely forgotten. But in staking claims to the property of their masters' lineages, ex-slaves and their descendants pushed facts about slave ancestry into the open. The resulting disputes helped perpetuate slavery's influence on the meaning of property long after slavery officially ended.

Some litigants argued that knowing one's genealogy proved kin membership. In court, ex-masters sometimes leaned on their former slaves and pawns as witnesses, who were valuable precisely because they knew so much of the history of their former masters' families. Mary Wharton called Effuah Addray, one of her family's former pawns, to the stand in the Cape Coast High Court and demanded: "You lived in my family house[;] state what you know about it what you were told by the elderly people." And indeed Effuah Addray knew a great deal, not only about the history of the disputed property but also about her old master's family history.[73] Her testimony helped her former masters win their case and claim their property. However, ex-slaves and ex-pawns could also use their detailed knowledge of these genealogies to claim family property for themselves. Sometimes ex-slaves knew more about the history of their masters' families than the masters did, and that knowledge made them tough to beat in a colonial court. In 1909, for example, former slaveowner J. D. Taylor tried to leave his former slave Kobina Kwansah out of the family inheritance. But the *Omanhene* who heard the case pointed out that although Taylor was "a principal party in the Nsona family" and was spearheading their interests in court, he "could not know the spot on which his ancestor lived and died." Taylor and his family had been Kobina Kwansah's masters, but they "seem not to have known much about the stool, house and lands now in dispute," other than what Taylor's uncle had hastily told them "of the history of the descent of their family."[74] In the *Omanhene*'s view, the plaintiffs knew less about their family history than the man they were trying to exclude from the family property. Kobina Kwansah kept his share.

Funerals were another arena in which slavery's grip on the meaning of property was perpetuated. Courtroom testimony in inheritance disputes often focused on funerals, and well into the 1930s, having the right to perform funeral customs "was interpreted as a sign of legitimacy in stool succession disputes."[75] Ex-slaves' interest in funerals was a variant on a view that all Akan shared: what was at stake was not merely property rights but a place in the family. As Kwame Anthony Appiah points out, funerals in Ghana are largely about belonging: who gets to bury someone helps define claims to kinship and inheritance. Those claims affect a whole range of people even beyond those standing at the graveside—the living, the ancestors, and those yet to be born.[76] Funerals, and the payments that went with them, were important occasions for publicly marking the social relationships among people, and hence they were also opportunities to shape those relationships. Just as free settlers now and then sent vegetables to landowners to publicly acknowledge the limits of their land rights, so funerals became occasions for ex-slaves to affirm their kin membership and to assert claims to family property.[77] "*Abusua dɔ funu,*" goes an Akan proverb—the matriclan loves a corpse. In the years after abolition, stories about the corpses of ex-slaves came right into the Cape Coast courts.

People usually argued about two related aspects of funerals: the right to pay for and participate in the ceremonies of death and burial and the placement of the physical remains. They watched closely to see who paid for funerals and whether rum and other presents were accepted or not. Many witnesses believed that the right to help pay for the funeral indicated a kin tie to the deceased, a kin tie that entitled a person to take the property of the deceased. "I paid the late William Scott's funeral expense because he was my cousin," said Abinabah Mensah in 1877. "Had he been a slave then defendant's family would have gone to the expense."[78] A plaintiff in another case told the court that his opponent "refused the [offering of] custom and did not take it." The chief who first heard the case explained: "When a party refuses the custom it means he says he is not the successor."[79] Many people believed that the activities surrounding funerals betrayed clues about people's origins. If those origins included slave ancestors, they could be used to cut off living descendants from family property. As a result, many litigants drew out detailed testimony about long-ago funerals as evidence of their claims to property.

Even when people agreed that a payment had been offered and accepted, they sometimes argued over what it meant. In about 1881, a man named Quesi Ahouron suddenly died and his older brother, Cobbina Saccoom, who was living in a different town, made ready to claim his property. But Ahouron had been a slave, and his former masters claimed that the property belonged to them. In court, Saccoom described what happened when a messenger brought the news of Ahouron's death: "A woman called Encroomah who was present said to Aucho [another in the group] that perhaps [funeral] customs for him had commenced. I asked who was making custom: Aucho said Quamin Sam and Odookoom, and Defendant were making Customs. He added that on the way he had met my brother's coffin and perhaps he was already buried. I sent my son, Quessi Yaboah, with Aucho to inform the three men not to bury my brother and that I would come in the morning." Saccoom set out to attend the funeral, he went on, "but [even] before my son and Aucho arrived, the body had been buried. I went myself and saw defendant and his two brothers: they told me how my brother had died: they gave my men rum: I took none." Instead, Saccoom "asked what expenses had been incurred." The three men told him that they were going to pay for the various items bought for the funeral custom, and that "they (the brothers) would take my brother's property for the debt. I did not agree to this. I said to Odookoom [one of the brothers] that Quesi Ahouron was my brother, and I had to pay the balance."[80] But Amoanee retorted: "No, you are not our family . . . we don't know you."[81] One can only imagine Saccoom's chagrin when these former slaveowners told him that "Quesi Ahouron was my brother when alive but not when dead."[82] Amoanee and his family insisted that since Quesi Ahouron had been their slave, his property belonged to their family, and that Saccoom—his blood relative—was not really his brother. Although slavery was illegal, the Cape Coast High Court ruled in this and other cases during the 1870s and 1880s that "Native law" did give the descendants of slaveowners the right to seize family property from the descendants of slaves.[83] Years after the abolition ordinance, slavery continued to shape the meaning of property in southern Gold Coast, both in popular practice and in the formal law.

Where people were buried was sometimes as important as who buried them. It was popular for people to bury their relatives inside the grounds of their family house, and some masters had allowed settlers, slaves, or pawns to bury their relatives in the piece of ground they occupied. According to the cousin of one former master, it "[h]as been [the] practice of our family to allow a stranger who has been living in the house to be buried there." When the pawn who had lived in their house died, he "was buried under the floor by . . . his nephews."[84] Graves were important symbols of kinship and could literally be inserted into land in order to form the basis for a claim of ownership. The presence of a body in the land often carried powerful meanings for both property rights and family membership, but when the body belonged to a slave and the question was of slave ancestors, all bets were off. One woman accused the heir of her old family slave of "desecrating" the graves of her ancestors by digging out foundations for a new house; her opponent retorted that the workmen had dug up nothing but cow bones.[85] There were graves in the land, both sides admitted, and somebody's ancestors were buried in them, but it would take months or even years of negotiation to decide to which family they—and the land—belonged.[86] In cases such as this, both sides relied on testimony about burials and slave ancestry as proof of ownership.

Burial made the legal or social connection between the family and its property palpably real, but it did not put that connection beyond dispute. Instead, burials and the memory of burials became a focal point for debates over who had been a slave or pawn, who had enjoyed rights in the family property, who had participated in family ceremonies, and so on. In court, people argued in both directions: either that one wasn't a part of the family if one's relatives were not buried in the house, or that if one wasn't a part of the family, one did not have any rights in the family property. Testimony in property cases suggests that emancipation did not end slavery's power to shape property and kinship. But emancipation did change the ways in which people negotiated and thought about the ideology of slavery as kin incorporation, and what it implied for people's economic rights.

The constant lawsuits that Akan ex-slaves and ex-masters kept pressing in British courts after emancipation etched deep grooves in that hybrid legal system. As both property cases and testimony on custom mounted up on the dockets, the courts increasingly demanded a systematic statement of what had been (under native custom) the rules of succession between masters and slaves. In 1881, a lawyer for an ex-master suing to recover his property from his former slave crystallized the problem for the court: "Are the slave born children living with their master [since] the abolition [to] have any right to hold property [and] live independently[?]"[87] As it turned out, there was no easy answer. During the 1910s and 1920s, Britain formally enshrined its old dream of separating British from African law in an official policy it called "indirect rule": as much as possible, Britain would rule its African colonies through native authorities and govern by native custom. Unfortunately for these plans of efficient government, discerning exactly what native custom was, particularly on issues of property and slavery, proved very difficult. Losing "traditional" native institutions would undermine the cornerstone of British colonialism in Africa, but British officials were convinced that their very presence in Africa was making native custom a thing of the past and that many of the native institutions had "got so mixed up with English law, that they are now hopelessly muddled."[88]

British officials took three approaches to fighting this alleged drift into a cultural and legal "muddle." First, they gingerly avoided disturbing practices they thought were traditional. British officials in Cape Coast and elsewhere believed that the abolition ordinance carefully exempted any coercion that might arise from lawful "contracts of service between free persons," or any coercion "not being repugnant to the law of England" that might arise "out of the family and tribal relations customarily used and observed in the Colony."[89] Unfortunately for them, slavery was deeply rooted in tradition and tangled up with many other "tribal relations" that were still quite legal, such as property and family.

Second, largely in order to sort out the confusing history of Akan tradition, British officials increasingly seated Akan chiefs in British colonial courts as "native assessors" to act as expert witnesses on customary law. Native assessors had sat beside British magistrates in the Cape Coast court since the 1840s.[90] But as more and more Africans came to colonial courts to pursue cases that British officials considered to be matters of "customary law"— which included slavery, succession, inheritance, and witchcraft—it routinely deferred to its native assessors.[91] Indeed, as Lovejoy and Hogendorn point out, one reason British officials relied on native courts in the years after emancipation was that these courts had rules to govern slavery, whereas British law did not, except to abolish it.[92] Yet many Fante chiefs owned slaves themselves, and slavery had long played an important role in the politics of all the Akan states.[93] Nevertheless, courts relied on chiefs to distinguish slavery from "family and tribal relations,"[94] even as they steadily reduced the chiefs' power to make and enforce decisions on their own.[95]

Western-educated Afro-Europeans joined the fray, too. John Mensah Sarbah published two books on Fante "customary law." Others began vying to become chiefs, sparking competition over "traditional" political office and heated debates in the local newspapers about what "native custom" really

Gold Coast Legislative Council, 1919. Akan and British men made and administered the Gold Coast's legal system in a complex process of cultural and legal interaction dating back as far as the 1700s. Note the variety of dress among the Akan representatives (from *Gold Coast Photographs 1914–1930*, courtesy of the Foreign and Commonwealth Office Library, London).

was.[96] In their role as advisers in colonial courts, as well as in their other dealings with colonial administrators, chiefs helped define a past for tribes that courts could use in deciding property cases. Chiefs (some of whom were Western educated) increased their power by sculpting an image of custom that was fixed, systematic, and deeply rooted in the history of their region or "tribe." As chiefs presented colonial courts with definitions of slavery, family, and tribe, they had a stake in drawing a rigid line between slave and free. That distinction helped foster the impression that systematic rules governed property and political succession and that chiefs were the traditional keepers of such knowledge. It is likely that chiefs influenced much of the testimony in the colonial court cases analyzed here, encouraging plaintiffs and defendants to present their property claims as consistent with "customary family and tribal relations," relations that often constrained ex-slaves and their descendants from claiming property.

The third approach to fighting cultural and legal "muddle" was to collect information on African law from authorities outside the courts. "[E]ducated Africans" were urged to make "scientific . . . investigations . . . into the customs and institutions of their own land and people" and publish them in a new journal.[97] An Anthropology Department was founded in Asante. Most spectacularly, the Colonial Office in London repeatedly sent out its district commissioners with detailed questionnaires about "native custom" to administer to hundreds of chiefs. These surveys can be viewed as political documents, in which chiefs and British officers negotiated new meanings for customary law. The chiefs' responses are remarkable for their descriptions of how property and lineage authority were bequeathed, a process called "succession." One respondent even drew a chart to illustrate succession in his division. "Being the paramount chief of the Winneba Effutu Division," he told the surveyors, "any differences arising in respect of the above are referred to me for settlement and therefore I am the only authority [illegible] cases in the Division."[98] British officials' faith in customary law gave chiefs an incentive, in certain contexts, to make sharp distinctions between the descendants of slaves and the descendants of free people. The head of Edwumaku Division gave a typical response to the question on the customary law of succession: "The order of successions are: His mother's grandchildren; His mother's sisters' grandchildren according to age, then Domestic [slave] born with blood family; then head-domestic, or domestic and then member of the Tribe by age (Male is preferable). . . . (In any of the above cases the heir is superseded for right cause, such as Extravagance, drunkness, imbecility &c.)"[99] These descriptions of succession may or may not have been accurate, but when they noted the possibility of someone superseding an heir "for right cause," these responses gave an impression of systematic fixity to a process that had been and still was highly contingent.[100] Moreover, chiefs' emphasis on "domestic" ancestors in their descriptions of the customary laws of succession may have helped preserve slavery as an active force in shaping claims to property.

Chiefs were not the only ones keeping slavery's legacy alive. The ex-slaves themselves helped nurture it by pursuing their interests within the ideological framework of kinship—the same framework that had structured slavery—and affirming their kin ties to masters. And as British courts increasingly took over the job of defining property and judging ownership, the connections among slavery, kinship, and property became institutionalized.

To this day, despite many attempts to codify a clear set of rules based on customary law,[101] rights in property continue to be contested along with (and often through) social relationships, in seemingly endless disputes. Because these disputes so often pivot on local history and genealogy,[102] the "legacy of slavery," as historian Akosua Perbi puts it, is an important factor.

Slave ancestry is not a total bar to economic success in Ghana, and "[m]ost families assert that there is complete incorporation of such people."[103] It is still considered impolite to talk about people's enslaved ancestors, and the descendants of masters are content to let the descendants of their slaves live in the family houses.[104] Yet the memory of origins lives on, and when real economic or political power is at stake, the polite veneer of secrecy strips away. History is marshaled, Perbi writes, to make "it clear to the members that a section of the household does not really belong to the family. The motive behind this is to safeguard property belonging to the family and to make sure it remains in the family proper."[105] The process of incorporation has been neither inevitable nor uniform. Just as they did in the 1870s, people of slave descent are waging fierce, if furtive, battles to control the memory of their past.

Still, ex-slaves' claims to property did influence the course of emancipation, giving legal status abolition some real impact on Fante life in ways that were both similar to and different from the ways emancipation affected slaves in the United States. By suing in colonial courts for family property—rather than for freedom—ex-slaves were able to challenge their masters and improve their lives materially, without necessarily cutting all ties to their masters and the property of their masters' families. Indeed, many of them tried to affirm their ties to the people who owned them, turning long-standing ideologies of slavery to their own advantage. No violent revolt or mass migration convulsed Fante society after the abolition ordinance. Instead, the meaning of freedom was worked out family by family, in such humdrum settings as gravesides, yam fields, or courtrooms.

Emancipation significantly changed the ways in which both ex-slaves and ex-masters enjoyed and asserted their claims to property, but it did not eliminate slavery's power to shape property or kinship in Ghanaian society more generally. Because family membership had long been intertwined with rights to property, when one of the most widespread and problematic of dependent relationships—slavery—was legally abolished, a galaxy of possibilities opened up for people to contest both their status in relation to the family and their rights to property—often at the same time. Legal status abolition gave some people an incentive to try to draw a sharp line between slaves and free people and to argue that the law automatically disqualified slaves from certain kinds of property rights. But the law was riddled with gaps and contradictions from its inconsistent attempts to combine British and African law. Aided by British officials' interest in finding a coherent body of African custom, ex-masters and ex-chiefs tried to put the authority of the past behind these arguments by elaborating an image of custom as fixed and systematic, and by marshaling family histories into genealogies with distinct slave and free branches. In this they did not succeed, partly because other people—especially ex-slaves—had an interest in obscuring this distinction. Nearly everyone, regardless of their ancestry, had a stake in a system in which claims to property and family membership never stopped shifting, in which seldom discussed genealogies and long-dormant facts could be brought to life at the right moment.[106] Neither the 1874 Abolition Ordinance nor the many laws passed to regulate the transfer and ownership of property stopped the contestation or confined it to rigid channels of customary law. Rather, the meaning of property continues to be contested because people still invoke ancestry—especially slave ancestry—as a means of claiming property. Slavery and pawnship continue to shape people's claims to the social and economic resources that come with being one of the family.

This case study of the late-nineteenth-century Gold Coast helps make clear the assumptions that anchor the rest of the book. This book does not argue—and indeed suggests that it is not necessary to argue—whether African Americans' ideas of property and family came from Africa. Instead, this analysis uses methods and insights from a case study of African history and anthropology to raise new questions about African American history.

Examining the ways that slaves and ex-slaves in southern Gold Coast experienced kinship and property yields useful comparisons with the United States. There were parallels between the two regions' experiences of slavery and emancipation, particularly in the meaning of property. First, in both the United States and the Gold Coast, ownership often included multiple, overlapping, and sometimes competing claims. People who transferred property did not always give up all claims to it. Even American law permitted multiple claims on property; for example, heirs, creditors, and hirers all had legally recognized interests in the slaves that masters legally owned. In both countries, what made a possession into property was not always "freehold" rights —a person's legal right to exclude all rival claims to something—but rather its entanglement in a network of claims and interests that had little to do with the law.

Second, in both regions the ending of slavery brought ordinary people face to face with a strange new legal system, one that seemed poised to replace the practices and laws they had known all their lives. It did not replace them, however, partly because federal and colonial officers wanted to preserve what they viewed as traditional local institutions (like county courts and "native custom") and partly because ex-slaves stubbornly insisted on pursuing their interests in both legal and extralegal institutions. The officials who came to administer the Gold Coast and the U.S. South saw themselves as outsiders and tried to base their government on a foundation of local custom. By relying on "expert" testimony to interpret "custom," officials in both regions boosted former slaveowners into a new and relatively powerful position even as they dismantled the system of slavery.

Third, in both regions, slavery persisted as a powerful factor shaping claims to property for decades after its legal status vanished. If Abraham Lincoln's Emancipation Proclamation of 1863 was a loud promise of freedom not far distant, then the Gold Coast Abolition Ordinance of 1874 was a bashful stage whisper, seemingly aimed at almost anyone but the slaves themselves. And long after slaves had grasped their freedom, many former masters in both countries lovingly preserved slave ancestry as a stigma, and used it to snatch property away from the children and grandchildren of slaves.

A final similarity was the mutual influence between property and social relationships. In Gold Coast, slavery helped fashion kin ties among fellow servants, and it incorporated slaves—people who by definition were cut off from their blood relatives—as junior members in the lineages that owned them. Rights over "family property" were a privilege of being one of the family, as well as one of the things that proved family membership. Although kinship ideology did not structure master-slave relations in the United States the way it did in Gold Coast, it played a crucial role in relationships *among* American slaves. As we will see, kinship among enslaved African Americans depended on more than blood; sometimes it was shaped by their interests in property. And possessions were valuable not only because they were useful or saleable but also for the social relationships they embodied, ready to be called into action. Hence, disputes over property were just as likely to call forth the kin ties that created and gave meaning to property as to elicit talk of dollars and cents. Slaves and ex-slaves in both regions claimed ownership by calling knowledgeable witnesses and giving detailed genealogies of the ties among people and between people and their possessions. In Gold Coast, such historical knowledge could affect the status of people, not just property. Akan ex-masters and ex-slaves enlisted, altered—and even created—knowledge about origins in order to claim (and reject rival claims to) both membership in families and the economic rights that went with that membership.

Yet, whatever the similarities between the experiences of these two groups of black folk, it is the differences between them that makes comparing these cases so useful for historians. Take, for example, the manner in which slavery ended. Driven by the ferocious violence of a civil war, Union policy after 1863 took dead aim at the heart of the southern economy—the South's four million slaves. An army of freedom was on the march. By contrast, the British officials who passed abolition laws in Gold Coast were horrified at the upheavals they had seen in the Caribbean during the 1830s and the United States during the 1860s, and they took pains to avoid similar disruptions, even if it sometimes meant not telling the slaves they were free.[107]

Even bigger differences lurked in the ideological foundations of slavery in the two regions. American masters almost never recognized any kin tie with a slave, and then only when a slave was related to the master by blood. Family relationships between American masters and slaves existed only in whispered-about affairs or violent rapes and in some masters' paternalist idea that they ruled over one big plantation family.[108] Whereas few American slaves could seriously lay claim to their master's inheritance, slaves and former slaves in the Gold Coast took such claims to court, and often won. They won because slavery in Gold Coast was built around an ideology of kinship, rather than the ideology of race that structured master-slave relations in the United States. As a result, the end of slavery had very different implications for kinship in Gold Coast than it did in the United States. Kinship between American masters and slaves was unthinkable. And once blacks were legally free, whites had to go to new lengths to try to keep the possibility of kinship with blacks unthinkable. In Gold Coast, by contrast, where a person could be one of the family and still a slave, there was often no reason to deny kinship after slavery's end. Sometimes, there were good reasons to claim it.[109]

Finally, freedom meant something different to people in the Fante region than it did to white Americans. Historians of North America are used to defining freedom as autonomy, getting away from oppressive or unjust relationships. But the evidence in the court records of nineteenth-century Gold Coast suggests that in the Fante region, ex-slaves were looking less for autonomy than for more status and power within social groups; rather than trying to get away from their old masters' lineages, Fante ex-slaves often elbowed their way further in. Struggles over property both reflected and helped define what it meant to be one of the family, and in that way, they significantly shaped the meaning of freedom.

The rest of this book focuses on the American South, but it does not leave Africa behind. Throughout, the book draws comparisons with this case study of emancipation in Gold Coast and is permeated with many of the perspectives that underlie African Studies in general. Property was at the heart of African Americans' ideas about family and community and, after slavery ended, it helped mold their relationship to the state. In turn, black people's social ties helped "make" property. That connection between claiming kin and claiming property is central to recent work in African history and anthropology, and in the 1800s it defined an important part of everyday life in both Africa and America.

chapter two

Slavery's Other Economy

. . . .

September 30, 1799, was Denmark Vesey's lucky day. Just as thousands of middling and poor people did sometimes, he bought a ticket for one of Charleston's lotteries; like everyone else, he probably put it in his pocket and barely gave it a second thought. But thirty-nine days and several drawings later, number 1884 came up and lottery commissioners promptly put $1,500 into Denmark Vesey's hands. His master and mistress drove a hard bargain, but when he paid them their price, they signed his freedom papers without any fuss.[1] Denmark Vesey led an extraordinary life—after all, he not only won the lottery, he also was accused of plotting the biggest slave insurrection in American history. But there is something in the mundane details of his otherwise unusual life that raises a fascinating question about American slavery, and about southern society as a whole: why did the lottery pay $1,500 to a slave?

The "cardinal principle of slavery," according to one 1827 summary of southern law, was "that the slave is to be regarded as a thing,—is an article of property,—a chattel personal."[2] Because they were property, slaves could not legally own property. A slave could "acquire and hold *personal* property" but only "by the consent of his master,"[3] who granted it as a "favor."[4] In the eyes of the law, "[w]hatever he [the slave] may accumulate by his own labor becomes immediately the property of his master."[5]

Yet Denmark Vesey was not the first enslaved American to own property, and he would not be the last. In the 1800s, there was a significant informal economy of property ownership and trade among enslaved people throughout the South. Most enslaved people owned much less than Vesey, and they got it in more humdrum ways, working for themselves in "truck patches" or at the city docks or at crafting brooms and pails. Property ownership by enslaved people was not legal, and it often sparked angry arguments among whites, but it was an integral part of North America's slave system. Some people owned property even while they themselves were property. As we look into how they were able to do this, we will begin to pry apart a seemingly unified slave community, and we will search the margins of the law to explore what it meant for rural people—white or black—to "own" something.

SLAVES' ABILITY TO OWN and trade property was part of fundamental processes in the system of slavery. The conditions that shaped it varied from region to region, according to geography, the system of labor, and the tolerances of different masters. Some places may have afforded slaves opportunities to accumulate unusually large amounts of property, even thousands of dollars worth.[6] But for small and modest amounts of property, no single region stands out. The Low Country, where Pompey Bacon lived, stretched along the Atlantic seacoast through parts of North Carolina, South Carolina, Georgia, and Florida. It was a region of very big plantations, ranged along slow-moving rivers and on the sandy, swampy Sea Islands. All along this wide, flat floodplain, some of the nation's wealthiest citizens wrung out their fortunes from the sweat of dozens, sometimes hundreds of enslaved African Americans. If they could afford it, those citizens tended to spend the sweltering summers in Charleston and Savannah, far from dangerous "fevers" that sickened the people who made them rich. By 1860, black people outnumbered white people by three to one in some Low Country counties, and nearly all of them were slaves. They spent most of their lives cultivating rice, the region's reigning cash crop.[7] Working by tasks defined the everyday life of slaves in the Low Country. Unlike the gang system that prevailed in most other areas of the South, the task system assigned each slave a certain amount of work each day—a quarter acre to hoe, for example, or a hundred wooden rails to split.[8] The system permitted slaves to help one another in their work and, after they finished the task, allowed them to use their time as they wished, within certain limits. By working on their own time to raise more than they needed to eat, slaves accumulated property and created traditions of property ownership and trade. Once they had their start, many slaves invested in a succession of animals, beginning with poultry and moving to larger and more valuable animals like hogs, cattle, and, finally, horses. Jacob Quarterman, who claimed livestock, a wagon, corn, and rice, told the claims agent: "I bought mine sir by taking care of what little I could get."[9] This practice of organizing labor by task rather than by time was the taproot of property ownership by Low Country slaves.

Only a few dozen miles in from the coast, the landscape and the work system looked dramatically different. In the wide belt of cotton fields stretching westward from Georgia to Louisiana, and in the tobacco- and wheat-growing regions of the Upper South, the summers were still hot, but few slaveowners could afford to leave. Enslaved people dealt with their masters nearly every day and they worked primarily in gangs. Gang labor required slaves to work a specific amount of time rather than do a certain amount of work each day. Like the task system, the gang system was a harsh regime, one that could stretch from sunup to sundown. Yet gang labor also afforded slaves opportunities to accumulate property. By the early nineteenth century, most slaves in gang-labor regions customarily were not required to work for their masters on Sundays. Masters sometimes demanded Sunday labor during the heavy work of the harvest season, but at other times of the year, many masters gave their slaves part, or even all of Saturday, in addition to Sunday.[10] Slaves seized these allotments of time as their own, and many spent them working for themselves to accumulate property.

Throughout the South, slaves' independent economies were founded on an economy of time rather than an economy of land. Compared to their struggles over time, masters and slaves devoted little attention to land and many slaves throughout the South had relatively easy access to land. One Louisiana sugar plantation, for example, set aside 150 of its 1,500 cultivated acres for "the negroes for their own use," as well as gardens and chicken-yards attached to each cabin.[11] "All of the slaves on the place" where Ansy Jeffries lived, in Marshall County, Mississippi, for instance, "had patches of land . . . to work as there own,"[12] approximately two acres in size.[13] Jerry Smithson, from Yazoo County, testified that he "always had an acre or two of ground for my family & sometimes I had as high as 3 or 4 acres." The major constraint on his accumulation was that he could only work "it on Saturday evenings & on Sundays."[14] In the Low Country, slaves generally "were allowed all the land they could tend without rent,"[15] an average of perhaps four to five acres,[16] far more than any one person could tend. "Our master allowed us slaves to own property," one Low Country ex-slave summed up, "and give us as much land as we could work in our own time."[17]

Many plantations allotted slaves plots of land away from the slave quarters in addition to small gardens next to their cabins. However, there were no consistent rules about the size of those plots, the pattern of allotment, or what slaves could grow in them. Some slaveowners forbade their slaves from growing the South's cash crops—cotton, tobacco, and rice—on the grounds that slaves would steal from the masters' crop and pass it off as their own. "One of our settled plantation practices," according to a former slaveowner near Jackson, Mississippi, "was to allow our slaves each for his own account, to cultivate a piece of our land and make whatever corn or other crop he could, *except cotton*. Beyond what was estimated as a fair week's labor we *gave* each slave all the time he could save."[18] Many former slaves remembered having "truck patches,"[19] or "little gardens,"[20] for vegetables, "corn and water melons to make pocket change with."[21] However, other slaves had their masters' permission to make more than "pocket change," by growing valuable cash crops. Many masters in Missouri's tobacco region allowed slaves to work tobacco crops, though only "after sundown, and without plowing."[22] Sarah Benjamin's Louisiana master gave each slave a "little tobacco patch,"[23] and Martha Patton's uncles had cotton patches on the Texas plantation where they lived.[24] Even the North Carolina Supreme Court spoke approvingly of a master who paid his slaves for cotton they made in their "patches."[25] John McConnell, who came from the Appalachian foothills of northwest Georgia, believed that "never since I was 14 years old was a year when I did *not* have a cotton patch."[26]

Just as in their decisions about what slaves should be allowed to grow, when it came to allotting slaves land, variety was the slaveowners' hallmark. According to J. H. Ingraham, a northerner who had moved to the South, it was "customary for planters in the neighbourhood" of Natchez, Mississippi, "to give their slaves a small piece of land to cultivate for their own use."[27] On one plantation, near Virginia's Blue Ridge mountains, there was a distinct "Negro Lot," which the master clearly indicated on a sketch he drew of his lands. By contrast, on other plantations, slaves were only allowed to make "gardens, in some remote and unprofitable part of the estate, generally in the woods" and work them on Sundays. In upcountry Georgia, Charles Ball helped a family work a patch that "was about a mile and a half from our dwelling. We took with us some bread, and a large bucket of water; and worked all day."[28] Some masters carefully allotted each slave family a sepa-

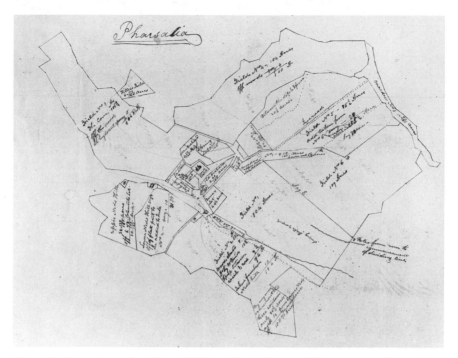

Pharsalia Plantation, 1847 (from William Massie Papers, CN no. 11401, Center for American History, University of Texas–Austin).

rate patch, but others simply set aside a "nigger field"[29] and left the slaves to sort out their claims.

Regardless of how the land was allotted, slaves asserted claims over particular plots of own-account land, even though those plots were located away from their cabins. On the upcountry Georgia plantation where Charles Ball lived, the patches were divided "and fenced—some with rails, and others with brush," to mark them as "the property of the various families."[30] Masters who did not give slaves access to a large, distant plot usually let slaves work a garden patch next to their cabins.[31] Slaves in the Low Country may have had access to larger plots than those elsewhere in the South. Slaves in the Chesapeake region usually had only a small garden beside their cabins rather than the "little plantations" and "private fields" that Low Country slaves had.[32] But regardless of where they lived, getting enough land was not typically the slaves' chief concern. Time was.

Masters restricted slaves' access to time much more than they restricted their access to land.[33] Within the economy of time that grew out of the strug-

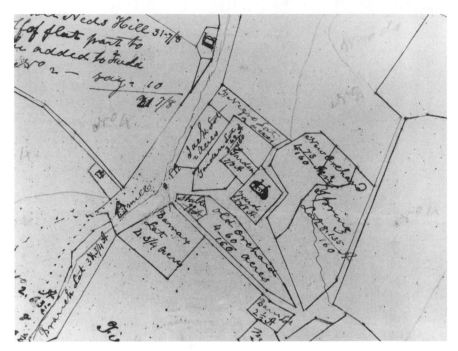

"Negro Lot of Pharsalia Plantation (detail)," 1847 (from William Massie Papers, CN no. 11402, Center for American History, University of Texas–Austin).

gle between slaves and masters, slaves used three avenues to accumulate property. First, some slaves could save time by working faster at their tasks and then use the leftover time to earn property. When the harvest was on, work days could stretch to sixteen hours,[34] yet some claimants testified that at other times of the year they could finish a task by noon or one o'clock or that they could "save . . . a whole day" by doing several tasks in a single day.[35] This option was not available to many slaves outside the Low Country, who usually did not work by the task. Yet they, too, had opportunities to manipulate time for their own use. For example, slaves harvesting turpentine in the piney woods of North Carolina had weekly quotas for "boxing," "chipping," and "dipping" and a set "district" of 3,000 to 5,000 trees. They could often finish these tasks by Friday afternoon.[36] Much of the "severe," deadly work of cutting the canal system in the South—one of America's biggest "public works" projects ever—was done by enslaved men working by the task.[37] And nearly every farm needed to spin wool, hoe cotton, or pull fodder, and these, too, were organized into tasks.[38] Depending on the season and the work, slaves in many parts of the South spent at least some of their time working by the task.

Second, although most slaves in the South worked in gangs, gang labor quickly developed its own customary standards of work and ideas about "the slaves' time."[39] Although slaves working in gangs could not "save up" time by finishing tasks quickly, they earned money by working beyond the customary expectations for a week, a season, or a year—on Saturday afternoons, Sundays, and holidays. This practice was called by various names. Ex-slave claimants in gang-labor regions from upcountry South Carolina to Alabama and Mississippi spoke of having earned property "by extra, & outside work"[40] and work done "after hours of general labor,"[41] by "overwork,"[42] "over time,"[43] and "night work."[44] No law required masters to grant such time, yet at least one state supreme court ruled that "slaves are entitled to the produce of their labor on Sunday."[45]

Third, for some slaves, a skill was a valuable and portable kind of "property" that could generate more income. As one former slave from Alabama put it, "I earned it by Working at night Making Cotton baskets horse collars brooms and Every other way that I could to make a dime."[46] Field hands who knew cooping could make small wooden pails called "piggins" and sell them to both slave and free. "I don't think anybody ought object to a man going into the woods and cutting the woods for pails and tubs and piggins and selling them," testified ex-slave William McIver. "This was the way I got my start."[47] Someone trained in carpentry could also make "tables & such things" to sell "after he knocked off for the evening."[48] Other skilled slaves spent their "over time" the same way field hands did, farming garden patches.[49] An ex-slave from Texas made money breaking wild horses, a man from North Carolina, by making hats,[50] a South Carolinian, by "work[ing] 'over time' at blacksmithing,"[51] and another, by "unloading steamboats . . . at night . . . in 'our time.' "[52] Enslaved people developed skills that fit the demands of their locale and used them to accumulate property.

Harvest season put enormous pressure on slave labor and threatened to swallow up the time slaves claimed as their own. "On cane plantations in sugar time, there is no distinction as to the days of the week," observed Solomon Northup, who lived in Bayou Boeuf near what later was called Louisiana's "sugar bowl." Yet it was "equally well understood that those who are hired . . . shall receive remuneration for it,"[53] an understanding of slaves' customary claims that even the Louisiana Supreme Court recognized.[54] Between September 1845 and January 1846, Northup himself earned $10 in what he called "Sunday money." As did those in the "sugar bowl," many slaves in the "cotton belt" received compensation for time that in other months they might have spent somewhere else, compensation that brought task work into the heart of the gang system. Charles Ball's overseer announced near the start of the cotton harvest that he was "fix[ing] the day's work [for adult men] at fifty pounds; and that all those who picked more than that, would be paid a cent a pound, for the overplus."[55] And, according to Ball, "This money was punctually paid to me every Saturday night."[56] Enslaved people in at least one Missouri county got the same rate for "breaking" more than their hundred-pound quota of tobacco.[57] "In cotton picking time," recalled a former slaveowner from Mississippi, the cotton was weighed each evening and the extra poundage was entered in "a daily a/c [account]" ledger of credits for the slaves.[58] According to another white observer, slaves watched the weighing and "would keep in their heads the amount to which they were entitled for their [extra] labor, so that they would know, at the end of the week, whether they received enough."[59]

Not every slaveowner permitted overwork, and even practices on neighboring plantations could be very different. Frederick Law Olmsted, a northern journalist, wrote popular books about his travels in the South during the 1850s. He met a planter near Lake Charles, in western Louisiana, who "was in the habit of making use of the Sundays of the slaves of the neighborhood," hiring them from their masters and paying them various amounts for hoeing.[60] But on the next few plantations Olmsted visited, slaves had to work for their masters on Sundays.[61] Such variations reflected the idiosyncratic choices of different masters, yet testimony from slaves and masters suggests that, despite variations, overwork practices recurred regularly throughout the cotton belt. Task labor in the Low Country moved to a different beat than gang labor in an Alabama cotton field or a Virginia wheat field, but all of these arrangements focused on time, rather than land. The goal for masters, as Ball pointed out, was to capture exactly as much of the slaves' time as the plantation's crop required at any particular moment while spending as little as possible to subsist the slaves.

Factories in the South afforded some slaves other opportunities to get property. Throughout the early nineteenth century, slaves at Buffalo Forge, an ironworks in the mountains of Virginia, received pay for working beyond what had come to be accepted over the years as the customary quotas for each task. Their master recorded this overwork and the amounts paid to the slaves in account books, deducting money when slaves missed their quotas.[62] Such practices occurred in other mines, too. Journal editor Edmund Ruffin scolded mine owners for letting their slaves "open two (not very deep) shafts to the coal, for their own private working." It was one thing to let slaves do "extra work for their own gain," but this was too "distinct and independent a footing."[63] Men like Ruffin—fiercely proslavery and experts on "scientific agriculture"—had no problem with slaves earning money, so long as it was managed the right way. By the 1840s, the overwork system was more than a hundred years old in Virginia's slave-run coal industry, and mine owners were even running newspaper advertisements aimed at enslaved people. "There is no work," boasted one ad, "in which slaves . . . have an equal chance [i.e., any better chance] of making money for themselves."[64] A hundred miles east of the coal mines, Frederick Law Olmsted reported that Virginia industrialists hired slaves and free people of color to process tobacco in their factories and offered "to pay the negroes a certain rate per pound for all the tobacco he works up beyond a certain quantity."[65] These "over-wages" were paid to the black workers "once a fortnight."[66] Only a minority of slaves ever worked in mines and factories, but the fact that these places had overwork payments and customary definitions of work quotas lends further support to the argument that the economy of time and opportunities for slaves to accumulate property were intrinsic to the system of slavery.

The economy of time offered another avenue for slaves to accumulate property: hiring out. Working on hire was a significant part of the black experience under slavery. On any given day in the South in 1860, about 6 percent of all rural slaves and about 31 percent of urban slaves were working on hire, and over a lifetime, their chances of being hired out increased.[67] Slave hiring worked in two ways. Some slaves were hired out, with their master negotiating payments and schedules directly with the hirer. A smaller number were permitted to hire themselves out. These slaves took the responsibility for finding an employer and paying their masters. Either way, the master got a cut. Interestingly, not all self-hired slaves were skilled elite; many of them were "farm labour[ers]" and "wood chopper[s]," and they often tended garden patches just as other slaves did.[68] Both arrangements could permit slaves to accumulate property. Slaves who worked under the hiring system were over-represented among the claimants before the Southern Claims Commission, accounting for 88 of the 498 successful claims by former slaves.[69]

Slave hiring sprang from many of the same factors that underlay the practice of overwork in the gang labor system. For white masters and hirers, it smoothed the uneven cycles of farming. For whites who owned no slaves it offered easy access to a cheap, temporary workforce.[70] Hired slaves released white women and men from toilsome housework, enabling middle-class southern whites both to boost their household income and to mold their households into a separate "domestic sphere," where white women could be ladies and even slaveless white men could be masters of their own small worlds.[71] For the people who actually owned the slaves, hiring cut down their subsistence costs and yielded profits even during slack times when they did not have enough for their slaves to do. Lewis Williams fed and clothed himself and paid his mistress a dollar a day, and other self-hired slaves paid nearly as much.[72] One white visitor to Alabama and Mississippi thought that the wages self-hired slaves paid to their masters made up a big part of many slaveowners' incomes.[73] "I don't know how he worked for his master," said a white witness, "but I know the custom was if I owned a servant & had no immediate employment for them I would buy a badge & tell them to go out & bring me so much a month."[74] Self-hiring represented the far end of a continuum of work arrangements built around the economy of time.

However, there were limits to what hiring themselves out could do for slaves. First, in many states it was illegal, and whites who hired out slaves had to either be willing to ignore the law or, as one former Mississippi slaveowner explained, be simply ignorant of it.[75] Second, the opportunities to accumulate property were probably better for the small minority of self-hired slaves than for those whose masters made agreements over their heads and received payments directly from hirers. Most important, slaves could accumulate property only if they earned more than the amount they paid for the privilege, and few activities paid as much as a dollar per day. Most self-hired slaves counted their earnings in nickels, not dollars.[76] So, self-hiring was always a harsh exchange for slaves. Even some whites admitted as much. Emily Burke thought that it was "quite common for a master to give his slave all his time if he will take care of himself after he has become so old and worn out as to be of no service to [his master]."[77]

No matter how slaves worked, owning property meant committing to long hours of toil after a hard day's labor for a master, "by the light of a torch at night"[78] or, as ex-slave Joseph James put it, "till the fowls crow for day, by moonlight & firelight."[79] Frederick Law Olmsted estimated that on plantations run by gang labor, slaves' workdays often lasted sixteen hours.[80] Moreover, much of the work slaves did in their own time—walking to fetch their firewood, grinding corn for their dinner, washing their clothes, or just fixing the drafty, ramshackle cabins they lived in—did not translate directly into property.[81] Then, too, many enslaved people had to spend some of their nights and mornings walking muddy roads to see their children, torn from them by masters.[82] Because of these restrictions on slaves' time, although many slaves owned property, most did not own very much.

Some people did earn a lot, though—enough to buy themselves out of slavery. Dozens of black claimants testified that they had purchased their freedom before the Civil War, "paying for it," as one man recalled, "out of careful earnings made by hard and constant work."[83] Some of the highest claims by African Americans, though, came from people who were set free only after the Union army came through. Benjamin Sterling Turner had amassed some $1,600 in gold by 1855 but was still in slavery in 1864. Why didn't people like Turner just buy their freedom?

Slaves faced grave dangers in working toward freedom and, once they grasped it, they found that it was a strange fruit. Many people bitterly remembered being cheated out of their freedom, sometimes more than once.[84] One Missouri ex-slave had "an uncle who was buying his freedom . . . and was almost paid out when marse Chris died, but he didn't know nothing 'bout keeping receipts so he was put on the auction block and sold again."[85] Some slaves simply were not allowed to buy themselves. Benjamin Sterling Turner's "master refused [to sell him] & sd. he wd. not take $5000 for him."[86] Several claimants who did go through with their self-purchase expressed disgust at southern state laws regarding free blacks, and much of their anger focused on the restrictions the law placed on their property ownership. Turner, who lost at least $4,958 worth of property to the soldiers, said that when he found out that Alabama law would require him to have a white guardian "who would stand in the relation of master to me, I preferred to remain with my old master and keep my money."[87] Horace Page pointed out to the commissioners that "a man who had bought himself . . . could not transact business in Virginia without having a white man to stand for him — that his business had to be done in [the white man's] name, even if he was worth a million dollars."[88] Such restrictions threatened to curtail free blacks' ownership of property but did little to curb it among slaves.

Slaves' ability to earn, own, and trade property directly boosted the formal economy of the plantation, and that is why so many masters allowed it. "The reader must not suppose," Charles Ball warned his northern audience, "that . . . we had nothing to eat beyond the corn and salt" their master gave them. "This was far from the case."[89] As many historians point out, by permitting slaves time to accumulate property, planters were able to shift "part or all of the burden of subsisting their slaves onto the slaves themselves,"[90] lowering production costs and raising the plantation's margin of profit.[91] Slaveowners stood to save a lot of money because the average cotton plantation spent more than one-fifth of its total output on feeding and clothing the slaves.[92] "The white folks didn't give us clothes," recalled two sisters who grew up near Opelousas, Louisiana. Instead, "Us daddy he work de ground he own on Sunday . . . to buy us shoes to put on us feet and clothes."[93] Alfred

Barnard remembered: "[M]y master never gave us any clothes or provisions —he used to sell all he made. He said that everything was too high [expensive]." Rather than buy such things from a merchant, Barnard's master expected his slaves to "find [them]selves"—to supply their own food and clothing.[94] Although few masters went that far, most expected their slaves to provide at least part of their needs from their own after-task earnings.[95] Permitting slaves to accumulate property also guarded the plantation business against the unpredictable cycles of nineteenth-century plantation agriculture. Slaves' gardens and property kept alive the slaves—who, after all, represented nearly half of the typical cotton planter's assets[96]—through dangerous floods and drought, failed crops, and bad prices. Lewis Miller tried to make enough from his corn patch "to keep me & family on during the summer when 'allowance' run short, so we would not have to steal or starve."[97] Even when the threat of starvation faded, slaves needed their gardens and property simply to survive because masters' typical rations left slaves vulnerable to malnutrition and cold. Without the fish, wild plants, livestock, and garden vegetables that the slaves produced for themselves, archaeologists argue, "many slaves would have surely died from diseases that are aggravated by undernourishment."[98]

Slaves seized the chance to work for themselves, but they refused to consider it a gift. One Low Country ex-slave, who had paid his master fifteen dollars a month out of his earnings as a wagon driver, was asked whether he was in debt to his former master. He retorted: "I do not owe him anything now. I think by rights, *he owes* me, for all the money I *paid him*."[99] "To ask the master for a knife, or skillet, or any small convenience of the kind, would be answered with a kick, or laughed at as a joke," wrote Solomon Northup, who spent twelve years in slavery in Louisiana. "Whatever necessary article of this nature is found in a cabin has been purchased with Sunday money."[100] Often, those who did not work overtime during the harvest season "were not able to provide themselves with good clothes; and many of them suffered greatly from the cold, in the . . . winter."[101] Moreover, because slaves would not let their friends and relatives starve if they could help it, masters who skimped on rations for their own workers ended up forcing slaves on neighboring plantations to siphon off their earnings. Ball met a slave in South Carolina who was "compelled . . . to lay out all his savings" to feed and clothe his wife and children, who lived on another plantation and whose master had begun to cut their rations.[102] Other slaveowners tried to recapture their slaves' time through plantation "stores." As a former slave from Missouri said, "You had to go to that store and get your needs and when the month was up you had nothing as it took all you earned to pay your bill."[103]

Permitting slaves to use part of their work week for themselves saved masters money on food and clothing; many whites also thought they could discipline slaves into a reliable workforce by threatening to take away their access to land or time. The slaves on one Tennessee plantation were actually required to raise chickens and vegetables, recalled one woman, because local whites thought it would keep them from stealing.[104] The owner of a big plantation in Mississippi told Frederick Law Olmsted that when his slaves ran away "he would make the rest of the force work Sundays, or deprive them of some of their usual privileges, until the runaways returned."[105] And on Moses Roper's first night at a Florida farm, his new master took "a bag of [Roper's] clothes . . . with him" to bed, "as a kind of security, I presume, for my safety."[106] Rather than undermining the system of slavery, allowing slaves the "privileges" of time and property ownership made plantations more profitable and easier to manage. "The slave is a kind of freeman on Sunday all over the southern country," said Charles Ball, but he benefited from "the exercise of his liberty on this day" only because that "liberty" also benefited his master.[107]

Moreover, property ownership did not make slavery any milder; on the contrary, it sometimes went hand in hand with the cruelest tortures. Masters who encouraged slaves to plant gardens or work overtime also dealt out brutal whippings, broke up families, and exercised a system of raw terror. Frederick Law Olmsted visited a Mississippi plantation where slaves earned money by "Saturday and Sunday work," kept gardens, and raised and sold fowls and eggs—and where the master sent vicious dogs to hunt runaways.[108] At another, the slaveowner blandly described the slaves' opportunities to accumulate, then a few minutes later turned to slash a young black woman with a whip.[109] Masters who permitted their slaves to earn and keep property were not necessarily "kind" or "indulgent" toward slaves, or even sympathetic to the Union cause when war broke out, although ex-slaves sometimes described them that way to northern visitors. During the Civil War, some planters tried to persuade their slaves to evacuate with them by offering to accommodate "to their little matters of property."[110] Others forced their slaves to pack up their "boxes, bedding, and luggage" and whipped them into the Union lines.[111] And one master, after years of permitting his slaves to earn property, "threatened to burn all his slaves rather than let the Yankees have them."[112]

The struggle to define the boundary between the master's time and the slaves' time was fought out in small episodes. The slaves on one Missouri plantation had to "stop . . . making splint brooms, baskets, &c., on Sunday" after their master "got religion" and started making them all go to his church.[113] Such struggles could also be sparked when a plantation changed owners. In Virginia, Frederick Law Olmsted met an overseer-turned-slave-owner who was convinced that "in general, a slave does not do half the work he easily might." As soon as he got a plantation of his own, the slaveowner bragged, he fired the overseer and "went to driving the negroes myself." What happened next reveals the dynamics of the unequal, half-masked struggle between masters and slaves all over the South. "In the morning, when I went out," the slaveowner continued, "one of [the slaves] came up to me and asked what work he should go about. I told him to go into the swamp and cut some wood. 'Well, massa,' said he, 's'pose you wants me to do kordins we's been use to doin'; ebery nigger cut a cord a day.' 'A cord!' that's what you have been used to doing, is it?' said I. 'Yes, massa, dat's wot dey always makes a nigger do roun' heah—a cord a day, dat's allers de task.'" One cord of wood is about 128 cubic feet, or a stack eight feet long, four feet wide, and four feet high.[114]

> "Well, now, old man," said I, "you go and cut me two cords to-day." "Oh, massa! two cords! Nobody couldn' do dat. Oh! massa, dat's too hard! Nebber heard o' nobody's cuttin' more'n a cord o' wood in a day, roun' heah. No nigger couldn' do it." "Well, old man, you have two cords of wood cut tonight, or to-morrow morning you will have two hundred lashes—that's all there is about it. So, look sharp!" Of course, he did it, and no negro has ever cut less than two cords a day for me since, though my neighbors still get but one cord.[115]

Doubling a task slashed the slaves' time. In a way, slaves' protests against breaking "usual" or customary practices were a sign of how fragile their claims to time were. Still, given the potential rewards of permitting slaves time to work for themselves, and costs of quashing slaves' resistance, many masters chose not to depart too radically from practices that slaves considered customary. For all his bragging, and although he managed to get two cords of wood a day from his slaves, Olmsted's Virginia informant had to threaten a whipping to do it and, moreover, his neighbors did not rush to copy his example. At least one North Carolina overseer died for taking away something a slave had made "in his own time."[116] And slaves "would play off on being sick," then "slip off & work for ourselves."[117] Many people throughout the South spoke of slave-owned property as a "custom," but such a description glossed over variations between different regions and tremendous struggle between masters and slaves. Those variations and struggles rumbled loudest over the precious allotments of time that slaves needed to make property.

Some of the most massive struggles over time and property accumulation may not have occurred in the context of any particular plantation or any confrontation between a master and a slave but as a result of mass migration. Between the 1790s and the 1840s, white southerners forced about one million enslaved African Americans to trudge from Maryland, Virginia, and the Carolinas westward to Mississippi, Alabama, and upcountry Georgia, where they tore open a new frontier for slavery.[118] It is likely that slaves and their masters thrashed out thousands of adjustments and conflicts during their first years in these new "cotton states." A faction of planters in the Chesapeake and Low Country had been complaining for years about the task system and slaves' internal economy. As planters moved westward they tried to "roll back" what they saw as too many privileges and tighten their control over their slaves.[119] They managed to put into place a gang labor system on the vast cotton-growing belt, from upcountry Georgia to Alabama and Mississippi.[120] Yet western planters also had to take account of a "customary" pace of work, "customary" levels of subsistence, garden patches, and personal property—"customs" that slaves carried with them from back east. Frederick Law Olmsted visited one Mississippi cotton plantation where the overseer demanded a share of the deer a slave had just caught in his spear trap. The overseer "justified himself to me," Olmsted remarked, by claiming that since this particular slave was a stock tender, he "had undoubtedly taken time which really belonged to his owner to set his spear." By contrast, "[g]ame taken by the field-hands was not looked upon in the same light, because it must have been got at night when they were excused from labour for their owner."[121] This master's and overseer's claims to ownership made several overlapping distinctions—between "stock tender[s]" and "field-hands," daytime and nighttime, "time which . . . belonged to [the] owner" and time when slaves "were excused from labour for their owner." As the seasons passed and the days grew shorter, or if the master sent the stock tender to the fields, masters and slaves presumably renegotiated the boundary between the master's time and the slaves' time.

Indeed, whatever they thought about the customs of slavery, many planters decided that the easiest way to get new land cleared for their precious cotton was to leave those customs alone. According to Moses Grandy, who escaped from slavery in North Carolina, "each colored person" was allotted a piece of forest "as large as he can tend after his other work is done; the women have pieces in like manner." They then "work[ed] at night, cutting down the timber and clearing the ground; after it is cleared, he has it for his own use for two or three years, as may be agreed on." Masters liked this arrangement for several reasons. The slaves' "new clearings" made a buffer that "saved . . . the planter's land" from marauding "squirrels and raccoons." Masters could keep watch over anything the slaves managed to coax out of the stingy ground. And as soon as the land became "fit for the plough" and bigger crops, masters took it and "removed [the slaves] to another new piece."[122] In using slaves to carve an empire out of dense forests, southern slaveowners followed the same trail that Asante had blazed in the late 1600s.[123] Moreover, in trying to redefine what was "customary" in southern slavery, masters prefigured debates about the slave past that would flare up in both Fante and the United States after slavery was gone.

Slaves established claims to time through constant struggles against the demands of masters. At times, the boundary between the master's time and the slaves' time[124] gradually became accepted as a custom. Yet when masters decided to expand or shrink their operations, switch to a different crop, or, as so many masters did in the early 1800s, move the whole business westward, those struggles broke out anew.

SLAVE-OWNED PROPERTY and the arrangements of land and labor from which it came were part of an important regional informal economy within the more formal economies of the plantation and the city. The former slaveowner Edward DeLegal, who owned a plantation in the Georgia Low Country, testified: "I never interfered with my people, they bought & sold these things at there own prices & spent the money as they pleased & this was customary in Liberty County & I suppose it was in other seaboard counties. . . . I know Mr Cay's people and mine used to raise cattle, horses, and more [illegible] than there were any use for."[125] Relatively free to trade the property they had, slaves exchanged goods, money, and labor with one another, with their masters, and with nonslaveowning whites. Some exchanges stayed on the plantation, as people traded corn for beans,[126] or bought a cow "from another of our women,"[127] or "traded . . . with colored people who came to the mill."[128] Some slaveowners tried to keep a lid on the situation by trading directly with their own slaves. For enslaved Louisianans, the end of the sugar harvest was "the time for settling up their outstanding accounts with each other, and [with] the master and mistress of the plantation."[129] Slaves' cabins also attracted buyers from outside the quarters. One slave traded from his plantation cabin regularly enough that witnesses spoke of him having "customers."[130] Far to the west, in Arkansas, Betty Brown remembered that there "Us' tuh be a coup'la pedluh men come 'round" to the slave quarters. Her mother, who "could hunt good ez any man," traded valuable mink, beaver, and deer skins with them "fer calico prints n' trinkets, n' sech-like."[131] Another woman recalled that her "grandpa made money sellin' wild turkey and hawgs to the poor white folks."[132]

Other kinds of trade happened along the roads. "A couple of negroes here passed along near us," wrote Frederick Law Olmsted, who had stopped to talk with a free black peddler and his son. "[T]he old man hailed them: 'Ho dah, boys! Doan you want to buy some backey?' 'No.' (Decidedly.) 'Well, I'm sorry for it.' (Reproachfully.) "[133] Roadside trading kept its own, intermittent rhythm, different from the regular pulse of trading in the towns. An ex-slave from Mississippi remembered leaving his cabin and going "out hunting for some person who had corn to sell."[134] Slaves across the South remembered trading with other slaves for horses, mules, rice, beehives and honey, hogs, dresses, and many other things. Most slaves did not get all that they needed from their masters, and many could not easily get to the nearest town; the internal economy permitted them to trade much closer to home for the things they needed.

Slaves were well-versed enough in market practices to handle adroitly the wild currency swings that plagued the South during the war. "I remember on one occasion," said Dudley J. Smith of a fellow ex-slave, "I had about one thousand dollars in Confederate currency. The claimant urged me to invest it in property," saying "that the United States Government would certainly succeed in the war, and that Confederate money would be worthless."[135] Another man invested his earnings in gold and two watches, "because I knew the Confederacy couldn't last."[136] When Confederate money became, as one witness put it, "no better than a newspaper after it is read," some slaves (when they could in their trade) began to insist on "silver and United States banknotes." Others accepted payment in salt, another wartime currency substitute.[137] Confederate notes did become worthless; Scott Hooper remembered that her father, who had saved $500 by 1865, "give it to us chillen to play with."[138]

Slaves also marketed their goods to the urban consumers in nearby cities. Indeed, much of the produce and small livestock that was sold in the markets of southern towns was raised and sold by enslaved African Americans. On Sundays, observed a white visitor, slaves on farms around Natchez were permitted

> to leave their plantations and come into town to dispose of their produce and lay in their own little luxuries and private stores. The various avenues to the city are consequently on that day filled with crowds of chatting, laughing negroes, arrayed in their Sunday's best, and adroitly balancing heavily loaded baskets on their heads. . . . Others mounted on mules or miserable-looking plough-horses . . . burthened with their marketable commodities, jog on side by side, with their dames or sweethearts riding "double-jaded" behind them; while here and there market carts returning from the city . . . or from the intersecting roads, pour in upon the highway.[139]

Sunday markets at Natchez, New Orleans, and Fayetteville were scenes of intense cultural mixing between white "boatmen" and slaves, and between slaves from different plantations.[140] Even small villages became incorporated into slaves' trade networks, as the 1826 trial of an enslaved Virginian named Peter reveals. One witness testified that he had been at Peter's "house twice on the day [of] the murder" and "got the prisoner to take some chickens in the morning of that day to Tappahannock to sell."[141] In 1826, Tappahannock, Virginia, was a sleepy village of 280 people,[142] a far cry from the hurly-burly of Natchez or New Orleans, yet it, too, drew enslaved people to buy and sell.

Slaves brought a wide variety of things to sell. As one white resident of the cotton belt explained, these things were usually small and relatively cheap but nevertheless were useful and of a high enough quality that local whites were glad to buy them.

> Here was one with half a dozen chickens in a basket—"jess big enough to fry, massa." Another had eggs carefully tied in a colored cotton handkerchief. . . . Another had brooms, made from old field-sedge, and very serviceable upon floors without carpets. Some had berries, some apples, peaches, and whatever other fruits might be in season. Shuck horse-collars and doormats were very abundant—most excellent articles they were too, and well worth their "quarter." [Other slaves sold] split-bottomed chairs, pine tables, and even pails and tubs, displaying no mean skill in their workmanship.[143]

People who lived in towns and villages willingly bought such items from slaves. In Alexandria, Virginia, African Americans sold "their baskets of berries, their chickens and eggs" right in the center of town, next to the municipal building in a courtyard shaded by a row of paper mulberry trees. "It was a busy scene" on Saturday mornings, reminisced one white resident years later, where crowds of people came to shop and socialize. White children who nagged their parents to take them to "Aunt Airey" for some yellow taffy[144] would have grown up used to the idea of patronizing—in both senses of the word—the "good old 'uncles' and 'aunties'" of their local markets.[145]

Black people nearly took over the trade in a few kinds of goods and services, like hauling, or baked goods, or chickens. When Frederick Law Olmsted got hungry while waiting for the ferry out of Portsmouth, Virginia, he "went into the market and got a breakfast from the cake and fruit stalls of the negro-women."[146] In New Orleans, immigrants from Europe owned the permanent stores, but slaves, especially enslaved women, did much of the town's trading from the streets. Visitors to Natchez and New Orleans remarked that a large proportion of the "picturesque multitude of holiday slaves" were women, and it is likely that many of these enslaved women spent their "holidays" in trading.[147] Black people's presence in urban markets is most evident—though it was not necessarily the biggest—in the Low Country. There, for more than a century, between 1755 and 1860, black women served as the major conduit of goods between white city dwellers and the slaves in the surrounding counties. Black women's marketing activity grew along with the cities. Soon after Savannah and Charleston opened their town markets, most of the people who traded in them were black women, and most of these were slaves.[148]

The preponderance of black women in urban markets allowed them to claim property—and to use public language—in ways that most enslaved men could not. Some whites felt that black women's voices turned town markets into "riotous and disorderly" places,[149] but for the women, words were a way of advancing their interests in the markets, of smoothing the wheels of business. Some words were aimed at customers. Black men and women marketers flattered white strangers by calling them "massa."[150] They pulled in new customers by filling the air with verbal advertisements. One visitor to New Orleans reported that on early mornings outside his hotel, "[b]lack women with huge baskets of rusks [a kind of sweetened biscuit], rolls and other appurtenances of the breakfast table, were crying, in loud shrill French, their 'stock in trade,' followed by milk-criers, and butter-criers and criers of every thing but tears."[151]

Much of what enslaved women said and did in markets was aimed not at white people but at other black people. They used banter and elaborate greetings to guard their relationships with other black traders. According to the northerner Ingraham, the black women in New Orleans "salut[ed] each other gayly as they met, 'Bo'shoo Mumdsal'—'Moshoo! Adieu,' &c.&c, and shooting their rude shafts of African wit at each other with much vivacity and humor."[152] The "wit" and salutations were probably just part of business among the traders. Today, in markets where bargaining still takes place, people often spend time joking and saying elaborate hellos before they get around to talking about prices.[153] In the 1800s, among traders who saw each other frequently, adding the formal "Mademoiselle" ("Mumdsal") or "Monsieur" ("Moshoo") to one's greetings would preserve good relations with a trading partner even through a round of hardnosed bargaining. Markets gave some slaves a chance to trade, to form new social connections and keep up old ones, and to have a little fun.[154] So did the trip to market.

Slaves had different ways of bringing their goods to market. People who earned enough to acquire a wagon and a horse or mule could then haul their goods to market on their own, carry passengers, or take up "draying" for other people. "Whenever I took people into the Country," recalled an ex-slave from Mississippi who drove a dray, "I bought butter, Eggs, chickens fruit & whatever I could sell at a profit and in this way I made considerable money."[155] At least one slave even sent goods by rail.[156]

For many slaves, rivers and creeks were the cheapest and easiest way of getting goods to town markets. But whereas black women dominated informal trading in the towns, most of the earning and trading that slaves did along rivers was done by black men. In the 1840s, as Frances Kemble was boating down a creek near her husband's plantation, she passed slaves on their way from the town of Darien, Georgia, in "parties of three or four [slaves] rowing boats of their own building, laden with their purchases." Like the black women in the town markets, these enslaved men enjoyed their time getting to town and back and expressed themselves out loud, "singing, laughing, [and] talking." Some of them "bawled" out across the water to tell the enslaved man who was rowing Kemble's boat "to 'mind and take good care of missis!'" For slaves, rivers were a man's world.[157]

Rivers were more than a means of transport; the river itself was a source of income and a marketplace, too. Some slaves owned boats and earned money by ferrying people across the South's myriad rivers and creeks. They made their own decisions about when to carry. One group of North Carolina slaves decided "that the job wouldn't pay" and left a group of white travelers stranded by the Roanoke River.[158] In the Sea Islands, these slave-run ferry services were sufficiently entrenched by the 1860s that, when the Union army set up its own ferries, it ran into fierce opposition from black ferrymen, who "seemed to claim the right of running [their] boat[s]."[159] Other enslaved men earned money working as porters and loaders for the steamboats that plied the bigger rivers. The arrival of a steamboat in Natchez, wrote Charles Lyell, a visitor from England, set off a "tumult" of "jabbering, hauling, pulling, kicking and thumping, of some score or two of ebony-cheeked men and urchins, who were tumbling over each other's heads to get the first trunk. 'Trunk, massa—trunk! I take you baggage.' . . . 'Carriage, massa—mighty bad hill to walk up!' "[160] Other blacks offered guided tours of the city.[161] For black people, eking out money from the steamboat trade required not only a strong body but also a sharp eye for customers and a willingness to use words to win business. The "tumult" and coaxing among the black porters, and their imagination in inventing new ways to make a dime, suggest that, like most property-owning slaves, they were poor. They and their work were almost invisible to whites, yet it was their back-breaking, casual labor that moved steamboats, cotton, and the luggage of well-to-do white visitors such as Lyell.

In addition, slaves turned waterways into a marketplace for the goods they and their fellow slaves produced on nearby plantations. Slaves in Calvert County, Maryland, wrote Charles Ball, were allowed to fish in the creeks and rivers that snaked through the land, and to sell their catch for money.[162] Here, as elsewhere, much of these earnings went to buy clothes and food that masters would otherwise have provided. Slaves who lived near the Mississippi and other big southern rivers earned small amounts by cutting and selling wood. Steamboats devoured wood at a fantastic rate, and their crews (which often included both blacks and whites) were often happy to buy it from whomever they hailed on the riverbank. "I used to buy wood from my fellow servants," recalled a slave who lived near the Mississippi River, "and on Saturday afternoons mo[o]nshiney nights & Sundays I used to haul it to the bank of the river where the overseer used to sell it to Steamboats."[163] Slaves supplied other things to steamboats, as well. Frederick Law Olmsted, who spent many days on southern steamboats, wrote that "[w]herever we landed at night or on Sunday . . . there would be many negroes come on board from the neighboring plantations, to sell eggs to the steward."[164] Selling from the riverbank linked plantation slaves with the swelling steamboat traffic of American rivers.

To be sure, trading with whites posed risks for slaves, who had a debased social status and no legal standing at all. Travelers on the rivers could cheat enslaved tradespeople and be gone the next hour or the next day, with no thought of a future reckoning. On a trip down a Kentucky river, one passenger saw a European buy "a string of fish" from an elderly black man who had come on board to sell, and then "refused to pay . . . and kept the poor black wrangling half an hour about a few cents. The needy cripple was at last compelled to take what he could get, and hobbled away, muttering . . . 'a mighty poor white man.' "[165] Faced with these risks, slaves may have preferred more lasting trading partnerships, even if that meant trading with an overseer, the man with the whip. Tacit understandings governed trade relations between slaves and whites, especially when the law seemed to forbid slaves from trading. Charles Ball and a group of slaves came to such an unspoken agreement with their overseer when they were put to work on a fishing seiner. The overseer permitted the slaves to run the seiner—and trade on the river— through the night, and in return, they permitted him to go to sleep early and earned him a bigger share of the fish than his contract called for.[166]

White storekeepers and small farmers also participated with slaves in informal, sometimes illegal, trading networks. Potentially, trading with slaves might have made some whites worry that slaves were breaking out of their cage at the bottom of America's racial order. It also might have angered their powerful slaveowning neighbors, on whom they sometimes depended for loans and other favors. But white storekeepers and small farmers found ways to trade with slaves without threatening either white supremacy or their alliances with planters. Whites in the cotton regions of upcountry Georgia kept stores "at some cross road, or other public place, in or adjacent to a rich district of plantations," where they could draw a share of the trade among slaves.[167] The storekeepers were "always ready to accommodate the slaves," wrote Charles Ball, "because the [slaves] always pay cash, whilst the [poor whites] almost always require credit."[168] Storekeepers in several Virginia counties even kept running accounts for enslaved customers.[169] Masters' restrictions on slaves' movements permitted storekeepers to overcharge slaves for some things and to pull in some of the trading among slaves who lived too far from the big towns. Those slaves "who have no other opportunity of making their little purchases," wrote a white observer, "crowd around the counters" of shops in Natchez, Mississippi. Perhaps because white merchants there did "more business . . . upon the Sabbath . . . than on any other" day,[170] the city did not outlaw such practices but instead regulated them with a sunset curfew. At four o'clock, a bell rang, "warning all strange slaves to leave the city." African Americans overlooked the annoyance and shame of having to hurry their belongings out of the city at the ringing of a bell.[171] For their part, white residents apparently felt that this curfew, with its penalty of forty lashes, preserved their domination over the black population while allowing them to profit from the slaves' time.

It is likely that a whole range of white southerners were used to seeing and dealing with property-owning slaves. Even going to college brought whites into contact with the slaves' economy. At least two slaves at the University of Alabama in Tuscaloosa worked on their "own account . . . at spare hours" making boots and shining shoes.[172] A cadet at the Georgia Military Institute in Marietta (near Atlanta) recalled two enslaved men "selling us such things as we could not get in the mess hall." They "did a pretty large business" giving haircuts, shining shoes, and performing other chores, and "used to furnish the boys . . . with their suppers when they would get up any little Society or meeting."[173] One enslaved man wrote poetry and sold it to students at the University of North Carolina at Chapel Hill.[174] The slaves' economy and the habits that went with it were thoroughly woven into the fabric of everyday life in the South. After losing a battle to Union general Grant's army in Virginia, a group of fleeing Confederate soldiers came to a river too wide to swim. They spotted an enslaved man named Jackson Hall and got him to ferry them across the river in his boat. Naturally, he would have been the last person to argue with a pack of grey-clad white men armed to the teeth. But when the soldiers got across, they paid him.[175]

Even though—or perhaps because—so many whites were used to dealing with property-owning slaves, slaves' market activity was a hotly disputed part of the slave system. By the 1790s, certain groups of whites worried that the informal economy encouraged slaves to steal and get drunk, that it broke the Sabbath, and that their towns were becoming dependent on slave produce. "One Negro woman's 'say so' controls the butter market," sputtered a newspaper editor in Natchez. "To her black majesty's nod all bow or go without buttered bread."[176] These whites urged new laws to regulate slaves' economic activities.[177] But too many other white people benefited from the informal economy for such laws to have much effect. In the 1820s, many white storekeepers, slaveowners, and consumers organized politically to block the new laws, and although Savannah's city council passed the laws, they proved "virtually impossible to enforce."[178] Alexandria's Sunday market stayed open, too.[179] In Mississippi, some whites accepted the "fact" of slave-owned property even as they admitted that "[t]he theory of our laws was that . . . slaves could not own real or personal property."[180] Years later, Vicksburg's former justice of the peace (and now mayor) testified that he was supposed "to supervise the Negro population" and then blandly mentioned buying a horse from a slave.[181] Any constraints on slaves' ownership and trading of property had to take account of the expectations and interests of a wide variety of white people. No law ever formally recognized slaves' ownership of property, yet many southern towns had laws to regulate slaves' marketing of property.[182]

During the 1840s and 1850s the sporadic attempts to restrict or stamp out slaves' trading grew louder and joined with a broader hostility toward blacks as a race. Alabama newspapers complained about "illegal and pernicious" trading with slaves.[183] Upcountry Georgia whites signed public oaths not to sell liquor to slaves or free blacks.[184] Whites in the Low Country formed the "Anti-Slave Traffick Association" in 1846. However, this association merely reprinted laws that were already on the books: laws that forbade slaves to hire themselves out, trade in liquor, or gather in large groups; laws that required slaves to wear a badge at the market; and laws that required masters to provide enough rations so that slaves would not need to go to market.[185] Still, white-owned newspapers, as well as the "anti-slave traffick" associations, fanned the fires of anxiety by constantly linking slaves' marketing with stealing and liquor-drinking; Richmond's enslaved tobacco workers were even accused of holding "champagne suppers."[186] Slaves did steal property, but whites' public pronouncements on the subject obviously did not accurately measure how much stealing there was, most glaringly because such pronouncements virtually ignored thefts *from* slaves.[187] The ebb and flow of "anti-slave traffick" laws and associations probably tell more about the current of whites' feelings toward the informal economy than any facts about the informal economy itself.

The noisy bleating of these voluntary associations suggests that whites themselves disagreed about whether slaves should be allowed to own and trade property and that many whites simply ignored the laws. Sim Neal, whose master took him to Tennessee, wrote home to his family in Virginia that he had "taken up a Small peasea of land . . . and laid it on the [illegible] plan" and that he "Exspe[cted] to have to pay up for my land Before long."[188] Edmund Moss testified that he had speculated in real estate, buying an Alabama farm lot cheap and selling it dear "afterward when the railroad came through." Legally, slaves could not obtain titles to land, yet, Moss insisted, "[i]t was not questioned that it belonged to me then, and I made deed to it."[189] Even more oddly from a legal standpoint, the federal government twice in the 1830s issued patents to an enslaved man from Maryland for corn harvesters.[190] These cases were probably unusual because they involved signed documents that guaranteed legal rights (to land and intellectual property), but even in the 1850s, it was difficult to get courts to convict whites of trading with slaves. "Three-fourths of the persons who are guilty, you can get no fine from," complained the *Charleston Standard* in 1854, "and, if they have some property, all they have to do is to confess a judgment to a friend, go to jail, and swear out," and then "go and commit similar offenses."[191] Some places had laws to regulate slaves' ownership of property, often by requiring slaves to carry "tickets" or written permissions to trade, and some masters paid attention to them, but they tended to call them "customs," not "laws."[192] "It was customary among us," testified a former Mississippi slave-owner, "when we sold a horse to a slave to say to his master when I first met him, that 'I have sold so and so a horse is it all right[?]' "[193] Many whites didn't even bother to do that. As Louisiana's high court pointed out, white passengers on steamboats and stagecoaches "cannot be expected to lose time in inquiring whether the boy be a slave or a free person . . . [or] whether he has his owner's permission. The law forbids the purchase of anything from a slave, without a written permission from his master, yet, many times, the most correct of our citizens buy a melon, or other trifling article, without the production of this permit. In such a case, the act is considered as justified by the maxim, *de minimis non curat lex*, or the proverb, *lo poco por nada se reputa*"[194] — literally, "the law does not concern itself about trivial matters." Whites' disagreements about the ownership of property by slaves tapped into deep splits among different segments of white society, as well as ongoing problems in the system of law.

Nevertheless, despite whites' involvement in the informal economy and their reluctance to ban it by law, larger changes in politics and the plantation economy may have curtailed slaves' independent economic activity by the 1860s. As the national argument over slavery caught fire during the 1850s, the "anti-slave traffick" associations gave way to "rifle corps" and "Vigilance Committees."[195] These militias were supposedly meant to root out abolitionists, but they also put new pressures on slaves' marketing activities. Moreover, as worldwide demand for cotton surged during the 1850s, slave-owners in the cotton regions may have tried harder than ever to gobble up more of the slaves' time. Whites lynched a slave in central Georgia during a dispute over "customary free time."[196] Henry Clay Bruce thought that "[f]rom

1857 to 1862 times had become rather hard on slaves" in his part of Missouri, and "very little better for the free Negroes."[197] A white Mississippian agreed: "A great many more privileges were allowed to the negroes . . . ten or eleven years ago . . . than are now allowed them" in 1863. Some planters were "concentrating the negroes" on large plantations, in barracks-type housing. "The tendency was," this witness believed, "to take away the capacity of the negroes to take care of themselves."[198] The forces that in the 1850s finally threatened to strangle slaves' ownership and trading of property had little to do with the law.

It is difficult to trace trends in the ownership of property by slaves, whether enslaved African Americans owned less property or more on the eve of the Civil War than at other times. However, it is possible to glimpse the scale and character of property ownership among southern slaves at one specific moment—the moment they grasped their freedom.

The records of the Southern Claims Commission provide direct evidence—if incomplete—about how many slaves owned property, and where. Of the 5,004 allowed claims whose records survive, ex-slaves filed 498, representing about 10 percent of the total. Their claims were scattered over 121 counties in every southern state except Texas and West Virginia, which sent very few claims of any kind.[199] An additional 104 successful claimants were slaves who became free before the Civil War broke out.[200] Freeborn people of color were responsible for 231 more.[201] These claimants met a stringent loyalty test and received at least partial compensation on at least one item. A claim could be wholly disallowed over questions of loyalty. However, because each item claimed was examined separately, nearly all claims were disallowed at least in part.

Former slaves accounted for a substantial percentage of the allowed claims in nearly every southern state. The bulk of the allowed claims came from whites, but in Georgia, Mississippi, and South Carolina, where white Unionists were relatively rare, more than a quarter of all the allowed claims came from former slaves. In Virginia, moreover, nearly one in seven of the state's allowed claims were by free people of color.

Comparing the distribution of claims by different groups, claims by ex-slaves were not much more geographically concentrated than were claims by whites. One-third of the successful claims by ex-slaves were filed in Georgia, a proportion not very much higher than the proportion of whites' claims that were filed in Tennessee. Tennessee, which was known for its population of white Unionists, accounted for fully one-quarter of the successful claims by whites. Moreover, although most of the slaves of the cotton belt worked

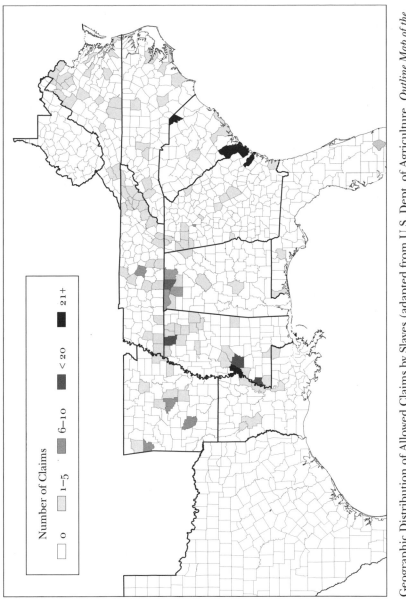

Geographic Distribution of Allowed Claims by Slaves (adapted from U.S. Dept. of Agriculture, *Outline Map of the United States*, June 1, 1870)

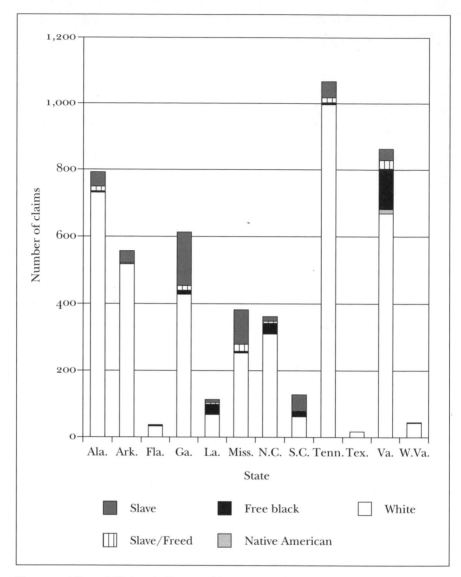

Figure 1. Allowed Claims, by Race and Prewar Legal Status

in gangs rather than by the task, they were still able to accumulate property. Of the successful claims by ex-slaves, one hundred eighty-one, or nearly two-fifths, came from the cotton-producing states of Mississippi, Alabama, and Arkansas. Three hundred thirty-one, or two-thirds, of the successful claims by ex-slaves came from counties outside the Low Country.[202]

Except for the very highest claims, the range of amounts claimed by former slaves roughly resembled that of white claimants.[203] Successful claims by ex-slaves claimed a median of $300 and received a median of $140, just under half of what they claimed. By comparison, white claimants, who claimed a median of $555, received a median award of $280.[204] Claims between $500 and $999 made up about one-fifth of the claims from both whites and ex-slaves. Claims between $100 and $499 accounted for roughly seven in ten claims by ex-slaves, and just under half of the claims by whites. Very small claims, those for less than $100, accounted for about the same proportion of ex-slaves' claims (4.5 percent) as for whites' claims (2 percent). The lowest amount claimed by an ex-slave, $30.50, by Taylor Thornton of Clark County, Virginia, was not much different from the lowest amount claimed by a white person, $50.[205] The lowest awards were even closer, with ex-slave James McQueen's $14 eclipsing the $10 awarded to a white claimant from Arkansas.[206]

Only at the highest brackets was the proportion of ex-slaves' allowed claims very much different from the proportion of whites' claims. More than three times as many whites as ex-slaves had successful claims for between $1,000 and $10,000, and no ex-slave claimed more than $10,000. Put another way, the median amount of the highest one-tenth of claims by ex-slaves was $1,172, compared with a median of $6,977.50 for the top one-tenth of claims by whites.[207] The highest successful claim by an ex-slave was for $7,804.40 by Benjamin Sterling Turner, who had run a livery stable in Selma, Alabama, while he was a slave. Turner was awarded $4,958.21.[208] By contrast, 118 whites made claims in excess of $10,000, higher than that of any ex-slave.

Thus, even though they could not point to any law or written document to back their claims of ownership, former slaves were remarkably successful in filing claims before the Southern Claims Commission. Certainly they faced fewer doubts about their loyalty. The government assumed that slaves had been loyal to the Union, whereas it presumed that white southern claimants had been disloyal until they proved otherwise.[209] Claimants such as Pompey Bacon, who testified that local whites "used to threaten me all the time and often very hard during the war because I was a friend to the Yankees," justified the government's assumption that slaves were loyal.[210] For their part, the ex-slaves felt that their property and their dangerous wartime loyalty to the Union deserved compensation. "I was on the side of the United States there was no *oder* way for me," replied David Stevens to the standard questions on loyalty.[211]

These claims were not evenly spread across the states. Unusual numbers of claims by ex-slaves came from a few counties; Liberty County, Georgia, alone accounted for ninety-one of them. But such clusters probably do not accurately reflect the distribution of enslaved property owners across the South. In order to understand this uneven distribution, we must keep four other factors in mind. First, the slave population itself was not evenly spread. Even in the Deep South, some counties had fewer than five hundred slaves, while in other counties more than seven of every ten people were slaves. Second, the wartime foraging that generated claims happened only in certain parts of the South. After all, the rules of the Southern Claims Commission said that it would only compensate people who lost property to the Union army for "legitimate army use," and many southern counties barely glimpsed the army. If the army did not go through a county, no one had any legitimate reason to file a claim. The third factor is the tactics the army used to get provisions. Normally, the Union army depended on its supply lines and did not do any systematic foraging in the countryside. In two significant campaigns, however—Grant's massive switchback march on Vicksburg and Sherman's march through Georgia—the Union army cut its supply lines and fed itself by foraging through the countryside. The counties with the highest number of allowed claims by ex-slaves—Liberty and Chatham Counties, Georgia; Warren and Hinds Counties, Mississippi—sat right in the path of those two campaigns. As a result, claims by ex-slaves were not distributed evenly, not even within the regions with the most claims. Some counties in the Mississippi Valley and the Low Country accounted for dozens of claims by ex-slaves, while others just next door had none at all. Where ex-slaves filed compensation claims after the war corresponded to where the army did unusual amounts of foraging, and the claims filed in these places do not reflect the full dimensions of property ownership by slaves. This book draws deeply on claims from Georgia, Alabama, South Carolina, and Mississippi, not because those states possessed stronger African cultural roots, but because most claims from former slaves came from these states.

Last, most people found it very difficult to file a claim before the Southern Claims Commission. Testimony from claimants and witnesses, as well as letters from the claims officials, make this clear. Former slaves who served as witnesses in claims cases frequently mentioned in passing that they, too, had lost property but had not reported it. Some of those witnesses said they had not known about the commission until after the deadline for filing. Others simply doubted that filing would do them any good. When asked why he had not filed to recover his own property, ex-slave Tony Law replied, "I have not put in my claim against the Government yet because I haven't seen those who put in get any money. I heard that some in 'Hilton Head' had got

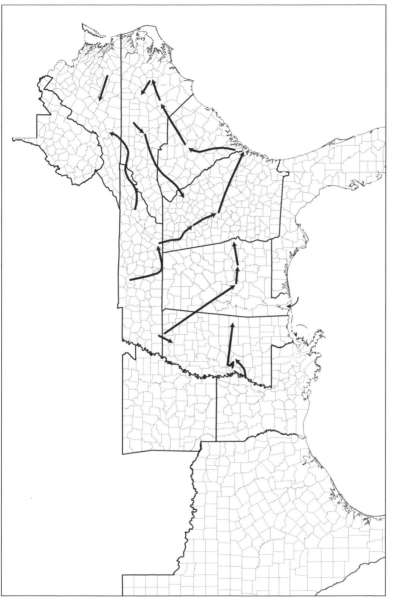

Major Campaigns by the Union Army, 1863–1865 (adapted from U.S. Dept. of Agriculture, *Outline Map of the United States*, June 1, 1870; James M. McPherson, *Ordeal by Fire: The Civil War and Reconstruction* [New York, 1982]; and Mark Grimsley, *The Hard Hand of War: Union Military Policy toward Southern Civilians, 1861–1865* [New York, 1996], 153, 192)

some money but I am afraid that there won't any ever come here in my life-time."[212] Most claimants "are in no hurry" to file, one agent wrote from Little Rock, Arkansas. "The fact is claimants want generally to wait & see some claims paid" before taking the risk of filing a claim.[213] Filing a claim was risky and expensive because it cost money to fill out the necessary paperwork. In Liberty County, Georgia, both Special Commissioner Virgil Hillyer and Raymond Cay Jr., the local lawyer who filed for most of the county's ex-slaves, received fees and percentages that left some successful claimants with as little as $15 of an official award of $130.[214] Claimants had to have a lawyer, but sometimes, said the chief clerk, the lawyer "actually brought some of them [the black claimants] in debt to him for advances, expenses and commissions."[215] And since the rules permitted both the lawyers and the special commissioners to block decisions until their fees were paid, arguing with one's lawyer only delayed whatever payment the claimants were due.[216] Many claimants probably accepted these reduced awards, reasoning that $15 was better than no money at all. But if some former slaves had trouble collecting on an approved claim, others saw their claims just vanish altogether. An ex-slave whose claim was somehow rescued from oblivion testified that after he gave his papers to a lawyer, "I never heered anything more about em. . . . I heard he was in Nashville . . . in the penitentiary . . . for robbing the Government about some claims."[217]

Filing a claim was expensive, confusing, politically risky and, in the end, more than likely to fail. These obstacles in the claims process probably deterred many former slaves from filing claims for lost property. The 498 ex-slave claimants compensated by the commission represented only a tiny fraction of the four million slaves who lived in the South in 1860. Yet, as we have seen, slaves' ownership of property crops up in a whole range of records other than the Southern Claims Commission, including many (such as narratives by runaway slaves and repentant ex-overseers) that sought to emphasize slavery's harshness.[218] Even in counties where ex-slaves filed only a few successful claims, or none at all, the commissioners of claims sometimes spoke of property ownership by slaves as "customary."[219] Some spectacular savers, like Sam Williams, who kept a bank account in Lexington, Virginia, never appear in the claims records.[220] Considering all these factors, it seems likely that the allowed claims of the Southern Claims Commission represent only a tiny fraction of the South's enslaved property owners.

What do these statistics, and the other evidence presented in this chapter, reveal about the ownership of property by slaves? First, the evidence demonstrates that slaves were very poor. This may seem obvious, but it is worth emphasis because it is so tempting to see slaves as budding capitalists.[221] They were not. The median amount of the claims made by former slaves was $300, about $3,877 in 1991 dollars.[222] More than nine-tenths of them were for less than $1,000. Like informal economies in Africa and Latin America, the slaves' economy did much for African Americans, but it also helped prop up the white-dominated formal sector while offering little chance of transforming southern society as a whole.[223] Enslaved African Americans could not increase the time they spent working for themselves. And although many slaves had access to gardens and provision grounds, they did not own those lands and could not borrow against them to expand their operations. As dozens of former slaves explained in their testimony, it could take a lifetime to buy a horse when the only way to earn money was raising chickens or loading at the docks. Such painfully slow, incremental accumulation suited masters just fine because masters were only interested in reducing their expenses, not in seeing their slaves become wealthy. Moreover, even the small amounts of property that slaves owned represented work that slaves did in addition to the exhausting, grinding labor they did for their masters. Owning property probably meant spending Sundays, evenings, and nearly every spare hour at work. Many enslaved people probably could not endure such an unrelenting pace, or chose not to. It is not likely that slaves were developing a neocapitalist mentality in the 1800s, both because of these harsh restrictions on their time and credit and because (as we will see) property meant much more to them than acquisitive individualism.

Second, the evidence suggests that property ownership by slaves was not just a special condition of the task system or a Low Country phenomenon. Property ownership by slaves seems to have existed at some level throughout the slave states, from the halls of the University of Alabama to the leafy creeks of rural Maryland, from bustling streets in Natchez to grassy ranchlands in Texas. The evidence also suggests that property ownership by slaves was not confined to special categories of skilled or privileged slaves. Slaves who had skills used them to accumulate property, and skilled slaves may have been over-represented among the claimants. Yet hundreds of ex-slave claimants had been ordinary field hands. Slaves seized hold of the everyday processes that made up the institution of slavery and used them to create property. Far from a special case, property ownership was generic among slaves, and, whatever conundrums it posed within the law, it was perfectly compatible with the institution of slavery.

Third, the evidence presented here hints that although slaves were poor, as a group, they were not propertyless. No precise figure can describe what all southern slaves owned, but the median amount claimed by slaves before the Southern Claims Commission, $300, can usefully be compared with the holdings of ordinary Americans who were not in bondage. One recent study of the Philadelphia Savings Fund Society in the mid-nineteenth century indicates that working-class northerners kept between $50 and $225 in their savings accounts.[224] Another study estimates that the average daily wage for American laborers in 1856 was $1.22; for artisans it was $1.94; and for clerks, $2.31.[225] These comparisons are not meant to suggest that southern slavery was mild in any way; on the contrary, as we have seen, the ownership of property by slaves was an integral part of a system built on savage whippings, murders, and grinding economic oppression. Instead, the comparison lends support to what Frederick Douglass, Charles Ball, and many recent historians have said: slaves did not have to be propertyless in order to be oppressed.[226] In other words, although we are used to thinking of property ownership as a pillar of freedom, the story of the slaves' economy suggests that owning property does not, by itself, make a person free.

Fourth, slaves' ability to own and trade property required the participation of many masters and nonslaveowning whites, or at least their tacit acceptance. Along with free people of color and visitors from outside the South, many southern whites participated with enslaved African Americans in an informal economy. The informal economy, and the relations of labor and land from which it came, played an important role in the formal economy of southern plantations, towns, and cities. Slaves buying and selling small items was probably a familiar sight for people in nearly every part of the South before the Civil War.

The fact that slaves owned property opens up new perspectives on African American history. It broadens our attention beyond the master-slave relationship to consider how relations among the slaves might have shaped what slaves did with their property, how they earned it, and how they were able to own it. Moreover, it prompts us to reconsider what slaves' ownership of property might have meant during the turbulent years of Emancipation and Reconstruction, questions explored in the chapters that follow. In their testimony before the commission and elsewhere, former slaves insisted that both property and freedom mattered to them, but in order to understand exactly how and why those things mattered, we must first discover what they meant when they talked about property.

chapter three

Family and Property in Southern Slavery

· ·

Dear Husband I write you a letter to let you know of my distress," wrote Maria Perkins. It was early October 1852, a season when chill winds began to blow through the foothills of the Blue Ridge Mountains, down the pretty, white-pillared "Lawn" of the University of Virginia, and across the Charlottesville courthouse square, where nearly every "court day" people were auctioned off to the highest bidder. Maria Perkins's master had sold her son to a slave trader, she wrote, and now "myself and other child is for sale also. . . . [M]y things is in several places some is in staunton and if I should be sold I dont know what will become of them. I dont expect to meet with the luck to get [out] that way till I am quite heart sick."[1] This remarkable letter draws attention to two key dimensions of African American life in the 1800s. As she sat picturing the courthouse steps where she would soon be sold away, Maria Perkins's first concern was for her family. Her second was for her property.

At first glance, it seems clear that the story of American slavery is a story of struggle between white masters and black slaves. From this viewpoint, the fact that slaves could not own property was the low-slung roof on the dungeon of their oppression, one whose other pillars were beatings, killings, and the threat of the slave trader. Between master and slave, where both violence and resources were at stake, there was a grinding, deadly antagonism. It seems natural to assume that the slaves were a community, united by the oppression they all lived under. Other than the little privileges their master might bestow, there was not much at stake among the slaves, and therefore not much to divide them.

Property obviously played an enormous role in the struggle between masters and slaves: masters made a fortune by forcing black people to work for no pay. But what role did property play in relationships *among* enslaved African Americans? As Maria Perkins's poignant letter suggests, both family and property mattered to enslaved African Americans. The connection was more than an accident. In testimony before the Southern Claims Commission, black people from across the South asserted that they had owned property while they were slaves with the tacit cooperation of their masters and nonslaveowning whites. Moreover, slaves' ownership of property depended not just on concessions from their masters but also on their relations with other slaves. Even having a master's permission to own property meant little to enslaved people unless they could get their fellow slaves and neighboring whites to recognize their claims of ownership. This chapter attempts to bring into focus what property and social relationships meant among poor Americans, meanings that often departed from what the law said.

FEW SLAVES COULD EARN much by working alone. When enslaved people accumulated property, they usually did it by finding someone else to work for them. Slaves negotiated for access to others' time through kin and communal relationships, hiring, and plantation privileges. In task system areas, where slave drivers had less extra time than the slaves they supervised, drivers sometimes had the right to have other slaves work their personal plots.[2] There is no way to estimate occupations from the claims records, since few claimants mentioned what they worked at during slavery, but ex-drivers were probably over-represented among the successful black claimants.[3] One white overseer complained in 1828 that in measuring out tasks to his fellow slaves the driver could "screen favorites" and "apply their time to his own purposes."[4] Slaves resented being forced to spend their time and energy working on the driver's extra crop. Years later, when witnesses stood before the claims commissioner, they sometimes gave only lukewarm support to the black men who used to "drive" them. "Some big headed drivers were not always Union," grumbled one former field hand.[5]

Slaves who ranked lower in the master's hierarchy found other ways of getting workers. Testimony from across the South reveals that some slaves were able to hire and pay other slaves to work for them, sometimes on a regular basis.[6] An ex-slave from Vicksburg testified that his employer "was also a slave but she hired her time and hired me . . . from my master" to drive a dray.[7] Benjamin Sterling Turner, who filed a claim for $7,804.40, the largest claim by any ex-slave, hired enslaved men to chop and haul wood, and to drive hacks in Selma, Alabama. The men collected money from customers and "would turn it over to him [Turner] at night," who then, presumably, used a portion of it to pay their masters.[8] For others, hiring themselves out to fellow slaves involved occasional, irregular work, with no questions asked. This was probably most common in cities. Charles Ball captures the flavor of these arrangements: "Whilst we were at our breakfast, a black man came along the street [in Savannah], and asked us if we knew where he could hire a hand, to help him to work a day or two" unloading cotton bales at a wharf. "This man was a slave, but hired his time. . . . He did what he called job work, which consisted of undertaking jobs, and hiring men to work under him, if the job was too great to be performed by himself." For this particular job, Ball remembered, the man "had seven or eight black men, beside me, all hired to help him."[9] Many of the slaves who hired other slaves were self-hired slaves (slaves who hired their own time from their masters). In a few cases, the hired slaves of hired slaves began hiring slaves of their own. Emily Frazier testified that because her "health was poor," her master "put me to work for Danger Rhodes a colored man who belonged to a man in Tennessee." While Rhodes and his other hired hands worked at brick-burning, Frazier "cooked for his hands and at the same time I took in washing on my own account." Once Frazier had enough money, she asked Rhodes to buy a hog and mule for her; she then began hiring the mule back to him "to haul water and tramp mortar." Finally, she hired a man to drive a wagon team for her "out in the country" of Limestone County, Alabama. Yet rather than strike out on her own — to pursue autonomy — she stayed on as Rhodes's cook.[10] Much as Fante people did in nineteenth-century Gold Coast, some American slaves took advantage of self-hiring both to earn property and to build up networks of dependents.

In some places, self-hired slaves met regularly enough that they formed networks, organized jobs, roomed together, and lounged together between jobs. Rural slaves like Samuel Harris "could name . . . a doz[en] others . . . who worked on jobs with me at different times."[11] But it was the black draymen of the South's cities and towns who formed the most enduring networks of self-hired slaves. Drays were two-wheel flatbed carts, handy for any kind of hauling or odd jobs. Black draymen were part of the economic lifeblood of many southern towns. In 1821, for example, six black men —

three of them slaves—were hauled before the Mayor's Court of Fredericks-burg, Virginia, for illegally "running their drays thro' the streets." The court fined them, not because slaves could not own draycarts, but for running them "in a gallop."[12] Although some enslaved women had men driving drays for them,[13] draying, like riverside trading, seems for the most part to have been confined to the realm of men. Richard Johnson remembered the group that developed around the Florida stable of another enslaved man, Wiley Jackson: "I was a hack man at the same time and we hack men would often meet at Wileys Stable to arrange our business."[14] William Chase, who lived in Natchez, Mississippi, testified: "I drove the dray & mules for John Young a colored man who owned the team." Black draymen sometimes shared rooms, socialized, and talked about business. Chase lived "about one block or square" from another slave, who owned his own team, and, he said, "we generally used to hitch up at the same time."[15] A black man from the neighborhood of Jackson, Mississippi, who "wagoned drayed and hacked in them times," re-membered: "Jackson was small, and I knew every man who owned stock for draying or wagoning purposes."[16] For those slaves who, as one ex-slave put it, could "get ahead enough to own . . . horses,"[17] the Civil War made draying more profitable than ever. "Such work was very profitable at that time," re-called a former slave from Mississippi. "The Rail Road was broken up and there was a great deal of hauling to be done from Big Black River to and about town." Enslaved draymen risked their lives to command the "high prices" whites were willing to pay because "there was great risk from the army about."[18] As the Union armies drew near to southern towns, some slaves who had previously worked on wharves or plantations sold their hogs, chickens, and other property and bought mules, harnesses, and carts, anticipating good business.

But the vast majority of enslaved people were not draymen, nor did they hire out or use masters' special grants to drivers. Most slaves got their prop-erty by drawing on their social relationships with each other. Men frequently revealed to the Southern Claims Commission that their wives and children had made much of the property they claimed. Of the property in his father's claim, Thomas C. Hampton testified: "[M]yself and an older Brother and sister both now dead helped raise that crop."[19] Husbands and wives expected their partners to work and contribute to the family. Enslaved people's mar-riages sometimes broke up over disagreements about dividing the work that kept up their households.[20] Robert Smalls, a slave in Low Country South Carolina, believed that concerns about property and labor influenced black women's decisions about marriage. A woman whose husband died, he testified in 1862, might cut short her mourning and start seeing someone new if "she is driven to it by want and must have somebody to help her." Likewise, some married women had to look outside their marriages even while their husbands were alive. "Sometimes a woman gets a lazy man," Smalls testified, "and she does this to help herself."[21] Enslaved men expected similar or even greater contributions from their wives, he went on. "The colored men in taking wives always do so with reference to the service the women will render." Smalls himself had wanted "a wife to prevent me running around—to have somebody to do for me and to keep me."[22] Although several claimants said they brought property to their marriages, it is not clear whether property was a prerequisite or even an incentive for marriage. But because masters forced slaves to carry much of the cost of their subsistence, some slaves may have married with an eye toward gaining property and labor, sizing up what a spouse might contribute to a limited family economy. Much as it did in the Fante region, concerns about property and labor helped shape one of the social ties that slaves cherished most—their marriages. Moreover, whether slaves worked by task or in gangs, their property owed less to individual achievement than to joint effort and negotiation.

Like most white Americans in the nineteenth century, many enslaved parents expected children to contribute time and work to their households. Most claimants who mentioned children too young to marry said that their children worked right alongside them on after-task work. Toney Elliott "had a son that helped him—worked only for his father & mother" up to the age of fifteen.[23] Mamie Barkley, an ex-slave from Jefferson County, Mississippi, remembered that she "used to hold a light for my grandfather as he worked," since her family's "truck patch had to be worked at night."[24] A few parents were even able to hire their children's time from their masters. "I hired the Childrens time as fast as they were old enough to earn anything," said one woman.[25] Martha Patton, a former slave from Hinds County, Mississippi, said that she hired her son's time from his owner and "made money" by having him drive a dray for her. The money belonged to her, she told the commissioners, not to her son or her husband.[26] Jane Dent recalled: "I used to send . . . my little boy . . . in with Eggs & chickens to Natchez" to sell.[27] Children did many of the repetitive, daily chores that maintained slave households, such as "mind[ing]" babies, fetching water, and taking care of hogs and chickens. As one young man testified about his father's claim for hogs, "I know I had sense enough [to] know [how many there were] because I had to tend them all the time."[28]

Even after they went to work in their masters' fields, young slaves kept working for their elders. On plantations that permitted overwork rather than task labor, "parents received pay" for any "few pounds of cotton" that their children managed to pick.[29] On plantations that operated by the task, many parents were able to control their children's after-task time directly. Joshua Cassell reported that "there was a fine lot of young people & they were jealous of one another & tried to see which would get their days work done first." Their master, Thomas Mallard, "used to come in the field, & tell the overseer not to balk we, if we got done soon to let us alone & do our own work as we pleased."[30] Clearly, Mallard benefited from this competition, but parents also may have encouraged it, for those young slaves would probably have gone to their parents' gardens after finishing their tasks. In this way, children helped to create family wealth and learned the importance of gathering property. Such arrangements were part of the constant negotiation that had characterized relations between Low Country masters and slaves since the 1710s, and no one underestimated children's value as workers. Under the task system, more children meant more property. "We could have all the land we could cultivate," remembered George Gould, and lucky was the man who had as large a family as his. He, his four children, and his wife all worked by the task, and when they finished, they "all worked the rice" in the family plot. His claim totaled a remarkable $580.[31] Of another Low Country ex-slave, one witness testified: "*He had a good many children to work for him.*"[32] Slaves were keenly aware of the value they placed on children's labor. "I was 30 years old before I married," testified Henry Stevens, "my children didn't help me much. I did most of it [accumulating property] myself."[33]

As children grew older and began to get property of their own, their relatives often helped them with loans, advice, and assistance in safekeeping their property. Some slaves got their start with a loan from a relative. A former slave from Fauquier County, Virginia, testified that "the first [horse] I ever owned" he bought with fifty dollars "borrowed . . . (from a cousin of mine who was [also] a slave), all in half silver dollar pieces."[34] Relatives often helped slaves take care of their property when they went away from home. One man called on his father, his younger brother, and his wife for help. "My father had money of mine that I had Saved up while I was a Slave," recalled William Hardin. During the war, Hardin left his Mississippi plantation, joined the Union army, and "placed [the money] in the hands of my father for Safe Keeping." More than just protecting the money, Hardin's father acted as adviser and agent for his son, buying livestock and keeping him apprised of his transactions. "[A]fter I came to Natchez," Hardin went on, "My Father came to me and told me he could b[u]y a nice mare If I would agree to it. I told him to b[u]y the Mare and Send her to me by My brother which he did."[35] Hardin's younger brother took the livestock to the home of Hardin's wife in Natchez and stayed with her "to take care of the Stock."[36] Hardin's father did not think it was wise to bring all the livestock into the city, but he followed his son's instructions and did it anyway.[37] On the other hand, Emily Frazier's father expected her to pay closer attention to his advice. She bought a horse in 1863, she said, "and my father whip[p]ed me for buying him. I never will forget that."[38] Even when relatives demanded such strict obedience, slaves worked hard to keep up with their relatives because these relationships gave them the trust and confidence that they needed to take care of their property under tough circumstances.

Not all cooperation occurred within slaves' immediate families. Partnerships and other economic exchanges linked blacks who were not married and who came from different families, had different occupations and legal statuses, and lived on different plantations. Windsor Stevens, who worked in the master's house and drove his master's carriage, did side-work washing and cooking for the field hands. "[S]ometimes they would bring their rations & I would cook them," Stevens recalled, "& they would offer some of their rations to me."[39] Some exchanges involved trading work for property. As a slave in Tippah County, Mississippi, Amanda Young received a mule from "a fellow servant [as payment] for work done for him."[40] Slaves' networks of exchange could become complex. A witness for Matilda McIntosh recalled, "She used to sew by the task . . . & after she got her task done she used to sew for the people down to the plantation & they used to pay her in rice & other things & I suppose she must have sold some."[41] In other words, McIntosh's after-task sewing was the road that connected the field hands' extra rice crops to the local markets. Simon Middleton had more than a trading relationship; he rented land in Savannah from a freeborn black woman, and, in time, Middleton said, he became "kind of an executor for her. There was a white man living on a part of it, & I used to collect her rent of the white man & turn it over to her."[42] While it was unusual for a slave to deal with white people in this way, economic links between slaves and free black people were common. For example, a free black Alabamian named Shanklin invested money in land on behalf of Moses, a slave. When Shanklin sold the land parcel, he turned over the money, and then asked to borrow some of the money back so that he could buy his own daughter, who was still in slavery.[43]

Other kinds of cooperation involved distant kin, people who were more than neighbors but not blood relations. Twenty-three-year-old Benjamin

Hines, a brick mason who had lived with his stepgrandfather at the time of the Union army raid ten years before, said he knew exactly how many turkeys, geese, and ducks the older man had owned because "I had the care of these —that was my business."[44] Whether his parents had sent him there or had themselves been sold away, the boy and his stepgrandfather shared obligations much like those binding immediate family members. Another case involved distant cousins. When Nancy Bacon's husband died in 1863, leaving all of their property at his quarters on another plantation, she enlisted her second cousin, Andrew Stacy, "to go there & bring them home & take care of them" and, it seems, move into her house. When Bacon's master took her to Walthourville, twelve miles away, she left her hogs and cattle again with Stacy.[45] These slaves called on their kin for help in caring for their property, even when those blood ties were distant or even vague. For them, as for most enslaved people in the 1800s, it took more than hard work to accumulate property; it took the help of kinfolk, too.

But just as families made property, property helped "make" family. Today, Americans are used to thinking of kinship as something with a definite structure, and less firmly structured relationships are commonly called "fictive kinship" or even "dysfunctional." But in the nineteenth century, many African Americans—and possibly whites as well—thought of kinship very differently. There was a whole rainbow of social relationships among people who were not related by blood or marriage, relationships that helped them overcome the hardships of getting and keeping property in the slave quarters. After Emanuel Armstead's wife died, he sent his children to live with his uncle, James Jackson, where they may have helped make the property in Jackson's claim.[46] Slaves who lost spouses or were disabled by age or disease often got by on the strength of hale, younger arms. "I had a boy to help me," said Eliza James of the crop she made in 1864 after her husband died. Another slave, Joshua Cassell, also helped her by measuring the grain into bushels, and when the army came through, yet a third slave followed the army to its camp and saw the soldiers dispose of Mrs. James's belongings.[47] Just as slaves who shared ties of descent or marriage did, slaves frequently helped out the needy, even if they weren't related by blood.

Sometimes, the nonblood social ties that slaves formed in the course of their economic efforts were so intense that slaves felt them as kinship. Caroline Walker, who lived in northern Alabama, testified that "Cousin Emily and Grandma and Sister Jennie and Uncle Ike were all there when [the soldiers] took the meat and the mule."[48] Yet, under questioning from the commissioners, her uncle revealed that Caroline, Emily, and Jennie were "orphans."[49] Years of making property together helped turn these strangers into a cousin, two sisters, an uncle, and a grandmother. In another case, John Wilson named, in addition to his wife and children, a "Sister Thompson" as one of the people who had seen his property taken. This turned out to be Charlotte Thompson, an elderly resident of Savannah and a former slave. "I have always been intimate with Mr. Wilson as a neighbor & friend," she testified. Prodded to state whether she had any "interest" in Wilson's claim, she went on, "[W]e are no relation, but he often visited the house as a friend until my sister died then he seemed like a brother."[50] Adopted parents and children created kin ties in similar ways. York Stevens, who received both property and his name from his adoptive grandfather, was so much a part of his adoptive family that in their testimony he and other ex-slaves often neglected to mention that the two men were not related by blood. Confused, the claims agent eventually went to the younger York Stevens's former master and took the following testimony: "Claimant was the son, or adopted son, of old York Stevens, a faithful old driver of Capt. Winn, this old driver, owned horses, cattle and hogs; and Witness understood that old York Stevens gave some of his property to claimant—Witness heard Capt. Winn say so."[51] Sometimes, it took the help of neighbors and friends to make these nonblood family ties take hold. After her husband died, Charlotte Thompson recalled, some of the slaves who lived near her brought "a young girl" to live with her out by the Savannah city limit. Thompson told the commissioners that the girl "was not related to me,"[52] but one of her witnesses said that the girl was Thompson's "niece,"[53] and Thompson herself said that the girl "was all the family" she had.[54] Statements like these suggest much more than "fictive kinship." In some cases, at least, kinship could be created; people could start life as strangers and *become* family.

Flexible understandings of kinship deepened the meaning of adoption and connected it to the slaves' informal economy. Some African Americans adopted not just children but grown people as well, using kinship as an idiom to organize and command labor from a larger pool of family labor. John Byrd, a free black man in Claiborne County, Mississippi, brought several black people into his business by widening the boundaries of kinship. When asked how Byrd accumulated his property, Thomas Richardson explained: "He had a quite large family of journeymen apprentices and children"— and at least one slave—all of whom helped Byrd in his various enterprises.[55] Richardson concluded: "I was a member of his family from [1853] untill [*sic*] the time of his death in 1865."[56] Another witness recalled: "[I] lived in the same house with them, I was the adopted son of Jno. Bird."[57] John Byrd stood at the center of a complex network of kin ties in which the property interests of blood relatives overlapped with those of "adopted" "members of his family." As historians of Africa and Europe have pointed out, blood ties are not always the most important ingredient to make up a family.

Kinship was flexible, but it was not limitless. The slave quarters was not inhabited by one big family; in fact, often the people living in a cabin did not see themselves as related. For one thing, death and masters certainly broke up families. At the same time, slaves themselves carefully set boundaries regarding who "their people" were. Consider what happened after Josiah Henson's master sold him away from his mother. Henson was only six: "He . . . put me into his negro quarters with about forty others, of all ages, colours, and conditions, all strangers to me. Of course nobody cared for me. . . . All day long I [was] left alone . . . lying on a lot of rags, thrown on a dirt floor . . . crying for water, crying for mother; the slaves, who left at daylight, when they returned cared nothing for me." Henson nearly died from neglect before being sold back near his mother, as he put it, "my best friend on earth."[58] "Sometimes I feel like a motherless child," ran a black spiritual from the early 1900s, and stories like Henson's make horribly clear what it meant for an enslaved person to be without kin. There was nothing automatic about black people's relationships with each other.

Thousands of enslaved people faced this horror every year between 1810 and 1850, when North America's internal slave trade forced them from the Chesapeake and the Low Country to the new "cotton kingdom" in Mississippi and Alabama, "sold down the river," an expression many people use even today. As Burwell McShane told the commissioners at Lauderdale County, Mississippi: "I left all my kin in Edgefield District South Carolina when I was about fifteen or sixteen years old."[59] What happened to people like McShane, teenagers sent to live among strangers? As the narrative of Charles Ball suggests, they needed to make kin, relatives who would help them deal with their grief and anger and provide loans, gardens, and extra hands to help them start earning property again. Ball's master thrust him into a cabin with another slave family, but being black and enslaved did not automatically render them anything more than strangers to one another. For fifty pages of his narrative, Ball never mentions the names of the family; he dwells instead on his sadness at losing his wife and children in Maryland. Ball's involvement with the occupants of this cabin really began when they agreed to share property and labor: "I therefore proposed to her and her husband [Nero]," Ball recounted, "that whilst I should remain a member of the family, I would contribute as much towards its support as Nero himself; or, at least, that I would bring all my earnings into the family stock, provided I might be treated as one of its members, and be allowed a portion of the proceeds of their patch or garden. This offer was very readily accepted, and from this time we constituted one community, as long as I remained among the field hands on this plantation."[60] Agreeing to share economic interests went hand in hand with the formation of new social ties, so that a newcomer like Ball became a "member of the family" at the moment when he began to participate in its economic life. Enslaved people arriving in Jamaica found themselves in similar relationships, claiming and being claimed by kinfolk. "[O]ld established Negroes" took on the newcomers "in the room of children they had lost by death, or had been deprived of in Africa," observed one slaveowner, and they assured him that "they had the means of supporting the strangers without difficulty." However old they were in biological terms, these "strangers" now "considered themselves as the adopted children of those by whom they were thus protected, calling them parents, and venerating them as such."[61] Such testimony suggests that, when death or the slave trader forced slaves to make new lives for themselves, they often spoke in the language of kinship.

Slaves who took in children and strangers or who worked for elderly neighbors were manifesting more than kindness or solidarity based on a common experience of oppression. Kinship and property were interrelated among slaves, but, precisely because the meaning of kinship was so complicated, property did not merely follow lines of "blood" and marriage. Slaves' efforts to raise and keep property were built largely on their relationships with one another, especially with family members. At the same time, family ties were flexible and negotiable, influenced by many factors other than marriage and descent, including people's shared interests in property.[62]

Inheritance permitted slaves to accumulate property over generations, beyond the lifetime of any individual owner. In a sense, inheritance gave back to children much of the labor they did for their relatives. It was one of the most important ways slaves got their start as property owners. "When my Father died he had 20 head of cattle," said Samuel Elliott, "about 70 head of hogs. Turkeys Geese Ducks and Chicken a plenty—he was foreman for his master . . . and had been raising such things for years. When he died the property was divided among his children and we continued to raise thing[s] just as he had."[63] Benjamin Stenyard, who lived in Warren County, Mississippi, testified that his father "had at his death Six horses which he left to me his Son and heir."[64] Sometimes, even masters and neighboring whites acknowledged how slaves were passing down their property. A white witness from Mississippi testified that "[t]he property of slaves was generally recognized & when a parent died it descended to his heirs in the usual manner." This witness knew, by "common report," of at least two slaves on plantations near him who bequeathed property.[65] Ex-slave claimants across the South mentioned inheriting chickens, one or two hogs or cows, or sometimes a horse from their enslaved parents.

Slaves and free blacks do not appear to have had any overarching rule on inheritance. The many different forms it took mirrored the flexibility of kinship and the fact that people often shared claims to property. One ex-slave claimant mentioned inheriting property from his cousin;[66] another inherited from her husband.[67] Claimants often recalled bequests made by fathers, less frequently by mothers.[68] Some spoke of inheriting property from both parents.[69] Slaves left property to both their sons and their daughters, but generally, far fewer women than men mentioned inheriting horses or cattle. When free black Charles Williamson's parents died in the early 1860s, under the law their property should have gone to him and his siblings, but instead it went to his grandmother.[70] Some recalled inheriting along with their siblings; other bequests came individually. As in Fante, the oldest child did not necessarily take the lead in claims on "heirs property" if the family as a group settled on someone else. Such was the case with the Williamson family, who emphasized, "It was with all our consent that brother Charles put in this claim" against the federal government.[71] Some families shared ownership of inherited property. At least one Mississippi claimant owned his late father's property jointly with his mother, until she, too, died.[72] But other ex-slave claimants testifying before the commission insisted that they were the sole owners of their property and that their children had "no more interest than any child" in the claims they filed.[73] One woman explained that her children were not "joined" in her petition to the commission because "they will only acquire an interest in [the property] at my death."[74] Still, such sweeping claims of ownership did not discourage children from testifying on their parents' behalf. Seen through the prism of their inheritance practices, flexibility and change were fundamental to slaves' ideas about kinship.

Inheritance practices expressed slaves' decisions about how property should move among family members. It is difficult to pick out one consistent inheritance rule because kinship itself was flexible. Slaves used bequeathed wealth to outline and strengthen the obligations they felt toward each other, obligations that stretched across past generations, sometimes as much as thirty years back in time, and future ones.[75] Part of property's value for slaves, apart from its capacity to be used or consumed, lay in the social relationships it embodied, ready to be called into action.[76] In this respect, property mattered to enslaved African Americans for some of the same reasons it did to Fantes. By bequeathing property, slaves over and over again defined not only *what* belonged to them but also *who*.

At the same time, these shared property interests among slaves posed a significant threat to the security of slave-owned property. So did theft. Slaves certainly stole from one another, and some former slaves continued to do so after emancipation. Visitors to southern plantations sometimes wrote of seeing "padlocks" on the doors of slave cabins.[77] However, there is little evidence of stealing in the southern claims testimony. The commission asked only about the large-scale theft by Union soldiers. Claimants and witnesses had little reason to volunteer stories of what other people stole, since they might have weakened their cases by giving the impression that there had been something uneasy or unstable about property ownership.[78]

Masters, who maintained legal rights over everything their slaves possessed, posed a more serious threat. One man from Florida remembered that his parents "lived in constant fear that their master would confiscate most of their vegetables; he so often did."[79] Some people reported that their former masters would ask before taking anything belonging to a slave. But, of course, it was hard for a slave to refuse such a "request." Behind the veneer of custom and good faith, said former house slave William Gilmore, the masters "were not any of them too good, they would not allow you to talk of your rights."[80] According to one white witness, "every planter had his own rule" regarding slaves' owning property, and a single master could change the rules capriciously. Perhaps in order to protect themselves, many slaves constantly sought "advice" and "would hardly ever do anything" with their property until they had consulted with their masters.[81] Nevertheless, few masters seem to have taken advantage of their legal rights, not even when they put their slaves on the auction block.[82] Joseph Bacon understood that, "legally," slaves had no right to property, but he insisted that "a master who would take property from his slaves would have a hard time." His own master, he said, "never interfered with me and my property at all."[83] Why not?

SLAVES PROTECTED their claims to property by using public occasions and public spaces to display their possessions and to secure acknowledgment from their masters and fellow slaves. The physical arrangement of the plantation was essential to this practice. Most big southern plantations clustered the slaves' cabins together in rows somewhere near where the master or the

The "quarter," shown here, provided slaves with a space to negotiate and change their economic and social ties. Slaves did their chores in the same place that they socialized and kept most of their movable property outdoors, in their yards. Clearly visible here are the kinds of property, such as livestock, wagons, and a washtub, that former slaves later claimed (from G. N. Barnard, *Slave Quarters on an Old South Carolina Plantation*. ca. 1865, Collection of the New-York Historical Society, negative no. 48169).

overseer, if there was one, lived. Slaveowners liked this layout because it kept slaves in "sight of his watchful and jealous eye."[84] Slaves stored their belongings separately. "In the rear of each cottage, surrounded by a rude fence,"[85] they kept "vegetable gardens, chicken coops, pig pens, rice ricks, and little store houses," under the control of individuals and families.[86] In cities, where enslaved people lived in attics or backlot sheds, slaves' "huck patches" were even easier to monitor.[87] Ex-slaves' testimony substantiates this picture and distinguishes what belonged to whom.

"Plan of Druid Hill Garden, Drawn and Written by Lloyd N. Rogers." Plat of an urban slave quarter, with its "huck patch" (at top right, below "Hog Pen") (The Maryland Historical Society, Baltimore, Maryland).

How enslaved people asserted their claims of ownership depended partly on what kinds of property they owned. In the early and mid-1800s, wandering hogs were one of the most important items of property not only among slaves but also among nonslaveowning white southerners and working-class whites in northern cities.[88] As one journalist joked: "What is a hog, but fifteen or twenty bushels of corn on four legs?"[89] Enslaved southerners knew that hogs could eat up waste scraps and turn them into valuable meat and that hogs would multiply without much effort or expense if turned loose to forage for their food. "We don't look after our hogs every day," explained a former slave. "Sometimes [we] don't see them for two (2) months at a time."[90] It was more difficult to raise hogs in the city, and urban slaves may have preferred other kinds of livestock. Lydia Brown commented that "the only way we could keep our hogs" was "by being on the outskirts" of Savannah.[91] But in the countryside, at least, the practice of letting hogs forage for their food pulled together masters, slaves, and local whites in tacit cooperation. Hogs and cows were valuable possessions, costing about $7 for a hog and about $19 for a cow,[92] yet they usually were not penned at all. Instead, these animals foraged for their food, mixing with those of the master and often wandering into the fields of neighboring whites.

But allowing animals to forage on other people's land might have multiplied the number of competing claims on property, dangerously blurring people's claims of ownership. Larger animals were easy to recognize since there were few of them relative to smaller stock like chickens. Claimants generally described mules, horses, and cows individually in great detail in their testimony, and could recognize them even in faraway army camps.[93] A white witness in an Alabama case insisted that, even though none of the animals belonging to his enslaved "near neighbor" was branded, "[t]his stock was known and understood by the neighbor[hood] to belong to Claimant."[94] Women as well as men paid attention to the animals their neighbors kept. Of her neighbor's claim for a horse, Matilda David testified: "I had seed Henry Hobbs driving and working the horse so much I knowed him wherever I seed him."[95]

Sometimes "neighborhood understanding" had to be helped along. Many of the things that slaves owned ran in flocks and herds too numerous for people to pick out so easily. In order to protect their ownership of wandering hogs (and sometimes cows and horses), some slaves branded the animals' bodies with distinctive cuts, and secured acknowledgment of those marks from other slaves, their masters, and neighboring whites.[96] In allowing slaves to "raise . . . hogs or mark them in their mark," said the North Carolina Supreme Court, masters permitted slaves to cross the line into "acts of dominion and ownership."[97] Yet some masters gave their slaves "a mark for their hogs," such as "an upperbit in one ear & a crop & a hole in the other,"[98] and told white neighbors that "the Masters had to be present when their slaves' hogs were marked."[99] In fact, slaves may have wanted the masters to be there. Moreover, some slaves went further, paying white neighbors to do the marking for them. From then on, those local whites could vouch for the slaves' claims of ownership by describing the marks in detail.[100] Southern whites knew how to spot such marks because they relied on the same informal system to protect their own claims on livestock. As one observer wrote, one of the first things that any newcomer did when he came to the Arkansas bottomlands was to "cut his hogs' ears in some mark or other [and] turn them out to root for themselves."[101] Such marks, said the North Carolina Supreme Court, "are the ordinary indications of ownership" of animals.[102] And although at least one county went to the trouble of keeping a "Record Book of Marks & Brands,"[103] such written records merely reflected the detailed knowledge of sizes, colors, and what one witness called "particular mark[s]" that undergirded nearly everyone's claims, whites' and blacks' alike, on wandering animals.[104]

Yet brands and marks were not enough. Most of the items that ex-slaves claimed—chicken coops, beehives, hogs, small gardens—were stored in their yards, where they were visible to other people. Cabins and storehouses closely adjoined, and, with four or five slaves living in each cabin, people could see from their own yards what their neighbors had.[105] One man recalled that his neighbor's "fowls & ducks" "were so near to mine that I counted them to know the difference. . . . I was living close by him & knew as much about his things as he did himself."[106] Often the display of property was more intentional. "We staid door to door to each other," testified Clarinda Lowe about her neighbor James Anderson, "& when we got any thing new we always showed one another."[107] One person's chickens, eggs, grains, money, and hogs were hard to tell apart from anyone else's. Among slaves, counting and measuring such property helped secure acknowledgment of their claims of ownership. An ex-slave from Warren County, Mississippi, recalled that she and one of her neighbors in the slave quarters "used to count the chicken[s] every other night, after they went to roost. [I]t used to take ½ half hour to count them."[108] Some slaves turned the counting of property into a public display and peppered these sessions with boasting and joking. "I used often to count them when he fed them," recalled Henry Harris of his friend Samuel Osgood's hogs. "We used to brag over things, & see who would get the most."[109] Another ex-slave remembered that he and a friend "always measure[d]" their rice "to see how much we had to laugh at one another."[110] Rachel Osgood recalled: "[I]n them times [we] hadn't much else to think about & we wanted to know who was getting along the best."[111] Counting out loud in the yards helped slaves secure their ownership of those things that were most difficult to keep track of.

Slaves frequently gathered in their yards to socialize. When slaves visited one another, whatever property was cooped, penned, or stacked there became more or less public knowledge. "I was backwards and forwards every day," recalled Henrietta McLaughlin, an ex-slave from the town of Jackson, Mississippi. "[I] lived only a door from Mrs. Lee [and] I knew what property she had. I didn't know every thing she had in her trunks and boxes, but knew what was in sight, such as provisions and bedding."[112] As Samson Bacon, an ex-slave from the Low Country, testified: "I know it was his because every man on one place know every other man's property. . . . [H]e can't help from knowing it. All go in his yard before his door."[113] Although their masters designed the slave quarters with their own interests in mind, slaves used the layout to their advantage as well.

Some of the property that slaves owned was not kept out in plain view and was not set apart by fences, walls, or other features of the plantation layout. Slaves on one Louisiana plantation put "pictures on the wall[s]" of their cabins, pictures they bought from itinerant "picture men [who] come thru the country."[114] Some masters provided a general storage space called the "nigger house" for slaves to store their corn, bacon, and other property.[115] Other kinds of property were stored inside the slaves' cabins, which commonly housed people from different families. Slaves often permitted their neighbors or relatives to store property with them in their cabins or, if they had them, in "smokehouses" nearby.[116]

Such common storage required careful attention to claims of ownership. Even people who lived together, worked together, and were members of the same family distinguished their property from that of their relatives or co-residents. John Swinney, who lived with his wife and her mother and stepfather, helped to kill and dress his father-in-law's hogs, putting the meat, along with "200 lbs Bacon" of his own "in [the] same Smoke house," which was "close by the front door of the house" they shared.[117] The "smoke house belong[ed] to my wifes step father," Swinney testified, and both he and his father-in-law concurred that although the bacon was "all put in [the] same smoke house," it "was kept separate."[118] Like those who owned storehouses, slaves who stored property in their cabins used the physical layout of the cabin to distinguish their property from that of the other people who lived with them. Essex Dargan testified that he lived with his wife and her parents "all in the same room" and that they stored several hundred pounds of bacon in the cabin. But, he insisted, the bacon owned by his wife's parents "was all separate from mine."[119] Samuel Fuller, who had been a slave on the same plantation, testified, "I knew it was [Dargan's] property because it was on his side of the room, and I suppose he kept all his property on the side he lived on with his wife. He also said it was his."[120] Fuller, who filed his own claim with the commission, recalled that he, too, stored property for one of his cousins and her husband, "but," he insisted, "it was all kept separate from mine."[121] In spite of limited storage space, which enslaved people often shared with relatives and friends, they kept track of what belonged to whom.

Unlike with corn and animals, the evidence suggests that slaves were discreet with their money. It was the most fungible and portable kind of property that anyone owned. Designed to be passed around quickly and easily, one person's money looked exactly like anyone else's. Slaves adopted different tactics to protect their claims on money. One tactic was to turn it into something that was harder to steal, like a wagon. "When I came to Nashville [in 1862] I had some two hundred dollars in gold and silver that I had saved while a slave," testified Richard Traynor. Right away, he spent it on mules and drays.[122] Another way slaves protected claims on money was simply keeping it hidden in trunks within their cabins. Asked to testify about what Jacob Quarterman, a field hand, had owned, fellow slave Joseph Bacon testified that he "knew all about what he owned & what was his," except for his money. "He is a man what had money," Bacon insisted, but people "never see his money. [H]e too cunning to show any body his money."[123] Another ex-slave witness in Quarterman's case told the special commissioner: "The gold & silver is something which few men could tell anything about, but he was the kind of man who would have money & I heard him crying out about it that [the soldiers] took it."[124]

Black people who hid their money were not necessarily worried about being robbed. Instead, hiding money reflected the fundamentally social character of all the property slaves owned. Since each piece of property embodied the interests of several different people, and cash could be divided easily, slaves who owned cash might have worried that other slaves would ask them for some of it, thus breaking up their savings into smaller, less useful amounts. It is possible that some slaves may have bought expensive things, like horses, precisely to avoid such family dilemmas.

Another way slaves secured their ownership of money was to pay attention to how the bills and coins looked and felt. Indeed, nearly all Americans, not just slaves, drew distinctions between the different kinds of money that circulated in the United States during the 1850s and 1860s.[125] In their testimony, ex-slaves distinguished "bank money" from "confederate" money,[126] coin from paper, and "good Yankee Money—old kind of money"[127] from the quickly worthless new bills that the rebel government issued during the war. Still others registered their ownership with a confidential witness by asking someone to count their money for them. Philip Hart knew exactly how much his neighbor Julia Ann McCaskell paid for her mule because he "counted the money for her" at the Mississippi slave quarters where they lived.[128] Alexander Kenner, a white witness from Kentucky, testified that one of the slaves who lived "on a neighboring plantation . . . used to get him (Alexander) to come and count his dollars." This slave, said Kenner, "knew by the appearance or weight whether it was all right or not" and "nobody could take any of the money without his knowing it," but, nevertheless, "he wanted to know the exact number."[129]

When someone did steal from them, slaves dealt with it by skillfully manipulating the power of the spoken word and the physical landscape of the countryside. Jacob Stroyer described special committees that publicly questioned suspects and sometimes used divination objects like string-tied Bibles and graveyard dirt to detect thieves.[130] Charles Raymond described what an enslaved woman named Maria did when someone stole her chickens. Maria went about her work until Raymond and his host were relaxing on the veranda, and then she sang out "a strong, high-keyed, nasal plaint, indignant and doleful, half chant, half recitative, and most profoundly earnest":

'Oh-h-h-h, Jesus! Oh-h-h-h, Jesus!
An' dey make long prayers,
An' dey sing long psalms,
But dey steal my chick-ins, Lord;
Oh-h-h, Jesus! Oh-h-h, Jesus!'

"Then, as an interlude, would follow a continuous humming sound, as if gathering up her feelings into metrical shape; and again would the plaint burst forth":

'. . . But dey'll all be damned
In dat drefful day;
For dey steal my chick-ins, Lord.'[131]

Although Raymond did not mention any other listeners, such a song was intended for an audience, one that included her master, her fellow slaves, and whoever stole her chickens.

Away from the eyes of their masters, slaves' verbal jousting became less oblique, more pointed. For example, a slave recorded only as West sarcastically told his fellow bondsman Hubbard "to be more of a Gentleman" and pay back the fifty cents he owed him, adding "that he was the rong man for Hubbard to fool with."[132] Henry Deedes, a white man who was traveling near Montgomery, Alabama, described an "altercation between two negroes" on a riverbank over a theft. The two black men shouted out threats to one another and made as if to fight. "You d—d nigger, what you come for to steal my gourd?" exclaimed the older man, who was a ferryman. "Oh! You go 'long with you," the younger man retorted, "I not steal your gourd, I only take him. I'll tell you, ole man, I'll smash your wool skull in if you call me tief." "Oh you tam rascal!" replied the older man. "First steal my pie and then say you'll break my head! Should like to see you! Will kill you where you stand if you not take that gourd back to where you found it." But they did not fight, nor did the older man summon "the law" to get back his property. Instead, he relied on the power of his words—"tief," "rascal"—to attract attention from the people watching from the riverbank. Deedes characterized this altercation as "a piece of melodramatic acting," and, in a sense, he was right.[133] Whites almost never noticed arguments between African Americans unless one of their slaves seemed likely to end up dead.[134] More often, the tight layout of the plantations, and the threat of harsh punishment from masters, led slaves to find other ways of dealing with their disagreements. Black people's words darted and drifted on the air of the South, ignored by whites and thus safe from censure because much of what they said was aimed at other black people.

Slaves also took advantage of special occasions to affirm their property claims, moments that often drenched their belongings with social meaning. Church visits enabled some slaves to testify in great detail about other slaves' property, even about the property of people who lived miles away from them. Cyrus Kirkman, for example, "was often at claimants house" in Alabama "on business connected with the Baptist church of which the claimant was the pastor and affiant was Deacon."[135] Enslaved people took only their best things to church, imbuing those items with personal and religious significance. Slaves and planters alike were deaf to the familiar preacher's complaint that "on Sunday many *garnish* themselves and go to church for show; they hear but do not attend."[136] Although the practice may have seemed a petty distraction to white preachers, slaves "showed" their property on Sundays for practical, social, and deeply spiritual reasons. For example, Charles Cox, a skilled miller enslaved in Maryland, picked through the ashes of the mill house after it burned in 1783, "crying and seemingly in great distress . . .

that he could not find a piece of the silver coin, a guinea, nor any of the yellow metal buttons which had been in his Sundays clothes that were in [his] chest."[137] Pompey Bacon, who gladly "clothed and fed" the Union soldiers, refused to part with his "nice" overcoat and shirts until the soldiers "hustled me round till they carried" off even those items. Bacon took especially hard the loss of "some nice linen shirts I used to go to communion in & they took *them* and I grieved . . . I wanted them to meet the '*Lord.*' "[138] Indeed, many of the things slaves owned had both practical uses and poignant, personal meanings for them. People waiting in the soul-killing "slave pens" sometimes had a few "boxes or bundles" of "baggage" filled with clothes, shoes, bedding, and maybe something to remember their loved ones by.[139] However forlorn these things seemed to white onlookers, they meant the world to those who stood on the auction block. "My heart was so full that I could say very little," remembered Moses Grandy of the day he said goodbye to his wife. "I gave her the little money I had in my pocket, and bade her farewell. I have never seen or heard of her from that day to this. I loved her as I loved my life."[140]

The spiritual and practical meanings that enslaved people associated with their belongings took on additional, social significance in the context of public worship. Some people, if they could afford it, kept certain possessions apart to use less frequently. They wore their "common everyday coarse clothes" during the week and saved their town-bought "finery" to wear on Sundays. William Gilmore, who owned a "spring wagon," said that he "only used it to go to Church on Sunday."[141] James Miller and Paris James did the same with their good saddles.[142] Some people even walked to church barefoot, "carrying their shoes and stockings in their hands."[143] All of these practices tended to ease wear and tear on their property, at the same time marking Sunday as a special day. Although friends and neighbors frequently visited one another in their yards, Sunday services were one of the few occasions for slaves to socialize in large groups. As they did so, they brought their best clothes, driving buggies, and quilted leather saddles out where people could see them. Recognition of the Sabbath was intertwined with the informal system of display and acknowledgment that secured slaves' ownership of property.

Sometimes, churches served as forums for settling disputes among enslaved people. Slaves probably preferred not to get tangled up in southern courts, because from the local courts of Oyer and Terminer to the lofty orbit of the governor, the South's legal system was not interested in getting to the bottom of black people's disputes with one another. For example, the Mayor's Court of Fredericksburg, Virginia, hauled in two black women for "fight[ing] and creating a riot." Once it discovered that an enslaved man was "keeping both women in the capacity of wives," the court had a quick solution: it had all three of them whipped.[144] Black people were unlikely to take an argument to court; instead, as the saying goes, they "took it to Jesus." The First African Church of Richmond apparently spent much of its time in the 1840s acting like a court, calling slave churchmembers to answer to charges like "drunkenness and riot" or "marrying a woman whose husband was still living" and sending deacons to "investigate . . . the case[s]."[145] Black churches could get under the surface of slaves' lives, to the knotty truths of a woman "provoked, by the blows of a fellow-servant" or of a man whose new wife's ex-husband had "maltreat[ed]" her and "gone off and married another wife."[146] It is hard to imagine any white judge taking the time to probe this deeply into a dispute between slaves. But right from its founding in 1841, the members of Richmond's first black-run church brought (or permitted others to bring) their most delicate secrets to be aired before the congregation.

Enslaved people also settled disputes outside the church. Archaeologists have discovered evidence that, in addition to storing food, tools, and clothing in lofts and on floors, slaves hid other items in the walls of their cabins, such as patent medicine bottles, coins, buttons, mirrors, musical instruments, chalk, bird skulls, ocean shells, scales, and small cloth bags filled with plants.[147] It is likely that some of these things were part of "conjure," in which special objects like these were used to channel supernatural power into "fixing" people's problems with one another. Some kinds of conjure targeted other black people, as when the teenaged Henry Bibb bought something to make girls fall in love with him.[148] Other kinds of conjure were aimed at whites. Frederick Douglass used "a certain *root*" gotten from another slave to win his epic battle with the slave-breaker Covey.[149] Fanny was said to have given mysterious objects to fellow slaves at their south central Virginia plantation: "a small whitish root . . . given in water," for example, would kill their master; and to Jacob she gave "black stuff to put on his Jacobs face to make his master love him."[150] In another case, Billey testified that Dick, one of his fellow slaves, "came to him at home and told him that he wanted to go to" a conjurer, saying "that his Master was so bad he could not please him and that he would go and get some Stuff to put his Master away."[151] Conjure objects were hard to come by; it took money to get them and connections to know whom to ask. Dick conferred with two other slaves before going over to the next plantation to see Frank about the "Root," saying "he would Poison his Master at the risqué of his life he would Procure Poison if it took every Rag of his Clothes to pay for it."[152] Another group of people heard of "a great conjuror living ten miles away, made up a purse and sent for him" to stop their master from sending them to Alabama.[153] Conjure straddled this world and the next; it was all about social relationships that knit together the living and the dead. But conjure was also a business, with standard fees[154] and competition between men who drummed up business by calling other conjurers "quack[s]."[155] Slaves traded the property they earned for property that could create or change social ties—or even kill.

Enslaved people also sank much of their time and their property into churches, both black-owned and those controlled by whites.[156] As northern commentators learned in the 1860s, black church property in the South was legally owned by free blacks, "[b]ut the slaves contribute towards it . . . very largely" and "do the most towards getting it."[157] After visiting a black church in New Orleans in 1847, newspaper correspondent Charles A. Raymond exclaimed, "Who would have expected a plate full of silver from slaves!" It was probably unusual for slaves to put thirty dollars into the collection plate of any Southern church.[158] More typical were the slaves of Frankfort, Kentucky, who contributed little by little "towards the support of the Methodist churches . . . in small sums" earned from "their patches and pigs & poultry."[159]

Black churchgoers did not have much money to give, and some churches took advantage of their layout—pews, pulpit, walls—to fill the collection plate. "After preaching," wrote the journalist Raymond, the minister "would remind the congregation of their duty . . . and announce that 'de collection for de poor members would be receive on dis present occasion.'" Rather than have the deacons walk through the pews, the whole congregation was supposed to come up front. As one of the deacons explained, people needed "pers[u]asion," even in church. "If you pass de hat nobody observe de consequences," Peter said. "But when dey comes forward to de table, de obser-[v]ations is perspicuous, and dey gibs berry much wid dere anxiety."[160] As anyone who goes to church knows, the size of the collection often depends on how it is taken.

Black-owned churches used the money they collected for a variety of purposes. The pastor of a Colored Baptist Church in St. Louis testified in 1863 that "the colored churches have each a poor fund . . . and when a man dies without leaving any property, we bury him. We have always done that, because we don't like to have the white people think we can't take care of ourselves."[161] A northerner visiting the Sea Islands in early 1864 caught a glimpse of another way that black communities took care of their own. One of the former slaves told him that a slave named "Prince Rivers used to be President of a Mutual Aid Society the colored people had—slaves and all. Each person deposited some money with him every week, and when anyone was sick his wife was aided from this fund—the money to be refunded when he became well."[162] Like the churches, black southerners' "poor funds" and "mutual aid societies" put some economic stability into their lives.

Black people in the South dealt with one another in their yards, on the roads and rivers between plantations, at church services, and at weddings. These social interactions nourished their hearts and minds and fostered a sense of community. They also helped make it possible for slaves to own property. The informal economy was built on a foundation of shared understandings about what property was and how people owned it. It nurtured a whole range of different practices, from conjure to churches. Those practices also tied free blacks and slaves into networks of "colored people," networks whose character was neither wholly social nor completely business oriented.

Yet, because slaves relied so heavily on their neighbors and kin to make property, their negotiations over property were impossible to separate from those over community and family. Indeed, in many ways, these negotiations were one and the same. Consider marriage, for example. Marriage among slaves called for careful attention to the public dimension of personal property ownership because it rearranged the property interests of two people and their families, often splitting property between two households. With the exception of those who hired themselves out, if enslaved people married off their plantations, their masters usually did not let them live together.[163] A slave who lived with his or her spouse was thought to enjoy "rather an unusual privilege,"[164] one that was probably granted most often to men who hired themselves out. Most slaves who married off the plantation were obliged to maintain two households, more or less complete with gardens, utensils, and all the other necessities of life. Property flowed back and forth between the households as spouses, usually husbands, shuttled between them. "Saturday nights," wrote Robert Quarterman Mallard, "the roads were . . . filled with men on their way to 'wife house,' each pedestrian, or horseman, bearing in a bag his soiled clothes and all the good things he could collect during the week, for the delectation of his household."[165] Depending on the season and what their masters permitted, slaves often kept property at each of their houses. "He had his things home to his house and I had mine to my house," recalled Harriet Smith of her husband.[166] Rarely did enslaved husbands keep property for their wives. Instead, slaves viewed the wife's house as the husband's primary residence, and the bulk of a couple's property usually stayed there with her. Henry Hall "[k]ept his horses & mule and other property at the place of his father in law where he lived," testified an Alabama witness.[167] Prince Stevens was known to have "lived with his wife—nights—and she took care of his property that was the custom generally." "Sometimes he would have some things at his home," said a witness in Stevens's case, but only "to use up the slops of [his wife's] house."[168] In spite of the masters' intentions, the flow of slave-owned property signaled that slave couples considered themselves to have one "home," though they had two cabins, with property at each. Faced with these restrictions on their mobility, slaves made the home—that is, the slave cabin, the multifunctional yard, and the garden—a locus of authority over property.

Uniting possessions under one roof helped secure them against threats from outside the household, but it also sparked negotiation within the household. Spouses contributed jointly the labor needed to earn property, and the work of looking after it. But joint effort did not rule out the possibility that in some situations slaves had an interest in asserting individual claims. How did people know who owned those household possessions?

Many couples distinguished items on the basis of who had "made" them, that is, who had contributed the labor that earned those items. A woman enslaved near Mount Vernon, Virginia, got her mistress to certify that she had acquired a long list of items "solely by her industry without the least assistance from her husband."[169] Thomas Drummond, who "was always trading," was only able to trade, testified Martha Bradshaw, because "we women, & his Mother kept house for him" and helped raise the livestock he purchased.[170] In addition, Drummond's mother "made ice Cream, & Sold to the Car Passengers" on the Mississippi railroad.[171] This way of distinguishing items gave enslaved women substantial claims because they did much of the work that "made" slaves' property. Asked why her husband had not "joined" in her claim against the government, Martha Patton explained: "[W]e belonged to different owners and he had to work for them whereas my mistress allowed me almost all of my time and I had a chance to make and save money. . . . I made the property and controlled it and every body knew it was mine."[172]

Enslaved husbands and wives recognized each other as having separate interests in the property they earned, even though American law before the 1900s generally gave husbands substantial claims on their wives' property. A witness in Maria Carter's claim testified: "The property has always been in her name, and known as hers, even before she was free. . . . I don't know whether her property could have been taken for her husbands debts. I dont know anything about such things. I know that the property was always called hers by both white and black."[173] Another witness recalled that Carter "managed everything" and "had everything in her name. . . . I call a husband's property his wifes, but I believe this was really in Maria Carter's name."[174] "William Verkins in his life time told me that he had given this property to his wife Sarah Verkins the claimant," testified one ex-slave witness. "[T]o my knowledge he never claimed the property as his, and always when speaking of it, called it his wife's property."[175] Some women even convinced their husbands' co-workers and friends about their separate claims over property. "I think his wife had a sow that used to come to the stable to eat up litter," testified Arthur Harris, the black owner of a Florida stable where ex-slave Wiley Jackson had kept his dray and horses during slavery. "He [Jackson] had no hog of his own."[176]

Slaves' careful recognition of inheritance and their willingness to be flexible about rules of descent also strengthened black women's control over property. Abraham Walthour, who claimed a horse and a colt, testified that the horse had belonged to him because he "rais[ed] it" but that "the Colt was given to my wife by her Father when [it was] about one year old."[177] Two other ex-slaves confirmed that Mrs. Walthour had inherited the colt from her father.[178] Asked why her husband was not a party to her claim, Elvira Anderson explained: "My father Ben Holley bought the two cows and calves and gave them to me before I was married."[179] Three other ex-slaves, including her husband, confirmed Anderson's account.[180] Slaves took care to remember who had earned or inherited the various things they owned. That knowledge helped black women maintain claims to property that might otherwise have been claimed by black men.

Custody could carry just as much weight as labor investment or inheritance in negotiations between husbands and wives who lived apart. Because men, not women, did most of the shuttling between houses, they tended to be familiar with—and possessive of—the property stored at the wives' cabins. William Cassels walked the half mile to see his wife most nights and "knew as much about my things there as at my own home." The property belonged to them both but to him most of all: "She doesn't claim anything separate from me we are all one."[181] Draymen, moreover, had much of their property in horses and equipment that were not in the house.[182] Women were not allowed to travel as much as men and could not have controlled property that was stored elsewhere, but a woman may have been able to control and claim her husband's belongings because they were stored at her house. One woman insisted that, "except the horse which was bought by my former husband," the property in her claim "never belonged to my husband for it was taken in Floyd Co. Georgia . . . before I came to Alabama."[183] During slavery, the prevalence of split-residence households and the importance of display and acknowledgment meant that custody and knowledge were likely to override other factors in determining which spouse controlled property and in turning control into claims of ownership. Since married couples living apart tended to keep most property at the wife's house, enslaved black women probably had substantial claims over household property.

After the war, men's tendency to claim household property as their own increased both because black households began to consolidate and because the Southern Claims Commission required women to prove separate ownership from their husbands. Male claimants faced no such requirement. Thus Prince Stewart testified that, although some of the things he claimed had "belonged to, and were taken from, my wife . . . 'wesm' are all one now so I put them into my claim."[184] "No person in the world but myself has any interest in this claim," Toney Barnes said of the property he and his wife had "made" under slavery in Mississippi. "I spose I might put my wife in, but we is all us one."[185] One man even claimed that "[i]t was the custom here among us" for married people "to keep our things together . . . and whatever was claimed by the wife belonged to her husband."[186] Married people's joint efforts to raise property and their common interest in safeguarding it did not stop their negotiations over control and ownership.

To make sure that the property interests of their children, nieces, and nephews stayed secure after marriage, some slaves relied on the public character of the wedding itself. Slaves treasured the public rituals surrounding marriage because they legitimized social and economic ties that the law did not recognize.[187] Giving property as part of the marriage ceremony publicly affirmed the bonds between newlyweds and their relatives. Public giving also permitted the new couple to avoid confusion or hard feelings in the future in that it spread knowledge about how each piece of the couple's property had come into the marriage, something that was especially important for enslaved women. Susan Bennett explained that although she and her late husband had earned some property together, not all of the property she claimed was jointly earned. "We both had pigs when we married," she remembered.[188] Nancy Hardeman testified that some of the property in her husband's claim belonged to her: "[M]y father gave me one of the mules . . . when I was married."[189] Jane Holmes took care to distinguish between her things and those that had belonged to her two husbands: "I did not get any property by either one of my husband's," she testified. "I kept the property my husband had when the raid came for his son to attend to. I had no children by him so when he died his property went to his son."[190] Enslaved men recognized their wives' ownership of the property they received from their relatives as wedding presents. And if anyone was inclined to forget where their household property had come from, those relatives were often there to remind them. "I made the bed myself & gave it to my daughter when she married claimant," said Martha Berry of a valuable goose-feather bed claimed by her son-in-law Albert Deval. "I lived in the same yard with my son in law & knew just what he had."[191]

This careful attention to the ways property came into the marriage made each spouse's claim to ownership stronger and, to some extent, offset the tendency men had to claim all household property as their own. Enslaved Americans paid close attention to the property dimensions of major life changes, much like Fante people preserved memories of who had done what at long-ago funerals and marriages. Moreover, because slave families provided so much of the labor that raised property, the knowledge that protected it, and the rules of inheritance that passed it down, married people's claims to property tended to get their relatives actively involved in their household affairs.

In the absence of legal protection, the claim a slave had to property seems to have depended on his or her long association with a thing, an association that had to be visible to as many eyes as possible. "I seen it in her possession, and her master knew it, and everyone considered it her property," said a witness in an Alabama case.[192] Testifying in the case of Prince Stevens, ex-slave Samson Bacon explained that he "never heard [Stevens's] master claim his horse. No sir no such thing as that, he had been riding the horse too long back & forth between there & his master's."[193] What from a legal perspective might have seemed merely rights of use or possession translated over time into real claims of ownership. As another witness put it, "I know it was his because it was right there under his 'controlment' & no one else claimed it."[194] Much of property's public visibility—through the multipurpose slave yards, inheritance practices, transfers at marriage, showy dress, and buggies at church—performed an important function. In effect, by dragging their personal property into public view, the slaves cemented their claims to own property in a society whose laws did not admit that possibility.

On the other hand, because of the constraints of the system of slavery, slaves could not use public display in their *conflicts* over property and social relationships as easily as they used it to *secure* their claims of ownership. Masters controlled the physical layout of plantations, and they had an interest in suppressing any disputes among slaves that might hurt the plantation's profits.

Nevertheless, wherever masters did not care, or were not there to see, slaves sometimes engaged in verbal jousting, loud talking that aimed to mobilize and influence their social ties with other slaves.

THE SIMPLE FACT that slaves owned property in the South raises fascinating questions for the study of slavery, southern history, and African American history. Slaves had no property rights but they frequently had property. They participated with white masters and nonslaveowning whites in an informal economy of time, land, and property that overlapped and supported the formal economy of the plantation even as it let slaves push back against the oppression of the system. The things slaves did to make property, keep it, and pass it down the generations shaped the very meaning of ownership among them. It is easy to assume that property meant one person's private, or exclusive rights over a thing. For slaves, however, an object became property by being associated publicly with people. Each piece of property usually represented the labor and interests of several people, including the master. What made ownership possible for slaves was that their property was enmeshed in several overlapping, sometimes competing, social relationships, often expressed in an interchange of display and acknowledgment.

Studying property ownership among slaves suggests new ways of looking at kinship and other social ties. Many of the perspectives in this chapter come from African Studies rather than southern history. Anthropologists and historians of Africa came to the study of slavery armed with a long tradition of linking property with the study of how kinship worked. They argue that kinship—including ties of marriage, descent, and other kin relations—is one of the most important ways that Africans have gotten access to resources. Because of the influence of anthropology, Africanists have argued that masters' domination over slaves was rooted in kinship, rather than in an exclusive legal right to the slave as property. Whereas Americanists tend to think of property as the legal and social foundation of slavery, most Africanists argue that family was one of the basic building blocks of all claims to property, labor, and other resources, including claims of slavery. It was this kin-based ideology of slavery that figured so strongly in the Atlantic slave trade and in the myriad court disputes between Fantes after emancipation. This perspective opens up new ways of thinking about property, family, and slavery in the South. Many scholars have recognized that African Americans treasured family and community relationships, especially in the face of racial oppression. The evidence in the slaves' claims suggests that while African

Americans struggled against masters, they also negotiated among themselves over economic resources, and that social relationships were integral to such negotiations. Because of the interdependence of economic claims and social ties, family became a place in which black people cooperated, negotiated, and sometimes argued over property and labor.

At the same time, just as social relationships helped people make claims to property, property ownership and slaves' hunger for productive workers shaped, maintained, and sometimes even created social relationships. In other words, "blood" and a common experience of oppression were not the only ways that African Americans related to one another. Just as in Fante, their varied and flexible social relationships and their ongoing negotiations over property and labor were mutually influential. By looking more deeply into the experience of oppression we may see how this intertwining of social and economic relationships came to define an important part of life in the nineteenth-century United States.

By the 1860s, many southerners, white and black, held assumptions about property and kinship that would not have made much sense to anyone trained in law. The Civil War not only destroyed slavery, it also promised to transform the role that formal institutions like law played in people's daily lives. Formal law had always been there, but with the arrival of military courts, the Freedmen's Bureau, and agencies like the Southern Claims Commission, formal law reached out to people and places it had up until then touched only indirectly. In these forums, northern officials, southern whites, and freedpeople would have to confront the differences in how they thought of property, community, and family.

chapter four

In and Out of Court

. . . .

Reconstruction in America, like colonialism in Africa, dramatically changed the way that black people related to the law and other state institutions. For the first time in American history, ex-slaves had legal rights and could defend their property and family ties in court. Winning the right to vote for black men was arguably the most important struggle of the decades after the Civil War, one that set the terms in which other issues were debated.[1] Yet much evidence indicates that African Americans went into the jury box, the Freedmen's Bureau court, and the polling place with their eyes wide open. Long after the law cracked open its doors, blacks held onto a wide range of forums outside the sphere of formal politics and law, such as church meetings, family meetings, and public arguments.[2] Like those in precolonial Africa, early modern Europe, and elsewhere, these extralegal forums seemed perfectly legitimate to southerners who had used them for years, but not to the officials who came to replace them with law. African Americans did embrace the law after 1862, but that fact is only part of a more complex story of ambivalence, change, and creative tension between legal and extralegal systems in the South, a story that emerges more fully in what people actually said in court.

Ex-slaves often pursued their claims to property and family through both the newly available legal settings—such as military courts and government agencies—and in extralegal settings, many of which had existed in some form before emancipation. African Americans did not draw a sharp line between these different venues. Like people in Africa then and now, African Americans in the 1860s and 1870s often took their concerns from the yard and the church into the courtroom, and sometimes back again, pursuing their interests wherever they saw an advantage. As a result, though government officials badly wanted to reconstruct the South on the trusted bedrock of law, in practice, legal and extralegal processes were hopelessly, vibrantly mixed together.[3]

IN THE 1860s the U.S. government extended legal rights and protections to four million black southerners through three major institutions: the provost courts, the Freedmen's Bureau, and the Southern Claims Commission. Each of these forums had a different mission and structure, but they all seemed to promise that ex-slaves might soon leave behind the uncertainties of plantation "custom" for the evenhanded formalism of law. The provost courts were originally supposed to maintain order within the Union army, disciplining soldiers for offenses as minor as drinking on duty or as deadly serious as desertion. However, during the Civil War, as the Union army took over vast regions of the South, the provost courts widened their jurisdiction beyond the confines of the army and began trying civilians. The federal government decreed that the South's civil courts could not be restored to power unless they granted blacks formal equality under the law, in particular, by letting blacks testify against whites. In many regions of the South, the army provost courts continued to act as a substitute legal system after the war ended. The Freedmen's Bureau, also a branch of the army and staffed by army officers, extended and institutionalized the provost marshal's legal protection of freedpeople. Like the British magistrates who set up courts in their new Gold Coast Colony, bureau and provost judges took over duties that local officials, such as sheriffs, justices of the peace, and civil judges, had performed before the war. But in one important respect, they reached much further than either prewar southern officials or Crown Colony magistrates had: they permitted newly freed people to claim the protection of law.

Beginning in March 1865, military courts offered freedpeople alternatives to the South's civil legal system, which was biased and hostile toward African Americans. In the civil courts, black defendants received harsher punishments than whites. Often, when black property owners could not be frightened out of their property, whites conspired with the civil courts and the police to rob them by legal means. Blacks who went to civil court as plaintiffs

Provost marshal's office, Aquia Creek, Va., February 1863. In buildings such as this, army provost marshals handled everything from writing safe-passage passes to holding trials. Until southern state governments were readmitted and their courts restored, the local provost marshal's office and its staff was the legal system (from *Gardner's Photographic Sketchbook of the American Civil War, 1861–1865* [Washington, D.C., 1865], courtesy of The Albert and Shirley Small Special Collections Library, University of Virginia Library).

often found their cases tied up for months, while their debts piled up dangerously high. "All those persons holding [land] Leases from the Government," complained a committee of freedpeople in Savannah, "are Summoned into Court by Tens and Twenties with large Sworms of witnesses on both sides." The judges "then put off these cases from day to day and from Week to Week." The freedpeople knew that the delays were intended "to compell these Freedmen to give up their Leases and hire-out to their former Masters," something they dearly hoped to avoid.[4] If a land case in a southern court was bad for blacks, a criminal case was worse. One white man flatly "state[d] that he would hang any negro in whose case he was called to sit as a juror."[5] Ex-slaves rightly believed that they could not "receive . . . full and equal justice before the" civil courts, and they asked to have their trials moved into the military courts whenever possible.[6]

The arrival of northern teachers, the Freedmen's Bureau, and the army courts aroused high expectations among ex-slaves about the promise of ac-

cess to formal law. Ex-slaves "never expect to receive justice from white people," observed teacher Laura Towne, yet they entered freedom with a "very
strong . . . idea of Justice" and "nothing arouses their indignation more than
to be treated unjustly." John Roy Lynch, Mississippi's first black justice of the
peace, recalled that some African Americans "were determined to take advantage of the smallest," as well as the most serious, "offense[s] to 'come to
law.' "[7] Moreover, young people were beginning to associate "justice" with
officers of the Freedmen's Bureau. "The children shout when a dispute oc-
curs at marbles 'I want justice,' " Towne noticed, "and when they want to
complain of anything they say 'I am going to Gen. Saxton for justice.' "[8]
These statements were mostly metaphorical, part of the joking and fussing
that all children do at play. But if Assistant Commissioner Rufus Saxton ever
heard them, he might have understood that he had become a symbol for
blacks' new access to regular courts, the Union army, and freedom all at once.

The Freedmen's Bureau effectively withdrew from the South in the summer of 1868 and closed its doors for good in 1869, but in the early 1870s the
federal government opened another legal forum within which ex-slaves
could assert claims over property: the Southern Claims Commission. Congress created the Southern Claims Commission in 1871 under the Treasury
Department to hear claims from Unionist southerners who had lost "stores
or supplies . . . taken or furnished for the use of the [Union] army" during
the Civil War. Virgil Hillyer, who heard Pompey Bacon's claim, was one of
106 special commissioners sent to towns across the South to gather information and to hold formal compensation hearings. Between 1873 and 1880 the
special commissioners forwarded more than 22,000 claims, testimony from
some 220,000 witnesses, and their official recommendations to Washington, D.C., where the three commissioners of claims passed final judgment.[9]

The commission originally sought to compensate white Unionist southerners. President Ulysses S. Grant signed into law the bill establishing the
commission amid stormy debate over whether the government should pay
citizens of a section that was barely six years past a bloody rebellion. Since
rebels deserved no compensation, nearly half of the "standing interrogatories" that commissioners posed to each claimant concerned loyalty during
the war.[10] White claimants had to refute the suspicion of disloyalty before
their property losses would be compensated. The original list of "interrogatories" for claimants did not mention slaves or free people of color.[11]

Much confusion stemmed from the assumption, widespread in the North,
that slaves knew nothing about property, marriage, or personal responsibility and that they would have to learn such concepts from northerners. An

1863 report to Congress from the American Freedmen's Inquiry Commission, which gathered information about the freedpeople from dozens of observers throughout the South, had confirmed white northerners' suspicions that "the laws of Slave States" had left African Americans without any "notions of the sacredness of property" and "no just conception of what the family relation was" or of "the relation between man and wife."[12] Ex-slaves, testified one of the Freedmen's Commission's investigators, had no "perception of the relative value of money and what it purchases."[13] Freedpeople should not be allowed to have money, said white witnesses, "until they are prepared for its proper use."[14] White northerners believed that they would have to inculcate "the ideas of northern men as to the rights of property [and] the honor of women."[15] Spurred in part by that report, groups of teachers, missionaries, and energetic capitalists had been coming to the South Carolina Sea Islands since 1863, offering the black residents an odd mixture of schooling, moralistic preachments, and profit-seeking exploitation.[16]

These early northern arrivals found, however, that many blacks did not need to be taught to respect and "regard the rights of property among themselves."[17] Reports of slaves who owned property flowed into the American Freedmen's Inquiry Commission from all over the South. From slave-owners in Kentucky (where slavery was still legal in 1863), the commission heard that slaves there "have some property that they call their own; they have the[ir] little cabins, and some furniture, and pigs & chickens, and they are as tenacious of their property as the whites are."[18] From Leavenworth, Kansas, where "nine-tenths" of the black residents "had been slaves within the last four years," officials were "astonish[ed]" to find many of them "own-[ing] their own homes" and farming small "patches of from one to ten acres," and not merely for subsistence but "as market gardens."[19] Indeed, according to a witness from the South's western edge, the Creek Indian Nation was relying on its enslaved African Americans as "the interpreters, traders and business men of the nation."[20] Dozens of white witnesses explained how slaves amassed property, why masters let them, and what slaves spent their "proceeds" on.[21] Among Sea Island blacks, reported one early observer, "If a man has a claim upon a horse or sow he maintains his right and his neighbors recognize it."[22] Those whites who had come to educate and inculcate were pleased but puzzled to find ex-slaves who already exhibited "a passion for ownership," who "delight[ed] in accumulating" property.[23] To most northerners, however, it seemed obvious that property could not own property; logically, only free people could own things. As a result, neither the Southern Claims Commission's founders nor its agents in the field expected many claims from former slaves. However, the new commission's emphasis on local knowledge in finding facts about the loyalty of white claimants—and its searches for both written and oral evidence—opened opportunities for ex-slaves to assert claims to property, and even to revive the extralegal practices that had secured ownership during slavery.

Unfortunately, these three government agencies were much too short-lived and never had enough funding or staff to meet the needs of black southerners during Reconstruction. Both the Freedmen's Bureau and the provost courts lasted only a few years in a limited area of the South. The Freedmen's Bureau, for example, never had more than 900 agents in the South at one time.[24] Undoubtedly, many ex-slaves who needed a hearing in court could not get one. Nevertheless, from roughly 1863 to late 1868, and again in the early 1870s, the federal government maintained dozens of courts and court-like arenas scattered across the South. Having an officer of the Freedmen's Bureau at the county seat or a provost marshal at a nearby army camp meant that, for the first time, at least some former slaves could go to a formal, legal arena to protect their marriages, their families, and their property.

Just as in Gold Coast, however, the opening of courts and official agencies to ex-slaves did not push aside the extralegal practices that had anchored property claims during slavery. Faced with a legal system that was often hostile and racially discriminatory, ex-slaves turned to the familiar practices of public display and acknowledgment to make claims to property, extralegal processes that involved family meetings, church meetings, "committees of Colored People," conjurors, and public displays of argument and insult. Moreover, African Americans began to use those forums to make claims not just to property but to kinship as well, asserting both their membership in families and their authority over their kinfolk.

Some of the extralegal forums that flourished after the Civil War grew out of people's experiences during the war or during slavery. Many of the bi-racial political organizations of the late 1860s—such as the Republican Leagues—could trace their roots back to a secret group like the one that Dudley Smith described: "A few of us colored men in Tuscaloosa had a Club or society, which was for the purpose of communicating with the loyal whites and learning how the war was progressing. . . . [W]e often met at night" to keep it secret.[25]

For ex-slaves, who were fervently buying marriage certificates and tracking down lost relatives, families became an important forum for working out problems, for deciding their claims both to property and on other black folk. Emancipation made it possible for many ex-slaves to call family meetings, and while these could not do much in disputes with white people, they had enormous weight in disputes among blacks. For example, when black women and men argued, women's families often took them back in and then met to decide on a collective response, such as demanding a public apology from the man.[26] Families gave their members advice concerning what to do about problems in their marriages and sometimes took over in negotiating apologies or settlements between the spouses. Often, families convened a meeting after one of the spouses made an appeal for someone to act as witness. When rumors of adultery were flying about ex-slaves June and Maria, June went to Amelia, the older sister of Maria's husband, Moses, and asked her to come watch him apologize to Moses. "June came and called me," Amelia recalled, and "we went to Moses' house. June said to Moses 'I beg your pardon for what I have done to your wife.' " June then "told Maria she must also beg pardon of Moses."[27] Such apologies were intended to do more than simply make peace between a married couple. Because ex-slaves often asked kinfolk to settle problems or witness potentially explosive confrontations, it seems likely that the line between personal and family business was easy to cross.

Ex-slaves also created "committees" of non-kin to judge the disputes that came up between them. In Tennessee, South Carolina, North Carolina, and possibly elsewhere, Freedmen's Bureau courts sometimes took their cues from the proceedings of black-run "committees" that had preceded them.[28] At least one black-run Odd Fellows' Lodge intervened in its members' personal lives, including their marriages.[29] Dinah Nelson's family took her grievance against Anderson Sanders a hundred miles north of their home to a "Committee of Colored People at Statesburg," which met periodically "to settle personal difficulties." There, Sanders apologized to Dinah Nelson and "begged her husband's pardon" for beating her up.[30] Sanders later recalled: "We went before it [the committee]. I begged her pardon & she accepted it. We shook hands and she said it was never to be heard again thro' this life."[31] The "Committee of Colored People" helped arbitrate between the two freedpeople and their families and put their seal of approval on the peace they made together.

Former slaves also turned to their churches to settle disputes. African Americans founded hundreds of churches after the Civil War, "theirs" for the first time, free from the oversight of white ministers. Much as they had been during slavery, these new black-run, black-owned churches were more than just places of worship. The church was also a place for politics, for socializing, for educating children, and for mediating disputes between its members.[32] During the 1870s and 1880s, for example, the First African

Church of Richmond continued to hear a wide range of disputes between African Americans. One member was "charged with giving a cake walk."[33] Another meeting cited a man "for refusing to live with his wife and his wife for disobeying her husband."[34] Black people even brought their business disputes to the church. "Bro. Lewis Dixon stated that Bro. Johnson owed him $27.42 & he has refused to give him His Part," read the minutes of another meeting, "he made it Quite Lengthy."[35] Churches had mediated disputes between slaves before emancipation,[36] but because whites had put heavy constraints on blacks' authority within the old black churches, the churches could not step in as often or directly as they did now. It is likely that African Americans felt much more comfortable airing their disagreements in front of black deacons and ministers than they had under white church overseers.

The church was not the only otherworldly force in people's lives. In some cases, black people consulted conjurers and fortune-tellers to weigh in on inheritance disputes,[37] to bring back lost husbands and wives,[38] and to find thieves.[39] At least some of the men recruited into the Union army were conjurers who intervened in black soldiers' disputes with one another.[40] One provost judge scoffed that fortune-tellers were merely "vagrants" who leeched a living from "the great ignorance of colored people." He was sure that "with a full knowledge of the law & the consequences" ex-slaves would not have put their faith in fortune-tellers.[41] Whatever the army lawyers thought, African Americans may have seen fortune-tellers as more accessible for airing disputes; in addition, fortune-tellers played a different, more openly partisan role in disputes than courts did.[42]

While slavery had forced African Americans to disguise or suppress their worst disagreements, emancipation cleared the way for people to take such disagreements out into public, often using what one Mississippi witness called "loud talking."[43] Much of this public speech took place in yards, partly because people gathered there both to work and to talk about local issues while they worked. Northern teacher Elizabeth Ware Pearson saw one group of women "washing outside their doors . . . holding forth . . . upon the subject" of a neighbor's marriage.[44] Quarreling Sea Islanders, she asserted, "excel all other people I ever saw with their tongues," producing "tremendous noise, terrible gestures, the fiercest looks."[45] Ex-slaves honed the verbal skills that could fill the house-yards (or marketplace) with sympathetic listeners.[46] Similar observations were made outside the South. "When negroes quarrel," wrote a visitor to the Caribbean, "they seldom look each other in the face. Nay, generally they turn back to back and seem to appeal to the bystanders, who usually answer each speech made by the belligerents at each other with a shout of laughter, until it comes to: 'I mash you up.' 'I cut your t'roat.' " At that point, friends and bystanders "judiciously interfere."[47] Many disputes between African Americans followed a similar pattern. Black people from Mississippi to the Carolinas testified about going up "in front of her House,"[48] "to her . . . yard gate,"[49] or "to the door"[50] to hurl creative, sometimes obscene, insults at one another.[51] "I was at the Dossy house," testified David Drayton, "when I heard [Henry] Mack curse my wife twice" from the yard. "I came down to the house and they were talking low. Mack had gone away from my house. I went into my house. Mack was in Coaxem's yard and told him my wife [was a] St Helena nigger and would not pay her debts." Mack was just next door now, in the neighbor's yard, and when Rina Drayton heard him say *that*, she went outside and threatened to "split [his] brains out." Then her husband came outside and told Mack "not to cuss my wife. We talk heap [and Mack] said he done cuss my wife and what I going to do about it." What David Drayton did was take a stick and beat Mack until another freed-man pulled him off. Then Rina Drayton hit Mack in the teeth with a brick.[52] What is striking about this testimony is not so much that freedpeople hit each other; it is the complex pattern of disrespect that led up to it: a series of verbal and spatial boundary-breakings. Henry Mack's accusations did not get much of a response from the Draytons until he put Rina's business in the street—that is, loud talking in a close-rowed string of yards so that the whole neighborhood could hear about her supposedly unpaid debts. In the yards and doorways of postwar black settlements, words were not always separate from deeds; they were not simply a means of saying what you were about to do—words *were* deeds. That is why arguments like these involved more than just the two people swapping insults; loud talking brought in a whole range of friends and relatives, people who might stick up for them, or hold them back just before a real fight broke out.[53]

Often these public demonstrations invoked family ties. Arguments often ended up in front of the home of someone's parents or some other relative. Phoebe Parson witnessed an argument of this type between her next door neighbors Frances and her husband, William. When Frances "started to go from her home to her Mother's," refusing to go back as her husband com-manded, William blocked her and said "he would carry her back home."[54] This pattern—a confrontation followed by a move to a parent's house—also occurred among men. After Charles Frazier attacked Marcus Brown, for example, two groups of people quickly gathered and parted them. "Both parties with many others then proceeded to [the] house of" Marcus Brown's father, loudly arguing as they walked.[55] Black city dwellers used streets in similar ways. "There was right smart of folks standing around"[56] when Ben Glass and Jacob Cooper tangled "in front of Mr Paxtons foundry," testified witnesses in a Vicksburg murder case. "They stood up and cussed each other."[57] Freer than ever from the strictures of whites, spoken words had the power to call out the wicked and the ugly, to rally friends and warn enemies.

Even more astounding, blacks, who had rarely been able to talk this way to one another, now began to use loud talking against whites. "I never was abuse[d] somuch before by anybody; as I was by Jennie," complained one North Carolina landowner. "She followed me for about two miles" into town, cursing, then stood near "Captain Phillips house . . . and said something about there was the man that had beaten her daughter."[58] Another North Carolina freedwoman stood in her landlord's yard and "said she was talking for her rights and would talk as mad as she pleased and as loud as she pleased."[59] Whites who had barely noticed disputes among blacks during slavery now confronted black women and men who refused to "hush."[60] For a few minutes at a time, ex-slaves turned yards, houses, and city streets into public forums where raising your voice at the right time could win you allies. They were drawing on extralegal processes of public display that had been established long before emancipation and that now nestled alongside the official sphere of courts and claims commissions.

What did people argue about? Although courts did not always keep good records, the many complaint registers and transcribed testimony that do survive disclose that African Americans had a stunning variety of concerns as they emerged from slavery. Courts in Mississippi, for example, handled everything from domestic violence to child support,[61] from debt to charges of using "conjure" to commit fraud.[62] Northern teachers in the Sea Islands heard "cases of assault and battery, and general plantation *squows*,—then . . . a divorce case,—last Sunday . . . a whiskey-selling affair; a calf-murder is still on the docket."[63] Remarkably, although victims of rape often hesitate to go to court even today, in the 1860s a few black women found the courage to bring rape allegations to the military courts, against both white men and black men.[64]

By far the most violent confrontations blacks had were with whites. Ex-slaves' newly won access to the law and legal institutions became vitally important during the mid-1860s because white people across the South launched vicious campaigns of terror against blacks. Between 1865 and 1868, federal officers, who recorded the freedpeople's complaints in ledgers, compiled a staggering catalogue of "outrages" by whites against the freedpeople.[65] White landowners cheated blacks out of their wages and property in every way

imaginable and bullied them when they could not be cheated. Judy Fitzsimmons's boss "cursed her" for asking about her pay, "& said he did not mind
the niggers being free but he would not take any sauce from them."[66] Former slaves knew these words were a warning. White people murdered black
people for trivial "offenses," such as not taking off a hat or "using insolent
language." Other white people did not even try to justify what they did: one
white Texan said he "wanted to thin out the niggers a little," while another
wanted "to see a d—d nigger kick."[67] These threats, beatings, and murders
may have seemed random to some, but they had a calculated goal: to maintain white supremacy as the South's guiding principle. But despite the risks
of speaking out, many African Americans went to the provost courts and
Freedmen's Bureau to demand justice.

Legal institutions promised more than a way to stop white terrorists. Ex-
slaves also used them to lodge claims against the U.S. government. One
Union officer who "sent out and gathered up horses & cattle" from around
Beaufort was stymied when "[t]he negroes soon after came in from all parts
of the Island claiming this property, stating they had want of it and it had
been given to them for special services performed." The army's foraging of
property owned by slaves, he reported, "has been a fruitful source of contro-
versy ever since."[68] Former slaves who lost property to both local whites and
Union soldiers lodged property claims with both the Freedmen's Bureau
courts and the military courts during the 1860s. In many cases, the courts
ruled in the ex-slaves' favor and ordered soldiers to give them back their property.[69] And in the 1870s the Southern Claims Commission, as we have seen,
awarded property compensation to 850 African Americans, of whom nearly
500 had owned property as slaves.

Moreover, although many freedpeople went to court to protest white outrages, many others went to court to argue with other freedpeople.[70] Henry
Judd, a northern officer who served in the Low Country during the Civil
War, expected to mediate between ex-slaves and their former masters but
was surprised to find that "[a]bout as much of my time is taken up in adjust-
ing difficulties among the colored population as in anything else."[71] The
provost marshal at one Louisiana post recorded dozens of "complaints" between African Americans, ranging from domestic abuse to stolen property
to one in which an ex-slave accused another of "[k]nocking his horse down
without any provocation."[72] Like any other farmers, black people who part-
nered in the spring to make a crop might end up suing each other in a military court in the fall. "Did not I gather your crop for you last year?" demanded
John Harvey. "You helped," admitted James Harris. But, Harris insisted, "I

dont owe you for it for you sued me and I cast you before the Justice."[73] In the civil courts at Natchez and Davis Bend, Mississippi, where the justices of the peace were black men, dozens of black people squared off every year.[74] One scholarly study indicates that a large percentage of the 1,023 cases heard before the Freedmen's Bureau courts of Kentucky, South Carolina, and Virginia (in which agents recorded the race of both parties) were disputes between ex-slaves.[75] Forty-four percent of the debt cases and 52 percent of the property cases in those states were brought by blacks against other blacks.[76] Few blacks committed assaults on whites, yet blacks were defendants in 56 percent of the assault cases in those Freedmen's Bureau courts, suggesting that black-on-black assault made up a significant proportion of the violence committed against blacks after the Civil War.[77] At the Freedmen's Bureau court of Yorktown, Virginia, former slaves began to lodge complaints almost as soon as the Civil War ended, complaints that ranged from "non-payment of wages" to "assault."[78] Although many African Americans had hired and traded and argued with one another during slavery, going to court over hiring and trading was an entirely new experience for them.

Disputes among black people also appeared in the military courts of the Lower South. Although whites committed the vast majority of violent acts against blacks in Louisiana, black-on-black homicide was far from unknown.[79] The 551 cases of black-on-black homicide made up 13.7 percent of all the homicides recorded in Louisiana during Reconstruction.[80] In Texas, during the first three years after emancipation, black-on-black crime accounted for 48 cases of homicide (6 percent of the total prosecuted in courts), 90 cases of assault and battery (14 percent of the total prosecuted), and 17 cases of assault with intent to kill (13 percent of the total prosecuted). Of all violent acts prosecuted in Texas courts between 1865 and 1868, 8.3 percent were committed by blacks against other blacks.[81]

It is important to be careful in interpreting these statistics. Emancipation did not unleash a wave of black criminality, either against whites or against other blacks. For example, only about 10 percent of Louisiana's 3,494 documented homicides between 1865 and 1876 were committed by blacks against other blacks.[82] White people committed the vast majority of Louisiana's homicides during Reconstruction, and most black victims of homicide were killed by white people. Even the reported rate of intraracial violence (among blacks) was lower than it was among whites.[83]

Still, much evidence suggests some level of conflict among African Americans. These records probably underestimate the frequency of conflict among ex-slaves, as well that between whites and blacks, because huge numbers of violent acts never made it to any court. For example, some Union officers refused to hear the vast majority of the black people who asked for military trials and instead sent them to the civil courts.[84] Black people soon found that those civil courts seized on their marital problems and conflicts as an excuse to prosecute and send them, especially black men, to the chain gang.[85] If this wasn't enough of a deterrent, high fees made the federal courts even less welcoming. Worst of all, some federal courts actually abused former slaves. At one post, said John Picksley, an ex-slave, Union soldiers were "in the habit of going around with the Citizens drinking and carousing and aiding them in their cruelty towards the Freedmen."[86] Yet, in spite of these obstacles, the Union military courts provided not only the most reliable protection from southern whites but also an inexpensive—and therefore accessible— way for ex-slaves to resolve disputes among themselves.[87] The courts' records contain evidence of disagreement and even violence among ex-slaves, evidence that reveals much about black life after emancipation, with both its solidarity and its social and economic tensions. Taken together, they suggest that at the end of the Civil War, much was at stake and there was a host of unresolved issues between ex-slaves.

More than anything else, ex-slaves used the courts to make claims to property and kinship. "Nine tenths of [their disputes] grow out of domestic difficulties," reported the American Freedmen's Inquiry Commission in 1863. In addition, ex-slaves brought many "other cases concerning the ownership of property, and trespasses upon premises," the report added. "[T]here seems to be a passion characteristic of the negroes for the ownership of horses or some animal."[88] In many cases, ex-slaves' "passion" for ownership was entangled with their "domestic difficulties." Testimony in Texas Freedmen's Bureau courts reveals that when black men and women agreed to get married, they often sealed their promise by loaning or sharing house rent, clothes, and other property. The many freedpeople who filed complaints after breaking off a marriage or engagement may have been trying in part to get back whatever things they had handed over to their partners. Much of the property involved in lawsuits over divorces and broken engagements belonged to black women.[89] Other things belonged to couples jointly, and these sometimes became sore points between them, as divorced men and women walked off with household clothing, chickens, ducks, and kitchenware.[90] "One day," wrote teacher Elizabeth Hyde Botume, "we met an old man and woman with two young witnesses marching to town. The old man immediately began to tell his story,—some trouble about his pigs, etc. Whatever it was, he decided he couldn't stand it any longer, and he was bound to go to the trial justice. Thereupon the woman pushed him aside, exclaiming,—'Pshaw, boy! Go 'long, an' let me talk.' Then she gave her version."[91] Testimony from northerners and hundreds of ex-slaves reveals that disputes over property went hand in hand with "domestic difficulties" and other troubled social relationships.

Although the claims officials and judges would not have recognized it, in the daily practice of making claims and disputes there was often little distinction between legal and extralegal processes in the South during Reconstruction. Ex-slaves pursued claims to property in all of these arenas and frequently came to the military courts only after making a claim through public display or a church or family meeting. Ex-slaves in Sumter District, South Carolina, summoned a former slaveowner to watch an "interview between Pompey and Dick" over a cow, then took the matter to an army captain, and only then to the provost court.[92] Other people went to court after their churches had already ruled on their cases, rulings that often put them "out of good standing [in the church] for stealing" and other misdeeds.[93] Richard Hamilton and Robert Francis, ex-slaves from coastal Virginia, found that they "could not agree as to the balance of accounts" between them, and "they agreed to let the Church decide the matter." Both men were "satisfied with the decision" of the church; the case later wound up in the Freedmen's Bureau court at Yorktown, Virginia, because Francis could not come up with the money.[94]

Like disputes over property, problems in family life also led African Americans to shuttle between legal and extralegal systems. Children whose parents would not or could not take care of them sometimes found a haven with their aunts, uncles, or cousins. Reporting a dispute over the custody of an eleven-year-old boy, a bureau agent at Knoxville, Tennessee, wrote that, before approaching the bureau, the boy's aunt had brought her case first to a group called the "Central Committee." Composed of "col[ore]d men of the most respectable character," this committee heard witnesses and put the boy in custody of his uncle Robert Bell.[95] Another man called on both systems to protect his niece from being abused by her stepfather. One "Sunday morning," Edmund Brown recalled, he "took Gentry up before witnesses," probably one of the extralegal "committees" among the freedpeople. This hearing before witnesses did not stop the abuse, so Brown finally had Gentry hauled before the local provost court. "She had no protector," Brown told the court, and as "her own uncle," Brown "would protect [her] if it cost him the last dollar."[96]

Former slaves sometimes combined elements of both legal and extralegal processes to make claims and resolve disputes. In many situations, ex-slaves wanted to avoid going to court, if possible, yet they dangled the possibility of a lawsuit as a way to leverage their negotiations out of court. Damaged crops, stolen hogs, even accidental shootings could be settled with an apology and some money.[97] A Mississippi man who killed a hog "agreed to pay for it and return what he had not used" to the woman who owned it.[98] James Wilson, who had been beaten by another freedman, "was going to sue him for damages," but he agreed to drop the matter when the man "finally . . . said [he] would give me 35$ if I would not sue him."[99] In order to put teeth into these out-of-court settlements, African Americans summoned local people to act as witnesses, taking care to include people with power, as well as sympathy. One morning Alfred Pack told his foreman that "he was very uneasy" about something and "he wanted witnesses to go to his house." The foreman fetched Mrs. Garrett, their white employer, and together they went to Pack's house. When they got there, "Pack was out of doors. Pack told [Garrett] he killed her sow[,] was very uneasy, & wanted to satisfy her Said he was poor & not able to pay much & would [she] take $15 for it. Isaac [the foreman] was present [and] said he would give her $15. Gave his note. He called Smiley to write [the] obligation. Pack said he wanted him [to] write a note for the hog [Garrett] had lost. He did not say he stole it from [her]."[100] By combining an extralegal demonstration before witnesses with the written, legally binding "note," Pack settled a potentially dangerous problem with his boss. And he did it without having to say whether or not "he stole it from [her]." Rather than cutting off the old practices of slavery times, courts became another forum for protecting black people and their interests in property.

Those legal and extralegal processes meshed in important ways. Judges and claims agents often relied on information generated by meetings of church and kin groups, and especially by practices of display and acknowledgment. In some provost courts, good oral testimony could trump written receipts in deciding who owned property, especially when a witness testified along these lines: "I know this boat by nature . . . known it all my life."[101] One provost judge insisted that witnesses be "allowed to see" the property in question before deciding a case.[102] Disputes over wandering hogs and other kinds of property reveal that in the late 1860s, property ownership still depended on local understandings and knowledge about animals and even grains. As one white yeoman put it, "I think the law is that if I see a hog with my mark, it is mine."[103]

Even when people had written, legally valid proofs of ownership, those receipts themselves were full of information from extralegal processes. Written records of movable property were scarce in the mid-1800s. Few of the

South's small property owners, black or white, could show a receipt for any of the property they owned. So what little written evidence of ownership did exist was often drawn up not by a lawyer but by the owners themselves, or by somebody else who knew how to read and write. During the Civil War, friendly Union soldiers sometimes wrote out receipts for freedpeople's horses or other property, using the backs of envelopes or other scraps of paper. "This is to certify that Michael Cain is the lawful owner of a horse," read one receipt written by Union officer Stephen Smails. "[S]aid horse is a bay about 15 hands high and was bought from George Morgan in my presence. Stephen A. Smails, 1st Lt. 54th Mass. Vols. Signed at hdqtrs, Barrows SC, August 3, 1865."[104] Receipts could help prove that people owned the things in their possession; they could also function as IOUs for things they expected to possess in the future. For example, "Sorrow Gray, col'd, working in Eloughs Mill owes Warren Campbell, Col'd, Dr Parkers plantation $7.00 for a table and dish bought from him March 15, 1866."[105] But while some northerners rejoiced that a "torn and dirty scrap" of paper could "now serv[e] to right many an ancient wrong,"[106] such written descriptions lost weight once they were taken out of the social context in which they were produced. When receipts were introduced as evidence in courts, they had to be scrutinized and interpreted to recover any social context that could make them more than just dirty scraps of paper.

The story of the Southern Claims Commission captures perfectly the interdependence of legal and extralegal processes in the postwar South. Even though it came from outside the South, it came to rely on understandings and practices developed during slavery almost as much as did any southern court. When claims officials began their inquiries in 1871, they expected to hunt (as their chief clerk put it) for "evidence of facts"[107] using county court records, receipts, deeds, maps, and documents seized during the war from Confederate archives.[108] Such records, one judge felt, were the "corner-stone" of any legitimate system of property ownership.[109] But few of the South's poorer property owners, and none of its slaves, could produce any documentary evidence about their property before the war. "It is a terrible job to discover just what they had, *which was all their own*," complained Robert Avery, one of the commission's traveling special agents, "I know not the name of a single colored claimant, free-born or slave, whose name is borne on the tax rolls of Chatham Co[unty]." Yet local residents, he continued, "tell me this is no evidence that the person did not own property, because [in order to be listed on the rolls] the law requires them to hunt up the assessing officer at the Court House and give in to him a list of property. Many white persons, who consider themselves honest and pretty well off, are not to be found on the tax rolls."[110] Agents could not dismiss the property claims of ex-slaves for lack of written evidence because nearly all southerners, white and black, also lacked such documents for most of the things they owned. Consequently, the commission leaned heavily on witnesses to provide the information about property that it could not find in duly recorded legal documents.

Although the Southern Claims Commission was a formal, legal organization, the practices it adopted to investigate claims ensured that it would be drenched with local politics and prejudices from outside its hearing rooms. Nearly every step in the claims process was visible to the public. In order to get the information they needed, agents often talked to as many local residents as they could "to find out 'who's who' in the vicinity."[111] Special Agent Robert Avery tracked down scattered claimants from the countryside by going to some of the black churches on Sundays. Word of his mission spread, and within two weeks, Avery was "besieged from early morning by claimants and persons who had lost 'hogs, cow and fowls,' and had heard I was to leave tomorrow."[112] In order to encourage witnesses to step forward, postmasters across the South were told to put up lists of claimants in their offices and to have those lists read aloud at churches.[113] An agent in Tennessee reported that he had put a "notice" in what he termed "a darky paper published here" called the "Weekly Planet." The notice read: "COLORED MEN NOW IN MEMPHIS, Who lived during the war, in the following localities, may hear of something to their advantage by leaving their name and addresses at this office within a week."[114] Advertisements like this one must have struck black people as vague, coy, and possibly dangerous. Only six years after the Civil War, the stigma of having been a slave or a unionist still stood out in local communities across the South, raising yet another obstacle to claimants. Among other things, filing a claim was a political act, one that often made neighbors and friends angry.

The public nature of the claims process tended to make claimants (and sometimes agents) a focus for local resentment against the Union government. After all, many white southerners had pointed rifles at Union soldiers only a few years before. Agents sometimes resorted to holding their "examinations" in their hotel rooms, but in Savannah even this tactic faltered when "the landlady objected to claimant's or witnesses visiting" the room "as [because] they were colored—maybe improper characters."[115] Outside the hotels, hearings became essentially public events. These public examinations, wrote a claims official from Nansemond County, Virginia, were "almost invariably attended by secessionists & Rebels who would have been glad to throw discredit on the claimant."[116] As a result, some agents found it "almost impossible to get a white man to testify in a colored man's case at all."[117] To make matters worse, wrote a lawyer, "the old rebel element" went around "telling the negroes they will not succeed, & otherwise discouraging them from following up their claims."[118] Even blacks were sometimes reluctant to testify about their black neighbors, especially since special agents sometimes thought they could get more candid answers if they did not reveal their mission. To ex-slaves, claims agents were just white strangers who appeared suddenly, asking difficult questions about their neighbors and relatives without saying what they were up to. One agent wrote that ex-slaves frequently "would deny any knowledge of a colored man—didn't know him, and never heard of him." Ex-slaves only gave out information, the agent reported, after they "learned my business."[119]

As the commission began its work in dozens of towns across the South, it breathed new life into the old system of display and acknowledgment by which slaves had held property, making it relevant once more. In claims filed by ex-slaves, the commission relied on witnesses, not written documents, to prove ownership. Prewar living conditions, the system of display, and the intense affective ties created by shared interests in property fostered detailed knowledge about property, and this knowledge enabled ex-slaves to marshal large numbers of witnesses to testify about their property in intimate detail. Especially on the big Low Country plantations, where the slave trader cut a relatively narrower hole through the slave quarters during the last few decades of slavery, by 1873 former slaves were able to call as witnesses people they had known for twenty or thirty years, from birth to middle age, from youth to old age, or, as one witness put it, "since I had sense."[120] The layout of plantations permitted even people who belonged to different masters to live "fence to fence," to call one another "nigh neighbor," and to see one another "every day" or "every night."[121] The people in this situation were at a significant advantage in their claims before the commission compared with those who had moved around since the war. In one particular case, it took an unusually perceptive claims agent to realize that "the reason that they Cant give any reference here [in Cherokee County, Alabama] was that . . . the Claimant lived in Georgia at the time the property was taken."[122] Being able to call fellow ex-slaves as knowledgeable witnesses thus continued to be important long after blacks won their official property rights.

In other ways, however, the commission's reliance on witnesses hurt ex-slave claimants. When investigating claims by former slaves, claims agents tended to trust the ones that offered testimony by at least one white witness.

This put black claimants in the difficult and sometimes strange position of needing supportive testimony from the very people who were least likely to give it. Edmund Moss, for example, ended up presenting a witness who used to be an Alabama county tax assessor and had "assessed him as . . . slave property."[123] By testifying as witnesses for ex-slaves, white planters, at least for a time, revived their role as protectors of black property ownership. "I know he had a horse," vouched a white Alabamian in another case. "I never heard it disputed. If a negro in those days had a horse that was not his own somebody would have disputed it sure."[124] Yet, however supportive they were of individual ex-slaves before the commission, and however willing they had been to participate in the prewar system of slave-owned property, ex-masters did not value property in the same way that ex-slaves did. Slaves had valued some objects not only for their worth in exchange but also because those objects were enmeshed in a network of social relationships that made them personally and culturally precious. Ex-slaves' attempts to translate those components of their value system into money splintered on the testimony of ex-masters. Pompey Bacon, as we have seen, "grieved" when the soldiers took his "nice linen shirts" because, as he put it, "I wanted them to meet the '*Lord.*'" But the investigating claims agent reported that the former slaveowner he interviewed about Pompey Bacon's claim thought that "the bed clothing and house hold effects [were] valued too high." This white witness admitted that he "could not state what they were worth, but thought [that] as a general thing, the bed clothing, and household effects, of negroes were not worth as much, as claimant claims."[125] Suspicious of fraud, casting about for clues about the validity of slaves' claims, northern agents quickly latched onto the paternalistic language that the "respectable gentlemen"[126] and "reliable citizens . . . of this vicinity"[127] used in speaking about slave-owned property. Part expert witnesses, part character witnesses, the white "gentlemen" consistently supported the ex-slaves' claims but scoffed at their "greatly overstated" values.[128] And planters' skepticism about the quality of slave-owned property had the same effect as if they had disputed its quantity.

Ex-slaves used language that was similarly marked. Indeed, the widespread acceptance of informal guidelines about what slaves could own can be seen as a logical corollary to the unofficial but widely observed rules that governed the "slaves' time." In this way, vague and general knowledge about "what was done" in the neighborhood could be distilled to a simple racial vocabulary and applied to specific instances.[129] Judging claims without written records required "some careful guessing," one agent admitted.[130] So agents quickly took up the former masters' race-specific, generalized notions about property and rounded them out with their own general impressions.[131] Some agents saw extreme poverty among the freedpeople in 1878 and apparently decided that they must have been just as poor in 1864 when the army came through and raided them.[132] In making final judgments, agents and commissioners applied the white "gentlemen's" opinions and their own assumptions like a formula, reducing the awards of even free blacks according to a set of racial preconceptions about property. "I suppose [it was] one of the finest in the county," the former slaveowner William Winn said of a horse claimed by one of his family's former slaves. Then, catching himself, he clarified: "I mean the horse was one of the finest of those owned by the negroes."[133]

Ex-slaves' experience with the commission was part of their larger adjustment in the South to new, more purely capitalist relations of land, labor, and capital. Ironically, establishing ownership through social claims under slavery proved easier than winning cash recognition from federal officials. Much of property's value for slaves could not be compensated in cash. Although slaves had long participated in a cash economy, they valued property in part for its social and personal significance, "use" values that former masters and federal agents did not understand and that had no equivalents in the monetary awards of the commission.

African Americans' experience with the Southern Claims Commission was emblematic of the way formal institutions came into their lives in the 1860s and 1870s. Rather than putting all their hopes into one institutional basket, ex-slaves tended to combine and move between legal and extralegal arenas. This interaction and fluidity had important consequences for the claims that ex-slaves made to property and kinship. How black people used— or did not use—the formal legal system would play an important role in deciding what would happen to the social relationships they generated under slavery now that slavery was finally over. Some elements of the old system survived, but the basic economy of land, time, and property had changed, and what survived now meant something different.

chapter five

Remaking Property

· ·

The end of the Civil War laid bare a set of wrenching questions about property. Years of half-hidden struggle had settled into fragile, yet widely recognized customs that gave slaves claims of access to land and a portion of their labor time. Slaves, masters, and other whites had built a system of owning and trading property that was anchored not in the law but in the yards and back roads of everyday life. The ending of slavery threw these complex understandings and practices into question. What was property? Who owned it? And what did ownership mean? Wherever black people turned—working a crop, buying a cow, renting a house, or even getting compensation for things soldiers had taken from them—they confronted new ideas about property. Black life after slavery involved intense, far-reaching negotiation with northern bureaucrats, white landlords, and other black folk about the ownership and meaning of property.

IN 1865, FORMAL LAW seemed poised to sweep aside extralegal understanding as the anchor of black people's claims to property. For the first time since their ancestors made the Middle Passage, African Americans had the legal right to own property. White people had always cherished their property rights, and they had shoved the slaves' economy off to a legal netherworld of "custom" and "usage"[1] that only seldom leaked into judges' written opinions. But when slavery ended, formal law did not sweep aside extralegal understandings of property; instead, it often nestled alongside, or even absorbed, those understandings. During the 1860s and 1870s, many former slaves found themselves making their claims to property in front of white men who had come from the North to work for the Freedmen's Bureau, the provost courts, and the Southern Claims Commission. In order to understand what happened when formal law came into black people's lives, we must first explore what those northern officers of the law thought property was.

The officials who went south in the 1860s and 1870s represented a northern society that, during the previous ninety years, had come to embrace two major assumptions about property: that law defined property and that property was an indivisible, individual possession. Between the 1780s and the 1860s, legal theorists and judges had transformed the law of property in the United States in ways that responded to and helped create the massive economic and political changes that took place in those years.[2] For centuries, when Europeans and European Americans had thought about property, their basic conceptual reference point had been land. In the early 1800s, chattels, especially business stocks and African American slaves, became more valuable and prominent in everyday life, and these kinds of property gradually pried land from its traditional place at the heart of European Americans' ideas about property. By the mid-1800s, many judges came to believe that America's prosperity depended not on anchoring a republican citizenry in the ownership of stable kinds of property like land but on putting property into flow, freely alienating it in the market.[3]

The problem, many judges thought, was that when it came to ideas about property, America was a howling wilderness of popular misunderstanding. "We all know who are the usual *scriveners*, or drawers up of last wills and testaments," warned a prominent judge in 1814: "the school-master of the neighborhood . . . or some one that has been about the courts and has some reputation for clerkship."[4] This gap between the formal legal system and ordinary people's understandings of law, judges believed, tied up property transactions—and choked the American economy—in a tangle of technical mistakes and confused intentions. In order to smooth the flow of commerce, judges wanted to bring property out of the wilderness and firmly into the realm of law. They tried to simplify and make accessible the country's arcane property laws. Similarly, judges' concerns about "the apparent legal soundness of titles" to property led them to redefine and clarify the meaning of "vested rights." People who transferred property had to know exactly when that property "vested" in the buyer (that is, when the buyer became the legal owner of an item) and how secure the buyer would be in her ownership if anything went wrong elsewhere along the chain of transactions (say, if a horse turned out to have been stolen). Legal thinkers agreed that uncertainty about property rights would deter Americans from investing, buying, and selling and thus strangle the nation's economy.[5] By working to develop a body of property law that property owners could use easily and consistently, judges and legal theorists made three key innovations to the concept of property in America: they succeeded in making property a *legal* entity, something that the law defined. They managed to consolidate, as one judge put it, all "rights and powers of ownership" into one tight package. And they put alienation —the ability to buy, sell, or transfer a thing—at the core of the concept of ownership.[6]

The Civil War put legal theorists' evolving ideas of property to the test. Instead of nurturing people's freedom to alienate their property on the open market, armies created barriers to trade. Instead of protecting the "sacred right" of property, both armies confiscated and destroyed property. As the war progressed, more and more of the South's property—slaves, houses, horses, hogs, and cotton—was either destroyed, consumed, or placed under the control of the U.S. government. In July 1862, with the passage of the first Confiscation Act, Congress gave its official blessing to "foraging," something soldiers had been doing unofficially for months. President Lincoln's private messages to his generals went even further. In order to "clear out . . . organized enemies" from the South, Lincoln ordered the army to arrest "active sympathizers" and confiscate their property. "Handle that class without gloves," he wrote to General Ulysses Grant, "and take their property for public use. As soon as the corn gets fit for forage get all the supplies you can from the rebels in Mississippi. It is time that they should begin to feel the presence of the war."[7] "Foraging" became an officially sanctioned way for both armies to get supplies, one that devastated whites, free blacks, and enslaved people.[8]

For white southerners, emancipation was a revolution in property. Slaves were *the* major wealth in the antebellum South, even though only a quarter of white southerners owned any slaves at all. By one estimate, the two million slaves in the five cotton-producing states (South Carolina, Georgia, Alabama, Mississippi, and Louisiana) were worth $1.6 billion in 1860, or 45.8 percent of the total wealth held by every resident of those states. This was nearly twice the value of all the farmland and buildings in those states, which was only $868 million. In 1863, President Lincoln's Emancipation Proclamation set in motion legal changes that eventually moved all four million of the South's slaves out of the category of property.[9]

Confiscation and emancipation devastated many southern property owners, yet the northern government carried out those measures in ways that *affirmed* property, especially legalistic, individualist notions of property. Both were war measures, intended to undermine the Confederacy's war effort and bolster the Union's. But confiscation and emancipation raised deeply troubling issues for the northern public and its army in the South. Northern officials knew that their handling of confiscated property, including slaves, would affect southerners' political choices during the war and beyond, and they desperately wanted to fan the embers of southern unionism.[10] One way to encourage southern unionism was to promise that unionists would be repaid for at least some of the property they lost. No federal official, however, wanted to pay compensation to disloyal southerners, or to liars who simply wanted to feast at the government's expense. Nor would the government compensate owners for their slaves, because the Emancipation Proclamation declared that slaves were no longer property. Most important, the armies' broadening attacks on property undermined bedrock principles of white Americans' political and social ideology.

In order to reconcile wartime exigencies with common doctrines of property, northern politicians and army officers adopted a two-pronged approach: first, they tried very hard to find some "undoubtedly constitutional" justification for confiscating property.[11] The second Confiscation Act, for example, was firmly grounded not only on the "laws of war" but also on Article III, Section 3, of the Constitution, which gave Congress the power to punish treason.[12] Congress's power to levy taxes provided the Union government with another constitutionally legitimate way to confiscate southerners' property. Reasoning that rebellious southerners would not pay taxes to the federal government, in 1862, Congress levied a "direct tax" on land. This measure permitted the government to confiscate much of the land that the Union army conquered. Second, in order to deal with the vast torrent of property that poured through the hands of its soldiers, the Union government developed a comprehensive system of accounting. Federal officials hoped that carefully accounting for each confiscated item would accomplish two goals. It would smooth the process of compensation after the war, and it would create a property regime that people would accept as legitimate during the war, one that was consistent with popular notions of what property was and how people owned it.

At the heart of this system of accounting were ledgers and receipts. They created a trail of paper that would document and preserve the link between person and object through the storm of a long war. Eventually, the paper trail would enable the government to determine who had owned what and to pay owners for the property it took. In 1863, the Treasury Department set up a procedure for "fully and distinctly marking all property" that came into the hands of its agents and for "making such a record of these marks, signs and numbers, and of all facts known in relation to the property, the identity and status of the alleged owner or agent, and . . . other information."[13] Dozens of agents and "forage clerks" were appointed to follow the army into the field and "receive and collect abandoned or captured property."[14] Before the agents sold the property or sent it away they gave each property owner a receipt:

> Received of _____ bales of Cotton [or hogsheads tobacco or sugar as the case may be, briefly describing it] estimated [insert weight or value, or both, of each parcel, and the aggregate] captured by the forces of the United States or seized under military or naval orders, and claimed to be the property of _____ . . . and marked and numbered as follows _____ [let the marks and numbers be distinct]

Then the agents made a written record for each item: "where [it was] captured or abandoned: under what circumstances: by whom owned or alleged to be owned: by whom captured or abandoned: by whom received or collected: from whom received: all names, marks, signs or devices (whether distinct, indistinct or partially erased, upon such property[)]: together with all other information which may in any way serve to identify or make known the history of any particular lot, or to trace the same or the proceeds thereof, from the earliest period possible to its final disposition."[15] This practice generated thick ledgers of confiscated property, arranged in lots, inventoried and indexed: "*Achilles* Cotton"; "*Amelia* Isld. Lumber"; "*Beaufort* Furniture"; "*Schooner* Bertha."[16] Where land and buildings were concerned, agents also recorded a "proof of ownership," usually a written title or deed, or some "documentary evidence."[17] Treasury agents compiled a mountain of these "proofs," a giant assemblage of numbers, measures, and descriptions that sits in the National Archives today.[18] The department clearly intended for southerners to bring these written records to special agencies, such as the U.S. Court of Claims and, later, the Southern Claims Commission, where they could prove ownership and loyalty.[19]

The chaos of wartime confiscation worried both the southerners who lost property and the northerners who took it. Treasury agents brought a sense of order out of the chaos. Their record keeping, and the promise that some-day compensation would be paid, preserved the idea of private property for Americans even as the armies violated and destabilized it. In effect, agents produced thousands of little "histories" of property in the South, stories that served much the same purpose as those orally remembered genealogies of ownership that North American slaves and Gold Coast residents had used to anchor ownership. But in the process, the agents began to change the meaning of property. By introducing this written system of receipts and ledgers into people's lives, the federal government laid the groundwork for a system of property ownership based on formal law rather than on display and acknowledgment, and one that aimed to reduce the complex social networks of southern ownership practices down to an exclusive, individual legal right.

In the 1870s, in the hearing rooms of the Southern Claims Commission, those legal assumptions about property ran into a challenge from an unlikely quarter: compensation claims from ex-slaves. Ex-slaves' claims could not succeed unless both they and the claims officials changed their assumptions about property. Agents, and especially the three commissioners of claims, came to the hearing room with highly legalistic conceptions of property and ownership, conceptions that were strikingly different from those held by the former slaves or even by the former masters. Northern officials expected that ownership was consolidated around one person (though it could be delegated), that property's value could be calculated in dollars and cents, that law validated ownership, and that property could not logically own property. Such understandings of property thus ruled out the idea of property owned by slaves.

Northern officials were prepared to evaluate the evidence found in contracts and to hear testimony about the clear, disinterested transfer of ownership from one person to the next.[20] But as one former slave put it, in those days many "black people did not understand about getting such things as a receipt and would not of known the use of them if they had got them."[21] Instead, officials heard witnesses tell of neighbors who helped one another keep animals and offer as proof of ownership the simple fact that they had seen the claimants use their possessions. Federal agents found such detailed anecdotal testimony useful for investigating claims brought by Unionist whites but problematic for those of former slaves. Asked why he relied on blacks' testimony to corroborate the claims of whites, Special Agent John D. Edwards explained, "I go to negroes because I find I can really get *detailed* information out of them. . . . They always know if a man was *really* loyal, they know if the cribs were full or not, often remember the names of the mules

[and] the oxen." By contrast, he went on sarcastically, "the rich white neighbors of the claimants" tended to "assert with a careless generality that 'so and so had between 50 and 100 head of whatnots, and the Federals took'm all sir; they took everything in the county, they robbed me, and broke me up . . . so and so lost ten times what he has charged the government.' "[22] By "interviewing darkies from all parts of the state" of Arkansas, boasted Edwards, "[I] have taken a lot of testimony that may save the Govt. a few thousands."[23]

Yet, if some agents considered blacks reliable witnesses in judging the property claims of whites, blacks' testimony was immediately suspect when given in defense of claims by ex-slaves because agents harbored powerful assumptions about the character of property in a slave society. Officials traveling to the South expressed disbelief at the claims of former slaves and at first tried to explain them away as claims to property "taken from their former owners"[24] or earned after emancipation.[25] Even the commissioners of claims in Washington apparently wondered "what is the use of taking testimony" in claims lodged by former slaves.[26] Ex-slave claims posed a problem not because claims officials mistrusted ex-slaves' ability to remember but because they believed that anything a slave may have possessed actually belonged to his master.[27]

Former slaves, on the other hand, believed that they *had* owned property and not merely as an extension of their masters' legal title to their bodies. Ex-slaves thought that what made an object into property was not that it disappeared into the private sphere of a single person but that it was associated publicly with people. These associations arose through cooperative labor and custody and the ongoing interchange of display and acknowledgment. Each piece of property embodied the interests of several people, including the master. Those multiple interests and associations made it difficult to calculate property's value strictly in individual and monetary terms, as the commission required. Claims officials had to evaluate claims without written evidence of ownership in a place where people who transferred property did not necessarily relinquish all interest in that property. Indeed, it was precisely the fact that property was enmeshed in several overlapping, sometimes competing, social relationships that made ownership possible for slaves and that turned possessions into property.

Many of the relationships that shaped and marked property also fit poorly with agents' assumptions about family structure, and even less with the rules of the commission, which required that witnesses state clearly what "interest" they had in the claim on which they testified. Ex-slaves who could discount blood family ties as a biasing motive were unusually persuasive witnesses. "I have done what I have out of neighborly kindness," said one, "& because he was a fellow servant in slavery times."[28] Agents usually accepted such statements at face value, perhaps because they did not expect that people who were neither linked by formal business mechanisms of debt and credit nor related by blood might share a "beneficial interest" in property. According to the rules of the Southern Claims Commission, however, the very strength of these social relationships could have undercut ex-slaves' credibility as witnesses. After all, slaves' claims to property mingled with their social relationships in ways that belied their statements of disinterestedness. Linda Roberts, for example, was "not related to" William Golding and had "no beneficial interest in his claim," but she had "known him since he was a little boy," had lived in his father's house, and had helped acquire the livestock, beehives, tea, and other property that Golding listed in his claim. In Roberts's words, Golding "made it there with 'we.' "[29] Observing the variety and flexibility of such personal relationships among slaves, with kinship, friendship, and economic connections mutually influencing one another, scholars today might conclude that many ex-slave witnesses did have an interest in the claims on which they testified, but claims agents accepted the avowals of disinterest. The arrival of the commission thus set in motion a complex process of adjustment. Successful claims had to resolve the conflict of expectations between ex-slaves and federal officials.

To a great extent, they did. But just as in the Gold Coast colonial courts, reconciling legal and extralegal understandings had ambiguous consequences for people's claims of ownership. Ex-slaves modified their expectations about property and freedom in order to convince the federal agents. Postwar events show that slaves also felt entitled to the land they lived on,[30] but ex-slaves did not list land among their possessions because the commission would compensate only "army supplies" and did not allow claims for things that soldiers could not carry off. The rules also disqualified many items that had been taken—such as buggies, chickens, beehives, clothing, and kitchenware, even peanuts, syrup, butter, sugar, and tea—but were deemed as having no legitimate army use. Even when they stuck to the eligible categories, ex-slaves sometimes had to change their conceptions of value. Soldiers confiscated some items that slaves valued primarily for their cultural or religious significance, items that were "owned" but whose worth as property was difficult to translate into dollars. Black claimants understood that the Southern Claims Commission would reject their claims if they argued that not only "the product of their taskwork" but also the rations their masters gave them and the land, buildings, and stock of the entire plantation all rightfully belonged to them. They purposefully—and necessarily—limited themselves to the definition specified in the commission rules: movable property taken by Union troops for legitimate army use.

Still, even the definition of movable property was subject to many different interpretations. When they could, claimants carefully conformed their testimony to the rules of the commission and the expectations of its agents. Some items clearly had been bought, used, and cared for by groups of slaves but were claimed by individuals. Linda Jones claimed a corn mill, taken from beside her house, which the plantation slaves had bought collectively "for their own use."[31] Other movables had been possessed and used by slaves but had been bought and given to them by masters. Indeed, the issue of rations could have undermined all of the ex-slaves' claims. As agents quickly learned, "Whatever [the slaves] raised for themselves saved so much to the owner in the necessary expense of Keeping them . . . and gave him so much more profit on their labor."[32] On this delicate issue, agents and ex-slaves moved carefully. Many claimants pointed to storage practices, distinguishing between "my corn-house" and that of the master.[33] Others emphasized function or quality. Sam Harris insisted that he used "his" wagon only for driving to church and for trips with his wife, while "my master's wagon was used for the farm work."[34] Another ex-slave, Jacob Dryer, summarized: "I had a good sum of clothes that master bought for me," including twelve yards of "white cob cloth" used "to dress the family with." He also had a new "suit of black, that I paid ten dollars for in Savannah." In all, he owned "five or six suits," but, he added, "all the good ones I bought for myself."[35]

Lawyers representing the ex-slave claimants found themselves in the odd position of arguing that the law was irrelevant to deciding ex-slaves' claims of ownership. "If it was right they should have had these supplies from the hands of their masters," insisted one lawyer, "no one will dispute their right of property & wish to evade legal responsibility by technical distinctions, arising out of abstruse questions of legal right."[36] Another pair of lawyers scolded the commissioners for their skepticism: "To say that this property belonged to the *master* & that therefore it should not be paid for does not look very well from the high moral anti-slavery standpoint." Anything the slave possessed, they went on, was "to all intents his property" because "he would have had the profit and enjoyment of it."[37]

At their office in Washington, the commissioners of claims received conflicting messages about property ownership in the South. On the one hand, several lawyers and agents sent them detailed explanations about the workings and logic of the informal economy. Some slaveowners had not only encouraged extra work, wrote one lawyer, they even "*forced* the Slaves, to supplement their Scanty rations by their own industry in that direction . . . & the negroes supplied the general market, with eggs & chickens."[38] On the other hand, many claims agents mistrusted claims from former slaves, and they relayed those doubts to their superiors back in Washington. Robert Avery considered black people "over grown children" who "know nothing of the value of money."[39] His attitude in hearings was so skeptical and patronizing that ex-slave Benjamin Lettuce got angry and blurted out:

> [Lettuce]: [Do you] Spose I'd tell you a lie[?] I'm used to money, Mister.
> [Avery]: I want you to stop and think every time before answering?
> [Lettuce]: I am thinking. I wouldn't lie for money. I'm used to money, I am. You are writing for a man that hasn't got much sense, but I'm used to money.[40]

Perhaps chastened by a similar tongue-lashing, another claims agent decided to take a studious attitude instead. "Doubtless the law as to the holding of property by slaves is well understood by the Commissioners," he began, "but [since] this is the first of the kind in which I have taken testimony," he thought it best to spell out what he had learned during his months in Alabama.[41] A few field agents, sympathetic to the former slaves and realizing that many of their fellow agents were extremely skeptical of claims by ex-slaves, added their own newly acquired knowledge to the fray.[42] Special Commissioner Virgil Hillyer described for his superiors a society in which respect for slave-owned property "was a law of honor with the best men," a "custom" that was equivalent, he argued, to the rights that northerners had to the improvements they erected on rented land. When the commissioners wondered how slaves could own valuable livestock, Hillyer explained to them that stock-raising was "little trouble or expense to any one . . . except the trouble of marking and branding the increase every year."[43] After hearing that one of the traveling special agents was stoking the Washington commissioners' doubts about slaves owning property, Hillyer wrote a passionate report: "[Y]ou ask what is the use of taking testimony in such cases? I answer how can I refuse?" Ex-slave claimants filled out all the required forms, he argued, and they found witnesses and appeared for hearings. Thus, "prima faciacly [*sic*] they have made out their case. If I am to suppose anything it is that the claimants will prove what they [illegible] can be proved in their petitions."[44]

Agents and commissioners modified their presumptive logic about slavery and property by drawing a line between "rations" and things that slaves bought or produced on their own. They began to base their awards on "what [slaves] would have on average at that season of the year, as the product of their task work."[45] They began to reject claims for things that they believed had been "measured out to them by the owners to do them for a specified time."[46] Thus, when William Cassels claimed 140 bushels of corn "because it was given to me before my master left . . . to feed my family and the rest of the people on the place," the commissioners compensated him only for the 60 bushels he had grown himself.[47]

In drawing such distinctions, the commission was essentially tracing the genealogy of slaves' possessions back to the last transaction it could recognize as "legitimate." By the standards of the North in the mid-1800s, this meant a cash sale from a free white to a slave or, failing that, a transaction between two slaves. In most cases, the commission excluded objects whose last involvement in a transaction had been a one-way transfer from master to slave, such as rations or gifts. Awards for drivers and plowmen were an exception that proved the rule. The commissioners viewed objects given to these slaves by their masters as legitimate compensation for not having access to their own after-task labor. Of course, this logic ignored the "reciprocity" implicit in all slave rations; to recognize rations as a kind of payment would have undermined the idea that slavery was the absolute opposite of "free labor"—an idea that had been a pillar of the Union's war effort and that was now shaping life in the South.[48] Nevertheless, this distinction between rations and legitimate property allowed the commissioners to accept the notion that southern slaves had owned property.

In May 1872, by an act of Congress, the commission revised its "interrogatories" to include "special questions for women and for colored persons."[49] Following a new set of "explicit . . . instructions" the commissioners in the field began to approve the claims of ex-slaves who could "furnish strict proof that they owned the property in their own right by such title as was recognized by their masters—a title that gave them absolute control & disposition of the property."[50] By the 1870s, whatever their initial assumptions and doubts, officials in Washington were recognizing not merely "possession" but "ownership" of property by slaves.[51] As things turned out, it would be much more difficult for ex-slaves to get their former masters to recognize their claims of ownership.

EX-MASTERS AND EX-SLAVES breathed in deeply from the slave past as they set about making a propertied future for themselves after 1865. For better or for worse, the understandings and practices that underpinned the informal economy were part of the fabric of everyday life and would profoundly influence the transition out of slavery. Thus, as white and black southerners squared off to grapple over the meaning of freedom, they began to fight over both legal and extralegal claims of ownership. Sometimes subtle, always ferocious, such struggles reached into the furthest recesses of people's lives because they went to the heart of what it meant to "own" something.

White landowners went into the postwar years with arrogantly big assumptions about their claims to land, crops, and the labor of former slaves. "Let everything proceed as formerly," wrote one white landowner, "the contractual relation being substituted for that of master and slave."[52] After all, said another, "[t]he emancipated slaves own nothing, because nothing but freedom has been given to them."[53] Former slaveowners wanted to preserve the system of centralized labor control. They expected their black employees to do all the different kinds of work a plantation needed, even work that had nothing to do with the plantation's main crop, and they expected to oversee it all. Most of all, they felt that the only reward black workers should expect in return was a wage. Working on the plantation, most ex-masters believed, did not give ex-slaves any rights to the crop, the land, or its buildings and equipment; those things would remain the exclusive property of the white proprietor. Although most ex-masters understood that the war had ended their property rights in black people, they nevertheless expected to keep their wide claims over land and movable property. Those claims had been the basis of the slave economy, and, if ex-masters could hold onto them, they would effectively keep blacks under their thumb.[54]

In some parts of the South, the northern government propped up these arrogant assumptions. Union troops guaranteed that ex-slaves owned their laboring time, but they also required that freedpeople sign contracts binding their labor to landowners for twelve months at a time. During the Civil War, army officers who were assigned to explore plans for ex-slaves' transition to "free labor" usually tried leasing the land to white people and then "supervising" the freedpeople in the fields. One Union general stationed in Louisiana testified in 1863 that the army leased plantations to "men who cared nothing how much flesh they worked off the negro provided it was converted into good cotton at seventy five cents per pound." The army drew up contracts that promised to freedpeople food, medicines, and "schools for the children," the general lamented, but these "were very seldom lived up to" in practice because "cotton has been the main thing, the negro is only a nigger."[55] Freedpeople at a Washington, D.C., camp agreed, saying that their superintendent was "better suited to [be] an overseer of a Southern plantation" than a director of a Union refugee camp.[56] In those areas of the South under Union army control, ex-slaves' lack of either land, tools, or money forced many, if not most, of them to continue working for their former masters, with Union soldiers acting as overseers. "The Negroes were mystified," one former master observed eight months after the raid in Liberty County, Georgia, "thunderstruck that they should receive such treatment (and in some cases very severe, even cruel) at the hands of their friends. Very soon they began to whisper that the said Yankees were only Southern men in blue clothes—that the true Yankees had not come yet."[57] While the grand slaveowning families complained of great privations, the county's black residents started with less and suffered more. As ex-slave Prince Maxwell put it, "all I got was my rations," and for him that was "hardly as good" as when they were slaves and had raised property after their tasks.[58]

New laws redefined claims to land in ways that threatened to bind black people back into dependency even after slavery was legally dead. Before the war, open-range laws had permitted poor southerners, both free and slave, to hunt, fish, and fatten their livestock on the unfenced portions of their wealthier neighbors' lands. But after emancipation, white landowners decided that those "customary" practices were tempting their obedient black workers away from the cotton and rice fields. Landowners began to limit the amount of "extra" land they permitted their workers to cultivate rent-free. Enclosure (or "fence") laws were passed, beginning in counties with high black populations, and landowners began to argue that landownership included an absolute and exclusive right over everything on it. Wild animals and plants that slaves and landless whites had previously used without much commotion were now off-limits.[59] In places where masters used to grant slaves relatively free access to land but had limited their access to "after-task" time, landowners now allotted only tiny half- or quarter-acre plots, on a yearly basis, and only to specific workers to raise "private crops."[60] People who hunted, fished, or grazed animals on someone else's land were now "trespassers," and if they were black, they were liable to be jailed and hired out as forced labor. Slavery's economy of time was becoming an economy of land.

This was the property regime that white landowners expected. But former slaves had their own expectations about property that rejected the sweeping claims of white landlords. Dealing with the Southern Claims Commission acquainted ex-slaves with legalistic notions of property, and evidence in postwar court cases allows us to glimpse a fundamental shift in their understanding of property, one that drew strength from the law but was not determined by it. These cases suggest that African Americans no longer accepted the notion that their claims to land, laboring time, and movable property depended on the sufferance—whether obtained by "custom," display, or asking permission—of a master.

Many former slaves fought back through law, defying white landlords by trying to legalize their claims to labor and property. Thousands of African Americans approached the Freedmen's Bureau during the late 1860s to complain about landlords beating them, refusing to pay wages or to divide the crop, kidnapping their children, or otherwise violating their lawful, duly signed contracts.[61]

Other freedpeople fought back by trying to buy land. While many slaves had access to land before emancipation, ex-slaves tried to replace those customary privileges of access with legal claims of ownership. In early 1865, it looked as though the government would help them. General William T. Sherman ordered some 400,000 acres of coastal Georgia and South Carolina to be set aside for freedpeople. Since most whites had run away, ex-slaves were able to stake out "possessory" titles to the so-called Sherman land. For the most part, they ignored Sherman's forty-acre rule and began dividing up their provision grounds and fields into plots of many different sizes and shapes. They allotted land by "household," but each household farmed more than one plot, in different fields.[62] Quickly, however, it became clear that the Union government would not redistribute its vast holdings of confiscated southern land to freedpeople. The government even went back and evicted some freedpeople from the "Sherman lands." As a result, although more than 30,000 black southerners owned some land by 1870, nearly 4.5 million others did not.[63] Even the few blacks who owned land rarely owned very much, and often had to work a sharecrop on the side to make ends meet.[64] As W. E. B. Du Bois observed, the "movement toward Negro property holding" was a "widespread accumulation of small sums in many hands."[65] The ranks of black landowners and the value of their holdings grew during the late 1860s and 1870s, but because most African Americans remained desperately poor, only a small minority managed to acquire the legal title to land that they so fervently sought.[66] Most had to approach some white person who did own land and agree either to rent, to work for wages, or to work on shares. Still, even the possibility of being a legally recognized landowner, rather than having mere claims of access to land, represented an important change from the days of slavery.

African Americans also asserted their ideas about property outside the strictures of legal rights. They transformed their relationship to southern towns and cities, visiting and moving in by the thousands, laying claim to the urban landscape and its economy.[67] Blacks in Richmond, Virginia, turned an old Main Street stable into a Baptist church in the winter of 1865; in the spring, they built a school and guarded it with their own brand-new black militia. And in 1867, a group of black men hammered loose the iron bars of the old Fifteenth Street slave-trading pen and turned it into a school.[68] African Americans asserted new claims even to places they did not own, such as yards, streets, and public squares. Starting in the summer of 1866, all-black militias began drilling and marching through the streets of several southern cities.[69] The old trade routes from the countryside continued to feed southern towns, but now some blacks began to set up the kind of permanent storefront shops that had been nearly impossible during slavery.[70] Ex-slaves began selling vegetables in and around Vicksburg almost as soon as the town surrendered;[71] and well into the 1900s, town markets in Washington, Annapolis, Charleston, Wilmington, Lynchburg, and Richmond thronged with black people selling everything from cigars to catfish.[72] But they and their carts moved through a different kind of urban landscape. As blacks left the plantations behind and moved into towns, they transformed both the cultural rhythm of the city and the old system that had linked it to the countryside.

Many white city dwellers resented the way that the growing influx of African Americans changed the sounds, smells, and habits of public spaces. Black people had always been there, working, trading, and talking, but they had been almost invisible to whites; now, blacks' presence seemed to jump out at them. At out-of-the-way railroad stations in Virginia, travelers were greeted by "[a] dozen or more Negroes, one or two men in Confederate gray, and some white women" selling "cigars, apples, and peaches at ten cents a dozen," along with ready-made lunches of chicken and cornbread.[73] In Vicksburg, whites literally looked down on the blacks living "in the bottom next to the RR" tracks, but they could not keep out Peter Johnson, who was "in the habit of going" up the hill into a white-owned grocery store, "lighting cigars and taking drinks too when I feel like it."[74] Some whites worried that ex-slaves were taking over the national holidays. Richmond's newspaper sneered that at the July 4 celebration of 1866, the "highways, byways, [and] Capitol Square were black with moving masses of darkeys."[75] Black residents of Memphis had to answer complaints about a "masked Ball" they had held at Hiztmer Hall on Shelby Street, even though the mayor had personally given them permission.[76] Even a former Union army colonel wrote an angry letter to the local Freedmen's Bureau officer, fuming at what he called "insolen[t]" behavior by his black neighbors. Several black families had moved into the kitchen and "back part" of the house next to his and, he complained, they were in the "habit" of "throw[ing] Melon rinds over the fence into my yard." One rind flew through the back door and hit his son; another barely missed his wife.[77] We may never know whether this man's neighbors were teasing him or just being careless, but one wonders whether the bureau officer kept a straight face.

Moreover, at the same time that African Americans changed the cultural rhythms of the city, they also altered the way that they related to it as earners and owners of property. One Freedmen's Bureau officer's conscientious investigation of a police shooting in Memphis has left behind a remarkable "map" in words and pictures of how blacks were building on slavery-era practices to forge an economic future for themselves in the city. Sixteen-year-old Tom Waller and his family lived in a house (marked "A") set back from the street, behind a vacant lot ("D") and the white-owned homes that fronted the street ("E," "F," "G"). In front of their house, the family kept a garden ("B"). "In addition to the garden," the officer wrote, "this colored family had an interest in an other garden on the Pigeon Roost Road . . . over a mile away . . . from which they have been marketing vegetables." Their "custom" was to gather vegetables on Tuesday evenings "for next mornings market." Early on one of these mornings Tom's mother woke up her two sons "and started them with sacks to the garden on the Pigeon Roost Road."[78] Only one of them came home. As much as Tom's death reveals about Memphis police brutality, his errand that fateful day also suggests how much the informal economy had changed since the days of slavery. Whereas slaves had been obliged to trek from the countryside into towns, enduring obnoxious curfews and miles of bad weather, these town-dwelling African Americans farmed their market gardens in and around town. Moreover, although they worked alone in the garden in front of their house, out in the more distant garden on Pigeon Roost Road they shared their ownership "interest" with other freedpeople. By mixing different kinds of ownership claims, and walking back and forth between home, garden, and market, this black family brought some of the practices of the plantation right into the city.

Change was just as subtle and sweeping out on the plantations. Former slaves did not get rid of the slavery era's system of display and acknowledgment, yet they transformed it to take advantage of the new possibilities of freedom. Under slavery, as we have seen, most large southern plantations had concentrated their main house, slave quarters, storage sheds, and work-buildings in one central place. Most of the buildings on the giant Millwood plantation in piedmont South Carolina, for example, had huddled onto just and in order to represent the facts more clearly, will insert a rude diagram of the immediate vicinity — in which the affair took place

Explanation

"A" is the lot on which the family, to which the deceased belonged, lives — "B" a garden cultivated by this family, "C" a vacant dwelling house, "D" a vacant lot on which the boy was killed, "E" the residence of Mr. Swire "F" the residence of Mrs Riley and "G" the residence of ———

The deceased's name was Tom Waller and not Sam Evans as given in the papers

It appears that in addition to the garden "B," this colored family had an interest in an other garden on the Pigeon Roost Road from which they have been marketing vegetables, during the whole season — Tuesday evening being cloudy and wet, vegetables were not gathered for next mornings market as had been the custom

On Wednesday morning about 3 o'clock A.M. Sally Waller waked up her two sons

A handwritten report on a Memphis police shooting by a Freedmen's Bureau officer. Local newspapers (which Walker clipped and attached to his report) fumbled even such simple facts as the name of the young man who was shot (Capt. T. A. Walker to Capt. W. W. Deane, July 21, 1865, Provost Marshal, Memphis, Tennessee, Entry 3545, RG 105).

thirty-two of its fifteen thousand sprawling acres.[79] Freedom broke down that centralized landscape and replaced it with a landscape of scattered clusters. At first, African Americans in many parts of the South worked under the "squad system," which modified the gang system and permitted them some choice in how they organized their labor. People who worked in squads went on to break up these "nucleated" living patterns and moved into clusters of cabins not far from the old slave quarters. At a plantation in the Sea Islands, reported Elizabeth Ware Pearson in 1868, fences and gates were removed, "[t]rees cut down, and houses moved and built in the middle of the field." Former slaves were busy "thinn[ing] out . . . the woods" and planting corn on the newly cleared fields.[80] Black homes kept dispersing decades after the squad system died, even in regions where few blacks owned any land, because tenants and sharecroppers insisted on quitting the old slave quarters and moving onto the plots they farmed.[81] "It was usual in slavery times to concentrate the 'quarters,' " wrote a traveler in Alabama, but freedpeople tended to "spread . . . more about, near [their] work."[82] In the late 1860s, and certainly by 1880, black people's fierce resistance to anything that smacked of slavery destroyed the plantation, not just as a labor system but also as a physical landscape.[83] Some whites complained at seeing "[t]he fine houses fallen to decay . . . the grounds neglected and grown over with weeds" and "stately date-palms ruthlessly burnt down by Negroes to make room for a small patch of corn."[84] But for African Americans, such changes marked a new beginning, not an ending.

The transformation of the plantation landscape made an enormous difference in how black people earned and owned property, especially movable property. Scattering the cabins took their daily life out of sight of their old masters. Breaking up the "quarters" also shortened the time it took them to walk each day between their cabins—with their attached garden plots— and the fields where they worked for a white landowner. Freedpeople could raise crops and animals for themselves much more easily if those things were close to the cotton and rice fields.

One of the most important consequences of breaking up the slave quarters was that it revamped the interchange of display and acknowledgment that had anchored property ownership for slaves. Under slavery, African Americans had used the centralized layout of the plantation, with its rigid "street" of slave cabins spread out under their master's watchful eye, to display their property and secure acknowledgment of their ownership. Nevertheless, although ex-slaves broke up the slave quarters, they still resettled in small clusters of families, "generally two or three near together," and they preserved

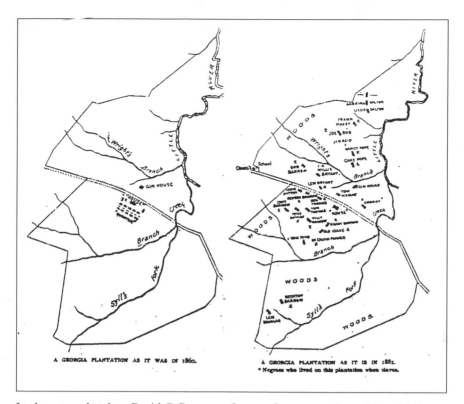

In these two sketches, David C. Barrow, a former slaveowner, showed how his former slaves changed the landscape of his piedmont Georgia plantation in the aftermath of emancipation (from David C. Barrow Jr., "A Georgia Plantation," *The Century Illustrated Monthly Magazine* 21 [1881], 832–33).

the house-yard pattern, with its calculated use of visible space. This setup minimized the walk to work and gave them some "elbow room" yet enabled them to keep up social networks that they could "call on . . . [w]henever they have heavy work to do."[85] Former slaves in Georgia built house-yard compounds, "smooth sand clearing[s]," often enclosed by "a reed and paling fence," with "three or four small unpainted wooden cabins, two connected by a narrow board walk just above the ground. Other smaller structures, sheds, and work tables were placed helter-skelter about the enclosure. There was some wire fencing, but dogs, cats, chickens, a litter of very young puppies, and an old rooster roamed at will."[86] While a house's back lot or the ground along the fence might be cluttered with shells or pots, the yards were spotless; even the grass was scoured away and the dirt swept clean every day.[87] Black people adapted their practices of public display and acknowledgment to take advantage of the new plantation landscape. Just as they had during slavery, they planted gardens and kept small livestock in their yards, but with plantations broken into clusters, masters no longer had a commanding view of their workers' cabins, of their work, or of the things ex-slaves owned.[88] This layout kept household property under the watchful eyes of the people who lived in the cabins and their neighbors but far from the oversight of their white landlord. Old ownership practices of the antebellum plantations continued, but the range of people who saw—and could vouch for—ex-slaves' claims over property had changed. By taking themselves and their property away from the oversight of white landlords, ex-slaves showed they no longer considered their property claims to be a custom or a privilege but a right. As we will see, such changes in the plantation landscape raised the stakes of negotiations *among* blacks—especially among kin. But they also set the stage for wide-ranging fights over property between whites and blacks.

Whites and blacks brought thousands of property disputes to court in the 1860s and 1870s, and their testimony in those cases suggests that legal theorists would face a tough battle if they expected to hack through the wilderness of untutored, popular ideas of property. "The law" became one of many weapons in southerners' ferocious disputes over property, and it often breathed new life into ideas and practices that dated back to slavery days. Many landowners still believed that "a garden, or truck patch, [or] a henhouse" would "engender . . . a home feeling" among black workers,[89] and thus many of the contracts signed during the first few years of freedom made a distinction between "private crops"—things ex-slaves raised on their own time—and the "general crop" that constituted the plantation's main income.[90] But although this distinction may have seemed clear enough in the precise legal language of a contract, ex-masters and ex-slaves seldom agreed about the boundary between private and general crops, any more than they had agreed about "the slaves' time" and "the master's time." Ex-slaves who asserted rights to private crops sometimes found themselves accused of stealing. One woman who ate rice from what she thought was her "private crop" was arrested for "stealing" because her employer had not specifically allotted her any extra land.[91] Another landowner, noticing that a freedwoman had planted a "private crop" on his land without his permission, loosed his cattle to trample it dead.[92]

Like the Fantes who appealed to "customary law" in British courts, many southerners—both white and black—made their claims in court by splicing together principles from both the legal system and the extralegal system it was supposed to replace. They combined the powerful yet somewhat ambiguous rule of law with assumptions and knowledge derived from practices of display and acknowledgment. Witnesses in court cases could speak in great detail about horses "fifteen and a half . . . hands high, rather weak eyes, a little white spot under the fetlock on the left hind leg,"[93] and they argued about whether a cow had an "under bit & small crop off of the right ear" or a "swallow fork in each ear."[94] Even hogs, which wandered around, had marks cut into their ears, making it possible for people to "Know" their neighbors' animals "by sight."[95] Sometimes, people put marks on things specifically to bolster their claims of ownership. When passing whites claimed to recognize "Private marks" on missing cradles and ploughs, it was often enough to land black people in court.[96] Whites drew on the same expectations and knowledge about property in their disputes with other whites. "Know the land and have known it for years," testified a white witness in North Carolina, "I helped to survey the land, carried the chain. I could go to the corners."[97] A Texas lawyer crafted exquisitely detailed arguments about "the identity of the pigs claimed" by his white client,[98] while witnesses in another case claimed to have "known the Pony . . . ever since it was foaled."[99] And one white Texan even interrupted his stroll along a low-ebbing river to "pick . . . up a hogs head which [he] recognized as belonging to" one of his neighbors and took it to a local judge.[100] Like the Southern Claims Commission and the Gold Coast colonial courts, the Freedmen's Bureau and the provost courts leaned heavily on such testimony in judging property disputes between middling and poor southerners of both races. Indeed, in one Baton Rouge trial, a witness was told to "Examine the horse pointed out to you . . . and tell the Court whether or not it is the same one which the accused offered to sell you."[101] One can only assume the court went outside to see the horse.

Nothing sparked as many fights as staple crops. With the odds of their becoming landowners stacked against them, black people took advantage of new laws that gave them a legal claim to rice, cotton, and corn. These things had become (ever since blacks themselves stopped being considered property) the single most valuable kind of movable property that ordinary people were likely to have. In the areas where the Freedmen's Bureau stationed officers, ex-slaves and ex-masters signed legally binding contracts and some ex-slaves were able to force landlords to pay the wages or crop shares that those contracts specified.[102] They sued white landowners in every kind of court available to them, demanding the share of the crop that was theirs by law. Ex-slaves took steps outside the courts, too, demanding to watch and critique the weighing and dividing of the crops. As one freedman recalled, "The crop was divided after January. . . . When we gathered the corn every fifth load carried to the house was set apart for our share. The other four loads we hauled to the house [were] set apart for his."[103] Nothing embodied the changes that emancipation wrought on the plantation's economy more than this once-a-year ritual of the crop division. For the first time, white landlords could no longer simply assume that they legally owned the plantation's "general crop" regardless of what the slaves did with their own "little matters of property."[104] By demanding their legal right to the "general crop," former slaves expressed a new understanding of property that defied the sweeping claims of ex-masters. Although slaveowners had commonly mortgaged their cash crops to "factors," they were not used to sharing ownership of those cash crops with their slaves, and they resented the freedpeople's new claims over the "general crop." They were convinced that the entire crop was theirs to dole out however they saw fit, and they refused to permit black workers to store any of it in their cabins. For former masters, there was little difference between letting the freedpeople store the crop and letting them steal it.

Rather than smoothing out these staple crop disputes, the law often only made them worse. Southern legislatures and judges after the Civil War tried to bring property into the world of law and to eliminate confusion over ownership, but the new laws—especially crop lien laws—often tended instead to multiply claims on property and to intensify, rather than displace, older practices of display and acknowledgment. Indeed, the crop lien laws passed during Reconstruction tended to focus not simply on who had the legal title to the crop but on what the crop looked like and where and how it was stored before it was divided between landowner and workers. Every year there were several months when one party legally owned the crop while the other had only an interest in it (in legal terms, a "lien" on the crop). This interested nonowner had the backing of law, but her or his interest would only be activated at the end of year, when the crop was harvested and divided. Everyone had to guard their interests jealously to prevent the others from selling the crop, taking out loans against it, or otherwise "encumbering" the crop before they divided it. Whether the state was under traditional landlord-tenant law (where tenants retained legal ownership of the whole crop until it was divided) or under the "Redeemer" laws of the late 1870s (which "gave the landlord legal possession of the crop until the tenant paid the rent"), the law put an emphasis on visibility, possession, and storage.[105] Under this system, people made it their business to know every day where the crop was and what was happening to it.[106]

Now the struggle over time that had rumbled in the background for 150 years of slavery broke into the open as disputes over movable property, disputes in which ex-slaves claimed a right to the staple crop and whites fought back by accusing them of stealing. Partly because of the law's emphasis on visibility, much of the postwar struggle over property between blacks and whites centered not on who legally owned things but on who possessed or controlled them. Landowners believed that black tenants were stealing from the piles of cotton and rice, and they constantly demanded to look into their tenants' houses to inspect "their" property. One day, three white men came to look at the corn stored in ex-slave August Macbeth's house and stood on his doorstep discussing whether "the corn looked like the Seed corn he had given to Jim Duggins to plant about a year ago."[107] White landowners in particular could get warrants to search their tenants' houses and confiscate any corn they could "Eyedentify" and bring it to the courthouse.[108] It was not unheard of for a planter to testify that he recognized some stolen corn by the red grains at the end of its cobs.[109] Another ex-slave recalled that his landlord brought him "some Rice in the ear . . . and showed it to me & asked me if I knew it. I said no."[110] White-owned newspapers advised cotton buyers to "demand proof" of ownership from black sellers, and when a white farmer's cotton went missing, "agents were sent out" to the local train station and cotton sheds "to inquire if suspicious cotton had been carried" there.[111] At a time when basic assumptions about "ownership" were in flux, southerners looked back to the practices of slavery and relied more than ever on what things looked like.

Black tenants, however, believed that their houses were not public spaces for looking at property and that the landowners had no absolute claims over a crop that had not yet been divided. "He asked me about cotton," said York Mikell of his landlord, but "I would not tell him because he rushed right in when my family was all naked."[112] Dock Baker said "he would break a stick over his [landlord's] head" if the man came looking for a missing axe at his house.[113] Despite black people's resistance, white landowners were convinced that "[t]her is agreat deel of steeling a goin on in this Cuntrey,"[114] and, as far as they were concerned, "no one is suspected save negroes."[115] Prosecutions for theft in southern civil courts reflected the anxieties of white landowners. In the grand jury rooms of Warren County, Mississippi, indictments for crimes against property began to crowd out those for other categories of crime— even violent offenses.[116] And just as white people's ideas about the nature of crime changed, so did the color of the criminal. In several Georgia counties, nine-tenths of the people charged with stealing were black and nine-tenths of the alleged victims were white, ridiculously skewed numbers that hide countless wrecked, innocent lives.[117] "It looks to me," said a black Mississippian, "that the white people are putting in prison all that they can get their hand on."[118]

Rural southerners probably could identify staple crops (which, to a novice, look almost exactly alike from one farm to the next).[119] Although both whites and blacks admitted that property like rice or chickens looked "very much alike" from one plantation to another, they insisted that, as one former slaveowner put it, those who were "familiar with" the property "can tell the difference."[120] It did not matter, said one Texas prosecutor, that "from their nature it was impossible to identify [things] such as money meal flour, &c." When a man was caught with coins "exactly similar to those stolen"— from their gold and silver denominations down to the "hole in . . . one of the twenty five cent pieces"—it was "prima facie evidence of guilt."[121] In their grim battle over the South's staple crops, white people went back to the old system of display and acknowledgment to turn stealing into a "negro" crime.

Like many of the property disputes argued in Gold Coast colonial courts, the courtroom arguments in theft trials probably reflected bigger concerns than the handfuls of corn and cotton that blacks were accused of stealing. Testimony at trials hints that the ending of slavery turned a smoldering negotiation over time into an open war over land and movable property. While black people claimed a right to the staple crop, whites, who felt that they had already been "robbed" of their property rights in slaves, fought back by accusing blacks of stealing. In the end, most ex-slaves still could make only fragile, limited claims to the crops they sweated over. The new crop laws of the 1860s and 1870s did not end crop disputes between whites and blacks, nor did they bring southerners' property claims completely into the world of law. Instead, evidence from postwar military courts hints that the laws permitted ex-slaves and ex-masters to combine legal and extralegal claims of ownership, to continue making claims based on display and acknowledgment while reinforcing those claims with the iron power of law.

ALMOST HIDDEN IN THE shadows behind black people's negotiations with northern officials and southern landowners was a third set of negotiations over property, just as important but less obvious because it happened inside black families and communities. In their testimony before military courts, former slaves outlined a world of black-black interaction where property continued to be embedded in social networks, especially kinship, and where ownership was secured through informal practices of display and acknowledgment. Indeed, scattering the slave quarters away from masters' prying eyes meant that for most blacks, owning property depended more than ever on the acknowledgment and support of other black people.

Trade between black people after the Civil War ran along the sinews of carefully nurtured social networks. Because of a severe money shortage and because most African Americans were desperately poor during the postwar years, relatively few of them could pay money for the things they needed.[122] They invented other ways to facilitate trading, practices that drew strength from social networks. In 1865, Shady Lewis bargained with a white blacksmith to fix his cart, agreeing "to pay for [the repair] in coals."[123] Other ex-slaves turned a shipment of hoes from northern charities into a circulating medium of exchange, almost like money.[124] In Alabama, the informal economy sprouted anew along roadsides and at little stores called "deadfalls," where poor whites and blacks bartered for what they needed. Much as they had during slavery, such small-scale, informal, often interracial markets stirred up self-righteous anger and a barrage of regulations from the judges and planters who ran these communities.[125] Somewhat less threatening than the deadfalls, all-black cooperative societies like the Daughters of Zion, the Colored Sons of Temperance, and the Poor Saints of First Baptist Beale Street made emergency loans, sponsored "feasts" and outings, and helped pay for funerals.[126] In the hours and days after someone died, people visited the person's house to bring food for the bereaved and to keep "watch over [the] corpse."[127] Black networks ensured that, no matter how poor a person was, she or he might, as was the case with Isaac Simmons, still have "some Society money to bury his father with."[128]

In a world where almost nobody used receipts and it could take weeks to pay off debts, ex-slaves looked to social ties for the knowledge and trust they needed to make trades. For example, selling a piece of property often took the combined efforts of parents, children, and neighbors. When Rachel Bostwick acquired a horse, she "gave the horse to [her] oldest son," two miles away in the Sea Islands, "who sent it to his sister Sally for sale." When Sally found a buyer, she gave the horse to the wife of another former slave, who "delivered the horse" to the buyer.[129] Another woman said her son had asked her to "collect pay for the cart" he had rented out before going "up in the County."[130] For some men, army service created the trust needed to make trades and extend credit. One black soldier "[g]ave his watch to" a soldier who had just been discharged and was going home, telling him "to sell [it] & pay proceeds to his mother."[131] When another soldier was sent to an Arkansas hospital, he entrusted $80 cash to one of his comrades with "instructions to send it to my Wife if I should die."[132] To guard against any fabricated deathbed requests, the soldiers summoned some men to act as "witness to the giving out of the money."[133] Freedpeople's economic activities adapted some of the creative practices of the old "slaves' economy" to the new realities of freedom.

Evidence hints that many African Americans may have used investments of labor or money to *create* social ties, ties that then, in turn, might give them claims to other people's property. Livestock, boats, and other nonperishable items made excellent investments for building relationships, since they could be loaned several times without being "used up."[134] Other people nurtured social networks by drawing out their trades over weeks, sparing their precious cash and keeping up relationships that might eventually come in handy. Rose Duggins testified that her neighbor August Macbeth, who lived "about 200 yards distant" from her, "bought ten Bushel[s of] Corn of my husband." Macbeth "[d]id not take all his ten bushel[s] at once," she testified; instead, he "came about once a week to get" it. Each time, she "measured out a two bushel basket full," Duggins explained. "That was the eighth time he had come for corn."[135] Why did Duggins let Macbeth take more corn than he had paid for? Perhaps because although ex-slaves cared about their property, they also valued the social networks that bloomed in the fertile ground of trade.

Such practices exasperated army judges because they blurred the distinction between selling and loaning and tangled up property in a thicket of claims that were difficult to sort out in court. One officer sternly lectured an ex-slave defendant that he "should not buy a boat unless he first assures himself that the party offering it for sale is lawfully possessed of the same."[136] For other northerners the problem had less to do with the law than with freedpeople's "wasteful[ly] generous" behavior.[137] "The man who at the end of the autumn had a hundred or two bushels of corn on hand," wrote another Union officer, "would suffer a horde of lazy relatives and friends to settle upon him and devour him before the end of the winter, leaving him in the spring at the mercy of such planters as chose to drive a hard bargain."[138]

But northerners who disparaged "[t]he thoughtless charity of . . . penniless Negr[oes]" could not see the complex understandings that lay behind it.[139] Black men and women had been nursing along useful acquaintances with whites since the days of slavery, painting a soft veneer of flattery and gifts over tough bargaining. To them, the whites who came south in the 1860s were more than just charity workers or bureaucrats; they were people with money and influence at powerful institutions. In short, the northerners were people worth knowing, and ex-slaves set about incorporating them into their networks of exchange and marketing. Beginning in 1862, dozens of northern teachers moved to the South to set up schools for the freedpeople. The freedpeople welcomed them with open arms and a rainbow of economic dealings. Some of their exchanges with teachers were clear money-for-work arrangements. One man told the northern teacher Laura Towne: "I craves work, ma'am, if I gets a little pay, but if we don't gets pay, we don't care—don't care to work!"[140] But other transactions were drawn out over time, with no payout to signal when they were finished. Often, former slaves "gave away" to teachers small items—such as poultry, sweet potatoes, and, above all, eggs—seemingly at random, and they refused to take anything in return.[141] When Lucy Haskell went out to distribute clothes around her North Carolina district, freedpeople gave her "rice, potatoes and one man promised to bring some Chickens."[142] In Charlottesville, Virginia, they "showered" their teachers with all kinds of "gifts."[143] At least one teacher thought there was more to these gifts than mere friendliness. "The negroes are pretty cunning," Towne opined. "They pretend they want us to stay . . . and . . . they do constantly offer eggs and they feel hurt if they are refused, for that is equivalent to refusing to make any returns." The "returns" ex-slaves wanted were not money but obligations, useful precisely because unlike money they were vague. "Old Susannah, the cook, often sends to the table fish or other delicacies," Towne continued. "When I ask her where she got them, she says a friend gave them to her and she gives them to us. She doesn't want pay— no, indeed. She always gave such things to her old 'massas,' and they in return gave a little sweetening or something good from the house."[144] These ex-slaves were far from "thoughtless" with their property. A freedwoman named Rina "brings out from her store one pretty thing after another to furnish [our] table and house," Towne went on. "She will not sell these things, but lends them."[145] Through Rina, Towne found out that still another ex-slave, named Hastings, "had a tureen at home and would like to lend it, but . . . was afraid I would want to buy it." Hastings eventually sent the tureen, but only after getting Towne to promise that "I would not wish to buy what he did not wish to sell."[146] As the northerners settled into their new homes in the South, they ran into complicated, sometimes unspoken, traditions of black-white negotiation that had been evolving since the days of slavery. Hastings, Rina, and Susannah wanted to give things to the teachers, but they also wanted to control what that giving meant. It seems likely that for these ex-slaves, giving and lending helped build up social ties and obligations in a way that selling could not. Accepting payment would have made their swaps legal, but then the teachers would not owe them anymore. Among African Americans, as well as among many whites, social relationships were both a necessary tool for enabling trade and an end in themselves.[147]

Freedpeople's dealings with land were even more bound up with social relationships. Unlike their claims to clothes, chickens, or tureens, slaves' claims to land had almost never amounted to anything more than claims of access, so those former slaves who managed to acquire land after emancipation had to establish new traditions of landownership. To help establish these traditions, they drew upon their experiences during slavery and their fast-reunifying networks of kin. Evidence in military court records and elsewhere hints that many African Americans imbued land with intense personal and social meaning. In places where plantation workforces had been relatively stable during the 1850s, freedpeople tended to claim the particular parcels of land that, for them, meant "home." "Never was there a people . . . more attached to familiar places than they," reported one Union officer in February 1862.[148] The "contrabands" had a "love of locality" that made it "almost impossible to drive them from their homes," reported an officer in Louisiana.[149] As Julie Saville has observed, "Attempts to maintain a link with particular land led some freedpeople to plant a patch on the old 'home place' " after they went to live somewhere else, while others stayed on in the old quarters and walked to work new fields.[150] These "local attachment[s]" to "home places" put a distinctive stamp on black people's ideas about land just at the moment they were beginning fierce efforts to acquire it.

Evidence suggests that ex-slaves called on kin ties to claim land. Brothers, aunts, uncles, and grandparents banded together to buy land that was otherwise priced out of their reach.[151] Those who were already living on land sometimes invoked kin ties to protest being evicted. "We has a right to the land where we are located," protested Bayly Wyat at a freedpeople's settlement near Yorktown, Virginia. "Our wives, our children, our husbands, has been sold over and over again to purchase the lands we now locates upon," he said. "For that reason we have a divine right to the land."[152] In Georgia, freedpeople told federal officials that they were reluctant "to leave their old Homes and often Speak of the Relatives upon the Lands[,] that their Fathers and Mothers cleared those Swamps and Marshes, and Made them the Fruitful Rice Fields they are."[153] Such statements wove ancestors and sweat equity into a seamless argument about property. In at least some cases, ex-slaves devoted special attention to old people, many of whom knew about the kin ties (usually unknown to whites) that underpinned land rights among blacks. White landowners who tried to save money by shoving elderly blacks

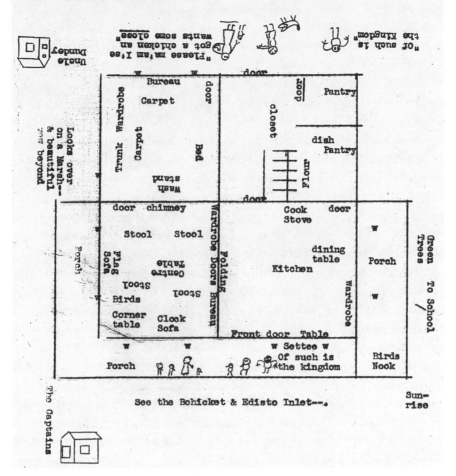

Martha Schofield's sketch of the layout of her Sea Islands home, 1865. Schofield came to the South to teach freedpeople. Clearly visible at the top of her sketch are several freedpeople, one of whom offers a teacher a chicken in exchange for clothes (from Martha Schofield Diary (1865), p. 67, typescript copy, #999-z, Southern Historical Collection, Wilson Library, University of North Carolina at Chapel Hill).

off their plantations[154] ended up disrupting political authority and property claims for the rest of the workers as well. For Samuel Boles, who argued on behalf of 200 St. Catherine islanders, land rights came from their ties to "21 of the old Founders of the place" who had not been "refugeed" away during the war. These "old Founders" were a living connection to "their Fathers and Mothers," long-dead ancestors who may have done the work of stump-clearing and ditch-digging that had established the plantation back in the distant past.[155] Much as people in nineteenth-century Fante invoked genealogy and testimony about long ago burials to make claims to land, some African Americans strengthened their claims to land by invoking long chains of ancestors.[156]

Because kinship often anchored ex-slaves' claims, what little land they acquired often came under the control of families, not individuals. Many black southerners cherished the land parcels their ancestors had acquired in the early years of freedom and tried to pass them down intact for generations.[157] One Southside Virginia landowner actually encouraged this tendency in the 1860s by encouraging his workers to make "six settlements" on his land, each "as far as practicable" made up of "hands and families who are related to each other."[158] For a group of 203 South Carolina slaves who were sent to Arkansas in 1859 and then "refugeed" to Texas during the Civil War, kinship became the organizing framework of an entire community. For decades after the move west, the Good Hope plantation people, who settled nearby each other and shared farm work along kinship lines, remained an easily identifiable subcommunity.[159] In Talbot County, Maryland, where Frederick Douglass grew up, ex-slaves built all-black hamlets on land they bought from local whites (including a white man who used to ship grain for slaves on the sly). In these black settlements, most people were related to dozens of other households, and claims to land were traced back to an original act of kin-cooperation, such as two brothers pooling money in 1866 to buy the town's first piece of land.[160] Black ideas of family had long gone beyond strict boundaries of blood and marriage, but the chance to own land and the end of the family-shattering slave auction block allowed some African Americans to establish traditions of "family land" that would bind kinship and land together for generations to come. Yet, as we will see, the meaning of family was itself being transformed, and black landownership absorbed many of the tensions and ambiguities that came with those transformations.

Ex-slaves fought desperately in the 1860s and 1870s to become landowners, partly because land meant independence from white people, but also because it meant interdependence among blacks. If reuniting and expanding their families enabled blacks to make landownership a reality, land also became a physical, tangible reflection of all the time and trouble that people put into family ties. Just as family "made" land, land, in turn, helped "make" family.

BY THE 1870s, much had changed about black southerners' ownership of property. They had seized legal rights to push back against white landlords. They had learned the tacit assumptions of northern judges and claims agents and had adjusted their testimony about property to conform to those assumptions. At the same time, they preserved and reconfigured the extralegal system of display and acknowledgment by transforming the plantation landscape. By taking themselves and their property out from under the "watchful eye" of a white landlord, former slaves told the world that their claims of ownership no longer depended on displaying to, or seeking "advice" from, a master.

However, although many ex-slaves tried to make their property claims less dependent on social ties with white landlords, when it came to other blacks they often did just the opposite. The evidence suggests that many former slaves continued to secure their claims to property through extralegal practices and social networks. They sold things without documentation and gave "gifts" that built up usefully vague obligations; they formed mutual aid societies and called on ancestors to claim land. Such evidence, although scattered and inconclusive, suggests that ex-slaves' understanding of property after emancipation did not conform to legal notions of private property. African Americans' first brush as free people with the mainstream of American economic life did not prompt a rush to embrace autonomy, individualism, or other tenets of free enterprise because the mainstream itself was full of ideas about property that were heterogeneous, intensely social, and remarkably impervious to the somber lectures of legal experts.

The American South of the late 1860s and 1870s was an only partly legalized world, where property ownership still depended in large part on informal display and complex social networks. Nowhere did the tie between claiming kin and claiming property glow brighter than in relations among African Americans. As surely as blacks became an impoverished racial underclass in the South, the ending of slavery widened the possibilities for inequality inside black families and communities. As Alabama sharecropper Nate Shaw put it, "all God's dangers aint a white man."[161] For that reason, understanding class differences between blacks and whites means taking account of relations *among* blacks, where property was often embedded in complicated social networks, especially networks of kin. Those social networks, and the often fierce struggles that flared within them, are the subject of the next chapter.

chapter six

Remaking Kinship and Community

. . . .

It was only a year or so after they won their freedom that Sarah Waite split up with her husband, Paul. Later that same year, Paul was living with somebody new. But the Waites had raised a crop together, and Sarah wanted her share of it. "When I got my corn," she remembered, "I went and asked Paul what he was going to do with the children! He said I must mind them. I told him I had lost my pease on account of him and that girl, Hester, prisoner, and I must have her peas to pay for mine." At that, Hester Scott "said she would like to see the one who would make her share her crop with me" and hit Sarah with an axe.[1]

Divorcing, remarrying, arguing over property: they were part of stories that thousands of Americans could have told in 1867, white and black, rich and poor.[2] Black families had surely broken up during slavery, either because someone was sold down the river or for emotional reasons all their own. For black people, however, just stepping out of the shadow of slavery, such stories meant something distinctive and new. In the late 1860s, former slaves began the joyous, bitter task of putting their kin ties back together again, family reunions of astonishing proportions.[3] These reconstituted families slowly began to accumulate more property than had been possible during slavery, when masters claimed all but a few of slaves' working hours. The world, at least in the 1860s, seemed bursting with possibilities.

But the new vibrancy and economic power of black families made defining what a family was and what it meant to belong both more difficult and more important than ever. As people like Sarah and Paul Waite claimed their relatives from their old masters, they looked back to older understandings of the ties and obligations between children and parents and husbands and wives; but emancipation changed the conditions in which those understandings had been forged. As was the case for Africans in the aftermath of emancipation in Fante, African Americans' new opportunities to reestablish families and accumulate property also raised difficult questions about kinship. What was a family? Who belonged in it? And what kinds of claims did kinfolk have on one another? This chapter draws on over 500 cases in the civil and military courts to explore what was happening inside black communities in the late 1860s and 1870s, the complicated, fast-changing, often angry relations between children and adults, between strangers and "home place" people, and between women and men. Looking at those interactions through the prism of African Studies lets us glimpse how African Americans' understandings of marriage, family, and community changed during the years after emancipation.[4] Ex-slaves argued with one another in the 1860s and 1870s not in spite of property's links to kinship but *because* of them. The ending of slavery in the South ushered in a new world of negotiation among black people over the claims of kinfolk, a world that comes to life if, rather than asking "whose daughter was this?" we ask instead, "what did it mean to be someone's daughter?"

EMANCIPATION CHANGED the economic conditions that had permitted slaves to make property together. Under slavery, children had done much of the work that raised property for slave families. After emancipation, many black people assumed that freedom would entitle them to claim their younger relatives' working hours, time that emancipation had pried from the master's fingers. Freedpeople fervently wanted to see their children educated in the new schools, "but they needed their help at home," noted a teacher in the Sea Islands. "So they came to beg us to give them their 'lessons quick,' and send them back" to work at home, explaining that "'the grass shines mightily in the cotton.'"[5] Years later, some former slaves had searing memories of the work their parents demanded from them in the 1860s and 1870s. Minksie Walker's mother remarried two years after the Civil War, "and," Walker recounted, "we started moving from place to place" around the Missouri countryside. Walker remembered his stepfather as "a mean man," who fed him on "parched corn" and "started hiring me out by de day" when "I couldn't have been more den ten years old."[6]

Cabbages by Thomas P. Anschutz (alternate title: *The Way They Live*). Artists such as Winslow Homer, Thomas Eakins, and Thomas P. Anschutz captured patterns of daily life among African Americans after the Civil War, including the mobilization of young people's labor (courtesy Metropolitan Museum of Art, Morris K. Jesup Fund, 1940. [40.40]).

Black people desperately wanted to avoid falling completely dependent on white landowners, and they leaned heavily on children to help fight this battle. Landowners wanted ex-slaves to spend all their time in the main plantation crop and use their wages to buy food, but instead ex-slaves turned back to the gardening, hog-raising, fishing, sewing, and hunting that had helped keep them going during slavery. As before, this strategy would not work unless everyone in their households pitched in, especially children. Now children joined "crowd[s] of colored men [and] women" at southern train stations, "vieing with each other" to sell trays of apples, eggs, fried chicken, and bread to the passengers.[7] Children took care of livestock for their parents, animals that sometimes cost as much as their parents earned in a year,[8] and helped out on hunting trips, too.[9] When they could, ex-slave parents shifted some of the work of running households onto children, too. One Alabama brick mason relied on his children to work the family farm while he earned money at his trade. "I work on my place until I get a good job," Robert Brandon testified, "then I take it, and let the boys 'run' the place."[10] A northern teacher saw a group of boys and girls "washing at washtubs" while others sat around taking care of even younger children.[11] Of course, children did not always do a good job at what their parents told them to do. Jack Washington got into a fight with his twelve-year-old cousin, perhaps because he was bored staying home on a Sunday to take care of his younger relatives. "I asked him [the cousin]," Washington testified, "what [did you say] and he said 'Nothing' I said 'you did.' He said 'if you touch me my father will squeeze the shit out of you.' I then went for him."[12] Still, even if children misbehaved, this was a time when black tenants were barely breaking even on their main crops of cotton or tobacco, and the dollar or two that children earned from the family garden or from quilting with grandparents at night could easily make the difference between success and going under.[13]

Of course, along with discipline, African Americans continued to give their younger relatives money, much as they had during slavery. A man in northern Mississippi, freed by the Union army, went to Memphis to borrow money from both his mother and another black man in order to start a bar business.[14] Adults also gave advice, and, as usual, young people did not always listen to it: those "who ha[d] charge of" their younger relatives, for example, sometimes complained (as one man said of his niece) that they weren't "sensible."[15] Unheeded advice turned deadly for Bester, who insisted on carrying a pistol around the Mississippi plantation where he lived. "Old people was constantly at him to put it down but he would tote it," recalled a witness, "Sort of a hard head boy."[16]

As black people claimed children and children's labor for themselves, they changed the black family and what it meant to be someone's child. It was up to children's black relatives to decide how, when, and by whom their labor should be claimed. Much evidence suggests that African Americans did not necessarily have anything against physical punishment for children, but they insisted that the child's parents, not white people, mete it out. Amelia, for example, described to a Jacksonville, Florida, military court what happened after her ten-year-old daughter broke two plates belonging to their white employer: "I went down to the yard and asked her how she happened to break these plates—she said her sister run up against her." Exasperated, Amelia "went to the house in order to give her a whipping," but when she returned, "The white lady had whipped her" already. "I said it was might hard to take up child and whip it all to pieces, when its mother was right there in the yard."[17] Amelia was risking her life to say such things— indeed, the "white lady" took out a gun and shot at her—but many black parents may have felt the same way: children needed discipline, but white people should leave that duty to the children's parents. It is difficult to know whether slaves beat their children during slavery, but much evidence hints that the ending of masters' authority permitted some ex-slaves to assert far-reaching, occasionally even severe discipline over children. "Reckons I shall beat my boy just as much as I please, for all Miss Chase," said a freedwoman to a disapproving northern teacher.[18] And in one court case, a procession of black men testified that a father could and should whip his son, if his son "was a slow hand" and careless with the livestock he was entrusted to watch.[19] As one of the men said, "Nero whipped James when he needed it."[20] Such testimony suggests that at least some former slaves expected to have wide-ranging authority over children's labor, an authority that changed the meaning of family.

As African Americans claimed children's labor from their old masters, they also widened the circle of people who could claim familial authority over those children. In the lean postwar economy, the calculus of raising and controlling children prompted some ex-slaves to petition for custody of children who had only distant blood ties. They went to Freedmen's Bureau offices to "demand" their "great grand child[ren]" and young cousins, saying that even if the parents were dead, those children should not have been "apprenticed" out to white planters "without the knowledge or consent of any of [their] kin people."[21] "[I]n every case where I have bound out children, thus far," groused a bureau agent in Louisiana, "[s]ome Grand Mother or fortieth cousin has come to have them released."[22] Whether the opponent was a white landlord or a black ex-husband, fighting to win back young relatives often widened the boundaries of black families and the authority of distant relatives.

Moreover, emancipation permitted some older folk to make grown-up children and grandchildren work for them, long past the age when masters used to put children into the "main crop." In North Carolina, one man "hired" his sixteen-year-old brother from their father,[23] and another couple settled their divorce by dividing up their grown daughter's share of the family crop.[24] A little to the south, Serena Blizer said that she worked all day for a white employer and that "[a]ll my extra time was employed with my father." Her "2 children" were also "in the crop," meaning that her father was claiming labor from both her and his grandchildren.[25] In some places, long residence had enabled certain elder African Americans to build up networks of kin, whom they could call on to work for them.[26] Bureau agents sometimes waxed cynical about what they were seeing. "Blood don't seem to thicken," wrote one bureau agent, "until children get to be about ten years of age."[27] Another believed that "freedmen" wanted "to live in a patriarchal manner by getting as many of the children of their kinsmen around them as possible" and be "supported by their labor."[28] Although few ex-slaves intended simply to stop working and live off their relatives, such testimony does suggest that kinship was becoming the language of choice among freedpeople for claiming authority over other black folk.

As black people widened their claims over children, they often ran into fierce resistance. Some of that resistance came from white landlords, who hoped to stave off the end of slavery by "apprenticing" black children into a new type of bondage.[29] In their complaints before the Freedmen's Bureau, ex-slaves did not deny that children were an important source of labor, or even that children should be hired. Instead, they said that "kinpeople," and not white landowners, were "justly entitled to the benefits of [their children's] services"[30] and should control when and where they worked.[31] Blacks battled over children not just against white landowners but also against other blacks. One freedman lodged a complaint that his wife would not "give back" their child,[32] and a freedwoman protested that her ex-husband, now remarried, "wants to take the child from me to aggravate me."[33] In Texas, African Americans brought so many child custody battles to the Freedmen's Bureau that one local officer asked his superiors for "definite instructions" about "who shall have possession of children born to them while living together as man and wife during slave times."[34]

And some of the resistance to blacks' claims on children came from the children themselves. Just as adults used courts to claim children, some children also went to court to challenge the claims of adults. Twenty-one-year-old Jane Brewer flatly told a North Carolina provost court that her former master "had no Right to Pay her Step Father" or make a contract over her head, even if the man was her stepfather.[35] One young man, whose father signed him to a year-long work contract, told the local bureau officer at Waynesboro, Georgia, that he had just gotten married and that his wife was expecting a child. For this reason, wrote the officer, he "now claims that his time is his own and refuses to be bound by his fathers action, or rather chooses to seek his own [em]ployment." In this case, the officer agreed, writing that the son's legal marriage made him "entitled to his earnings and was no longer under the control of his father."[36] For those young people who went to court in the 1860s and 1870s, the formal laws gave them muscle in conflicts with their parents and guardians. That legal recognition, and the state power that backed it, had a serious impact on black family life because it helped redefine relations between black youth and their elders.

Sometimes, though, young people asserted themselves in informal arenas and only later went to a court, if ever. In 1866 Charles Stewart and his father "had a difficulty" over the contract his father had made for him with a white planter. "We settled it," Stewart remembered, with an informal compromise: "I agreed to work the year out & was to get tobacco & whiskey on Saturday night."[37] Running off was an even simpler way for young people to wrest control of their labor from older men. James Tindall, whose father had put him to work for a white landowner and was taking all of his pay, broke his contract and ran away after the boss "knocked me in the corn field while I was hauling hay."[38] Children couldn't always understand why their relatives kept them in harsh jobs, and sometimes they lashed out clumsily in ways that hurt their relatives as much as the white bosses. One child said she was angry both because her mother made her keep working for a local white family and because her mother "made her stay" with an uncle she hated. She was in court on charges of burning down a house.[39]

As freedpeople claimed their relatives from their old masters, they relied on older understandings of what children and parents owed each other, but emancipation had changed the conditions in which those understandings had been forged. It freed children's working hours from the demands of a master, it permitted ex-slaves to reunite and expand their families and, in some places, it opened the legal system to ex-slaves. Increasingly, children found themselves under the care—and the authority—of a wider range of black adults, some of whom were only distant relatives, and they were expected to obey those relatives for a bigger piece of their lives than during slavery. By the 1870s, white landowners still stood at the top of the South's economic order, but few of them bossed black children in the fields anymore. Black grown-ups did. And black family life would never be the same.

THE STRUGGLE OVER CHILDREN went hand in hand with a broad (though far from uniform) expansion of black family. Hounded by poverty and short of decent housing, many black people in the late 1860s took in nieces, nephews, elderly parents, aunts, and uncles.[40] Others came up with new living arrangements that bent traditional notions of what a household looked like. It was not unheard of for middle-aged men to move in together and "go . . . to farming,"[41] for married couples to share rooms with bachelors,[42] or even for newlyweds to take in the groom's ex-wife as a boarder for a while to make ends meet.[43] As one observer said of freedpeople in Hampton, Virginia, "It was very common to hear of families that were helping not only their own relatives, but others who had no such claim of kindred upon them."[44] Because work and property had long been near the heart of African Americans' ideas about family and community, life after slavery demanded that blacks transform not only their economic lives but also their families.

For many ex-slaves, it was the experience of being a refugee that changed ideas about family and community. During the Civil War, thousands of African Americans left their plantations and slipped into the Union lines. As they did so, they organized themselves into large groups that they called "families." These "families" did not jibe with white officers' ideas of what a family looked like. "A 'family' of 205 persons came 30 miles to our camp" from a large sugar plantation, reported a Union army colonel from Louisiana, "they termed [their former master] "Old Cottonbeard." The colonel, who apparently expected members of a slave family to have followed a single occupation, such as field hand or carpenter, was puzzled because instead this family included "nearly every species of mechanic and artisan."[45] These families of refugees seemed much too big and diverse to be related in the way that northerners expected. Ex-slaves continued to form such groups after emancipation—in some places army policy required it[46]—and although some spoke of themselves as nothing but a work party,[47] others considered themselves members of a family. In Low Country South Carolina, an elder ex-slave named Roger approached the superintendent of freedpeople on behalf of a large group of ex-slaves, offering to forfeit their emergency rations in exchange for certain land rights. Roger told the officer that he had a family of sixty "parents", that is, relations, children included. He asked permission to take part of the land on the Oaks "to raise crop on." He said they would not require houses, but put themselves upon "a camp", that is, these little shelter-tents of palmetto, and walk to and fro from the village to the Oaks—nearly eight miles, through deep, sandy roads. Mr. Soule [the superintendent] gave his consent, and Roger's "family" began to cultivate the fields. . . . They walked to and fro, except the old persons and children who often stayed in the tents, or else at the village a few nights at a time.[48]

What does one say about a family with 205 members or sixty parents? Most whites at the time believed that black people had no family life worth speaking of. Stories like this simply made no sense to them unless they assumed that all ex-slaves were members of one big family.

Many white observers did exactly that. For white southerners that family was just an extension of the master's household. As one Louisiana woman put it, "Without regard to class age or any thing else, they are nearly all of one family and my own negroes."[49] White northerners who moved to the South in the 1860s were tempted to adopt similar ideas, especially when they heard blacks calling each other "aunt," "uncle,"[50] "brother," "sister," or "cousin,"[51] seemingly at random. Robert Smalls, a war hero and former slave, told the northerners that Sea Island blacks used the word "parents" to "mean relations in general; the same that they mean when they say 'family.' "[52] In fact, labor-hungry white landowners often had a stake in extended kinship patterns; they tried to "develop" squads of 200 cotton pickers from the "nucleus" of a "strong family group" by urging blacks to "attach other labour, and bring odd hands to work at proper seasons."[53]

But the tremendous expansion of kinship in the 1860s did not make freedpeople into one big family any more than the "quarters" had made slaves. They had to forge that bond of kinship themselves and hammer it to fit their needs in a rapidly changing world. The pains and limits of kinship became especially sharp during the Civil War, when thousands of displaced blacks sought new beginnings throughout the South. Their arrival sometimes caused friction, partly from competition over scarce resources. Most refugees were very poor—"vastly worse off than the plantation people" who did not migrate,[54] according to one observer—and they leaned heavily on longtime residents for help in getting started. Refugees also made it more difficult for longtime residents to bargain with whites for better labor contracts when they showed up "exceedingly anxious" to work and signed the

Group photograph of African Americans attending a wedding on or near the Mississippi plantation of Joseph Davis, brother of Confederate president Jefferson Davis. Such photographs circulated widely after the Civil War, often with captions that implied some social tie among the people in them, such as having the same master, or being members of a family, or simply being black. Although the people in this wedding group shared a history of slavery and race, they did not necessarily belong to the same family or community; they may not even have liked each other ("Slave—Joe Davis," ca. 1864, glass negative, photographer unknown, no. 164, from J. Mack Moore Photograph Collection, Old Court House Museum Collection, Vicksburg, Mississippi).

contracts as offered.[55] In places where landowners allotted their workers some land to raise crops outside the "main crop," freedpeople protested angrily when their bosses tried to add new "hands" after the crop was planted.[56] They realized that a boss would often use "the introduction of strangers" as an excuse to "claim . . . the whole" for himself.[57] Migrants helped resident ex-slaves raise valuable crops and animals, but they sometimes jeopardized other people's property, things that migrants had not earned. As a result, particularly in the Low Country but elsewhere as well, longtime residents and newly arrived refugees disagreed about who was part of their communities and over the obligations and privileges of community membership.

Land, which embodied both economic hope and ancestral identity, could divide black people as well as unite them. Samuel Boles, "the oldest Head Stevedore" at Savannah, wrote on behalf of more than 200 slaves from St. Catherine's Island who had been forced to leave during the war. When they came back, he wrote, they discovered "about 150 one hundred & fifty folks . . . from the main[land] that did not formaly live there."[58] These black newcomers, Boles argued, had no better claim to the land than his former master because they were "unacquanted [*sic*] with the Soil." What did it mean to be "acquanted with the Soil"? Boles argued that "those that was taken away" from St. Catherine's had a right to the land both because they had "give[n] there labor there all there Life" and because they "was Born & Raise on that Island & there parent is stil there." Like land claimants in Fante, they had, as Boles put it, "a knolledge of the soil" that included both the expertise of a lifelong farmer and the kinship claims of their ancestors.[59] The 150 newcomers "from the main" were poor and black and had searing memories of slavery; so did the 200 who were "Born & Raise on that Island," but that did not necessarily make the two groups one community. As African Americans established new identities and new claims to resources, race and the shared memory of slavery mingled and sometimes competed with powerful ideologies of kinship.

As much as kinship and community helped unify blacks against white oppression, they also became touchstones of difference, exclusion, and even conflict among blacks precisely because in order for them to claim property and labor from each other, increasingly they had to be part of the family or the community. For example, while Low Country blacks welcomed the refugees as workers, they tried to control the terms on which refugees were incorporated into long-standing social networks, the terms on which, for example, a new community might emerge in the Sea Islands. Beginning in 1862, some ex-slaves began to use terms like "Georgia" and "home place" to define the boundaries of an emerging community in which longtime residents were clearly distinguished from "strangers." Elizabeth Hyde Botume thought that her students were "rather unfriendly to the refugees, always passing them with a degree of scorn, and speaking of them as 'dem rice niggers.' "[60] Many of those who had grown up in the Sea Islands said that "the new-comers were 'only Georgia niggers' . . . 'low down country niggers.' "[61] Some of the newcomers gave as good as they got. On a November evening in 1866, Henry Mack went to remind Rina Drayton that "she owed me 75 cents," and the two ended up swapping curses. According to Mack, Drayton "told the girl" who answered the door "to shut [the] door in my face. She began to cuss me and I said yes you are a St Helena nigger and dont want to pay your debts . . . that is the way you damned St. Helena niggers does git in debt and then wont pay. . . . She then took up a brick and ran at me and struck me in the face and loosed my teeth."[62] These kinds of insults hint that

black people were tightly linking property claims to an emerging set of social identities, identities so intense that speaking them could start a fight, yet
so specific that only a local would have felt truly offended.

It is likely that new identities—and the possibilities for bonding and tension
—blossomed wherever black migrants came together. From Princess Anne
County, Virginia,[63] to Memphis, Tennessee,[64] from the banks of the Mississippi to the shores of South Carolina, African Americans watched rivers of
freedpeople from other parts of the South pour into their locales.[65] A group
of black men from Baton Rouge who had been free before the war petitioned "not to be placed on an equality with contrabands."[66] At a camp outside St. Louis, "a group of contrabands" from Missouri "disdained to associate with those from Mississippi, considering themselves far above them."[67]
Black Mississippians had their own prejudices. One of them reportedly yelled
out during a brawl: "He is nothing but a dam Louisiana cotton patch son of
a bitch."[68] In Greensboro, North Carolina, another ex-slave saw two black
women fighting next to the Freedmen's Church and tried to break it up. "I
went to Lyda [and] told he[r] She must be quiet," he testified. "She cursed
me Said no damd upper country Nigger Should run over her. . . . I took hold
of her and made her go with me up to near the graveyard and talked to her
and Shamed her until She became quiet and then I returned to Church."[69]
Not all of the geography-based names were insults. Some African Americans
picked up names to craft new identities out of old places they left behind.
A woman who took a live-in job with a black family in Alabama called herself "Tennessee King."[70] In the 14th U.S. Colored Troops, stationed in Chattanooga, Tennessee, in 1865, one of the men was nicknamed "'City Ohio' but
he always gave his name Columbus Friarson."[71] Even when newcomers held
onto their names, the memory of their origins lived on, much as it did in
Fante. Eliza Long, an ex-slave who had migrated to a plantation near Au-
gusta, Georgia, watched helplessly as another freedwoman named Phillis,
for reasons that are not clear, convinced local residents to close ranks against
her. Phillis "had been threatening to kill me for more than a year to the rest
of the Negroes," Long recalled. "[H]er folks told me that I would have to
keep out of her way." After a year of living and working on the place, Long
"f[ou]nd out . . . that all the black ones were against me" because of her origins. Her identity as an outsider sat dormant but alive, ready to be stirred up
by someone with a grudge. Yet by testifying that she "concluded to go home,
and leave them," Long implied that she herself had kept up ties to a "home"
that lay outside her adopted community.[72] African Americans created meaning out of the bewildering upheaval of mass migration, but this meaning did

not necessarily establish a common identity or a unified black community. It often emphasized the *differences* among black people: between refugees and those who had grown up on a place, between the free and the freed, between blacks from different regions, states, or even different islands.

If black families and communities were getting bigger, they were also becoming more unequal inside. On the one hand, the sheer size of families spread shelter over those who belonged in them. Take Bester, for example. After watching his white boss whip his young brother-in-law, Bester loudly announced that "if Richard Fitzgerald [the employer] staid on this place—he didn't call him by name[—]that he would sling the shit out of him." It was risky to talk salty to a white man in 1867, yet Bester willingly took that risk to protect even this relatively distant kinsman.[73] But strangers—along with the very young, orphans, and some women—lacked the social networks of kinship or long residence that shielded community members. Their vulnerability made it easy for longtime residents to integrate them as junior, inferior members of their families and communities.

Newcomers to a locale, far from their relations, could be absorbed into families on fairly unequal terms, in ways that implied both subordination and protection. They often found it hard to assert claims over the property they helped make. One person who knew this vulnerability firsthand was Sarah Breedlove, later known as Madam C. J. Walker: America's first black millionaire, Harlem Renaissance celebrity, and founder of a black-oriented cosmetics industry. Born in 1867 on a Mississippi plantation, she became an orphan when she was only seven years old. She went to live with her brother-in-law, a man she later described as "cruel" and who put her to work washing laundry. Within a few years, she took her things and ran away to work for herself.[74] Orphans like Breedlove—and in the turmoil of Reconstruction there must have been many—were part of a family but lacked the "relatives and influence"[75] that could shield them if adults made harsh demands on them.

For orphans and strangers, loud talking spelled out the powerlessness that came with not having a dense network of relatives. Amos Vandross savagely whipped a boy who was living and working with him in 1864 for losing Vandross's pistol. People in the nearby cabins heard him taunting the boy as he beat him, "asking what he mammy name & what he daddy name." As one witness recalled, Vandross "remark[ed] to the boy . . . that he would whip him until he would tell what the name of all the generation."[76] These words were sarcastic; Vandross was probably not trying to find out who Gallant's relatives were. Instead, when black people said they were "going to raise a nation to whip" someone,[77] or threatened "to talk about his people,"[78] they were turning kinship into *power*. For Vandross to beat the names of Gallant's whole "generation" out of him was to show the world that the boy had no family, that he could not make any claim to kin membership that anyone would respect. Gallant was not a slave, yet his suffering demonstrated the same logic of kinship-based power that underpinned slavery in Fante and other African slave systems. "There was a pounding going on,"[79] volunteered one witness, but no one went to stop it. For six hours, sounds of the whipping drifted on the evening air to the neighbors' homes and yards.[80] Gallant had no kinfolk to claim and protect him; he was at the mercy of men like Vandross. While it is likely that "family" had sometimes excluded strangers or orphans like Gallant before emancipation (recall Josiah Henson's experience as an orphan), during the first few years of freedom, when there were unusually high numbers of such strangers and orphans, kinship's power to exclude and subordinate may have become more obvious and widespread. And although the people involved in these incidents were not slaves, comparing these cases to those of colonial Gold Coast suggests that for the most vulnerable black southerners, belonging *in* a family could almost mean belonging *to* a family.

Conflict among former slaves was more than a by-product of blacks' continued oppression by whites. And it did not necessarily signal that love and commitment were breaking down in black families and communities any more than white people's family violence — of which there were many examples — heralded the breakdown of the white community.[81] Instead, as ex-slaves reestablished and expanded social ties, and as their control over labor and property grew, community and family ties may have become more important than ever before and thus more contested.

NOWHERE DID THE opportunities and knotty tensions of kinship's transformation crop up so starkly as in relations between husbands and wives. Emancipation opened both new opportunities for black men and women to earn property as a family — and new possibilities for conflict. At the same time, it overturned the old arithmetic of household labor and claims to household property. Slavery had swallowed up most of enslaved women's working hours yet had also permitted them a great deal of control over the small amounts of property they did earn. By marrying men who lived on other plantations, and by emphasizing the public character of marriages, some enslaved women and their relatives had asserted property claims that their husbands and other enslaved men had recognized. Indeed, many married men had stored the bulk of their own property at their wives' homes, permitting some women to assert claims even over things they made together. Similar to Fante, the end of slavery let ex-slaves dramatically transform their deepest social ties yet raised the stakes of that very transformation. Beyond the pans, chickens, and dresses, the mundane yet precious items of property that people talked about in and out of court, what was at stake in black men's and women's disputes was the meaning of marriage itself.

The stage was set in the late 1860s, when freedpeople shattered the old plantation landscape and gathered their families and property into clusters of cabins. The breakup of the slave quarters probably moved black women's workday under the watchful eyes of their husbands and relatives, who could legitimately invoke ties of kinship or marriage to claim their laboring time. For black women in southern cities, work and home were still usually in two different places. Doing laundry or cleaning in a white household took them as far away from home each day as field labor had during slavery.[82] But most black women lived in the country. Evidence from archaeology, courtroom testimony, and other sources suggests that although both women and men worked out in the fields, when it came to housework, the bulk of women's work happened in the inner yard, up to about twenty feet from the house.[83] Perhaps because so much of women's work was not paid work, women's male relatives often treated it blithely. They expected their sisters to pluck and clean turkeys[84] and handed over cloth to their mothers saying, "'[H]ere is some things I want you to make up Clothes for my children.' "[85] One Mississippi man, who was convicted of defrauding another ex-slave, paid off his fine using $7.50 worth of "washing done by his . . . Wife."[86] Elizabeth Hyde Botume believed that in the Sea Islands "[m]ost of the field-work was done by the women and girls." She commented sarcastically that men behaved as if they were "lords and masters" over the women, that one freedman "spoke of [his wife] as if she were his slave" and that this was a "manner most of the colored men had."[87] White northerners' comments on black marriages must be taken with a grain of salt, but much evidence suggests some level of struggle among African Americans over the control of women's work. White southerners, by contrast, thought that black women had actually stopped working in order to "play the lady."[88] Of course, freedwomen were still working, but the kinds of work they now did—washing, cooking, and making clothes— were (or were becoming) "women's work," a development almost invisible to white southerners because it was buried in the postwar tenant's house-yard. Yet the same changes that hid black women's work from whites made it *more*

"The Sign of the Pine," Hale County, Alabama, ca. 1890–1910. The kinds of work shown here—childrearing, raising chickens, and washing clothes—were easy to see from the house but probably out of sight of most white people. After emancipation, black families increasingly assigned such work to women, putting much of their workday under the eyes of their husbands and other relatives (Edward Ward Carmack Papers #1414, Southern Historical Collection, Wilson Library, University of North Carolina at Chapel Hill).

visible to other black people, especially relatives, who now could legitimately claim it for themselves.

The shift from slave "quarter" to clustered tenant compound affected non-kin, too, because many black households got help from people who were not related by blood but who lived in or nearby. Ex-slave Rebecca Clegg testified that, while she lived with her grandmother, she also did work for her husband's parents and for the family of a black neighbor, Joshua Mitchell, who lived "a little distance from" her. "My business is about the house," she explained, "I go home before the rest to get dinner . . . Card and Spin & help make a crop."[89] Sometimes a son or daughter's marriage brought another pair of hands into the extended household. Maria "lives within a few steps of my house [and] she works with me in the field," said David Peter of his son's wife. "For a short time she cooked for my wife" and left the field early.[90] In many parts of the South it was common for freedpeople to move in with—and help out—their husband's or wife's parents.[91]

Angry arguments broke out when ex-slaves brought in non-kin to live and work with them and then tried to keep them from sharing in what the household raised. John Taylor "did not pay Ann wages," testified a witness in one North Carolina case, "but Said he would furnish money—at the end of the year."[92] Another black woman was furious at two of her neighbors, both freedwomen, for mistreating their live-in worker, Dora Godfrey. It was not "proper," she said, to "turn her off" after she had been "working for you all summer . . . made crops for you & y[ou]r husband to eat."[93] And sometimes, married men complained that their wives were being hired out to work by their in-laws, as one freedman put it, "being forced to do the same by *her* mother, against *his* will."[94] The question was not whether black women should work but rather where, how, and for whom. Much as in Fante, some of the fiercest struggles over labor happened under the sheltering umbrella of family.

During slavery, married slaves had negotiated and even argued over property, but after emancipation, as couples began to accumulate more property, growing uncertainty about the obligations and definition of marriage sparked a number of disputes between black men and women. Divorce created the most problems because it required husbands and wives to sort out their claims to the things they had raised together. One woman took care that "before she left his house she separated her things from his locking hers up."[95] Others "destroyed and hid away various clothing and furniture belonging to their Household"[96] or simply "put her things out of doors and went to another house."[97] But sometimes trying to divide family property ended up turning a divorce into a fistfight. For example, Dessica Bliging and her husband, August, planted and worked a crop together but then separated in August 1866. When the crop ripened, Dessica tried to protect her interest by asserting control over the process of dividing it. "I proposed to divide the ground nut patch in parts," she testified. "He refused to do so, but wanted to dig the whole & then divide." To bolster his claim, August then "got four people to go & dig the groundnuts," perhaps calculating that once they had put their work into the crop, they would want to help him control it.[98] According to a witness, Dessica "called to him to stop [digging] & said she come for dead which meant that one had to die."[99] August "said if I had any fuss with him," Dessica went on, "he'd beat me like the Devil. He commenced to dig and I put my foot on the hoe. He went to another place and I went and put my foot on the hoe again." Finally, her ex-husband tried to choke her.[100] Just as in their cash-crop disputes with jealous white landlords, it was hard for divorced freedpeople to sort out their property claims when that property was still growing in a field.

The speed and depth with which ex-slaves' social world was transformed during the 1860s created uncertainty and tension that sometimes led to violence between black couples. The number of wife-beating cases and the sense that it was a routine occurrence that surfaces in testimony suggest that some black men beat their wives to make them work and to seize control over the property that spouses made together, and that many more men considered it their right. Despite the dangers of taking such problems to a court, fully 5 percent of all the complaints that freedwomen brought to Freedmen's Bureau courts in Mississippi involved violence by their husbands.[101] "I told my wife to get me something to eat," said Tom Edwards, "and if she dont get it I'll be damned if I dont make her get it."[102] South Carolinian Prince Kennedy, who whipped his wife, Jane, with a wooden switch two weeks after she had given birth, explained to the court: "I whipped her . . . for jawing me. That was the only time."[103] Men expected their wives to work hard, and some accused men and their witnesses apparently considered violence an acceptable way to extract labor from their wives. According to a white witness in another case, Matt Spann said that he beat his wife "Fanny [because she] did not work & talked too much."[104] George Robinson "believe[d] he had a right to whip" his wife, Lavinia, and said he "[d]id not know [it] was against the laws."[105] "She had not attended to [the] crop," he testified, "Wife went off Sunday & did not come back till Tuesday 1/2 hour of Sun."[106] Robinson's witnesses, all black men, backed up his testimony. Paul Frierson testified that Lavinia "[i]s not an obedient wife. Don't obey orders. Don't humble her self or civil her self. Don't go to work when George tells her."[107] Prince Simons said that he "[h]eard George threatened to kill his wife. If he could catch her he would cut her throat." Simons admitted that he had "heard colored people frequently threaten to kill their wives" but insisted that he "never Knew them to do it."[108] The military court records suggest that although passion may have ignited the spark, the tinder for violence between ex-slave men and women was supplied by a basic change in power relations within their marriages, raising questions of who would control women's labor and its products.[109] What was at stake in these disputes was more than just work and property: it was the very bonds that gave married people claims on one another.

For African American couples locked in disputes, having access to law, with its universe of statuses like "husband" and "feme covert" (a married woman legally seen as under her husband's protection and authority), offered mixed blessings. Since formal laws and institutions like the Southern Claims Commission designated one "head" for each household, usually a man, bringing property claims to those forums tended to give black men legal claims to property that women, men, and children produced jointly. But the law also cleared the way for women to reshape their relationships with men, and, to some extent, to assert claims to property. Black women found that, in some situations, legal processes could strengthen their claims to property and ties of kinship. They noticed that the military and Freedmen's Bureau courts cared about regulating freedpeople's marriages, and they sometimes found the courts' preconceptions about women useful in their disputes with black men.[110] Nancy and Titus Bacon "raised a large family of children together" during slavery, but by 1867 "Titus had taken another woman and was depriving [Nancy] of the use of the better & greater part of four acres more or less of land purchased by their joint earnings." When Nancy lodged a complaint against Titus in the Beaufort Provost Court, she enlisted white witnesses to testify that Titus "was domineering, unfaithful, & living upon the labor of his wife." Titus agreed "to give up all the land purchased between them" if Nancy would give up her claims on him.[111] Other women discovered that they could get leverage for their claims by taking advantage of the Freedmen's Bureau's intense concern over their sexual morality. If a woman could prove that she had been legally married to a man, she could sue him for desertion or alimony, and the bureau would help her claim property from him. But it was not easy for a woman to sue an ex-husband in a Mississippi court if all she could say was "that they were married five years ago at Celma Alabama."[112] For women who had moved with their families since the war, protecting their property claims often meant convincing courts that their marriages ought to be considered legally valid. Sarah Robinson showed the court a marriage certificate and got the A.M.E. minister who performed the ceremony to testify that he had married Sarah and her husband "in [the] Kitchen of the Portious house."[113] She won her case. Although black men also took their ex-wives to court,[114] black women's lawsuits represented a startling, brilliant use of the legal system and its attitudes about gender.

Thus, while thousands of African American men went to great lengths after the war to make their marriages official, others tried hard *not* to. Some women who had had "broomstick" marriages during slavery or who had "taken up" with men after the war were dismayed when these men refused to get legally married.[115] Savannah resident Rosa Freeman's testimony about how she received a beating from her husband tells us much about how formal law was beginning to change ex-slave households. She testified: "On Saturday night he came to my room, took all his things, some four linen sheets & Some underclothes belonging to me & tore up two nice dresses of mine— he told me he would rather keep a woman than be married because she could not carry him to law & I could." Rosa Freeman had gotten the military authorities to lock up her husband once before and was perfectly willing to see him go, but she insisted that "if he wanted to leave me" he must first "get a Divorce." David retorted: "[I]f I can get a Divorce without paying for it; I'll get it for you, [but] if I can't I wont give it to you; you can go without it."[116] Both David and Rosa Freeman understood that, without the official legitimacy of a legal divorce, Rosa would lose the protection that the law gave to married women, including protection for her property. As David Freeman taunted, she could start a liaison with another man but not a marriage.

Some black leaders were also anxious about how the legal system might affect relations between black women and men. "Stay out of the Police court with your petty quarrels," warned the editors of the black-run *Richmond Planet*. The *Savannah Colored Tribune* complained that it was "intolerable" for "colored women [to] . . . arrest their husbands every time they have a family quarrel." As one black Alabama politician put it, "All that is wrong—you can settle it among yourselves."[117] Image-conscious black editors and politicians hated to see such quarrels because married people's disagreements touched both property rights and marriage, and many whites pointed to black conduct within those very same institutions as proof that "negroes" were a savage race. It was better, they seemed to say, for blacks to keep their dirty laundry inside the community than to hang it out where white supremacists could turn it into a cruel, racist joke.

Many people did not need any encouragement to stay out of court. As we have seen, rather than be dragged into the white-run legal system, with its dangerous pitfalls and prejudices,[118] blacks often pursued their interests in a whole range of extralegal settings. Some women just hit back when men tried to bully work out of them, "blow for blow," as one Mississippi husband said.[119] Mary Ward's husband, said a witness in another case, "told her that she had to go home & stay there that he was going to whip her after he got there, [but] she told him that she would not go home with him . . . that if they started home [together] she would Kill him before they got there"— and she did.[120]

Often, women reached out to their relatives, getting a brother-in-law to beat up an abusive husband[121] or going to live with their parents when their husbands beat them. A soldier stationed near Memphis complained to his superiors that his mother-in-law refused to move out of his house and that she was the "cause of much trouble between himself and his wife."[122] Women negotiated with their husbands from the safety of their parents' homes, sometimes sending out messengers until they felt ready for a face-to-face talk.[123] When cases went to court, it was often women's male relatives who filed the charges.[124] Although men sometimes called on their relatives for protection, too,[125] the practice usually involved women.

Sometimes, like lineages in Fante who jealously guarded their prerogatives, women's families stepped in without being asked. "Charles Reddick my father came up while [my husband] was sticking me," testified twenty-year-old Frances Ross about a beating her husband William gave her, "& raised a hoe over William's head & threatened to kill him, if he struck another blow."[126] Charles Reddick recalled: "He was beating my daughter & I told him to stop. . . . I told him not to beat her more, as he had beaten her Enough." The provost judge asked Reddick whether he was living with his daughter and son-in-law at the time of the beating:

A: I was not.
Q: Do you consider it your business to interfere between him & his wife?
A: I did.[127]

As the meaning of marriage changed in the 1860s, parents increasingly may have been the only people for whom it was socially acceptable to step between a married couple. In contrast to Charles Reddick's confident intervention, people who were not part of the family spoke more cautiously when they tried to stop family beatings. Witnesses testified that Alexander Black was out looking for his wife on the day in question and "[s]aid if She did not go home he would whip her." A freedman named "Mike said he should not whip her and should not have a fuss there. [Black] asked Mike 'if he took it up.' Mike said No, he 'did not get in between him and his wife, nor no other man and his wife' but he [Black] 'should not whip her.' "[128] In the end, Black killed Mike, for what he called "interference with my family relations."[129] Such testimony suggests that in many black communities, a woman's family could "interfere between [a husband] and his wife," but other people had to be careful when "get[ting] in between" them.[130] Women's families helped them fend off men's sweeping (and occasionally violent) claims to their property and labor, but the same assumptions that allowed women to call on their relatives may have isolated them from non–family members who might otherwise have helped.

Loud talking could rally help from outside the family, but for African American women, such verbal skill was sometimes a double-edged sword.

On the one hand, loud talking helped some women shore up local opinion behind their claims to property they earned jointly with men. Louisa Thigpen, who was already angry that her husband was giving vegetables to another woman, lost her temper when he ordered her "to go get a goard [of] water." In a voice loud enough to attract passersby, she said that "she did not care for no damed man."[131] In another case, Lucy Bryan temporarily stopped her husband from paying off a debt to a man named Tony Bowles with a boat that she believed was hers. "[I] heard her a long way off talking loud," Bowles said later. "She said, 'To night is Sunday night and any bod[y] see me coming down to the landing may know the Devil is in me.' Before she got to the landing she said 'Before any body shall have this boat I will take an ax and cut it up.' " She called Bowles's name three times before she got there and "then said 'Tony you scap gallous rascal, your meanness carried you away from here, and that is what brought you back!' "[132] Like Louisa Thigpen, Lucy Bryan tossed her salty words not just at Bowles but also at the people working nearby. By the time her "cussing" goaded Bowles, as he said, "to break my peace with you,"[133] other people were on hand to stop the fight, then block Bowles from collecting her boat, and even act as witnesses when Bryan filed a lawsuit against him for assault and battery.[134]

Men, however, could turn these public episodes back on women and invert the power of their outspokenness. Lucy Bryan used loud talking to claim a flat-boat, but Julius Monroe, one of the people who stepped in between Bryan and Bowles, dismissed her claim to the boat by saying that women, as a group, lacked social authority. "She went on talking very rash," he recalled, "and I advised her to go away and leave this to her husband. . . . I said to Bowles to not mind her as she was but a woman and had not got sense."[135] The idea that women did not have "sense" bundled a gender stereotype into popular understandings about maturity and kinship. As a white observer noted in 1864, having sense meant being "old enough to know."[136] Black Sea Islanders used the same phrase in the 1970s to denote the social authority and maturity people needed, among other things, to make claims to property. Those who had not yet begun to "have sense" were still "children"; they did not possess (or did not understand) the kin ties that would allow them to contract economic debts responsibly, or count on those social networks to back their debts.[137] That Monroe was not the only one to use the term "sense" suggests that his statement may have reflected broader struggles during the 1860s over what family members owed each other.

Nearly all former slaves counted on their families for protection and assistance, but ties to family sometimes reinforced familial discipline. Ex-slave women often found that leaving the claims of a husband could end up bringing other claims from their kin groups. Nathan Gibson killed Joshua Newell —his father-in-law and the man he lived and worked with—"because he was beating the girl (Lavinia) [Newell's] daughter, whom Newell had given to him for a wife."[138] Another woman who had quarreled with her neighbor told friends that she "was willing to settle it but her family was not" and that they refused to let her shake hands with the man.[139] In other words, the decision was not up to her. Such disputes suggest that, much as in Fante, the story of how newly freed African Americans strengthened their family ties and claims to property is also a story of quickening struggle over what it meant in the first place to be one of the family.

VIEWING THE HISTORY of ex-slaves' negotiations over property and social ties through the prism of African Studies brings into focus a whole world of black-black social relationships. Lifting our eyes from the familiar ground of white-black race relations reveals black kinship and black community life on their own terms, with all their dynamism and noisy dissent, rather than as mere side effects of their dealings with whites.[140] The evidence in military court records suggests that black life after emancipation cannot be understood solely in terms of ex-slaves' accommodation and resistance to whites' continued oppression, or as a shift from communal "African" cultural values to American individualism. Indeed, our brief look at emancipation in Fante shows just how complicated African cultures were in the 1800s, a complexity that American historians can use to rethink the history of the black family, the black community, and life in the nineteenth-century South.

Under slavery, ties of kinship and community had given African Americans not only emotional support but also the muscles they needed to accumulate property and the social networks to claim it. In the years after emancipation, ex-slaves rebuilt their families, often widening them to embrace new members. From their old masters they wrested away more control over their labor and property than ever in their lives. Ex-slaves took their swelling amounts of property and their brand-new control over labor and applied older, kin-based understandings of controlling labor and property. Just at the moment when black people began seizing new opportunities to accumulate, they drastically changed the social networks that still anchored their claims of ownership. Hence, black-on-black negotiations transformed their lives as much as anything whites did. Such insights shine clearly when black life in the South is placed alongside an African society such as Fante, where most slaveowners were black, where family members could be slaves, and where the meanings of property, family, and slavery were changing dramatically year by year.

The reestablishment and expansion of family networks after the Civil War and the growth of property controlled by families meant that family became more important to African Americans than ever. The evidence in the military court records of conflict among former slaves did not mean that the black family was weak or broken. On the contrary, as the Fante case suggests, such conflict reflects how expansive kinship became after emancipation, how strong its claims on people, and how important it remained for people's access to property and labor. For African Americans and Fantes alike, emancipation both opened new opportunities to strengthen their families and sparked fiery struggles over the meaning of kinship. Perhaps as much as official ordinances and emancipation proclamations, it was this remarkable surge in the claims of kinfolk that made the 1860s and 1870s a turning point in so many people's lives.

conclusion

. . . .

In 1937, Zora Neale Hurston laid out a guiding principle for understanding the black community. One good place to watch this principle in action (she volunteered helpfully for anyone who had not ridden there) was in the Jim Crow section of a train. Here and there in the crowds of traveling black folk, Hurston wrote, were some "sensitive souls" who "detest the forced grouping." "When somebody else eats fried fish, bananas, and a mess of peanuts and throws all the leavings on the floor, they gasp, 'My skin-folks but not my kinfolks.' And sadly over all, they keep sighing, 'My People, My People!'" Hurston's comments are salty and over-the-top, yet in their steady focus on black-black relationships, they point directly toward the central theme of this book. "Who are My People?" she asked rhetorically. Well, there were "Negroes, Colored folks, Aunt Hagar's chillum, the brother in black, Race men and women, and My People. They range in color from Walter White, white through high yaller . . . smooth black [to] coal black, lam black, and damn black." Still and all, Hurston said, "you can't just point [them] out by skin color." Instead, "when you find a set of folks who won't agree on a thing, those are My People."[1]

It is a pungent joke with a serious point: there is much more to being black than the struggle against white oppression. As Evelyn Brooks Higginbotham points out, one has only to consider the relative silence that surrounds AIDS among African Americans to realize how dangerous it is to assume that there is a unified, homogeneous "black community" somewhere in America.[2] With this book I intend to join a small but growing number of scholars in naming the internal diversity and conflict that has always been hidden in sayings like "My People, My People!"

Evidence is everywhere of a vibrant, creative tension between social solidarity and difference among African Americans. Take landownership, for example. Well into the 1970s, many black farmers classified much of their land and houses as "heirs property," property that was owned by a large and complicated network of kin, and not any single person.[3] But many people, black and white, came to believe that "heirs property" was "a very serious problem" for African Americans because "although you pay taxes on the land, you don't own it and can't build a house on it or anything."[4] Indeed, as black-owned farmland in certain parts of the South became more valuable, many whites exploited legal loopholes in "heirs property" to force blacks to sell their land. By then, many of the heirs lived far away from the "home place" and often did not realize that developers would use their claims to push their country relatives off the family land.[5] Today, black communities from Alabama to the Caribbean are struggling to reconcile the need to preserve the "home place" with younger members' desire to "sell out their portion."[6]

Even those with no "home place" to preserve have often commented on, and sometimes chafed at, the threads between claims to kinship and claims to resources. "Rich relations give crusts of bread and such," wrote Billie Holiday, who grew up being shunted around the parlors and spare bedrooms of various Baltimore uncles, aunts, and cousins. "You can help yourself, but don't take too much. Mama may have, Papa may have. But God bless the child that's got his own."[7] And, as Hurston pointed out, there were other kinds of diversity in black communities, too. The National Association of Colored Women's motto, "lifting as we climb," and the Urban League's exhortations to "refrain from loud talking and objectionable deportment" in public places, are just a couple of examples of how African Americans have been simultaneously united and divided by class.[8] Negotiations among black people are a rich part of black history, a part that overlaps African Americans' struggles with whites but is not determined by those struggles.

It was black people's relationships with one another, as much as their struggles with whites, that shaped their experiences during the years of slavery and Reconstruction. While some observers say that slavery's tendency to break up black families and its corrosion of supposedly traditional African gender roles, and especially slaves' utter lack of property, ingrained a legacy of "broken" black family life and "dysfunctional" economic decision making,[9] others think that the dysfunction argument is tantamount to blaming black people for their own victimization. The latter argue that the black family, the black community, and black traditions of property ownership have been the only things keeping black people from total annihilation. Acknowledging both the power of white oppression and black people's resistance to it, this book is guided by the principle that black people's lives involved far more than their relations with whites.

Understanding the inner dynamics of black social relations in the 1800s may require changing some of our basic assumptions about property, kinship, and the way communities work. That is why this book compares African Americans' experiences with those of Fante people, and is partly built on the interpretive frameworks developed by anthropologists and historians of Africa. Studies of Africa demonstrate that kinship is fantastically rich and hard to freeze in place, either in terms of "structure" or in terms of any single analytical framework like "resistance" or "culture."[10] And, like the history of African Americans in the South, what Europeans did to Africans is only part of the story. African historians' long tradition of analyzing conflict and connection among black people provides models for how American historians might start to rethink African American history. It is precisely because Fantes and African Americans were different that they are worth comparing.

Viewed through the prism of African Studies, property in the nineteenth-century South becomes richer and more interesting than formal law makes it out to be. As colonial officers and World Bank officials have ruefully admitted over the years, although property is a venerable institution in Africa, it usually does not fit Westerners' commonsensible notion of it as individuals possessing exclusive legal rights over a thing. In West Africa and the Caribbean, where policy makers have repeatedly tried to "rationalize" property along the lines of Anglo-American law, the courts still recognize "family land" and permit lineages to make overlapping, often competing, ownership claims to it, and to many other kinds of property as well.[11] Moreover, many people in Africa responded to colonialism by shuttling back and forth between European, Islamic, and precolonial local institutions; for black southerners after 1865 it was the county court, the military court, and the house yard. In short, property was less an institution or a legal right than a social process. What made slaves' possessions into property were complex networks of social relationships, where being an owner meant getting masters, neighboring whites, and other enslaved people to recognize their claims of ownership, displaying things in yards or at church, loaning them out, or, in the case of animals, having neighbors cut marks in their ears. This notion about property contributes to a long-standing effort by legal historians to "de-naturalize" property, to take it out of its abstract cubbyhole and put it back into the messy swirls of history.[12]

Drawing insights from African Studies also helps us see that there was

nothing inevitable about the history of the black family, least of all its structure. In fact, whether we are hunting for two-parent families, female-headed,
nuclear, or otherwise, our very hunger to find structure in nineteenth-
century black families tends to obscure some of what is most fascinating
about them: their ability—even eagerness—to change as they pursued their
interests, the conflicts that sometimes rumbled inside them, and their close
association with work and property. In Fante, widely accepted links between
claiming kin and claiming property helped give meaning to the word "slave"
and maintain slavery as a system. Those same links enabled African Americans to make claims on each other through one storm after another: the internal slave trading of the early 1800s, the chaotic migrations that followed
the Civil War, and possibly even the massive turmoil of the Middle Passage.
Thus, ex-slaves' efforts to "reunite" their families in 1865 were part of a long
history of constant change in the claims of kinfolk. Through negotiations
with one another and with white people, black people throughout the diaspora made the meaning of family over and over again.[13]

Thus, ties of family and community were intricately laced with property
and labor. It is worth noting that conflict in slave communities did not necessarily break along lines of color or status, the idea reflected in the old
clichés of "house Negroes" and "field Negroes." Since field hands could own
property right alongside carpenters and house slaves, conflict among slaves
spilled out in all sorts of messy, unpredictable ways: field hands surely grumbled against drivers, but so did husbands against wives, neighbors against
neighbors, even black stranger against black stranger on a riverbank. In
short, black-black conflict over property sheds light on what slave communities looked like and what it meant for African Americans to be part of "the
slave community."

When freedom dawned for black southerners, kinship became one of the
key languages that expressed their social world and what it might become,
complete with all its bridges and myriad fractures. No one knew what shape
black families would take, or who would control their labor and the property that they amassed. With the Fante example in mind, it is possible to see
how calling someone "nephew" or "sister" could express powerful claims on
people; in Fante, sometimes nephews and sisters were slaves. With so many
ex-slaves trying to reunite divided families, and with so much labor and property coming under the control of these newly reunited families, the shape
and meaning of family became a heated issue, one that played out in the
courts, Freedmen's Bureau offices, and blacks' informal negotiations over
property.

Did property mean something different for African Americans than for whites? Were black people's families, communities, and ideas of property derived from African, and not European, traditions? Possibly. But in working to make property, black southerners were not necessarily turning from the values of "traditional Africa" to embrace "modern" Anglo-American values of acquisitive individualism. For one thing, although many slaves were acquisitive, they lacked individual legal rights to property, the key ingredient in acquisitive individualism. They and their descendants joined the informal economy for many reasons, and maximizing income was only one of them. Much of what black people did on their own time was simultaneously economic accumulation *and* an investment in social ties. Moreover, the evidence in the claims and elsewhere suggests that although enslaved African Americans probably brought many practices from Africa, they were not the only people who negotiated access to resources through social, rather than legal, claims. After all, many white people also lacked written records of ownership in the 1800s and relied heavily on social relationships with kin and neighbors in matters of work and property.[14] Wealthy ex-slaveowners, who also filed claims before the Southern Claims Commission, leaned on testimony from their overseers and former slaves to prove ownership.[15] This should not be surprising, since a large chunk of any plantation's assets stood growing in a field, with no price tag or receipt attached. The plantation's biggest asset—the slaves themselves—often embodied the property interests of several different white people.[16] And even someone as famous as Martin Van Buren could not prove "under the closest scrutiny" that he owned property; twice, the future president's political opponents stopped him at the polls and made him swear publicly that, among other things, he "possessed a freehold estate" big enough to qualify him to vote.[17] The fact that southern whites and, later, northern whites took part in an extralegal, noninstitutional system of black property ownership challenges common assumptions about how white Americans conceived of family, property, and slavery in the 1800s—and perhaps even now.

Still, in America today, the connection between markets and freedom is part of our cultural heritage. How could slaves own property without undermining slavery, or at least moving themselves a little closer to freedom? After all, every day in the 1800s, black southerners set prices, made loans, worried about the strength of the nation's currency, and saved up for their children, but they were still enslaved, and nothing they did with their property weakened the slave system at all. Indeed, their pursuit of property may have strengthened it. Viewed from the perspective of African Studies, it is easier to see why ownership of property did not necessarily undermine slavery or protect slaves from being harshly exploited. A growing literature in African Studies argues that access to resources "is predicated on social identity" and that "the definition of property rights hinges on the demarcation of social boundaries." Africans have struggled over resources for centuries, just as Europeans and Americans have done, but the terms of struggle have less to do with owning the means of production—depriving others of property—than with who is subordinated within the groups that define access.[18]

Viewing social relations as (among other things) a field of struggle over resources helps explain why so many slave societies throughout human history permitted their most exploited members—slaves—to own property.[19] Between masters and slaves in the United States, race provided the language and the justification for subordinating people of African descent. Most white southerners either supported the informal economy of slavery or did not care about it one way or the other. They did not have to deprive slaves of all property, because slavery and freedom were written on people's skin and hair for anyone to see.[20] But *among* black southerners and in many parts of Africa, it was kin who defined access to resources, and it was through a language of kinship, not race, that people rationalized and understood their claims on one another. Kinship mattered, both because it helped "make" property and helped people claim it, and because property—more precisely, people's interests in property and labor—helped "make" kinship. For African Americans, the meanings of property, race, and kinship were interrelated, and none of them stood still for long. That constant experience of claiming and belonging was an important part of life in the 1800s—and maybe beyond.

Notes

ABBREVIATIONS USED IN THE NOTES

AFIC   Records of the American Freedmen's Inquiry Commission, File O-328 (1863), Entry 12, Letters Received, 1805–89, Correspondence, 1800–1947, General Records of the Adjutant General's Office, Record Group 94, National Archives, Washington, D.C.

BRFAL   Records of the Bureau of Refugees, Freedmen, and Abandoned Lands, Record Group 105, National Archives, Washington, D.C.

CAP   Criminal Action Papers, Edgecombe County, North Carolina, North Carolina State Archives, Raleigh, N.C.

CBF   Condemned Blacks Executed or Transported, 1781–1865 (APA 756), Auditor of Public Accounts (RG 48), Archives Research Services, Library of Virginia, Richmond, Va.

CC   Criminal Cases, Warren County Circuit Court Papers

CWSAT   Records of Civil War Special Agencies of the Treasury Department, Record Group 366, National Archives, College Park, Md.

FCO   Library, Foreign and Commonwealth Office, London, England.

FSSP   Records of the Freedmen and Southern Society Project, College Park, Md. (with document identification number)

GNA   National Archives, Accra, Ghana

LV   Library of Virginia, Archives Research Services, Richmond, Va.

NCSA   North Carolina State Archives, Raleigh, N.C.

OCHM   Old Court House Museum, Vicksburg, Miss.

PCA   Entry 1520, Proceedings of the Provost Court, Apr. 1867–June 1868, Aiken, South Carolina, Records of Towns and Posts (with volume number) District (P), 1862–83

PCB, Sept. 1865–June 1868
            Entry 1548, Proceedings of the Provost Court, Sept. 1865–June 1868, Beaufort, South Carolina, Records of Towns and Posts

PCB, June–July 1868
            Entry 1549, Proceedings of the Provost Court, June–July 1868, Beaufort, South Carolina, Records of Towns and Posts

PCBerk   Entry 1394, Proceedings of Provost Court, Monthly Report of Cases Tried, and Other Records of the Provost Court, 1867–68, Berkeley District, South Carolina

PCNSC   Entry 4257, Proceedings of Provost Courts, Military Tribunals, and Post Court-Martial Cases Tried in North and South Carolina, 1866–68, Records of the Judge Advocate, Records of Staff Officers, Departments of the South and South Carolina and 2nd Military District (P), 1862–83

PCSum   Proceedings of the Provost Court, Sumter District, South Carolina

PMG   Entry 1758, Miscellaneous Records of District and Parish Provost Marshals, 1862–66, Subordinate Provost Marshals in the Department of the Gulf (with volume number)

PRO   Public Record Office, Kew

RG 153   Court-Martial Case Files, 1809–1938, Court-Martial Records, Records of the Office of the Judge Advocate General, 1808–1942, Record Group 153, National Archives, Washington, D.C.

RG 393, Part I
            Records of Geographical Divisions and Departments and Military (Reconstruction) Districts, Records of United States Army Continental Commands, 1821–1920, Record Group 393, National Archives, Washington, D.C.

RG 393, Part IV
            Provost Marshal Field Organizations of the Civil War, Records of United States Army Continental Commands, 1821–1920, Record Group 393, National Archives, Washington, D.C.

RRSCC   Records Relating to the Southern Claims Commission, Letters Received, 1871–80, General Records of the Department of the Treasury, Record Group 56, National Archives, Washington, D.C. (with microfilm publication number and roll number)

SCC   Case Files, Southern Claims Commission, Records of the Third Auditor, Allowed Case Files, Records of the U.S. General Accounting Office, Record Group 217, National Archives, Washington, D.C.

SCC-D   Case Files, Southern Claims Commission, Records of the Third Auditor, Disallowed Case Files, Records of the U.S. General Accounting Office, Record Group 217, National Archives, Washington, D.C.

SHC   Southern Historical Collection, University of North Carolina at Chapel Hill

UVA   The Albert and Shirley Small Special Collections Library, University of Virginia Library, Charlottesville

WSCC   Alabama Allowed Case Files, Southern Claims Commission, Microfilm Publication 2062, Wallace State Community College

INTRODUCTION

1. Claim of Pompey Bacon, p. 1, Liberty County, Georgia, SCC.

2. Claim of Prince Maxwell, p. 4; testimony of Gideon Jackson in claim of Prince Maxwell, p. 6; claim of Pompey Bacon, p. 1; and claim of Joseph Bacon, p. 5, all Liberty County, Georgia, SCC.

3. Claim of Pompey Bacon, p. 3; claim of Ned Quarterman, p. 2; testimony of Moses Quarterman in claim of Toney Elliott, pp. 5–6; claim of Peter Winn, p. 3, all Liberty County, Georgia, SCC.

4. Claim of Samuel Elliott, p. 3; testimony of Clarissa Monroe in claim of Samuel Elliott, p. 3; claim of Paris James, p. 2; claim of Pompey Bacon, pp. 1–6, all Liberty County, Georgia, SCC. Soldiers used such condescending phrases to slaves everywhere. Clarissa Monroe remembered them dryly: "I suppose Uncle Sam is the Yankee" (testimony of Clarissa Monroe in claim of Samuel Elliott, p. 3, ibid.).

5. Lt. Charles C. Jones Jr. to Rev. C. C. Jones (1862), in Robert Manson Myers, ed., *The Children of Pride: A True Story of Georgia and the Civil War* (New Haven, 1972), 987. See also Clarence Mohr, *On the Threshold of Freedom: Masters and Slaves in Civil War Georgia* (Athens, Ga., 1986), 102.

6. Testimony of D. B. Nichols, Supt. of Contrabands, p. 14, File 1, AFIC.

7. Testimony of Tennessee District witnesses, pp. 45–57, File 7, AFIC. In another case, William Jones and his wife recalled that they "packed up . . . our clothes . . . and some money we had saved from our earnings" and ran away to Camp Nelson, Kentucky, where a white guard confiscated it. See affidavits of William Jones and Marilda Jones, Mar. 29, 1865, reprinted in Ira Berlin, Joseph P. Reidy, and Leslie S. Rowland, eds., *The Black Military Experience*, ser. 2, *Freedom: A Documentary History of Emancipation, 1861–1867* (New York, 1982), 276.

8. Testimony of Capt. R. S. Hinton, p. 3, Dec. 14, 1863, File 8, AFIC.

9. Testimony of Col. T. W. Higginson, p. 189, File 3, AFIC. See also Cmdr. P. Drayton to Flag Officer S. F. Du Pont, Dec. 9, 1861, reprinted in Ira Berlin et al., eds., *The*

Destruction of Slavery, ser. 1, vol. 1, *Freedom* (1985), 117–18; and Lt. W. T. Truxton to Flag Officer S. F. Du Pont, June 13, 1862, reprinted in ibid., 126.

10. Claim of Jackson Daniel, Madison County, Alabama, reel 24, WSCC. Some freedpeople fought the Union foragers with fists and guns. See *United States v. Middleton Smith*, May 11, 1865, Proceedings of a Military Commission at Charleston, South Carolina, MM2433, RG 153.

11. Testimony of Corporal Sykes, p. 34, File 2, AFIC.

12. Testimony of unnamed witness from Tennessee District, Apr. 29, 1863, File 7, AFIC; Preliminary Report, p. 19, AFIC.

13. Testimony of D. B. Nichols, p. 14, File 1, AFIC.

14. E. L. Pierce to Hon. S. P. Chase, Mar. 14, 1862, BE 1861–64, Port Royal Correspondence Received by Sec. Treasury Chase, Nov. 25, 1861–Aug. 7, 1862, entry 574, CWSAT.

15. T. G. Campbell to Capt. A. P. Ketchum, July 29, 1865, entry 1025, Letters Received, Sept. 1865–Oct. 1865, Agent, Savannah, Georgia, Subordinate Field Offices, BRFAL.

16. Testimony of Mrs. Daniel Breed, pp. 22–23, File 1, AFIC.

17. Claim of Benjamin S. Turner, supplemental testimony, Apr. 21, 1871, Dallas County, Alabama, reel 6, WSCC.

18. Frank W. Klingberg, *The Southern Claims Commission* (Berkeley, 1955), 65–72, 76–84.

19. Gen. William T. Sherman, quoted in Christopher Waldrep, *Roots of Disorder: Race and Criminal Justice in the American South, 1817–80* (Urbana, 1998), 73.

20. For North America, see Philip D. Morgan, *Slave Counterpoint: Black Culture in the Eighteenth-Century Chesapeake and Lowcountry* (Chapel Hill, 1998); Philip D. Morgan, "Work and Culture: The Task System and the World of Lowcountry Blacks, 1700–1880," *William and Mary Quarterly* 39 (Oct. 1982), 563–99; Philip D. Morgan, "The Ownership of Property by Slaves in the Mid-Nineteenth-Century Low Country," *Journal of Southern History* 49, no. 3 (Aug. 1983): 399–420; Ira Berlin and Philip D. Morgan, eds., *Cultivation and Culture: Labor and the Shaping of Slave Life in the Americas* (Charlottesville, 1993); Betty Wood, *Women's Work, Men's Work: The Informal Slave Economies of Lowcountry Georgia* (Athens, Ga., 1995); Ira Berlin and Philip D. Morgan, eds., *The Slaves' Economy: Independent Production by Slaves in the Americas* (Portland, 1991); Roderick A. McDonald, *The Economy and Material Culture of Slaves: Goods and Chattels on the Sugar Plantations of Jamaica and Louisiana* (Baton Rouge, 1993); and Loren Schweninger, *Black Property Owners in the South, 1790–1915* (Urbana, 1990), 29–60. For the Caribbean, see Sidney Mintz, *Caribbean Transformations* (1974; reprint, New York, 1989). For Brazil, see Ciro Flamarion S. Cardoso, "The Peasant Breach in the Slave System: New Developments in Brazil," *Luso-Brazilian Review* 25, no. 1 (1988): 49–57; Stuart B. Schwartz, *Slaves, Peasants, and Rebels: Reconsidering Brazilian Slavery* (Urbana, 1992), 45–49; and João José Reis, *Slave Rebellion in Brazil: The Muslim Uprising of 1835 in Bahia*, trans. Arthur Brakel (1986; reprint, Baltimore, 1993), 160–69. Much of the work on slaves' "internal economies" in Brazil is written in Portuguese. The discussion that follows is based on those works that have been translated into English.

21. Linda Wheeler, "Excavation Reveals Slaves as Entrepreneurs," *Washington Post,* Oct. 13, 1998, B3. I am grateful to Susan and Bob Tobias for this reference.

22. Peter Kolchin, *American Slavery, 1619–1877* (New York, 1993), 153.

23. Kenneth Stampp was the first to frame slaves' culture in terms of "resistance," an idea that Eugene Genovese later elaborated and reshaped into a thesis about slavery as a dialectic of accommodation and resistance. See Kenneth Stampp, *The Peculiar Institution: Slavery in the Ante-Bellum South* (1956; reprint, New York, 1975); and Eugene Genovese, *Roll, Jordan, Roll: The World the Slaves Made* (New York, 1972). For a recent synthesis of these arguments, see Kolchin, *American Slavery.*

24. Morgan, "Work and Culture," 592.

25. Christopher Morris, "The Articulation of Two Worlds: The Master-Slave Relationship Reconsidered," *Journal of American History* 85 (Dec. 1998): 982–1007; introduction to Berlin and Morgan, eds., *Cultivation and Culture;* Larry E. Hudson Jr., *To Have and to Hold: Slave Work and Family Life in Antebellum South Carolina* (Athens, Ga., 1997), xiv.

26. Morgan, "Work and Culture," 592; Morgan, "Ownership of Property by Slaves," 399–420; introduction to Berlin and Morgan, eds., *Cultivation and Culture,* 45. For an extended discussion of "protopeasants," see Mintz, *Caribbean Transformations,* 146–55. See also Wood, *Women's Work, Men's Work;* Berlin and Morgan, eds., *Slaves' Economy;* and Schweninger, *Black Property Owners in the South,* 29–60. Historians of Brazilian slavery have made similar arguments about slaves' independent economic activities. See Schwartz, *Slaves, Peasants, and Rebels,* 49.

27. Ira Berlin, Steven F. Miller, and Leslie S. Rowland, "Afro-American Families in the Transition from Slavery to Freedom," *Radical History Review* 42 (1988): 89; Jon F. Sensbach, *A Separate Canaan: The Making of an Afro-Moravian World in North Carolina, 1763–1840* (Chapel Hill, 1998), 270.

28. Morgan, *Slave Counterpoint,* 511. On slaves' community, culture, and family, see Herbert G. Gutman, *The Black Family in Slavery and Freedom, 1750–1925* (New York, 1976); Sensbach, *Separate Canaan;* Stephen Gudeman and Stuart B. Schwartz, "Cleansing Original Sin: Godparenthood and the Baptism of Slaves in Eighteenth-Century Bahia," in *Kinship Ideology and Practice in Latin America,* ed. Raymond T. Smith (Chapel Hill, 1984), 35–58; Sylvia Frey, *Water from the Rock: Black Resistance in a Revolutionary Age* (Princeton, 1991), 48–49; Margaret Washington Creel, *"A Peculiar People": Slave Religion and Community-Culture among the Gullahs* (New York, 1988); Gwendolyn Midlo Hall, *Africans in Colonial Louisiana: The Development of Afro-Creole Culture in the Eighteenth Century* (Baton Rouge, 1992); and Hudson, *To Have and to Hold.*

29. Schweninger, *Black Property Owners in the South,* 9–11, 235–36; John Patrick Diggins, *On Hallowed Ground: Abraham Lincoln and the Foundations of American History* (New Haven, 2000), 270. As Schweninger puts it, "Nothing in their African heritage prepared them for the New World emphasis on land ownership and economic individualism."

30. For a fuller discussion of these historiographical issues, see Dylan C. Penningroth, "Claiming Kin and Property: African American Life before and after Emancipation" (Ph.D. diss., Johns Hopkins University, 1999), 10–23.

31. For a hilarious critique of misconceptions about African economic activity be-

fore colonial rule, see A. G. Hopkins, *An Economic History of West Africa* (New York, 1973), 9–10. The "myth of Merrie Africa," he writes, portrayed Africans as living in "a state of harmony" before colonial rule, their economic life dominated by "an anti-capitalist value system . . . primitive technology, communal land tenure and the extended family." Ironically, some of American historians' assumptions about property in Africa echo the assertions of the European officials who implemented colonial rule in Africa. For example, in 1919, a British judge in Kenya declared with "absolute certainty" that "the theory of individual ownership of land is absolutely foreign to the mind of any African until he has begun to absorb the ideas of an alien civilization" (Chief Justice Maxwell, quoted in Sara Berry, *No Condition Is Permanent: The Social Dynamics of Agrarian Change in Sub-Saharan Africa* [Madison, Wisc., 1993], 106). For an overview of historiography on the interaction between European and African conceptions of property in Africa, see Martin Chanock, "A Peculiar Sharpness: An Essay on Property in the History of Customary Law in Colonial Africa," *Journal of African History* 32, no. 1 (1991): 65–88.

32. Nell Irvin Painter and Evelyn Brooks Higginbotham have shown how assumptions of "strong black people" and "the overdeterminacy of race . . . ha[ve] tended to devalue and discourage attention to gender conflict within black communities," as well as many other possible "intragroup" relations (Nell Irvin Painter, "Soul Murder and Slavery: Toward a Fully Loaded Cost Accounting," in *U.S. History as Women's History*, ed. Linda Kerber, Alice Kessler-Harris, and Kathryn Kish Sklar [Chapel Hill, 1995], 125–46; Evelyn Brooks Higginbotham, "African-American Women's History and the Metalanguage of Race," in *Feminism and History*, ed. Joan W. Scott [New York, 1992], 183–208). Armstead Robinson ("Beyond the Realm of Social Consensus: New Meanings of Reconstruction for American History," *Journal of American History* 68 [Sept. 1981]: 291–93) urged historians to probe "[d]ivisions between groups within the Afro-American community," divisions that "emanat[ed]" not solely from their relations with whites, but from "the social structures of postslavery Afro-American communities." See also Darlene Clark Hine, "Rape and the Inner Lives of Black Women in the Middle West: Preliminary Thoughts on the Culture of Dissemblance," *Signs* 14 (Summer 1989): 912–20. On black-black conflict as a destructive force within black communities, see Kolchin, *American Slavery*, 109; Brenda Stevenson, "Distress and Discord in Virginia Slave Families, 1830–1860," in *In Joy and in Sorrow: Women, Family, and Marriage in the Victorian South, 1830–1900*, ed. Carol Bleser (New York, 1991), 103–24; and Orlando Patterson, *Rituals of Blood: Consequences of Slavery in Two American Centuries* (Washington, D.C., 1998), 3. A fuller discussion of these historiographical issues is in Penningroth, "Claiming Kin and Property," 10–23.

33. On "egalitarianism," see Deborah Gray White, *Ar'n't I a Woman? Female Slaves in the Plantation South* (New York, 1985), 153, 158, and Morgan, *Slave Counterpoint*, 533. The issue of conflict within slave communities is difficult to integrate into the resistance framework, but it is not new to historians. Several historians have discussed it and concluded that, whatever the conflicts among slaves, those conflicts were overshadowed by, subsumed within, or determined by the conflict between slaves and masters.

34. Patrick Manning, *Slavery and African Life: Occidental, Oriental, and African Slave Trades* (New York, 1990), 23.

35. Orlando Patterson, *Slavery and Social Death: A Comparative Study* (Cambridge, Mass., 1982). On modern-day slavery, see David Stout, "Passage in Senate Sends Bill on Forced Labor to President," *New York Times*, Oct. 12, 2000, A12; U.S. Department of Justice, "Two Men Plead Guilty in Southwest Florida Slavery Ring," May 26, 1999 (Washington, D.C.); Howard W. French, "The Ritual Slaves of Ghana: Young and Female," *New York Times*, Jan. 20, 1997, A1; Andre Corten and Isis Duarte, "Five Hundred Thousand Haitians in the Dominican Republic," *Latin American Perspectives* 22, no. 3 (1995): 94–97.

36. Marcia Wright, *Strategies of Slaves and Women: Life-Stories from East/Central Africa* (New York, 1993), 25–26; Igor Kopytoff and Suzanne Miers, "African 'Slavery' as an Institution of Marginality," in *Slavery in Africa: Historical and Anthropological Perspectives*, ed. Suzanne Miers and Igor Kopytoff (Madison, Wisc., 1977), 14; Anatole Norman Klein, "Inequality in Asante: A Study of the Forms and Meanings of Slavery and Social Servitude in Pre- and Early-Colonial Akan-Asante Society and Culture" (Ph.D. diss., University of Michigan, 1980); T. C. McCaskie, *State and Society in Pre-Colonial Asante* (Cambridge, Eng., 1995), 95–101.

37. Barbara M. Cooper, "Reflections on Slavery, Seclusion and Female Labor in the Maradi Region of Niger in the Nineteenth and Twentieth Centuries," *Journal of African History* 35, no. 1 (1994): 61–78; Wright, *Strategies of Slaves and Women*; Claire C. Robertson, "Post-Proclamation Slavery in Accra: A Female Affair?" in *Women and Slavery in Africa*, ed. Claire C. Robertson and Martin A. Klein, 220–45; Gareth Austin, "'No Elders Were Present': Commoners and Private Ownership in Asante, 1807–1896," *Journal of African History* 37, no. 1 (1996): 1–30. On state- and lineage-based forms of slavery, see Klein, "Inequality in Asante," 97–98; Richard Roberts, *Warriors, Merchants, and Slaves: The State and the Economy in the Middle Niger Valley, 1700–1914* (Stanford, Calif., 1987), 112–26; Kopytoff and Miers, "African 'Slavery,'" 55–69; and Justin Willis and Suzanne Miers, "Becoming a Child of the House: Incorporation, Authority and Resistance in Giryama Society," *Journal of African History* 38, no. 3 (1997): 479–95. The closest analogues to North American slavery were in the Sokoto Caliphate and the east coast of Africa. See Jan Hogendorn, "The Economics of Slave Use on Two 'Plantations' in the Zaria Emirate of the Sokoto Caliphate," *International Journal of African Historical Studies* 10, no. 3 (1977): 369–83; Frederick Cooper, *From Slaves to Squatters: Plantation Labor and Agriculture in Zanzibar and Coastal Kenya, 1890–1925* (New Haven, 1980).

38. This book does not investigate the thousands of other claims that also contain testimony but were "disallowed," or others that were barred without a hearing. Although some of the claims records have been used before to investigate slavery in particular counties, no study has explored what they may mean for the study of slavery—and emancipation—in the South as a whole.

39. Of these approximately 659 court cases, 36 are from the pre–Civil War United States, 521 are from the postwar U.S., and 102 are from Gold Coast. At the National Archives of Ghana, I focused on the courts at Cape Coast, Elmina, and Akuse, dur-

ing the period between roughly 1860 and 1920. I selected roughly eighty cases in which one or both of the litigants was a slave or a descendant of a slave, paying particular attention to cases of inheritance.

40. For example, see Dinesh D'Souza, *The End of Racism: Principles for a Multiracial Society* (New York, 1995).

CHAPTER ONE

1. In some parts of West Africa, slaves did do those things. See Richard Roberts, *Warriors, Merchants, and Slaves: The State and the Economy in the Middle Niger Valley, 1700–1914* (Stanford, Calif., 1987), 188; Paul Lovejoy and Jan Hogendorn, *Slow Death for Slavery: The Course of Abolition in Northern Nigeria, 1897–1936* (Cambridge, Eng., 1993), 33–63; Gerald M. McSheffrey, "Slavery, Indentured Servitude, Legitimate Trade and the Impact of Abolition in the Gold Coast, 1874–1901," *Journal of African History* 24, no. 3 (1983): 349–68; Carolyn A. Brown, "Testing the Boundaries of Marginality: Twentieth-Century Slavery and Emancipation Struggles in Nkanu, Northern Igboland, 1920–1929," *Journal of African History* 37, no. 1 (1996): 51–80; and Martin Klein, *Slavery and Colonial Rule in French West Africa* (New York, 1998), 159–77.

2. Anatole Norman Klein, "Inequality in Asante: A Study of the Forms and Meanings of Slavery and Social Servitude in Pre- and Early-Colonial Akan-Asante Society and Culture" (Ph.D. diss., University of Michigan, 1980); Joseph C. Miller, *Way of Death: Merchant Capitalism and the Angolan Slave Trade, 1730–1830* (Madison, Wisc., 1988). For an early statement of the kin-incorporation model of slavery in Africa, see Igor Kopytoff and Suzanne Miers, "African 'Slavery' as an Institution of Marginality," in *Slavery in Africa: Historical and Anthropological Perspectives*, ed. Suzanne Miers and Igor Kopytoff (Madison, Wisc., 1977), 3–81.

3. Sara Berry, *No Condition Is Permanent: The Social Dynamics of Agrarian Change in Sub-Saharan Africa* (Madison, Wisc., 1993), 101–66; Richard Rathbone, *Murder and Politics in Colonial Ghana* (New Haven, 1993); Sara Berry, "Oil and the Disappearing Peasantry: Accumulation, Differentiation and Underdevelopment in Western Nigeria," in *State, Oil, and Agriculture in Nigeria*, ed. Michael Watts (Berkeley, 1987), 202–22; Sara Berry, "Tomatoes, Land, and Hearsay: Property and History in Asante in the Time of Structural Adjustment," *World Development* 25, no. 8 (1997): 1225–41; Michael J. Watts, "Idioms of Land and Labor: Producing Politics and Rice in Senegambia," in *Land in African Agrarian Systems*, ed. Thomas J. Bassett and Donald E. Crummey (Madison, Wisc., 1993), 157–93; Mahir Saul, "Land Custom in Bare: Agnatic Corporation and Rural Capitalism in Western Burkina," in ibid., 75–100.

4. K. Poku, "Traditional Roles and People of Slave Origin in Modern Ashanti: A Few Impressions," *Ghana Journal of Sociology* 5 (Feb. 1969): 34–38; Akosua Perbi, "The Legacy of Slavery in Contemporary Ghana" (unpublished paper presented at University of Ghana, Legon, n.d.).

5. The phrase "slow death" for slavery is borrowed from Hogendorn and Lovejoy, *Slow Death for Slavery*. Scholars working on Africa see property, family, slavery, and

freedom very differently from the way American historians do. Their methods and perspectives offer exciting possibilities for American historians, many of whom are searching for new ways to think about master-slave relationships, culture, resistance, and accommodation. But despite the potential for comparative studies, Africanists and Americanists have largely worked in isolation from one another. Frederick Cooper, a historian of East Africa, noted this tendency more than twenty years ago in an Africanist journal. See Frederick Cooper, "Review Article: The Problem of Slavery in African Studies," *Journal of African History* 20 (1979): 103–25. On the historiography of North American slavery, see Christopher Morris, "The Articulation of Two Worlds: The Master-Slave Relationship Reconsidered," *Journal of American History* 85 (Dec. 1998): 982–1007, and Peter Kolchin, "Reevaluating the Antebellum Slave Community: A Comparative Perspective," *Journal of American History* 70 (Dec. 1983): 579–601.

6. On renegotiating dependency, see Richard Roberts and Suzanne Miers, "The End of Slavery in Africa," in *The End of Slavery in Africa*, ed. Suzanne Miers and Richard Roberts (Madison, Wisc., 1988), 3–6; Lovejoy and Hogendorn, *Slow Death for Slavery*, 157.

7. Staff Surgeon Second Class Thomas Colan, Journal of Her Majesty's Corvette "Rattlesnake," Cape of Good Hope and West Coast of Africa Station, Jan. 1, 1873–Dec. 31, 1873, ADM 101/141, PRO. *Asafo* companies, which are urban, hereditary, often quasi-military cooperative organizations, still go out to sea today.

8. Roger S. Gocking, *Facing Two Ways: Ghana's Coastal Communities under Colonial Rule* (Lanham, Md., 1999), 61; Colan, Journal, p. 99. On Jamaicans in Cape Coast, see *George Walters v. Quow Kootah*, n.d., SCT 5/4/102, GNA, and Roger Stephen Gocking, "The Historic Akoto: A Social History of Cape Coast, Ghana, 1848–1948" (Ph.D. diss., Stanford University, 1981), 116–17. On "Hausa" influences in food, see "Colonial Reports—Miscellaneous," vol. 33, FCO.

9. Larry W. Yarak, "Murder and Theft in Early Nineteenth-Century Elmina," in *Banditry, Rebellion, and Social Protest in Africa*, ed. Donald Crummey (Portsmouth, N.H., 1986), 33–47.

10. Surgeon A. G. Delmege, Journal of Detachment of Royal Marines, Gold Coast Station, June 9, 1873–July 28, 1873, ADM 101/142, PRO.

11. Gocking, *Facing Two Ways*.

12. H. J. Bevin, "The Gold Coast Economy about 1880," *Transactions of the Gold Coast and Togoland Historical Society* 2 (1956): 73–88. The British called it "legitimate commerce" because it was not a trade in slaves; they ignored the fact that it was a trade *on* slaves, so to speak.

13. Larry W. Yarak, "West African Coastal Slavery in the Nineteenth Century: The Case of the Afro-European Slaveowners of Elmina," *Ethnohistory* 36 (Winter 1989): 48.

14. Ivor Wilks, *Asante in the Nineteenth Century: The Structure and Evolution of a Political Order* (1975; reprint, New York, 1989), 126–27.

15. Klein, "Inequality in Asante," 34, 99–122.

16. Kwame Arhin, "Rank and Class among the Asante and Fante in the Nineteenth Century," *Africa* 53, no. 1 (1983): 15.

17. Gareth Austin, "'No Elders Were Present': Commoners and Private Ownership in Asante, 1807–1896," *Journal of African History* 37, no. 1 (1996): 19, 26–28; Claire C. Robertson and Martin A. Klein, "Women's Importance in African Slave Systems," in *Women and Slavery in Africa*, ed. Claire C. Robertson and Martin A. Klein (Madison, Wisc., 1983), 3–25; Toyin Falola and Paul Lovejoy, eds., *Pawnship in Africa: Debt Bondage in Historical Perspective* (Boulder, 1994); Barbara M. Cooper, "Reflections on Slavery, Seclusion and Female Labor in the Maradi Region of Niger in the Nineteenth and Twentieth Centuries," *Journal of African History* 35, no. 1 (1994): 68–74.

18. *Yowah Wooraduah v. Yaw Occootah*, June 1, 1877, High Court, Cape Coast, SCT 5/4/102, GNA.

19. *Quassie Bayaidee v. Quamina Mensah*, Sept. 8, 1877, ibid.

20. Testimony of Charles Cuthbert Brown in *Charles Cuthbert Brown v. Quaese Twah and Cofee Berryin*, June 30, 1874, ibid.

21. McSheffrey, "Slavery and the Impact of Abolition," 349–68.

22. Poku, "Traditional Roles," 35; Klein, "Inequality in Asante," 95; T. C. McCaskie, *State and Society in Pre-Colonial Asante* (Cambridge, Eng., 1995), 95–101.

23. Testimony of Effuah Adooah in *Effuah Adooah v. Cofee Awooah*, July 19, 1869, High Court, Cape Coast, SCT 5/4/91, GNA.

24. See, for example, the testimony of Quassie Ackarsahn in *Quabina Abakan v. Quassie Ackarsahn*, July 22, 1879, High Court, Cape Coast, SCT 5/4/102, GNA, and testimony of James Davis in *Aminah Mends v. James Davis*, Oct. 18, 1869, High Court, Cape Coast, SCT 5/4/91, GNA. Children were especially vulnerable to being pawned when their older relatives got into debt. See testimony of Quacoe Thatey in *Eccoah Incromah v. Quacoe Thatey*, Nov. 17, 1877, High Court, Cape Coast, SCT 5/4/102, GNA; *Regina v. Cudjoe Banee and others*, Mar. 31, 1883, High Court, Cape Coast, SCT 5/4/103, GNA; and testimony of Quamina Ahin in *Regina v. Accoful*, Apr. 9, 1883, ibid.

25. Gareth Austin, "Human Pawning in Asante, 1800–1950: Markets and Coercion, Gender and Cocoa," in Falola and Lovejoy, eds., *Pawnship in Africa*, 131–44. European traders suffered angry backlash when they blurred the line between pawnship and slavery (Paul E. Lovejoy and David Richardson "The Business of Slaving: Pawnship in Western Africa, c. 1600–1810," *Journal of African History* 42, no. 1 [2001]: 78).

26. Lord John Russell to President MacLean, July 14, 1841, HCA 30/1029, Royal Commission on Fugitive Slaves, Report of the Commissioners, Minutes of the Evidence and Appendix, with General Index, of Minutes of Evidence and Appendix, Presented to both houses of Parliament by Command of her Majesty, PRO; Gocking, "Historic Akoto," 102–5.

27. Colonial Office, Gold Coast, Domestic Slavery, The Jurisdiction of the Judicial Assessor, and the Legal Character and Limitations of British Power Upon the Gold Coast, Mar. 1874, CO 879/6, no. 47, PRO, 9.

28. On juries, see ibid. On "educated natives'" role in making "customary law," see Gocking, *Facing Two Ways*.

29. W. E. F. Ward, *A History of Ghana* (New York, 1963), 81–232; Roger Gocking,

"British Justice and the Native Tribunals of the Southern Gold Coast Colony," *Journal of African History* 34, no. 1 (1993): 93–113.

30. Inez Sutton, "Law, Chieftaincy and Conflict in Colonial Ghana: The Ada Case," *African Affairs* 83, no. 330 (1984): 41–62.

31. For inheritance among slaves, see testimony of Quacoe Dantee in *Adooah v. Awooah.*

32. Nana Dr. Irene Odotei, interview by author, Oct. 28, 1996, notes (in author's possession).

33. *Adjuah Abamba v. Quabina Otoo*, May 19, 1881, High Court, Cape Coast, SCT 5/4/100, GNA.

34. Testimony of Quow Quotah in *Quacoe Abban v. Sago*, Jan. 24, 1883, High Court, Cape Coast, SCT 5/4/103, GNA.

35. Gocking, *Facing Two Ways*, 56–57; Kristin Mann, "Owners, Slaves, and the Struggle for Labor in the Commercial Transition at Lagos," in *From Slave Trade to Legitimate Commerce: The Commercial Transition in Nineteenth-Century West Africa*, ed. Robin Law (New York, 1995); A. G. Hopkins, *An Economic History of West Africa* (New York, 1973), 124. "Legitimate" because it was not a trade in slaves.

36. Caption accompanying photograph "The Market Place Cape Coast," *Views from the Gold Coast: Wesleyan Missions, 1892–1893* (Ghana 5), FCO.

37. Gocking, *Facing Two Ways*, 54, 76 n. 5. On homelessness in Cape Coast, see Delmege, Journal.

38. Gocking, "Historic Akoto," 152–53.

39. Trevor R. Getz, "The Case for Africans: The Role of Slaves and Masters in Emancipation on the Gold Coast, 1874–1900," *Slavery and Abolition* 21, no. 1 (2000): 136–37.

40. Antony Hopkins, "Property Rights and Empire Building: Britain's Annexation of Lagos, 1861," *Journal of Economic History* 40 (Dec. 1980): 784–91; Raymond Dumett and Marion Johnson, "Britain and the Suppression of Slavery in the Gold Coast Colony, Ashanti, and the Northern Territories," in Miers and Roberts, eds., *End of Slavery in Africa*, 94.

41. A. N. Allott, "Native Tribunals in the Gold Coast, 1844–1927," *Journal of African Law* 1, no. 3 (1957): 166–69; A. N. Amissah, "The Supreme Court, A Hundred Years Ago," in *Essays in Ghanaian Law, 1876–1976* (Legon, Ghana, 1976), 1–3.

42. Gocking, *Facing Two Ways*, 74. One obvious example is the difference between Ga patrilineal inheritance and Fante matrilineal inheritance.

43. Gov. George Cumine Strahan, "Proclamation," Dec. 17, 1874, in *Great Britain and Ghana: Documents of Ghana History, 1807–1957*, ed. G. E. Metcalfe (London, 1964), 377–78.

44. Lovejoy and Hogendorn, *Slow Death for Slavery*, 127. See also [Earl of] Carnarvon to [Capt. G. C.] Strahan, Aug. 21, 1874, in Metcalfe, ed., *Great Britain and Ghana*, 371–74. Another interesting result, not explored here, was that, according to some witnesses in these cases, many freed slaves enlisted in the "Hausa police" and other colonial military units and began encouraging their enslaved northern "countrymen" (presumably, though not necessarily, people from Hausa-speaking areas) to

leave their masters. See, for example, *Ammah Ackoon v. Quaw Etroo,* July 13, 1880, District Commissioner's Court, Elmina, SCT 23/4/1, GNA, and testimony of Yamyardom in *Regina v. Ochay,* Apr. 7, 1875, High Court, Cape Coast, SCT 5/4/99[101], GNA.

45. Claire C. Robertson, "Post-Proclamation Slavery in Accra: A Female Affair?" in Robertson and Klein, eds., *Women and Slavery in Africa,* 222; Dumett and Johnson, "Britain and the Suppression of Slavery," 108.

46. Memorandum on Vestiges of Slavery in Gold Coast, by J. C. de Graft Johnson, African Assistant Secretary for Native Affairs, Accra, Oct. 17, 1927, CO 323/1027/7, PRO.

47. "'The Epwe Speaking People,' by the Late F. G. Crowther, Sec. for Native Affairs, 1909 to 1917 (Dated 22nd October, 1912)," *Gold Coast Review* 3 (Jan.–June 1927): 21.

48. Despatch from Gov. Sir B. Pine to Mr. Secretary Labouchere, Oct. 1, 1857, HCA 30/1029, Royal Commission on Fugitive Slaves, PRO. British officials sometimes exaggerated slavery's role in Akan societies. See Colonial Office, Despatches Addressed by the Earl of Canarvon to the Governor of the Gold Coast Respecting the Nature of the Queen's Jurisdiction in the Protectorate, and Domestic Slavery (Confidential), Sept. 1874, CO 879/6 no. 56, PRO, 10.

49. E. Fairfield, Memorandum on Gold Coast Slavery, and the Measures Recently Taken for Its Abolition, Mar. 14, 1876, HCA 30/1029, Royal Commission on Fugitive Slaves, PRO.

50. Colonial Office, Gold Coast, Domestic Slavery, Jurisdiction of Judicial Assessor. See also Colonial Office, Despatches Addressed by the Earl of Canarvon.

51. See, for example, testimony of Quassie Ackarsahn in *Abakan v. Ackarsahn,* and *Cudjoo Ekrofull v. Quaw Assimah,* Jan. 20, 1880, Elmina District Commissioner's Court, SCT 23/4/1, GNA.

52. *James Davis v. Quow Mensah,* Oct. 11, 1869, SCT 5/4/91, GNA; *Quacoe Appeah v. Bamin Agnafforol,* Aug. 15, 1871, SCT 5/4/96, GNA; *Quabina Awoosie v. Ahyarfell,* Aug. 19, 1871, SCT 5/4/96, GNA; *Cardon v. Danbogen and Appeah,* Sept. 5, 1871, SCT 5/4/96, GNA; *[?]amianaw v. Agin and Affil,* ibid. See also Getz, "Case for Africans," 132.

53. Testimony of Quacoe Abban in *Abban v. Sago,* Jan. 24, 1883; testimony of Sago, in ibid.

54. *Quamina Attah v. Quamina Sam and others,* Oct. 27, 1881, High Court, Cape Coast, SCT 5/4/100, GNA.

55. Asst. Sec. for Native Affairs J. C. de Graft Johnson to Sec. for Native Affairs, July 8, 1930, ADM 11/1/975, GNA. A much earlier case involving stool succession may be linked to this: *Arthur Hutton v. Quow Kootah,* Dec. 6, 1878, High Court, Cape Coast, SCT 5/4/102, GNA.

56. Testimony of Yowah Wooraduah in *Wooraduah v. Occootah.*

57. "Before Amonoo V," in *J. D. Taylor v. Kobina Kwansah* (1907), Appeal from Native Tribunal of Anomabo (Case No. 29/1909), ADM 11/1/40, GNA; J. D. Taylor to Sec. Native Affairs, Jan. 18, 1909, enclosed in *Taylor v. Kwansah.*

58. Colonial Office, Gold Coast, Domestic Slavery, Jurisdiction of the Judicial As-

sessor, 3, 7. This official report erroneously concluded that "[t]he great majority of the people of the Gold Coast are in actual slavery." With somewhat more justification, it identified debt as a major problem in nineteenth-century Akan society, and distinguished the "harsh . . . treatment of the imported slaves or 'donkos' " from that of the "native slave," who "sits at his master's table, eats from the same dish," and "marries his master's daughters."

59. Testimony of Kwamina Annan in *Kwow Amoasie v. Kwamina Annan*, Nov. 13, 1883, SCT 23/4/2, GNA. See also *Quabina Mensah v. Thomas Hamilton*, Aug. 15, 1877, SCT 5/4/102, GNA.

60. J. D. Taylor to Sec. Native Affairs, Jan. 18, 1909, enclosed in *Taylor v. Kwansah*.

61. See *Quasie Ammanee v. Agay-Koo Affaree*, July 22, 1879, High Court, Cape Coast, SCT 5/4/102, GNA, and *Abbrobah v. Chibboo*, Dec. 21, 1882, High Court, Cape Coast, SCT 5/4/103, GNA.

62. *Abban v. Sago.*

63. Testimony of Quow Attah in *Attah v. Sam.*

64. Testimony of Quamina Arhin in *Regina v. Quamina Arhin*, Dec. 20, 1869, High Court, Cape Coast, SCT 5/4/91, GNA. In Asante, it was illegal to reveal this kind of information. For later cases turning on slavery-related insults, see testimony of Coffee Abiasah in *Abbrobah v. Chibboo*, and Isaac Blay, Omanhin of Attuaboe, to Sec. Native Affairs, Feb. 13, 1907, enclosed in Attuaboe Native Affairs (Case No. 489/07), ADM 11/1/13, GNA; for the 1960s, see Poku, "Traditional Roles," 34–38; and for the 1980s, see Perbi, "Legacy of Slavery," 6–7.

65. Testimony of Abinah Mensah in *Regina v. Quamina Eddoo*, n.d., Court Record Book, Judicial Assessor, Cape Coast, SCT 5/4/19, GNA.

66. Cross-examination by plaintiff, in *Abinabah Mansah v. Samuel Watts*, Jan. 25, 1877, Court Record Book, Judicial Assessor, Cape Coast, SCT 5/4/19, GNA; see also *Mary Wharton and others v. W. E. Pieterson*, Apr. 26, 1877, High Court, Cape Coast, SCT 5/4/102, GNA.

67. Testimony of Immo-Coomah in *Mensah v. Watts.*

68. On village councils, see testimony of Coffee Abiasah in *Abbrobah v. Chibboo.* (Abiasah's testimony refers to an 1867 case.) On yards, public speech, and violence, see *Regina v. Arhin.* On inheritance, see testimony of Effuah Adooah in *Adooah v. Awooah*, July 19–23, 1869.

69. *Chief Eccra Qwacoe v. Johannes Bartels*, n.d., SCT 23/4/27, GNA. The court ruled for Qwacoe but awarded him only one farthing damages.

70. Omanhin Isaac Blay of Attuaboe, Eastern Appollonia to Sec. for Native Affairs, Feb. 13, 1907, ADM 11/1/13, Attuaboe Native Affairs (Case No. 489/07), GNA. For other cases of "abusive language" involving slave origins, see *Yamie Norsi v. Effuah Arcooah and Ekoom*, Dec. 11, 1883, SCT 23/4/2, GNA, and Birim District Appeals from decisions of Native Court (1907–9), ADM 11/1/1440, GNA.

71. Testimony of Yao Ottabaw in *Amanee v. Affaree*, July 22, 1879, High Court, Cape Coast, SCT 5/4/102, GNA. See also testimony of Effuah in *Cudjoo Ekrofull v. Quaw Assimah*, Jan. 20, 1880, Elmina District Commissioner's Court, SCT 23/4/1, GNA. Sara Berry confirmed my suspicion that women played an influential role in inheri-

tance disputes and chieftaincy succession cases because they are seen as the people "who really know who is descended from whom" (Sara Berry, e-mail communication, Oct. 18, 2001 [in author's possession]).

72. Testimony of Samuel Watts in *Mansah v. Watts*.

73. *Wharton v. Pieterson*. See also testimony of Brembah Insongh in *Imbrah v. Yami et al.*, July 20, 1877, SCT 5/4/102, GNA.

74. Judgment of King Amonoo V, in *Taylor v. Kwansah*, Mar. 10, 1909, ADM 11/1/40, GNA. See also Robertson, "Post-Proclamation Slavery in Accra," 226. On slaves' special role in safeguarding knowledge and producing family histories, see Mamodou Diawara, "Women, Servitude, and History: The Oral Historical Traditions of Women of Servile Condition in the Kingdom of Jaara (Mali) from the Fifteenth to the Mid-Nineteenth Centuries," in *Discourse and Its Disguises: The Interpretation of African Oral Texts*, ed. Karin Barber and P. F. de Moraes Farias (Birmingham, Eng., 1989), 109–37.

75. Gocking, *Facing Two Ways*, 197.

76. Kwame Anthony Appiah, *In My Father's House: Africa in the Philosophy of Culture* (New York, 1992), 181–92. Thanks to Richard Roberts for helping me think through the implications of Appiah's work.

77. See, for example, *Adjuah Ashon v. Abrabah Aidooah*, Oct. 31, 1876, Court Record Book, Judicial Assessor, Cape Coast, SCT 5/4/19, GNA. Michelle Gilbert ("The Cracked Pot and the Missing Sheep," *American Ethnologist* 16 [May 1989]: 227 n. 1) writes that funerals play a major role in matters of inheritance, politics, and social life in Akuapem, Ghana, today, and "everybody hopes to be buried in his hometown."

78. *Mensah v. Watts*.

79. Testimony of King Amonoo in *King Amonoo v. Quasie Gan*, Jan. 20, 1881, High Court, Cape Coast, SCT 5/4/100, GNA.

80. Testimony of Cobbina Saccoom in *Cobbina Saccoom v. Amoanee*, July 26, 1881, ibid.

81. Testimony of Amoanee in ibid.

82. Testimony of Cobbina Saccoom in ibid.

83. *Saccoom v. Amoanee*; judgment in *Mensah v. Watts*.

84. Testimony of Accu Mensah in *Abbosroe v. Isaac Jones*, Feb. 5, 1870, High Court, Cape Coast, SCT 5/4/91, GNA. Note that the term "stranger" was often a euphemism for "slave" in Akan usage. See also *Abinabah Ahkery v. Quabina Awoosie*, Sept. 17, 1869, ibid.

85. Testimony of Cudjoe Salmon in *Wharton v. Pieterson*.

86. Testimony of Ambah Bessemah in ibid.

87. *Attah v. Sam*.

88. J. W. Breckinridge to Sec. Native Affairs, Sept. 2, 1909, enclosed in "Laws and Customs of Native Communities" (Case No. 169/07), SNA Board 150, Jan. 12, 1907–Nov. 8, 1910, ADM 11/1503, GNA.

89. Acting Colonial Secretary C. H. Hunter to Acting Chief Commissioner, Ashanti, Apr. 23, 1908, File D234, Kumasi Regional Archives, GNA. I am grateful to Prof. Akosua Perbi for this reference.

90. Allott, "Native Tribunals in the Gold Coast," 165.

91. See Amissah, "Supreme Court," 7.

92. Lovejoy and Hogendorn, *Slow Death for Slavery*, ch. 4.

93. Getz, "Case for Africans," 133; Klein, "Inequality in Asante."

94. See *Abakan v. Ackarsahn* and *Amanee v. Affaree*. As Roger Gocking has observed of matrilineal inheritance, the introduction of the colonial legal system could work to preserve African practices that the British considered "outmoded," as well as to open up a wide field of "judicial ambiguity" for skillful litigants to exploit. See Roger Gocking, "Competing Systems of Inheritance before the British Courts of the Gold Coast Colony," *International Journal of African Historical Studies* 23, no. 4 (1990): 602.

95. For a discussion of the cross-cultural interactions between English and Fante judicial practices, see Gocking, "British Justice and the Native Tribunals," 93–113. For an important early statement on the history of "tradition," see Terence Ranger, "The Invention of Tradition in Colonial Africa," in *The Invention of Tradition*, ed. Eric Hobsbawm and Terence Ranger (Cambridge, Eng., 1983), 211–62.

96. Gocking, *Facing Two Ways*, 149–70.

97. C. W. Welman, Sec. for Native Affairs, Accra, "Introductory," *Gold Coast Review* 1 (Aug. 1925): 3–4, FCO.

98. Native Customary Law of Succession to Property Other than Stool Property, Winneba Division (Case No. 22/1925), ADM 11/1/919, GNA.

99. Ibid., Edwumaku Division. French officials in the Sudan sent out similar questionnaires (Richard Roberts, "Conflicts over Property in the Middle Niger Valley at the Beginning of the Twentieth Century," *African Economic History* 25 [1997]: 89).

100. A. K. P. Kludze divides today's Ghanaian law into what he calls "the *practised customary law*" made by litigants, and "the *judicial customary law*" made by superior court judges who try "to set down elaborate and often stringent formalities which they regard as the customary law." The "customary law of succession" in Ghana between 1876 and 1976, he suggests, was shaped by an interaction between these two. See A. K. P. Kludze, "A Century of Changes in the Law of Succession," in *Essays in Ghanaian Law*, ed. Gordon R. Woodman (Legon, Ghana, 1976), 233–65.

101. See, for example, John Mensah Sarbah, *Fanti Customary Laws* (1897; reprint, London, 1968), and N. A. Ollennu, *The Law of Succession in Ghana* (Accra and Kumasi, Ghana, 1960). On rising land litigation in Ghana, see William Malcom Lord Hailey, *An African Survey: A Study of Problems Arising in Africa South of the Sahara* (London, 1957), 793–94, and Sara S. Berry, *Chiefs Know Their Boundaries: Essays on Property, Power, and the Past in Asante, 1896–1996* (Portsmouth, 2001).

102. Recent studies have explored fascinating connections between history and politics, though not in the context of slavery. On Ghana, see Gilbert, "Cracked Pot," 222–26; on Nigeria, see Karin Barber, *I Could Speak until Tomorrow: Oriki, Women, and the Past in a Yoruba Town* (Washington, D.C., 1991), 183–247; on Kenya, see David William Cohen and E. S. Atieno Odhiambo, *Burying SM: The Politics of Knowledge and the Sociology of Power in Africa* (Portsmouth, N.H., 1992); on Malawi, see Landeg White, *Magomero: Portrait of an African Village* (Cambridge, Eng., 1987), 240.

103. Akosua Perbi, "Domestic Slavery in Asante, 1800–1920" (M.A. thesis, University of Ghana at Legon, 1978), 229.

104. Naa Kwaale Dove, interview by author, notes (in author's possession).

105. Perbi, "Domestic Slavery in Asante," 229. Perbi continues: "Those who become too haughty or too presumptuous and who have slave ancestry are likely to be reminded of it." See also Poku, "Traditional Roles," 34–38, and Perbi, "Legacy of Slavery." As Poku argues, ex-slaves and their descendants did not try to "escape" from "traditional society" but rather to "participate more fully in" its rituals and stool histories. The ambiguous result of this strategy has been that slave descendants are normally treated like anyone else, but the knowledge of their origins has been retained orally and is "re-inforced from time to time" by certain acts. In the 1960s, Poku saw one woman abuse a group of men by yelling "at them their own history" of servitude. For similar conclusions on East Central Africa, see Marcia Wright, *Strategies of Slaves and Women: Life-Stories from East/Central Africa* (New York, 1993), 36, 169–70.

106. This interpretation draws on conversations with Sara Berry, 1995–97, and an unpublished historiographical essay by the author titled "Fixity and African Historical Production" (in author's possession).

107. McSheffrey, "Slavery and the Impact of Abolition," 354.

108. Several authors have explored the tensions that paternalist ideology created for American slaveowners, particularly those stemming from sex between masters and slaves. See Michael P. Johnson, "Planters and Patriarchy: Charleston, 1800–1860," *Journal of Southern History* 46, no. 1 (1980): 45–72, and Drew Gilpin Faust, *James Henry Hammond and the Old South: A Design for Mastery* (Baton Rouge, 1982).

109. I am grateful for Sara Berry's keen insights on this score.

CHAPTER TWO

1. Douglas R. Egerton, *He Shall Go Out Free: The Lives of Denmark Vesey* (Madison, Wisc., 1999), 73–74; *Charleston City Gazette*, Oct. 1, Nov. 9, Dec. 4, Dec. 9, Dec. 11, 1799.

2. George Stroud (1827), quoted in Thomas D. Morris, *Southern Slavery and the Law, 1619–1860* (Chapel Hill, 1996).

3. John Belton O'Neall, *The Negro Law of South Carolina* (1848), quoted in Morris, *Southern Slavery and the Law*, 350. State supreme courts across the South consistently supported this position. See *Francois v. Lobrano*, 10 Rob. 450 (1845); *Livaudais' Heirs v. Fon*, 8 Mart. 161 (La. 1820); and *Graves v. Allan*, 52 Ky. 190 (1852). Yet the Louisiana court also ruled that slaves were "entitled" to their earnings on Sundays. See Thomas R. R. Cobb, *An Inquiry into the Law of Negro Slavery in the United States of America* (1858; Athens, Ga., 1999), 235 n. 3, and below.

4. Cobb, *Inquiry into the Law of Negro Slavery*, 235.

5. Ibid.

6. Several ex-slave claimants were awarded more than $500 by the Southern Claims Commission. Horace Page, of Fauquier County, Virginia, was awarded $1,320. Benjamin Sterling Turner, of Dallas County, Alabama, was awarded $4,958.21. In each case, the awards were much smaller than the amounts claimed.

7. United States Census Office, *Population of the United States in 1860; Compiled from the Original Returns of the Eighth Census* (Washington, D.C., 1864), 66–67, 73; United

States Census Office, *Agriculture of the United States in 1860; Compiled from the Original Returns of the Eighth Census* (Washington, D.C., 1864), 22–27.

8. For a contemporary's description of the task system, see Frederick Law Olmsted, *The Cotton Kingdom: A Traveller's Observations on Cotton and Slavery in the American Slave States, 1853–1861* (1861; New York, 1996), 191–95.

9. Philip D. Morgan, "Work and Culture: The Task System and the World of Low-country Blacks, 1700–1880," *William and Mary Quarterly* (Oct. 1982), 565–71; claim of Jacob Quarterman, p. 1, Liberty County, Georgia, SCC. For a comparison of the task system with slave labor organization on the Upper Guinea Coast in the eighteenth century, see Judith Carney, "From Hands to Tutors: African Expertise in the South Carolina Rice Economy," *Agricultural History* 67 (1993): 26.

10. Peter Kolchin, *American Slavery, 1619–1877* (New York, 1993), 106–7; John Campbell, "As 'A Kind of Freeman'?: Slaves' Market-Related Activities in the South Carolina Upcountry, 1800–1860," in *The Slaves' Economy: Independent Production by Slaves in the Americas*, ed. Ira Berlin and Philip D. Morgan (London, 1991), 141; Ralph B. Flanders, "Two Plantations and a County of Ante-Bellum Georgia," *Georgia Historical Quarterly* 12 (Mar. 1928): 10–11; testimony of unnamed Georgia informant, "Kicked Around Like a Mule," in George P. Rawick, ed., *The American Slave: A Composite Autobiography*, vol. 18, *Unwritten History of Slavery (Fisk University)* (Westport, Conn., 1972), 107.

11. Thomas Bangs Thorpe, "Sugar and the Sugar Region of Louisiana," *Harper's New Monthly Magazine* 7 (Oct. 1853): 758–59. See also claim of Polyte Powell, pp. 11–12, Point Coupee Parish, Louisiana, SCC; Elizabeth Ross Hite, interview (ca. 1940), quoted in Roderick A. McDonald, *The Economy and Material Culture of Slaves: Goods and Chattels on the Sugar Plantations of Jamaica and Louisiana* (Baton Rouge, 1993), 51; and Catherine Cornelius, interview (ca. 1939), quoted in ibid.

12. Testimony of Ansy Jeffries in claim of Miller Jeffries, n.p., Marshall County, Mississippi, SCC.

13. Claim of Miller Jeffries.

14. Claim of Jerry Smithson, pp. 3–4, Yazoo County, Mississippi, SCC. See also the claim of Waller Wade, ibid.; claim of Peter Jackson, p. 2, Warren County, Mississippi, SCC, and H[enry] C[lay] Bruce, *The New Man. Twenty-Nine Years a Slave. Twenty-Nine Years a Free Man. Recollections of H. C. Bruce* (York, Pa., 1895), 62. For upcountry South Carolina, see claim of Peter Stanton, p. 2, Marlborough County, South Carolina, SCC.

15. Testimony of Richard Cummings in claim of Lafayette DeLegal, quoted in Philip D. Morgan, "The Ownership of Property by Slaves in the Mid-Nineteenth-Century Low Country," *Journal of Southern History* 49, no. 3 (1983): 415.

16. Loren Schweninger, *Black Property Owners in the South, 1790–1915* (Urbana, 1990), 30–33.

17. Testimony of Elsie Davis in claim of Benjamin Platts, p. 5, Beaufort County, South Carolina, SCC. Similarly, on plantations in the Sokoto Caliphate (in today's northern Nigeria), slaves divided their work between *gandu* (master's fields) and *gayauna* (private plots). See Jan Hogendorn, "The Economics of Slave Use on Two 'Plantations' in the Zaria Emirate of the Sokoto Caliphate," *International Journal of African Historical Studies* 10, no. 3 (1977): 374–75.

18. George T. Swann to Charles F. Benjamin, clerk, Mar. 1, 1877, in claim of Peyton Robinson, Hinds County, Mississippi, SCC. Emphasis is in original. Swann, who had owned Robinson, was now a special commissioner for the Southern Claims Commission. Robinson was born in Virginia and sold to Mississippi in 1836.

19. Claim of Anthony Friend, pp. 6–7, Limestone County, Alabama, reel 21, WSCC. On truck patches in Charles County, Maryland, see Josiah Henson, "Autobiography of the Reverend Josiah Henson," in *Four Fugitive Slave Narratives*, ed. Robin W. Winks (Reading, Mass., 1969), 19; on those in Kentucky, see Francis Fedric, *Slave Life in Virginia and Kentucky; or, Fifty Years of Slavery in the Southern States of America* (London, 1863), 35, 89; and in North Carolina, see James Curry, "Narrative of James Curry, a Fugitive Slave," *The Liberator*, Jan. 10, 1840.

20. George Simmons in Rawick, ed., *American Slave*, vol. 5, pt. 4, Texas Narratives, p. 24.

21. Testimony of Daniel David in claim of Anthony Friend, p. 22, Limestone County, Alabama, reel 22, WSCC.

22. Bruce, *New Man*, 84–85.

23. Sarah Benjamin in Rawick, ed., *American Slave*, vol. 4, pt. 1, Texas Narratives, p. 71. See also testimony of unnamed Georgia informant, "Kicked Around Like a Mule," 107.

24. Martha Patton, in Rawick, ed. *American Slave*, vol. 5, pt. 3, Texas Narratives, p. 173. See also testimony of Mariah Calloway, quoted in Schweninger, *Black Property Owners in the South*, 31, and testimony of Lorenza Ezell, quoted in ibid.

25. *Thomas Waddill v. Charlotte D. Martin*, 38 N.C. 562 (1845).

26. Claim of John McConnell, pp. 6–7, Chattooga County, Georgia, SCC. Emphasis is in original. See also Charles Sackett Sydnor, *Slavery in Mississippi* (New York, 1933), 97; John Hebron Moore, *The Emergence of the Cotton Kingdom in the Old Southwest: Mississippi, 1770–1860* (Baton Rouge, 1988), 101–3, 136; and the testimony of Samuel B. Smith, Esq., Nov. 19, 1863, pp. 1–2, File 7, Kentucky, Tennessee, and Missouri, AFIC.

27. [J. H. Ingraham], *The South-West. By a Yankee* (New York, 1835), 1:54–56, Huntington Library Rare Book Collection, San Marino, Calif.

28. Charles Ball, *Slavery in the United States: A Narrative of the Life and Adventures of Charles Ball* (Lewistown, Pa., 1836), 166–67. In Louisiana's sugar regions, masters put "Negro grounds" away "on the borders of the forest," whereas kitchen gardens were near the big house (McDonald, *Economy and Material Culture of Slaves*, 52). See also the testimony of William Bass in claim of Silas Cook, p. 3, Marlborough County, South Carolina, SCC.

29. Testimony of Sterling Jones in claim of Sandy Austin, p. 7, Liberty County, Georgia, SCC. For a discussion on how the geography of garden patches changed between 1800 and 1830, see Betty Wood, *Women's Work, Men's Work: The Informal Slave Economies of Lowcountry Georgia* (Athens, Ga., 1995), 32–35.

30. Ball, *Slavery in the United States*, 166–67.

31. See, for example, the claim of Pompey Lewis, p. 1, Marlborough County, South Carolina, SCC; and claim of Alexander Dudley, p. 3, ibid.

32. Philip D. Morgan, "Task and Gang Systems: The Organization of Labor on New

World Plantations," in *Work and Labor in Early America*, ed. Stephen Innes (Chapel Hill, 1988), 213.

33. An economy of time appeared in the Caribbean as well. Woodville K. Marshall writes that in the Windward Islands there was a "scramble" among slaves "for labor services," one that "was probably more intense than the competition for land, because labor was the slaves' scarcest resource." See Woodville K. Marshall, "Provision Ground and Plantation Labor in Four Windward Islands: Competition for Resources during Slavery," in *Cultivation and Culture: Labor and the Shaping of Slave Life in the Americas*, ed. Ira Berlin and Philip D. Morgan (Charlottesville, 1993), 218. Masters' tendency to shunt "Negro grounds" to distant corners cut down available time for slaves in Louisiana (McDonald, *Economy and Material Culture of Slaves*, 52).

34. Elizabeth J. Reitz, Tyson Gibbs, and Ted A. Rathbun, "Archaeological Evidence for Subsistence on Coastal Plantations," in *The Archaeology of Slavery and Plantation Life*, ed. Theresa A. Singleton (Orlando, 1985), 166.

35. Testimony of Richard Cummings (1873) and Scipio King (1873) in Morgan, "Work and Culture," 586.

36. Morgan, "Task and Gang Systems," 192; Robert S. Starobin, *Industrial Slavery in the Old South* (London, 1970), 99–100. On "over task" payments to slaves hired out by their masters as sawyers in North Carolina, see Catherine W. Bishir, "'Severe Survitude to House Building': The Construction of Hayes Plantation House, 1814–1817," *North Carolina Historical Review* 68, no. 4 (1991): 386.

37. Moses Grandy, *Narrative of the Life of Moses Grandy, Formerly a Slave in the United States of America* (Boston, 1844), 22–24; Starobin, *Industrial Slavery in the Old South*, 100–101.

38. Martha Ann Carter Dettor Collection (Accession 34298), The History of Lawrence Creek, ca. 1934, Personal Papers Collection, LV; Moses Roper, *A Narrative of the Adventures and Escape of Moses Roper, from American Slavery* (London, 1834), 9, 22, 18–19. On task work in Virginia woodcutting, see Olmsted, *Cotton Kingdom*, 106–7, and in Mississippi's timber industry, see John Hebron Moore, *Emergence of the Cotton Kingdom*, 152; on seasonal task work in Kentucky, see Brian W. Thomas, "Power and Community: The Archaeology of Slavery at the Hermitage Plantation," *American Antiquity* 63, no. 4 (1998).

39. This term comes from the introduction to Berlin and Morgan, eds., *Cultivation and Culture*. For a Virginia slaveowner's expression of the line dividing plantation time, see Thomas Jefferson to Hugh Chisholm (1807), quoted in Barbara J. Heath, *Hidden Lives: The Archaeology of Slave Life at Thomas Jefferson's Poplar Forest* (Charlottesville, 1999), 50.

40. Claim of William Green, p. 4, Warren County, Mississippi, SCC.

41. Testimony of David Robinson in claim of Solomon Wharton, n.p., Madison County, Alabama, SCC.

42. On "overwork," see the claim of Littleton Barber, p. 1, Adams County, Mississippi, SCC; on overwork in North Carolina, see Allen Parker, *Recollections of Slavery Times* (Worcester, Mass., 1895), 15, 20, 65; on overwork in Virginia, see Austin Steward, "Twenty-Two Years a Slave and Forty Years a Freeman," in *Four Fugitive Slave Narratives*, ed. Robin W. Winks (Reading, Mass., 1969), 11.

43. Claim of Edward Broaddy, p. 1, Marlborough County, South Carolina, SCC.

44. Claim of Alexander Dudley, p. 1, ibid.

45. *Rice v. Cade et al.*, 10 La. 288, 1836 WL 746 (La.).

46. Claim of Benjamin Thompson, p. 1, Colbert County, Alabama, SCC.

47. Claim of William Cassels [Cassell], p. 3, and claim of William McIver, p. 3, both Liberty County, Georgia, SCC.

48. Testimony of Bob Simmons in claim of John Cuthbert, p. 5, Chatham County, Georgia, SCC.

49. Claim of Furgus Wilson, p. 4, Liberty County, Georgia, SCC.

50. Curry, "Narrative of James Curry."

51. Claim of Edward Broaddy, p. 1, Marlborough County, South Carolina, SCC.

52. Tom Holland in Rawick, ed., *American Slave*, vol. 4, pt. 2, Texas Narratives, p. 144; claim of Essex Dargan, p. 1, Marlborough County, South Carolina, SCC.

53. Solomon Northup, *Twelve Years a Slave: Narrative of Solomon Northup, a Citizen of New-York, Kidnapped in Washington City in 1841, and Rescued in 1853* (Auburn, N.Y., 1853), 195.

54. *Rice v. Cade et al.*

55. Ball, *Slavery in the United States*, 217, 273; quotation is on 217. The "overplus" for elderly slaves and children would begin at twenty-five pounds, and for women with small children, at forty pounds.

56. Ibid., 271–72.

57. Philip V. Scarpino, "Slavery in Callaway County, Missouri: 1845–1855," *Missouri Historical Review* 71, no. 3 (1977): 24–25.

58. Testimony of George T. Swann in claim of Peyton Robinson, pp. 1–2, Hinds County, Mississippi, SCC. See also Sydnor, *Slavery in Mississippi*, 96.

59. Testimony of Samuel B. Smith, Esq., Nov. 19, 1863, p. 2, File 7, AFIC.

60. Olmsted, *Cotton Kingdom*, 323.

61. Ibid., 329–30.

62. Charles Dew, *Bond of Iron: Master and Slave at Buffalo Forge* (New York, 1994), 108–9; Ronald L. Lewis, *Coal, Iron, and Slaves: Industrial Slavery in Maryland and Virginia, 1715–1865* (Westport, Conn., 1979), 124; Starobin, *Industrial Slavery in the Old South*, 102.

63. Edmund Ruffin (1837), quoted in Lewis, *Coal, Iron, and Slaves*, 120.

64. Lewis, *Coal, Iron, and Slaves*, 124; *Richmond Whig and Public Advertiser* (1846), quoted in ibid., 120.

65. Olmsted, *Cotton Kingdom*, 109.

66. Ibid., 77. An 1865 petition by black tobacco workers of Richmond and Manchester referred to tasks and overwork payments in 1858 and 1859 (J. T. Trowbridge, *The South* [1866; reprint, New York, 1969]), 230–31). See also Starobin, *Industrial Slavery in the Old South*, 99–103.

67. Kolchin, *American Slavery*, 109–10.

68. Claim of Mack Duff Williams, p. 1, Charleston County, South Carolina, SCC; testimony of James K. Hyman in claim of John Holdman, p. 11, Adams County, Mississippi, SCC.

69. Calculated from SCC. The actual number may be higher, since testimony did not always indicate occupations during slavery.

70. Sarah S. Hughes, "Slaves for Hire: The Allocation of Black Labor in Elizabeth City County, Virginia, 1782 to 1810," *William and Mary Quarterly* 35 (Apr. 1978): 260, 275, 282.

71. Keith C. Barton, "'Good Cooks and Washers': Slave Hiring, Domestic Labor, and the Market in Bourbon County, Kentucky," *Journal of American History* 84 (Sept. 1997): 436–60. The phrase "masters of small worlds" is taken from Stephanie McCurry, *Masters of Small Worlds: Yeoman Households, Gender Relations, and the Political Culture of the Antebellum South Carolina Low Country* (New York, 1995).

72. Testimony of Charlotte Knight in claim of Lewis Williams, pp. 9–10, Hinds County, Mississippi, SCC.

73. Ingraham, *South-West*, 2:251.

74. Testimony of Henry Smith in claim of William Anderson, p. 9, Chatham County, Georgia, SCC.

75. George T. Swann to C. F. Benjamin, Mar. 1, 1877, enclosed in claim of Peyton Robinson, Hinds County, Mississippi, SCC.

76. Calvin West-Widener in Rawick, ed., *American Slave*, vol. 11, pt. 7, Arkansas Narratives, p. 104.

77. Emily P. Burke, *Reminiscences of Georgia* (Oberlin, Ohio, 1850), 88, Huntington Library Rare Book Collection, San Marino, Calif.

78. Duncan Gaines in Rawick, ed., *American Slave*, vol. 17, Florida Narratives, p. 133.

79. Claim of Joseph James, p. 2, Liberty County, Georgia, SCC.

80. Olmsted, *Cotton Kingdom*, 431.

81. Interview of Mandy Morrow in Rawick, ed., *American Slave*, supp. ser. 2, vol. 7, pt. 6, Texas Narratives, p. 276; Frederick Douglass, *Narrative of the Life of Frederick Douglass, an American Slave, Written by Himself*, ed. David W. Blight (1845; reprint, Boston, 1993), 17.

82. Douglass, *Narrative*, 13.

83. Claim of Moses Hampton, p. 5, Cherokee County, Alabama, reel 2, WSCC.

84. Venture Smith, *A Narrative of the Life and Adventures of Venture A Native of Africa, But Resident Above Sixty Years in the United States of America. Related by Himself* (1798; Middletown, Conn., 1897), 19; Grandy, *Narrative of the Life of Moses Grandy*, 16.

85. Jane Simpson in Rawick, ed., *American Slave*, vol. 11, pt. 8, Missouri Narratives, p. 315.

86. Claim of Benjamin S. Turner, judgment, Dallas County, Alabama, SCC.

87. Claim of Benjamin S. Turner, supplemental testimony, Apr. 21, 1871, Dallas County, Alabama, reel 6, WSCC.

88. Cross-examination of Daniel Barber by Horace Page in claim of Horace Page, May 25, 1876, Fauquier County, Virginia, SCC; cross-examination of William Murray in ibid. According to the records of Page's exchange with Barber, Page said that "a slave man could not transact business," but other testimony in the case, particularly his subsequent exchange with Murray, strongly suggests a transcription error.

89. Ball, *Slavery in the United States*, 189. Allen Parker, a fugitive from North Carolina, made a similar point in his *Recollections of Slavery Times*, 20.

90. On planters' stake in the informal economy, see the introduction to Berlin and Morgan, eds., *Slaves' Economy*, 19.

91. Supreme courts in North and South Carolina said the same thing. See *Thomas Waddill v. Charlotte D. Martin; Richardson v. Broughton*, 3 Strob. 1 (1848).

92. Roger L. Ransom and Richard Sutch, *One Kind of Freedom: The Economic Consequences of Emancipation* (New York, 1977), 4.

93. Pauline Johnson and Felice Boudreaux in Rawick, ed., *American Slave*, vol. 4, pt. 2, Texas Narratives, p. 225.

94. Claim of Alfred Barnard, pp. 2–3, Chatham County, Georgia, SCC. On supplementing skimpy clothing rations in North Carolina, see Curry, "Narrative of James Curry."

95. See Ball, *Slavery in the United States*, 194; claim of Lewis Quick, p. 4, Marlborough County, South Carolina, SCC.

96. Ransom and Sutch, *One Kind of Freedom*, 53, table 3.5.

97. Claim of Lewis Miller, p. 5, Chatham County, Georgia, SCC.

98. Reitz, Gibbs, and Rathbun, "Archaeological Evidence for Subsistence," 185. For archaeological evidence of slaves hunting and gardening in Virginia, see Heath, *Hidden Lives*, 59–60.

99. Claim of William Harris, p. 3, Chatham County, Georgia, SCC. Emphasis is in original.

100. Northup, *Twelve Years a Slave*, 194–95. For a similar statement by a slave from Virginia, see Steward, "Twenty-Two Years a Slave," 11; for North Carolina, see Grandy, *Narrative of the Life of Moses Grandy*, 18–19.

101. Ball, *Slavery in the United States*, 271–72.

102. Ibid., 108. See also claim of Allan Quick, p. 1, Marlborough County, South Carolina, SCC.

103. Sarah Frances Shaw Graves in Rawick, ed., *American Slave*, vol. 11, pt. 8, Missouri Narratives, p. 138.

104. It didn't work. According to this unnamed informant, "But we would steal anyhow—that is, the grown folks would. They would have sweet potatoes and steal the white folks' sweet potatoes" (quoted in "One of Dr. Gale's 'Free Niggers,'" Rawick, ed., *American Slave*, vol. 18, p. 11). Virginia slaveowner Hill Carter believed much the same thing. See Genevieve Leavitt, "Slaves and Tenant Farmers at Shirley Plantation," in *The Archaeology of Shirley Plantation*, ed. Theodore R. Reinhart (Charlottesville, 1984), 156. See also John Hebron Moore, *Emergence of the Cotton Kingdom*, 101.

105. Olmsted, *Cotton Kingdom*, 456. On whites using "privileges" to discipline slaves in the Low Country, see testimony of Oliver P. Bostick in claim of Andrew Jackson, p. 9, Beaufort County, South Carolina, SCC. For Alabama and North Carolina, see James O. Breeden, ed., *Advice among Masters: The Ideal in Slave Management in the Old South* (Westport, Conn., 1980), 259–60.

106. Roper, *Narrative of the Adventures and Escape*, 80.

107. Ball, *Slavery in the United States*, 273. Ex-slaves from other regions agreed. On Missouri, see Bruce, *New Man*, 84–85; on North Carolina, see Grandy, *Narrative of the Life of Moses Grandy*, 22.

108. Olmsted, *Cotton Kingdom*, 431.

109. Ibid., 447–56. For a similar account in Virginia, see Steward, "Twenty-Two Years a Slave," 11–12; for North Carolina, see Grandy, *Narrative of the Life of Moses Grandy*, 16.

110. Clarence L. Mohr, *On the Threshold of Freedom: Masters and Slaves in Civil War Georgia* (Athens, Ga., 1986), 102. See also letter from Lt. Charles C. Jones Jr. to Rev. C. C. Jones (1862), in Robert Manson Myers, ed., *The Children of Pride: A True Story of Georgia and the Civil War* (New Haven, 1972), 987.

111. Maj. Frank H. Peck to Gen. J. W. Phelps, June 15, 1862, and Brig. Gen. J. W. Phelps to Capt. R. S. Davis, [La.], June 16, 1862, reprinted in Ira Berlin et al., eds., *The Destruction of Slavery*, ser. 1, vol. 1, *Freedom: A Documentary History of Emancipation, 1861–1867* (New York, 1985), 210, 215. See also affidavit of Fanny Ann Flood, Mar. 7, 1866, Louisville, Ky., reprinted in ibid., 587–89.

112. Claim of James Brutus, p. 1, Marlborough County, South Carolina, SCC.

113. William Wells Brown, *Narrative of William W. Brown, a Fugitive Slave. Written by Himself* (1847; reprint, Boston, 1848), 35.

114. *Webster's New Universal Unabridged Dictionary*, 1st ed., s.v. "cord."

115. Olmsted, *Cotton Kingdom*, 106–7. For a similar struggle (this time over spinning) between an enslaved woman and her mistress, see Curry, "Narrative of James Curry."

116. *State v. Will*, Dec. term, 1834, North Carolina Supreme Court, case 2191, NCSA.

117. Claim of Peter Miller, pp. 2–3, Liberty County, Georgia, SCC. The literature on this and other kinds of day-to-day resistance is too large to list here. Some examples include Raymond A. Bauer and Alice H. Bauer, "Day to Day Resistance to Slavery," *Journal of Negro History* 27 (Oct. 1942): 388–419; Eugene Genovese, *Roll, Jordan, Roll: The World the Slaves Made* (New York, 1972). James C. Scott's influential work on peasants in twentieth-century Southeast Asia expanded these ideas into a framework of "weapons of the weak." See James C. Scott, *Weapons of the Weak: Everyday Forms of Peasant Resistance* (New Haven, 1987).

118. Kolchin, *American Slavery*, 96.

119. Steven F. Miller, "Plantation Labor Organization and Slave Life on the Cotton Frontier: The Alabama-Mississippi Black Belt, 1815–1840," in Berlin and Morgan, eds., *Cultivation and Culture*, 167.

120. Miller, "Plantation Labor Organization," 164; Joseph P. Reidy, "Obligation and Right: Patterns of Labor, Subsistence, and Exchange in the Cotton Belt of Georgia, 1790–1860," in Berlin and Morgan, eds., *Cultivation and Culture*, 138–54. A few ex-slaves in the southwest reported working by the task. See the deposition of Octave Johnson, Corporal, Co. C, 15th Reg't., Corps d'Afrique, p. 34, File 11, AFIC; claim of Cyrus Ward, p. 1, Oktibbeha County, Mississippi, SCC; and claim of Polyte Powell, pp. 11–12, Point Coupee Parish, Louisiana, SCC.

121. Olmsted, *Cotton Kingdom*, 448.

122. Grandy, *Narrative of the Life of Moses Grandy*, 36–37. A similar account of masters using the slaves' economy to get new land cleared is in Curry, "Narrative of James Curry." See also Dumont [de Montigny] (1853), quoted in Joe Gray Taylor, *Negro Slavery in Louisiana* (Baton Rouge, 1963), 15.

123. Ivor Wilks, "Land, Labor, Capital and the Forest Kingdom of Asante: A Model

of Early Change," in *The Evolution of Social Systems*, ed. J. Friedman and M. J. Row-lands (London, 1977), 487–534.

124. Morgan, "Work and Culture," 578–79; introduction to Berlin and Morgan, eds., *Cultivation and Culture*, 14–16, 41–43.

125. Testimony of Edward DeLegal in claim of Tony Axon, p. 7, Liberty County, Georgia, SCC.

126. Ball, *Slavery in the United States*, 194. See also claim of Benjamin Lettuce, p. 3, Lauderdale County, Alabama, SCC.

127. Claim of Nancy Jones, p. 3, Madison County, Alabama, reel 25, WSCC.

128. Testimony of Joel L. Easterling in claim of Crawford Turnage, p. 2, Marlbor-ough County, South Carolina, SCC.

129. Thorpe, "Sugar and the Sugar Region of Louisiana," 767; McDonald, *Economy and Material Culture of Slaves*, 76–78.

130. Testimony of Simeon Walthour in claim of William Golding, p. 10, Liberty County, Georgia, SCC.

131. Betty Brown in Rawick, ed., *American Slave*, vol. 11, pt. 8, Missouri Narratives, p. 53. For peddlers on sugar plantations, see Thorpe, "Sugar and the Sugar Region of Louisiana," 767.

132. Millie Ann Smith in Rawick, ed., *American Slave*, vol. 5, pt. 4, Texas Narratives, p. 43.

133. Olmsted, *Cotton Kingdom*, 163.

134. Testimony of James Pinkett in claim of Henry Watson, p. 11, Warren County, Mississippi, SCC.

135. Testimony of Dudley J. Smith in claim of Henry Hall, n.p., Dallas County, Al-abama, reel 6, WSCC. See also Trowbridge, *South*, 437.

136. Trowbridge, *South*, 437.

137. Testimony of Edward DeLegal in claim of Tony Axon, p. 7, Liberty County, Georgia, SCC; claim of Jacob Quarterman, p. 2, ibid.; testimony of Tony Law in claim of Linda Roberts, p. 12, ibid. Salt was an essential resource. People working under the hot sun, as most slaves did, needed as much as one pint every two weeks. It was crucial to the war effort, especially for preserving meat. Salt thus made a solid invest-ment and a stable currency substitute. On currency and its substitutes, see the testi-mony of William Bacon in claim of Patsey Campbell, p. 3, ibid.; claim of Jacob Dryer, supplemental testimony, ibid.; claim of Tony Axon, p. 5, ibid.; claim of Pompey Bacon, ibid.; and *First Annual Report of the Boston Educational Commission for Freedmen* (Boston, 1863), 22.

138. Scott Hooper in Rawick, ed., *American Slave*, vol. 4, pt. 2, Texas Narratives, p. 157.

139. Ingraham, *South-West*, 2:54–56.

140. Ibid., 55–56; Thomas H. Clayton, *Close to the Land: The Way We Lived in North Carolina, 1820–1870*, ed. Sydney Nathans (Chapel Hill, 1983), 61–62.

141. Testimony of Peter in *Trial of Peter* [no relation], Oct. 16, 1826, Court of Oyer and Terminer, Essex County, Virginia, Order Book 45, 1823–26, Microfilm Reel 94, Local Records, LV. For slaves' participation in Sunday markets in Alexandria, Va., see Mary V. Thompson, "'They Appear to Live Comfortable Together': Private Life of

the Mount Vernon Slaves," unpublished paper dated Jan. 20, 1999, 4–5. For Louisiana, see McDonald, *Economy and Material Culture of Slaves*, 68. For Huntsville, Alabama, see Daniel S. Dupre, *Transforming the Cotton Frontier: Madison County, Alabama, 1800–1840* (Baton Rouge, 1997), 214–15.

142. James B. Slaughter, *Settlers, Southerners, Americans: The History of Essex County, Virginia 1608–1984* (Salem, W.Va., 1985), 125.

143. Charles A. Raymond, "The Religious Life of the Negro Slave," *Harper's New Monthly Magazine* 27 (1863): 676. See also Ellen Payne in Rawick, ed., *American Slave*, vol. 5, pt. 3, Texas Narratives, p. 178. For other references to slaves' marketing, see Flanders, "Two Plantations," 6, 18.

144. Mary G. Powell, *The History of Old Alexandria, Virginia, from July 13, 1749 to May 24, 1861* (Richmond, 1928), 58–59. I am grateful to Mary V. Thompson for this reference.

145. *Alexandria Gazette* (1876), reprinted in T. Michael Miller, ed., *Pen Portraits of Alexandria, Virginia, 1739–1900* (Bowie, Md., 1987), 281–82. I am grateful to Mary V. Thompson for this reference.

146. Olmsted, *Cotton Kingdom*, 126.

147. Ingraham, *South-West*, 2:55–56. On enslaved women marketers in Brazil, see João José Reis, *Slave Rebellion in Brazil: The Muslim Uprising of 1835 in Bahia*, trans. Arthur Brakel (1986; reprint, Baltimore, 1993), 161–62, and Mary Karasch, "Suppliers, Sellers, Servants, and Slaves," in *Cities and Society in Colonial Latin America*, ed. Louisa Schell Hoberman and Susan Migden Socolow (Albuquerque, N.M., 1986), 251–83.

148. Wood, *Women's Work, Men's Work*, 80–87; Robert Olwell, "'Loose, Idle and Disorderly': Slave Women in the Eighteenth-Century Charleston Marketplace," in *More than Chattel: Black Women and Slavery in the Americas*, ed. David Barry Gaspar and Darlene Clark Hine (Bloomington, Ind., 1996), 97–110.

149. Olwell, "'Loose, Idle and Disorderly,'" 104. On networks among black women during and after slavery, see Deborah Gray White, *Ar'n't I a Woman? Female Slaves in the Plantation South* (New York, 1985), 119–41, and Tera W. Hunter, *To 'Joy My Freedom: Southern Black Women's Lives and Labors after the Civil War* (Cambridge, Mass., 1997), 63–97.

150. Raymond, "Religious Life of the Negro Slave," 676.

151. Ingraham, *South-West*, vol. 1, 99–102.

152. Ibid. Ingraham's attempt at "dialect" can be translated: "'Bonjour, Mademoiselle'—'Monsieur! Good-day.'"

153. This interpretation draws from my own experiences with bargaining, which took place in the fall of 1996 in markets, homes, and taxis in Accra, Ghana; Ho, Ghana; Abomey, Benin; and Cotonou, Benin. Of course, I did not bargain with slaves; the comparison is meant to suggest similarities in bargaining practices, regardless of the bargainers' status.

154. Robin D. G. Kelley has argued persuasively that historians should take seriously the aesthetic dimensions of blacks' self-expression. See Robin D. G. Kelley, *Yo' Mama's Disfunktional! Fighting the Culture Wars in Urban America* (Boston, 1997), 15–42.

155. Claim of Henry Banks, pp. 9–10, Warren County, Mississippi, SCC. For simi-

lar statements on Georgia, see claim of Jacob Quarterman, p. 2, Liberty County, Georgia, SCC. On Kentucky, see [Samuel Allen], "Sketches of the West," in Eugene L. Schwaab, ed., *Travels in the Old South: Selected from the Periodicals of the Times* (Lexington, Ky., 1843), 289–91.

156. Testimony of Richard Livingston in claim of William Golding, pp. 1–3, Liberty County, Georgia, SCC. The commission disallowed the items of Golding's claim because it could not distinguish them from items belonging to Golding's master, who sent his own goods in the same shipments.

157. Frances Anne Kemble, *Journal of a Residence on a Georgian Plantation in 1838–1839* (New York, 1961), 90. See also Charles Lyell, *A Second Visit to the United States of North America* (New York, 1850), 2:13. With apologies to James Brown.

158. Frederick Law Olmsted, *A Journey in the Seaboard Slave States* (New York, 1859), 313. On an enslaved ferryman in Virginia, see Thomas Holcomb, interview by Craig Baskerville, Apr. 27, 1976, audio recording in author's possession.

159. See the series of suits initiated by two of the government's black franchisees, George Holmes and Robert R. Sams: *George Holmes and Robert R. Sams v. Bacchus Mitchell*, Apr. 23, 1866, PCB, Sept. 1865–June 1868, RG 393, Part IV; *Holmes and Sams v. Harry Johnson*, Apr. 27, 1866, ibid.; *Holmes and Sams v. William Washington*, Apr. 23, 1866, ibid.

160. Lyell, *Second Visit*, 2:200–201.

161. Ingraham, *South-West*, 2:17–18. The Louisiana High Court described stagecoach and steamboat landings in similar terms, suggesting that many white southerners were familiar with such scenes. See *Rice v. Cade et al.*

162. Ball, *Slavery in the United States*, 43–44. For such activity in the Low Country, see Charles Nordhoff, *The Freedmen of South Carolina: Some Account of their Appearances, Character, Conditions, and Peculiar Customs* (New York, 1863), 5–6, Huntington Library Rare Book Collection, San Marino, Calif.

163. Claim of Thomas Bradshaw, n.p., Warren County, Mississippi, SCC.

164. Olmsted, *Journey in the Seaboard Slave States*, 565.

165. James Hall, *Letters from the West; Containing Sketches of Scenery, Manners, and Customs; and Anecdotes Connected with the First Settlements of the Western Sections of the United States* (London, 1828), 141–42.

166. Ball, *Slavery in the United States*, 292–98. Ulrich B. Phillips in his *Life and Labor in the Old South* ([Boston, 1929], 238) rather gleefully noted a Virginia slaveowner who fired his overseer in 1828 for, among other things, selling whiskey to his slaves.

167. Ball, *Slavery in the United States*, 191.

168. Ibid., 191–92.

169. Heath, *Hidden Lives*, 51–53.

170. Ingraham, *South-West*, 2:60.

171. Ibid., 72. Fayetteville, North Carolina, and Alexandria, Virginia, used a similar system in the 1820s (Clayton, *Close to the Land*, 60; Ann Royall [1826], quoted in Miller, ed., *Pen Portraits of Alexandria*, 107). I am grateful to Mary V. Thompson for the Royall reference.

172. Lyell, *Second Visit*, 2:84.

173. Testimony of Robert H. Atkinson in claim of Crawford Monroe, p. 14, Fulton County, Georgia, SCC.

174. Clayton, *Close to the Land*, 21; "An acrostic Written by a Negro, at Chapel Hill," ca. 1846–49, PC 1533.1, Simpson and Biddle Family Papers, NCSA.

175. Thomas Holcomb interview. Jackson Hall was Thomas Holcomb's father and my great-great-great-uncle. He was enslaved near Farmville, Virginia.

176. Natchez *Free Trader* (1858), quoted in John Hebron Moore, *Emergence of the Cotton Kingdom*, 280. For angry editorials about black women marketers in Alabama newspapers, see James Benson Sellers, *Slavery in Alabama* (1950; reprint, Tuscaloosa, 1994), 233.

177. Wood, *Women's Work, Men's Work*, 140–48; Royall (1826), quoted in Miller, ed., *Pen Portraits of Alexandria*, 107.

178. Wood, *Women's Work, Men's Work*, 159.

179. Miller, ed., *Pen Portraits of Alexandria*, 107.

180. Testimony of James W. Gray in claim of Henry Banks, pp. 30–31, Warren County, Mississippi, SCC. On New Orleans slaves' ownership of real estate and race horses, see Loren Schweninger, "A Negro Sojourner in Antebellum New Orleans," *Louisiana History* 20 (Summer 1979): 312.

181. Testimony of Lay. Lindsey in claim of Henry Banks, p. 32, Warren County, Mississippi, SCC.

182. The North Carolina Supreme Court went even further than this, saying that the many statutes which regulated trading with slaves effectively

recognize a sort of ownership by slaves of certain articles, by permission of the master, forbidding them to have certain other articles or to sell or buy them; which shews, that there is an universal sense pervading the whole community, of the utility, nay, unavoidable necessity, of leaving to the slave some small perquisites, which may be called his and disposed of by him as his, although as against a wrong doer the property must be laid in the master, for the sake of the remedy, and although the master, if he will, may take all. (*Thomas Waddill v. Charlotte D. Martin*)

183. *Southern Advocate* (1827), quoted in Sellers, *Slavery in Alabama*, 233.

184. Flanders, "Two Plantations," 37.

185. "Preamble and Regulations of the Savannah River Anti-Slave-Traffick Association," Nov. 21, 1846, pp. 8–9, Huntington Library Rare Book Collection, San Marino, Calif. Virtually all prosecutions for liquor trading between whites and enslaved people came in the last forty years of North American slavery (Morris, *Southern Slavery and the Law*, 352).

186. Olmsted, *Journey in the Seaboard Slave States*, 102, 432–43. On "champagne suppers," see ibid., 102. Slaves drank but probably no more than whites did. See, for example, testimony of Caesar in *Trial of Bill Williams*, Sept. 7, 1807, Court of Oyer and Terminer, Norfolk, Virginia, and CBF.

187. Charles Ball and other slaves were once caught with stolen goods and managed to blame the crime on a poor white family nearby (Ball, *Slavery in the United*

States, 300–318). Others recruited "poor white" people to fence goods (Parker, *Recollections of Slavery Times,* 76–77).

188. Sim Neal to "Dear mother and brothers and Sisters," Sept. 8, 1827, no. 4370, Neal Family Papers, SHC.

189. Claim of Edmund Moss, p. 5, Shelby County, Alabama, reel 31, WSCC.

190. John Hope Franklin, *From Slavery to Freedom: A History of Negro Americans,* 3rd ed. (New York, 1967), 197. An 1858 ruling by the attorney general barred any more such patents. Yet in 1861 the Confederate Congress took steps to insure that enslaved inventors could receive patents.

191. *Charleston Standard,* Nov. 23, 1854, quoted in Olmsted, *Cotton Kingdom,* 196.

192. Testimony of Benjamin P. McCrany in claim of John Langford, p. 9, Madison County, Alabama, SCC; Sellers, *Slavery in Alabama,* 233; testimony of James Fraser in claim of John Bacon Sr., p. 24, Liberty County, Georgia, SCC.

193. Testimony of J. H. Ledbetter in claim of William Hardeman, pp. 6–7, Hinds County, Mississippi, SCC.

194. *Rice v. Cade et al.* See also Cobb, *Inquiry into the Law of Negro Slavery,* 235.

195. On these kinds of organizations in Georgia, see Mohr, *On the Threshold of Freedom,* 3; on those in Mississippi, see Natchez *Courier* (1838), quoted in John Hebron Moore, *Emergence of the Cotton Kingdom,* 280.

196. Mohr, *On the Threshold of Freedom,* 8–11.

197. Bruce, *New Man,* 76.

198. Testimony of Samuel B. Smith, Esq., Nov. 19, 1863, pp. 3–4, File 7, AFIC.

199. Texas sent seventeen, and West Virginia sent forty-six—and the absence of claims by ex-slaves can be seen as statistically insignificant. Amounts calculated from SCC. An additional 2,088 allowed claims are not considered here because they were either lost or filed with the records of other agencies.

200. Claims by people who became free before the Civil War are not included in the count of claims by ex-slaves, even though many of them also earned property while they were slaves.

201. Native Americans accounted for fourteen allowed claims. An additional seventeen allowed claims were filed by people identifiable as African American but for whom no status could be deduced. Three allowed claims were filed by slaves for property they inherited from whites. Eight claims contained no evidence of either race or status. It is difficult to identify property owned by women, since legal constraints frequently prompted men and women to file on behalf of spouses, children, and other relatives.

202. I include the following counties in the Low Country (number of allowed claims by ex-slaves appears in parentheses). Georgia counties include Camden (1), Glynn (0), McIntosh (0), Liberty (91), Bryan (0), and Chatham (43); for South Carolina: Beaufort (23), Colleton (0), Charleston (1), Georgetown (4), and Horry (0); for North Carolina: Brunswick (0), New Hanover (1), Onslow (0), Carteret (2), Craven (0), Pamlico (0), Beaufort (1), Hyde (0), Tyrell (0), and Dare (0); for Florida: Nassau (0), Duval (0), and St. Johns (0). Amounts calculated from SCC.

203. The total number of allowed claims does not match the total stated in Figure

1 because claim amounts could not be located for six white claimants. Amounts calculated from SCC.

204. All amounts are calculated from SCC. Thousands of additional claims, including claims by whites, blacks, Native Americans, and citizens of foreign countries, were barred or disallowed. Such claims went to the War Claims Commission of the U.S. House of Representatives, and persistent claimants could have them reconsidered before the U.S Court of Claims.

205. Claim of Taylor Thornton, judgment, Clark County, Virginia; claim of William Willbanks, judgment, Washington County, Arkansas; claim of William Rector, judgment, Claiborne County, Tennessee, all SCC.

206. Claim of James McQueen, judgment, Marlborough County, South Carolina, and claim of Henry Marshall, judgment, Washington County, Arkansas, both SCC.

207. Median amounts for 50 claims by ex-slaves and 412 claims by whites are calculated from SCC.

208. Claim of Benjamin Sterling Turner, judgment, Dallas County, Alabama, SCC.

209. Klingberg, *Southern Claims Commission*, 89, 100. Klingberg's study focuses on the top bracket of claimants; as yet, the only published information on ordinary claimants appears in two indexes by Gary B. Mills. See his *Southern Loyalists in the Civil War: The Southern Claims Commission* (Baltimore, 1994) and *Civil War Claims in the South: An Index of Civil War Damage Claims Filed before the Southern Claims Commission, 1871–1880* (Laguna Hills, Calif., 1980). Neither index identifies ex-slave claimants.

210. Claim of Pompey Bacon, p. 1, Liberty County, Georgia, SCC.

211. Claim of David Stevens, p. 1, ibid.

212. Testimony of Tony Law in claim of Linda Roberts, p. 12, ibid.

213. Frank [B. Howell] to "Father" [J. B. Howell, commissioner of claims], Mar. 12, 1872, entry 325, Letters Received by the Commission, M86, roll 2, RRSCC.

214. Letter from Rev. J. T. H. Waite to Charles F. Benjamin, clerk, Office of Commissioners of Claims, Feb. 1, 1877, in claim of Tony Axon, SCC.

215. Enclosure by Charles F. Benjamin, clerk, to Commissioners of Claims, Sept. 17, 1877, entry 325, M87, roll 8, RRSCC.

216. See Virgil Hillyer to Charles F. Benjamin, clerk, Office of Commissioners of Claims, Nov. 9, 1877, ibid.

217. Claim of William Richardson, pp. 14–15, Limestone County, Alabama, reel 23, WSCC.

218. For mention of the "slaves' economy" in an ex-overseer's abolitionist narrative, see John Roles, *Inside Views of Slavery on Southern Plantations* (New York, 1864), 9–10. On foraging from enslaved people in Fayetteville, North Carolina, see John Richard Dennett, *The South as It Is: 1865–1866*, ed. Henry M. Christman (New York, 1965), 177; on Alabama, see Trowbridge, *South*, 437–38. Many ex-slaves petitioned the army during the Civil War to go back and get children, beds, furniture, and clothing. See statement of Harriet Anne Maria Banks, Nov. 14, 1864, and statement of Jane Kamper, Nov. 14, 1864, both reprinted in Ira Berlin et al., eds., *The Wartime Genesis of Free Labor: The Upper South*, ser. 1, vol. 2, *Freedom* (1993), 518–19; and affidavit of Fany Nelson, Apr. 12, 1867, Louisville, Ky., reprinted in ibid., 712. For a pe-

tition from an Arkansas ex-slave to the secretary of war, see 1" Sergent Alex Shaw to Mr. E. M. Stanton, Nov. 19, 1865, reprinted in Berlin, Joseph P. Reidy, and Leslie S. Rowland, eds., *The Black Military Experience*, ser. 2, *Freedom* (1982), 776.

219. Claim of King Goodloe, judgment, Colbert County, Alabama, SCC. Only four allowed claims came from ex-slaves in that county.

220. John Rex to James D. Davidson (1855), quoted in Lewis, *Coal, Iron, and Slaves*, 126.

221. John Patrick Diggins, *On Hallowed Ground: Abraham Lincoln and the Foundations of American History* (New Haven, 2000), 270–71.

222. Amounts converted from 1877 dollars using John J. McCusker, *How Much Is That in Real Money? A Historical Price Index for Use as a Deflator of Money Values in the Economy of the United States* (Worcester, 1992).

223. Frederick Cooper, *From Slaves to Squatters: Plantation Labor and Agriculture in Zanzibar and Coastal Kenya, 1890–1925* (New Haven, 1980), 251 n. 55; Sara S. Berry, "Custom, Class, and the 'Informal Sector': Or Why Marginality Is Not Likely to Pay," Working Papers, African Studies Center, Boston University, n.s., no. 1 (1978), 19; Roderick A. McDonald, *The Economy and Material Culture of Slaves: Goods and Chattels on the Sugar Plantations of Jamaica and Louisiana* (Baton Rouge, 1993); Mary Karasch, "Suppliers, Sellers, Servants, and Slaves," in *Cities and Society in Colonial Latin America*, ed. Louisa Schell Hoberman and Susan Migden Socolow (Albuquerque, N.M., 1986), 251–83.

224. George Alter, Claudia Goldin, and Elyce Rotella, "The Savings of Ordinary Americans: The Philadelphia Savings Fund Society in the Mid-Nineteenth Century," *Journal of Economic History* 54 (Dec. 1994): 738.

225. Claudia Goldin and Robert A. Margo, "Wages, Prices, and Labor Markets before the Civil War," in *Strategic Factors in Nineteenth Century American Economic History*, ed. Claudia Goldin and Hugh Rockoff (Chicago, 1992), 101.

226. See, for example, Douglass, *Narrative*, 51, 64–65.

CHAPTER THREE

1. Maria Perkins to Richard Perkins, Oct. 8, 1852, quoted in Ulrich B. Phillips, *Life and Labor in the Old South* (Boston, 1929), 212. Warm thanks to David Brion Davis for this reference. Staunton is about fifty miles west of Charlottesville, just over the mountains. For a similar letter, see Sim Neal to "Dear mother and brothers and Sisters," Sept. 8, 1827, Neal Family Papers, no. 4370, SHC. On the Court Square area of Charlottesville, see Gayle M. Schulman, "Site of Slave Block?" *Magazine of Albemarle County History* 58 (2000): 64–86.

2. Testimony of William Golding in claim of Linda Roberts, p. 10, Liberty County, Georgia, SCC.

3. Ex-drivers filed five of the seventeen claims for over $500 in one task system county, even though they made up less than 1 percent of the slave population in the cotton belt in 1860. See Michael P. Johnson, "Work, Culture, and the Slave Community: Slave Occupations in the Cotton Belt in 1860," *Labor History* 27 (Summer 1986): 333. Three field hands, four skilled slaves, three house servants, one free black, and one white man filed the other claims over $500 in Liberty County, Georgia.

4. Roswell King, "On the Management of the Butler Estate" (1828), quoted in Julia Floyd Smith, *Slavery and Rice Culture in Low Country Georgia, 1750–1860* (Knoxville, 1985), 69.

5. Testimony of Simon Harris in claim of Thomas Irving, p. 2, Liberty County, Georgia, SCC.

6. Claim of William Richardson, p. 17, Limestone County, WSCC. Richardson had hired out for years but began hiring his young relatives "just before the war . . . bursted out." For testimony about slaves who hired other slaves, see the testimony of John Foddis in claim of John Aiken, p. 7, Clarke County, Alabama, SCC; claim of Benjamin Holder, p. 7, Chattooga County, Georgia, SCC; and claim of Austin Wright, p. 2, Fulton County, Georgia, SCC.

7. Testimony of Moses W. White in claim of Minerva Boyd, n.p., Warren County, Mississippi, SCC.

8. Testimony of John Ford in claim of Benjamin Sterling Turner, pp. 8–10, Dallas County, Alabama, SCC.

9. Charles Ball, *Slavery in the United States: A Narrative of the Life and Adventures of Charles Ball* (Lewistown, Pa., 1836), 505.

10. Claim of Emily Frazier, p. 3, Limestone County, Alabama, SCC.

11. Claim of Samuel Harris, p. 2, Liberty County, Georgia, SCC. See also claim of Pompey Bacon, p. 2, ibid., and testimony of Samuel Harris in claim of Peter Winn, p. 9, ibid. On hiring among rural slaves in the East Texas plains, see Kenneth L. Brown and Doreen C. Cooper, "Structural Continuity in an African-American Slave and Tenant Community," *Historical Archaeology* 24, no. 4 (1990): 15–16.

12. Proceedings of Mayor's Court, Fredericksburg, Virginia (no. 4141), Apr. 18, 1821, UVA.

13. Testimony of Moses W. White in claim of Minerva Boyd, Warren County, Mississippi, SCC; claim of Emily Frazier, p. 5, Limestone County, Alabama, reel 21, WSCC.

14. Testimony of Richard Johnson in claim of Wiley Jackson, n.p., Escambia County, Florida, SCC.

15. Testimony of William Chase in claim of John Holdman, p. 7, Adams County, Mississippi, SCC. On sharing rooms, see claim of Harrison Woodcock, n.p., Hinds County, Mississippi, SCC.

16. Testimony of Mark Austin in claim of Toney Barnes, p. 17, Hinds County, Mississippi, SCC. Austin was black but may or may not have been a slave.

17. Claim of Hamlet DeLegal, pp. 1–2, Liberty County, Georgia, SCC.

18. Claim of Frank Sheppard, p. 2, Hinds County, Mississippi, SCC. See also the claim of Frank Sheppard, supplemental testimony, Apr. 30, 1878, ibid., and testimony of Gallian Wickliff in claim of Henry Anderson, pp. 11–12, Adams County, Mississippi, SCC.

19. Testimony of Thomas C. Hampton in claim of Moses Hampton, p. 16, Cherokee County, Alabama, reel 2, WSCC. See also claim of Peter Stanton, pp. 1–3, Marlborough County, South Carolina, SCC; claim of Alfred Barnard, p. 7, Chatham County, Georgia, SCC; claim of Francis Keaton, p. 3, ibid.; and claim of Lewis Miller, pp. 3–5, ibid.

20. Frederick Law Olmsted, *The Cotton Kingdom: A Traveller's Observations on Cotton*

and Slavery in the American Slave States, 1853–1861 (1861; reprint, New York, 1996), 471; claim of Josephine James, supplemental testimony, Liberty County, Georgia, SCC.

21. Testimony of Robert Smalls, pp. 102–3, File 3, AFIC.

22. Ibid., p. 101.

23. Testimony of Peter Stevens in claim of Toney Elliott, p. 9, Liberty County, Georgia, SCC.

24. Mamie Barkley, Jefferson County, Mississippi, interview in John B. Cade, "Out of the Mouths of Ex-Slaves," *Journal of Negro History* 20 (July 1935): 331. According to an ex-slave from nearby Louisiana, "this [working truck patches] was called the edge of slavery." Annie Washington, quoted by A. W. Casterman in ibid., 332.

25. Claim of Joseph Sneed, p. 4, Chatham County, Georgia, SCC. See also the testimony of Celia Brown in claim of David Delions, p. 2, ibid., and claim of William Richardson, p. 17, Limestone County, Alabama, WSCC.

26. Claim of Martha Patton, pp. 1–2, Hinds County, Mississippi, SCC.

27. Claim of Jane Dent, p. 1, Adams County, Mississippi, SCC.

28. Testimony of J. H. Butler in claim of Thomas Butler, supplemental testimony, p. 2, Chatham County, Georgia, SCC. See also the testimony of Annetta Stewart in claim of Prince Stewart, supplemental testimony, Liberty County, Georgia, SCC. On minding babies and fetching water, see testimony of Benjamin Sneed in claim of Joseph Sneed, p. 12, Chatham County, Georgia, SCC, and Frances Anne Kemble, *Journal of a Residence on a Georgian Plantation in 1838–1839* (New York, 1961), 87.

29. Ball, *Slavery in the United States*, 272. In return, these parents "were obliged . . . to find the children in bedding for the winter."

30. Testimony of Joshua Cassels [Cassell] in claim of George Gould, p. 9, Liberty County, Georgia, SCC.

31. Claim of George Gould, p. 3, ibid.

32. Testimony of Rosanna Houston in claim of Primus Wilson, p. 10, Chatham County, Georgia, SCC. Emphasis is in original. See also the claim of Samuel Osgood, pp. 1–4, Liberty County, Georgia, SCC.

33. Claim of Henry Stevens, p. 4, Liberty County, Georgia, SCC.

34. Claim of Horace Page, p. 17, Fauquier County, Virginia, SCC.

35. Claim of William Hardin, pp. 2–3, Adams County, Mississippi, SCC.

36. Ibid., p. 3. Hardin's brother was a "boy" at the time, according to a witness (testimony of Benjamin Taxer in ibid., p. 9).

37. Testimony of Tolliver Taylor in ibid., p. 12. Crawford Monroe, whose master forced him to move to the outskirts of Atlanta, managed for years to keep up ties with his relatives back home. In 1864, as a battle raged around the city, Monroe recalled, "I took this property from [my house] in Marietta to Savannah," near where he was born, "& stored it with my brother John Monroe" (claim of Crawford Monroe, p. 12, Fulton County, Georgia, SCC). On storage at a father's house, see the claim of William Golding, p. 2, Liberty County, Georgia, SCC. On storage at a brother-in-law's house, see the claim of Henry Hall, n.p., Dallas County, Alabama, SCC.

38. Claim of Emily Frazier, p. 5, Limestone County, Alabama, reel 21, WSCC. For

a stern view of parent-child relations during slavery, see Jacob Stroyer, *My Life in the South* (1879; reprint, Salem, Mass., 1898), 21. Stroyer believed that "it was a custom among the slaves not to allow their children under certain ages to enter into conversation with them."

39. Claim of Windsor Stevens, p. 2, Liberty County, Georgia, SCC.

40. Claim of Amanda Young, n.p., Tippah County, Mississippi, SCC.

41. Testimony of Joseph Baker in claim of Matilda McIntosh, Liberty County, Georgia, SCC-D. The commissioners could not believe that an enslaved woman "would earn & own a horse & both a buggy & a wagon" simply by sewing after hours, and without white witnesses to testify, they disallowed this claim. See judgment, claim of Matilda McIntosh, ibid.

42. Claim of Simon Middleton, p. 6, Chatham County, Georgia, SCC.

43. Robert B. Robinson and James D. Hardy Jr., "An *Actio de Peculio* in Ante-Bellum Alabama," *Journal of Legal History* 11, no. 3 (1990): 365. This partnership is notable because Moses' new master claimed the money in court; the legal battle that ensued in 1846 led the Alabama Supreme Court for the first time to rule formally on the issue of property ownership by slaves.

44. Testimony of Benjamin Hines in claim of Paris James, p. 9, Liberty County, Georgia, SCC.

45. Testimony of Andrew Stacy in claim of Nancy Bacon, pp. 1–2, ibid.

46. Testimony of Emanuel Armstead in claim of James Jackson, p. 14, Pulaski County, Arkansas, SCC.

47. Claim of Eliza James, p. 2, Liberty County, Georgia, SCC.

48. Testimony of Caroline Walker in claim of Isaac Allen, p. 11, Limestone County, Alabama, reel 21, WSCC.

49. Claim of Isaac Allen, pp. 2–4, Limestone County, Alabama, reel 21, WSCC.

50. Testimony of Charlotte Thompson in claim of John Wilson, p. 7, Liberty County, Georgia, SCC.

51. Testimony of Raymond Cay Sr. in claim of York Stevens, supplemental testimony, Liberty County, Georgia, SCC.

52. Claim of Charlotte Thompson, p. 3, Chatham County, Georgia, SCC.

53. Testimony of Abraham Johnson in ibid., p. 13.

54. Claim of Charlotte Thompson, p. 3, Chatham County, Georgia, SCC. Isaac Allen said that, along with his mother, the three orphans who lived with him were "my family" (claim of Isaac Allen, pp. 2–4, Limestone County, Alabama, reel 21, WSCC).

55. Testimony of Thomas Richardson in claim of Rosetta Newsom (Byrd's wife), p. 25, Claiborne County, Mississippi, SCC.

56. Ibid., p. 40.

57. Testimony of Robert Boatsman in claim of Rosetta Newsom, p. 38, Claiborne County, Mississippi, SCC. All of these witnesses (Byrd's former workforce) denied any interest in this claim.

58. Josiah Henson, "Autobiography of the Reverend Josiah Henson," in *Four Fugitive Slave Narratives*, ed. Robin W. Winks (Reading, Mass., 1969), 18.

59. Claim of Burwell McShane, n.p., Lauderdale County, Mississippi, SCC. For a harrowing account of slaves' "worst fears of being sold down South," see Henson, "Autobiography," 51.

60. Ball, *Slavery in the United States*, 192–93.

61. Bryan Edwards (1801), quoted in *Sugar and Slavery: An Economic History of the British West Indies, 1623–1775*, ed. Richard Sheridan (Baltimore, 1973), 166. Edwards believed these "adoptions" often became "harsh" "apprenticeships." See his *The History, Civil and Commercial, of the British West Indies* (London, 1793), 2:56–77.

62. Crandall A. Shifflett ("The Household Composition of Rural Black Families: Louisa County, Virginia, 1880," *Journal of Interdisciplinary History* 6 [Autumn 1975]: 235–60) linked black familial structural change in the 1880s to economic factors. Ann Patton Malone (*Sweet Chariot: Slave Family and Household Structure in Nineteenth-Century Louisiana* [Chapel Hill, 1992], 32, 47, 258, 271), while still using the interpretive framework of structure and "desirable norm[s]," brilliantly draws out the "multiplicity of forms" of Louisiana slave families. The problem of defining the family as a unit of analysis is succinctly laid out in Megan Vaughan, "Which Family? Problems in the Reconstruction of the History of Family as an Economic and Cultural Unit," *Journal of African History* 24, no. 2 (1983): 275–83. For parallels in twentieth-century Africa, see Sara S. Berry, "Custom, Class, and the 'Informal Sector': Or Why Marginality Is Not Likely to Pay," Working Papers, African Studies Center, Boston University, n.s., no. 1 (1978), 18; Sara Berry, *No Condition Is Permanent: The Social Dynamics of Agrarian Change in Sub-Saharan Africa* (Madison, Wisc., 1993); Luise White, "Bodily Fluids and Usufruct: Controlling Property in Nairobi, 1917–1939," *Canadian Journal of African Studies* 24, no. 3 (1990): 418–38; and Landeg White, *Magomero: Portrait of an African Village* (Cambridge, Eng., 1987), 165–85. Anthropological and historical studies of Latin America have developed somewhat similar arguments, though not, to my knowledge, with the same attention to property and labor issues. See Ruth C. L. Cardoso, "Creating Kinship: The Fostering of Children in *Favela* Families in Brazil," in *Kinship Ideology and Practice in Latin America*, ed. Raymond T. Smith (Chapel Hill, 1984), and Stuart B. Schwartz, "Rethinking Palmares: Slave Resistance in Colonial Brazil," in *Slaves, Peasants, and Rebels: Reconsidering Brazilian Slavery* (Urbana, 1992), 103–36.

63. Claim of Samuel Elliott, p. 2, Liberty County, Georgia, SCC.

64. Claim of Benjamin Stenyard, pp. 6–7, Warren County, Mississippi, SCC.

65. Testimony of D. H. Alverson in claim of Alex[ander] Cash, n.p., Warren County, Mississippi, SCC. For inheritance across plantation lines, see the claim of Dennis Smith, p. 1, Chatham County, Georgia, SCC.

66. Claim of William Roberts, p. 1, Liberty County, Georgia, SCC.

67. Claim of William Drayton, judgment, Beaufort County, South Carolina, SCC.

68. Examples of bequests by fathers include the claim of Isaac Simpson, p. 1, Liberty County, Georgia, SCC, and claim of Wesley Jackson, pp. 1–2, Warren County, Mississippi, SCC. Examples of bequests by mothers include the claim of Henry Porter, p. 2, and claim of Harry Ripley, p. 2, both Liberty County, Georgia, SCC.

69. Claim of Henry Stephens, p. 2, Liberty County, Georgia, SCC. Stephens was an only child. See also the testimony of Jacob Dryer in claim of Samuel Maxwell, p. 5;

claim of William Cassels, p. 2; claim of Pulaski Baker, p. 2; and claim of Rachel Norman, p. 2, all Liberty County, Georgia, SCC.

70. Claim of Charles J. Williamson, p. 1, Beaufort County, South Carolina, SCC.

71. Testimony of Samuel Williamson in ibid., p. 10.

72. Claim of Belfield Hicks, p. 5, Warren County, Mississippi, SCC.

73. Claim of Frank James, p. 2, Liberty County, Georgia, SCC. See also claim of Martha Patton, pp. 18–19, Hinds County, Mississippi, SCC.

74. Claim of Maria Carter, p. 2, Hinds County, Mississippi, SCC. See also claim of Sarah Verkins, pp. 2–3, Warren County, Mississippi, SCC.

75. Testimony of Thomas Wright and of Hamilton Brown in claim of Hercules LeConte, p. 1, Liberty County, Georgia, SCC.

76. For an important formulation in African Studies of social networks as a form of wealth, see Jane Guyer, "Wealth in People, Wealth in Things: Introduction," *Journal of African History* 36, no. 1 (1995): 83–90, and Jane Guyer, "Wealth in People as Wealth in Knowledge: Accumulation and Composition in Equatorial Africa," *Journal of African History* 36, no. 1 (1995): 91–120.

77. [J. H. Ingraham], *The South-West. By a Yankee* (New York, 1835), 2:127, Huntington Library Rare Book Collection, San Marino, Calif.; William Howard Russell, *My Diary North and South* (1863; reprint, Gloucester, Mass., 1969), 77; Charles Lyell, *A Second Visit to the United States of North America* (New York, 1850), 1:264–66; Olmsted, *Cotton Kingdom*, 184–85. See also the testimony of Mary Dudley in claim of Alex Dudley, p. 1, Marlborough County, South Carolina, SCC. Records of a Louisiana plantation and archaeological digs in Virginia show that slaves used several different kinds of locks. See Roderick A. McDonald, *The Economy and Material Culture of Slaves: Goods and Chattels on the Sugar Plantations of Jamaica and Louisiana* (Baton Rouge, 1993), 145, and Barbara J. Heath, *Hidden Lives: The Archaeology of Slave Life at Thomas Jefferson's Poplar Forest* (Charlottesville, 1999), 63–64.

78. Freedmen's Bureau records contain far more evidence of theft among blacks than do the Southern Claims Commission records. See Registers of Complaints, 1866–68, Subassistant Commissioner for Savannah District, Georgia, Subordinate Field Offices, BRFAL. Only a few of the ex-slaves making claims before the Southern Claims Commission mentioned theft. See claim of Prince Cumming, Liberty County, Georgia, SCC, and claim of Millie Richardson, p. 3, Limestone County, Alabama, SCC. Some historians have discussed theft among slaves as part of a "moral economy" that sanctioned stealing from masters but punished stealing from fellow slaves. Such analysis treats theft as a form of resistance, a different framework than is emphasized here. See Margaret Washington Creel, *"A Peculiar People": Slave Religion and Community-Culture among the Gullahs* (New York, 1988), 181–82, 207, 239; Alex Lichtenstein, "'That Disposition to Theft, with Which They Have Been Branded': Moral Economy, Slave Management, and the Law," *Journal of Social History* 21 (Spring 1988): 413–40; and Eugene D. Genovese, *Roll, Jordan, Roll: The World the Slaves Made* (New York, 1972), 599–609.

79. Sam and Louisa Everett in George P. Rawick, ed., *The American Slave: A Composite Autobiography* (Westport, Conn., 1981), vol. 17, Florida Narratives, p. 126.

80. Claim of William Gilmore, p. 9, Liberty County, Georgia, SCC.

81. Testimony of William Winn in claim of David Stevens, p. 26, ibid.

82. [Mortimer Thomson], *What Became of the Slaves on a Georgia Plantation? Great Auction Sale of Slaves at Savannah, Georgia, March 2d & 3d, 1859. A Sequel to Mrs. Kemble's Journal* (n.p., 1863), 6, 10; Moses Grandy (1844), quoted in Walter Johnson, *Soul by Soul: Life inside the Antebellum Slave Market* (Cambridge, Mass., 1999), 64–65.

83. Claim of Joseph Bacon (1873) in Philip D. Morgan, "The Ownership of Property by Slaves in the Mid-Nineteenth-Century Low Country," *Journal of Southern History* 49, no. 3 (1983): 411. Many Louisiana plantations had house-search policies yet rarely exercised them (McDonald, *Economy and Material Culture of Slaves*, 148).

84. Emily P. Burke, *Reminiscences of Georgia* (Oberlin, Ohio, 1850), 112, Huntington Library Rare Book Collection, San Marino, Calif. Burke goes on to describe the slaves' gardens, their after-task work, their trading, and their purchases. On plantation layouts in North Carolina, see *Robert McNamara v. John Kerns et al.* 24 N.C. 66 (1841); on Virginia, see Larry McKee, "The Ideals and Realities behind the Design and Use of 19th Century Virginia Slave Cabins," in *The Art and Mystery of Historical Archaeology: Essays in Honor of James Deetz*, ed. Anne Elizabeth Yentsch and Mary C. Beaudry (Boca Raton, 1992), 200–210; on Louisiana and Tennessee, see John B. Rehder, *Delta Sugar: Louisiana's Vanishing Plantation Landscape* (Baltimore, 1999), 93–94, 99–100, and Brian W. Thomas, "Power and Community: The Archaeology of Slavery at the Hermitage Plantation," *American Antiquity* 63, no. 4 (1998): 537–39.

85. Thomas Bangs Thorpe, "Sugar and the Sugar Region of Louisiana," *Harper's New Monthly Magazine* 7 (Oct. 1853): 753.

86. R. Q. Mallard, *Plantation Life before Emancipation* (Richmond, Va., 1892), 18. See also Olmsted, *Cotton Kingdom*, 184–85. On nucleated plantations in northern Virginia, see Julian Ursyn Niemcewicz (1798), quoted in Mary V. Thompson, "'Better . . . Fed than Negroes Generally Are': The Diet of the Mount Vernon Slaves," unpublished paper presented at Montpelier Mansion, Laurel, Maryland, May 19, 1999, p. 12; on those in the Chesapeake region, see Patricia Samford, "The Archaeology of African-American Slavery and Material Culture," *William and Mary Quarterly* 53 (Jan. 1996): 87–114; on central Virginia, see Heath, *Hidden Lives*, 43–46, 62; Martha Ann Carter Dettor Collection (Accession 34298), The History of Lawrence Creek, ca. 1934, Personal Papers Collection, LV; and Douglas W. Sanford, "The Archaeology of Plantation Slavery in Piedmont Virginia: Context and Process," in *Historical Archaeology of the Chesapeake*, ed. Paul A. Shackel and Barbara J. Little (Washington, D.C., 1994), 125–27; on tidewater Virginia, see Henry C. Knight (1824), quoted in James B. Slaughter, *Settlers, Southerners, Americans: The History of Essex County, Virginia 1608–1984* (Salem, W.Va., 1985), 136; on southern Louisiana, see Thorpe, "Sugar and the Sugar Region of Louisiana," 753, 759; William Howard Russell (1863), quoted in McDonald, *Economy and Material Culture of Slaves*, 51; and Ingraham, *South-West*, 1:236. Not every master liked what slaves did with their yards. For criticism by an Alabama slaveowner, see James O. Breeden, ed., *Advice among Masters: The Ideal in Slave Management in the Old South* (Westport, Conn., 1980), 120.

87. Barbara Wells Sarudy, *Gardens and Gardening in the Chesapeake, 1700–1805* (Baltimore, 1998), 54–55. "Huck patch" was the term used for such gardens in Baltimore in the early 1800s.

88. Hendrik Hartog, "Pigs and Positivism," in *Folk Law: Essays in the Theory and Practice of Lex Non Scripta*, vol. 1, ed. Alison Dundes Renteln and Alan Dundes (Madison, Wisc., 1994), 711–50.

89. Samuel B. Ruggles, quoted by James Parton (1867), and reprinted in William Cronon, *Nature's Metropolis: Chicago and the Great West* (New York, 1991), 226. The fast-growing city of Chicago, as contemporaries observed, built much of its fortune on the agricultural wealth concentrated in hogs.

90. Testimony of Spencer Cummins in *Thomas Matthews v. James Clarke*, Dec. 21, 1867, PCBerk, RG 393, Part IV.

91. Testimony of Lydia Brown in claim of Lido Brown, p. 6, Chatham County, Georgia, SCC.

92. Rough estimates from judgments, Walker County, Georgia, SCC. In 1991 dollars, a hog would cost about $91 and a cow about $250. Amounts converted from 1877 dollars using John J. McCusker, *How Much Is That in Real Money? A Historical Price Index for Use as a Deflator of Money Values in the Economy of the United States* (Worcester, 1992).

93. Testimony of William Matthews in claim of Henry Hall, n.p., Dallas County, Alabama, SCC. See also claim of Linda Roberts, for estate of Caesar Roberts, deceased, p. 4, Liberty County, Georgia, SCC, and Julia Floyd Smith, *Slavery and Rice Culture*, 122.

94. Testimony of Francis Maples in claim of Henry Slaughter, p. 8, Madison County, Alabama, SCC. Union soldiers took two of Maples's horses at the same time, yet Maples did not try to weaken Slaughter's claim by saying all the horses really belonged to him. See also "General Affidavit" of Joseph W. Thompson in claim of Benjamin Thompson, Colbert County, Alabama, reel 6, WSCC.

95. Testimony of Matilda David in claim of Anthony Friend, p. 8, Limestone County, Alabama, SCC.

96. On foraging hogs and their "marks," see Olmsted, *Cotton Kingdom*, 185. On Low Country slaves' marking of poultry, see Russell, *My Diary North and South*, 77. In the same vein, Russell also noted that masters felt sure that slaves would not steal jewelry from them because jewelry was designed to be distinctive. An 1848 South Carolina Appeals Court decision mentioned hogs kept by slaves and "marked as their own." See *Richardson v. Broughton*, 3 Strob. 1 (1848).

97. *McNamara v. Kerns*.

98. Testimony of John Keyser in *Matthews v. Clarke*. Keyser owned only three slaves. As one of those slaves testified later, "This mark was common to all Mr. Keyser's people" and "there were five (5) people [including himself] that used this mark." See testimony of Spencer Cummins in *Matthews v. Clarke*.

99. Testimony of James Long in *Matthews v. Clarke*.

100. Testimony of John Hill in ibid.; testimony of James Murray in ibid.; testimony of George G. Murray in ibid. James Clarke, the white son-in-law of Mr. Keyser (Matthews's former master), killed three hogs that were wandering on or near his property; ex-slave Matthews sued Clarke for trespass and damages—and won. On masters weighing (and acknowledging slaves' claims on) tobacco for slaves to sell, see testimony of George S. Simmons in claim of Horace Herndon, pp. 3–4, Lauderdale County, Alabama, reel 18, WSCC.

101. Albert Pike, "Letters from Arkansas," 213, reprinted in Eugene L. Schwaab, ed., *Travels in the Old South: Selected from the Periodicals of the Times* (Lexington, Ky., 1973).

102. *State v. John Davis*, 24 N.C. 153 (1841).

103. "Record Book of Marks & Brands No. A," 037.908.1, Stock Marks, 1732–1809, 1835, Edgecombe Co. Misc. Records, NCSA.

104. Testimony of Meyer Levy in claim of Jackson French, pp. 24–25, Claiborne County, Mississippi, SCC. On marks belonging to a white woman, see testimony of James Clarke in *Matthews v. Clarke*. For other evidence of whites using marks, see testimony of John Mingoe in *Trial of Chance*, Sept. 26, 1805, Amelia County, Virginia, CBF.

105. On slave cabin occupancy, see Robert William Fogel, *Without Consent or Contract: The Rise and Fall of American Slavery* (New York, 1989), 184–85.

106. Testimony of Abner Wilson in claim of Albert Wilson, pp. 3–4, Liberty County, Georgia, SCC; testimony of Marlborough Jones in claim of Ben Howard, p. 7, ibid.

107. Testimony of Clarinda Lowe in claim of James Anderson, p. 6, Liberty County, Georgia, SCC.

108. Testimony of Malinda Ward in claim of Maria Smith, n.p., Warren County, Mississippi, SCC. Ward apparently had to convince the skeptical claims commissioner that she could "count 100 with rapidity and readily add numbers up as large as 13+14."

109. Testimony of Henry Harris in claim of Samuel Osgood, p. 6, Liberty County, Georgia, SCC.

110. Testimony of Peter Lambright in claim of William James, p. 4, ibid. For Mississippi slaves bragging over property, see the testimony of Louisa Lattimer in claim of Andrew Black, p. 13, Warren County, Mississippi, SCC.

111. Testimony of Rachel Osgood in claim of Samuel Osgood, p. 8, ibid.

112. Testimony of Henrietta McLaughlin in claim of Lucy Lee (Ennis Royal, administrator), p. 9, Hinds County, Mississippi, SCC.

113. Testimony of Samson Bacon in claim of Prince Stevens, p. 11, Liberty County, Georgia, SCC. See also testimony of Woodson Armstead in claim of Edmund Pool, supplemental testimony, Nov. 18, 1873, Lauderdale County, Alabama, reel 19, WSCC.

114. Martha Stuart, interview (ca. 1938), quoted in McDonald, *Economy and Material Culture of Slaves*, 146. When James Presley Ball, himself a free man of color, set up one of the world's first photographic studios in Richmond, enslaved people jostled with whites to have their pictures taken. See [James Presley Ball], *Ball's Splendid Mammoth Pictorial Tour of the United States, Comprising Views of the African Slave-Trade; of Northern and Southern Cities; of Cotton and Sugar Plantations; of the Mississippi, Ohio, and Susquehanna Rivers, Niagara Falls, &c. Compiled for the Panorama* (Cincinnati, 1855), 7–8.

115. This was the counterpart to the practice of allotting slaves a general "nigger field." See claim of York Stevens, p. 3, Liberty County, Georgia, SCC. See also Mallard, *Plantation Life before Emancipation*, 17–18.

116. Testimony of Alexander Seals in claim of Monroe Hill, n.p., Marshall County,

Mississippi, SCC; claim of William Cook, p. 1, Marlborough County, South Carolina, SCC. On storing rice in cabins, see claim of Adam LeCounte, p. 1, Liberty County, Georgia, SCC. On storing personal items in cabins, see Charles Nordhoff, *The Freedmen of South Carolina: Some Account of their Appearances, Character, Conditions, and Peculiar Customs* (New York, 1863), 17, and Breeden, ed., *Advice among Masters*, 128–29.

117. Testimony of John Swinney in claim of Edward Broaddy, p. 3, Marlborough County, South Carolina, SCC; claim of John Swinney, p. 2, ibid.

118. Testimony of John Swinney in claim of Edward Broaddy, p. 3, Marlborough County, South Carolina, SCC; claim of John Swinney, p. 2, ibid.; testimony of Edward Broaddy in claim of John Swinney, p. 3, ibid. For a similar arrangement between two brothers, see the testimony of Simon Mudd in claim of Jacob Allman, p. 15, ibid.

119. Claim of Essex Dargan, p. 1, Marlborough County, South Carolina, SCC.

120. Testimony of Samuel Fuller in claim of Essex Dargan, p. 3, ibid.

121. Claim of Samuel Fuller, p. 1, ibid.

122. Claim of Richard Traynor, p. 6, Davidson County, Tennessee, SCC.

123. Testimony of Joseph Bacon in claim of Jacob Quarterman, p. 9, Liberty County, Georgia, SCC.

124. Testimony of Edward Quarterman in claim of Jacob Quarterman, p. 11, ibid. See also claim of Daniel Bryant, p. 2, ibid., and claim of Nancy Bacon, p. 1, ibid. On money in Virginia slave cabins, see Heath, *Hidden Lives*, 63–64.

125. They continue to do so today. On the marking and "earmarking" of money by white Americans, see Viviana A. Zelizer, *The Social Meaning of Money: Pin Money, Paychecks, Poor Relief, and Other Currencies* (Princeton, 1997). Archaeologists have dug up coins from slave quarters in Virginia, Kentucky, and Tennessee (Heath, *Hidden Lives*, 51; Amy L. Young, "Task and Gang Labor: Work Patterns at a Kentucky Plantation," *North American Archaeologist* 18, no. 1 [1997]: 50; Thomas, "Power and Community," 545).

126. Claim of Jacob Quarterman, supplemental testimony, June 16, 1878, Liberty County, Georgia, SCC.

127. Claim of Rachel Bromfield, p. 6, Chatham County, Georgia, SCC.

128. Testimony of Philip Hart in claim of Julia Ann McCaskell, n.p., Warren County, Mississippi, SCC.

129. Testimony of Alexander Kenner, p. 98, File 7, AFIC. When one free black man in Virginia made a pricey bet with an enslaved forge-man at the local iron forge, he asked a white worker to act as "witness to the[ir] . . . bargain" (John Rex to James D. Davidson (1855), quoted in Ronald L. Lewis, *Coal, Iron, and Slaves: Industrial Slavery in Maryland and Virginia, 1715–1865* [Westport, Conn., 1979], 126).

130. Stroyer, *My Life in the South*, 57–59.

131. Charles A. Raymond, "The Religious Life of the Negro Slave," *Harper's New Monthly Magazine* 27 (1863): 824–25.

132. Testimony of Milly in *Trial of Hubbard*, Jan. 20, 1817, Southampton County, Virginia, box 3, CBF.

133. Henry Deedes, *Sketches of the South and West* (Edinburgh, 1869), 143–46.

134. See, for example, *Trial of Peter*, Oct. 16, 1828, Court of Oyer and Terminer, Essex County, Virginia, Order Book 45, 1823–26, microfilm reel 94, Local Records, LV.

135. Testimony of Cyrus Kirkman in claim of Stephen Coleman, p. 7, Lauderdale County, Alabama, reel 17, WSCC. For a similar account, see testimony of Lorena Smith in claim of Daniel Murfee, p. 12, Warren County, Mississippi, SCC.

136. Mallard, *Plantation Life before Emancipation*, 133. Emphasis is in original. On enslaved churchgoers' clothes in Missouri, see H[enry] C[lay] Bruce, *The New Man. Twenty-Nine Years a Slave. Twenty-Nine Years a Free Man. Recollections of H. C. Bruce* (York, Pa., 1895), 72, 84.

137. Enos Duvall (1783), quoted in John H. Sprinkle Jr., "The Contents of Charles Cox's Mill House Chest," *Historical Archaeology* 25, no. 3 (1991): 92.

138. Claim of Pompey Bacon, p. 1, Liberty County, Georgia, SCC. Emphasis is in original. Black churchgoers have long sung of preparing for death by putting on a "long white robe."

139. [Thomson], *What Became of the Slaves on a Georgia Plantation?*, 6, 10.

140. As Walter Johnson notes, several published slave narratives mixed memories of property with memories of being sold. Johnson, *Soul by Soul*, 64–65.

141. Claim of William Gilmore, p. 4, Liberty County, Georgia, SCC. On Sunday clothes in Louisiana, see Russell, *My Diary North and South*, 373, quoted in McDonald, *Economy and Material Culture of Slaves*, 150; and in North Carolina, see Allen Parker, *Recollections of Slavery Times* (Worcester, Mass., 1895), 20.

142. Claim of Paris James, p. 3, Liberty County, Georgia, SCC; testimony of Edward Miller in claim of James Miller, p. 9, ibid. See also Genovese, *Roll, Jordan, Roll*, 555–57, and A. J. H. Duganne, *Twenty Months in the Department of the Gulf* (New York, 1865), 79–80. The shoes the slaves owned often pinched terribly, so going barefoot was probably also the least painful way to get to church for those without wagons (Charles Joyner, *Down by the Riverside: A South Carolina Slave Community* [Urbana, 1984], 115–16). Elizabeth Ware Pearson (*Letters from Port Royal, 1862–1868* [Boston, 1906], 50) also noted blacks carrying their shoes, but she added that "[m]ost of them [the freedpeople] wear none."

143. Mallard, *Plantation Life before Emancipation*, 83. For a vivid description of slaves' Sunday clothes in Mississippi, see *American Cotton Planter and Soil of the South* (1861), quoted in John Hebron Moore, *The Emergence of the Cotton Kingdom in the Old Southwest: Mississippi, 1770–1860* (Baton Rouge, 1988), 106.

144. "Commonwealth agt. Matilda Grayson a free woman & Celia the slave of Mrs. Massey, of Spotsylvania," June 1, 1821, Proceedings of the Mayor's Court, Fredericksburg, Virginia (no. 4141), UVA.

145. "At a regular ch. meeting held Jany 2, 1842," p. 11, First African Baptist Church (Richmond, Virginia) Minute Books, 1841–1930, Miscellaneous Microfilm Reel 494 (Accession 28255), Church Records, LV. Thanks to Wallace Best for the phrase "take it to Jesus."

146. Ibid. "(This case was ably argued)," noted the church's recorder, suggesting that these proceedings may have looked something like a court. For an investigative "committee" of slaves within a white-controlled church, see Penfield Baptist Church Minutes (1856), in Edward L. Ayers, *Vengeance and Justice: Crime and Punishment in the 19th-Century American South* (New York, 1984), 124.

147. Samford, "Archaeology of African-American Slavery," 107–13; for Texas, see

Brown and Cooper, "Structural Continuity," 16–17; for Tennessee, see Thomas, "Power and Community," 545–47. As Samford notes, many archaeologists interpret these items as sacred objects slaves brought from Africa or reproduced items they remembered from Africa.

148. Gilbert Osofsky, *Puttin' on Ole Massa: The Slave Narratives of Henry Bibb, William Wells Brown, and Solomon Northup* (New York, 1969), 72–73. It didn't work; he got slapped by the first girl he tried to kiss.

149. Frederick Douglass, *Narrative of the Life of Frederick Douglass, an American Slave, Written by Himself,* ed. David W. Blight (1845; reprint, Boston, 1993), 49–50.

150. Testimony of Jacob in *Trial of Fanny,* Apr. 19, 1805, Charlotte County, Virginia, CBF.

151. Testimony of Billey in *Trial of Dick,* Mar. 18, 1802, Mecklenburg County, Virginia, CBF. On slaves prosecuted for poisoning, see Philip J. Schwarz, *Twice Condemned: Slaves and the Criminal Laws of Virginia, 1705–1865* (Baton Rouge, 1988), 200–205.

152. Testimony of Fanny in *Trial of Dick,* Mar. 18, 1802, Mecklenburg County, Virginia, CBF.

153. Bruce, *New Man,* 56. Their master changed his mind.

154. William Wells Brown, *Narrative of William W. Brown, a Fugitive Slave. Written by Himself* (1847; reprint, Boston, 1848), 91.

155. Osofsky, *Puttin' on Ole Massa,* 71.

156. Eugene Portlette Southall, "The Attitude of the Methodist Episcopal Church, South, toward the Negro from 1844 to 1870," *Journal of Negro History* 16, no. 4 (1931): 365.

157. Testimony of Hon. James Speed, p. 30, File 7, AFIC. On slaves' support of Charleston's black churches, see William F. Allen, Manuscript Diary and Letters, p. 16, Apr. 30, 1865, microfilm reel 33, roll 157, State Historical Society of Wisconsin, Madison. A black minister from Kentucky agreed. At the two large Methodist churches in his town, he testified, "a majority of the members are slaves" and their contributions paid off the bulk of the churches' debts. Rev. Bradwell himself was born a slave and accumulated enough money to buy himself. In order to "meet the requirements of the law," however, he made himself "nominally the slave of the church" at which he preached (testimony of Rev. Mr. Bradwell, p. 92, File 7, AFIC).

158. Raymond, "Religious Life of the Negro Slave," 482–83. For slaves' donations in Richmond, Va., see Ayers, *Vengeance and Justice,* 95.

159. Testimony of Rev. Mr. Ebbett, Sup't. of the State School for Idiots, Frankfort, Ky., Nov. 25, 1863, File 7, AFIC. See also Southall, "Attitude of the Methodist Episcopal Church," 365.

160. Raymond, "Religious Life of the Negro Slave," 480. For a similar account in Jackson, Mississippi, see Southall, "Attitude of the Methodist Episcopal Church," 365. As many readers will know, many churches, such as my grandparents' church in Paterson, New Jersey, still do this every Sunday. Others, like the one I grew up in, save this format for special occasions.

161. Testimony of Rev. Edward S. Woodson, Pastor of Colored Baptist Church, St. Louis, Mo., Dec. 1, 1863, File 7, AFIC.

162. Allen, Manuscript Diary and Letters, pp. 132–33, Feb. 21, 1864, microfilm reel 33, roll 157, State Historical Society of Wisconsin, Madison.

163. Fogel, *Without Consent or Contract*, 183. See also Mallard, *Plantation Life before Emancipation*, 50–51.

164. Claim of Samuel Harris, p. 2, Liberty County, Georgia, SCC.

165. Mallard, *Plantation Life before Emancipation*, 50–51.

166. Claim of Harriet Smith, p. 4, Beaufort County, South Carolina, SCC. See also claim of Jacob C. Allmon, pp. 1–2, 5, Marlborough County, South Carolina, SCC. On separate storage by a Maryland couple, see John Ridout (1783), quoted in Sprinkle, "Contents of Charles Cox's Mill House Chest," 91.

167. Testimony of William Matthews in claim of Henry Hall, n.p., Dallas County, Alabama, reel 6, WSCC.

168. Testimony of Samson Bacon in claim of Prince Stevens, p. 9, Liberty County, Georgia, SCC. See also claim of Prince Wallace, p. 2, Marlborough County, South Carolina, SCC; claim of Crawford Turnage, p. 1, ibid.; and claim of Matilda Anderson, pp. 2–3, Warren County, Mississippi, SCC.

169. Mary V. Thompson, "'They Appear to Live Comfortable Together': Private Life of the Mount Vernon Slaves," unpublished paper dated Jan. 20, 1999, 16. For a similar assertion by a slave woman from Kentucky, see the affidavit of Fany Nelson, Apr. 12, 1867, reprinted in Ira Berlin et al., eds., *The Wartime Genesis of Free Labor: The Upper South*, ser. 1, vol. 2, *Freedom: A Documentary History of Emancipation, 1861–1867* (New York, 1993), 712.

170. Testimony of Martha Bradshaw in claim of Thomas Drummond, pp. 5–6, Warren County, Mississippi, SCC; claim of Thomas Drummond, p. 3, ibid.

171. Testimony of Martha Bradshaw in claim of Thomas Drummond, pp. 5–6, Warren County, Mississippi, SCC. See also testimony of Mary Dudley in claim of Alexander Dudley, p. 3, Marlborough County, South Carolina, SCC.

172. Claim of Martha Patton, pp. 18–19, Hinds County, Mississippi, SCC.

173. Testimony of Mark Austin in claim of Maria Carter, pp. 11–12, Hinds County, Mississippi, SCC.

174. Testimony of Betsy Stamps in ibid.

175. Testimony of Levy Walker in claim of Sarah Verkins, p. 6, Warren County, Mississippi, SCC.

176. Testimony of Arthur Harris in claim of Wiley Jackson, n.p., Escambia County, Florida, SCC.

177. Claim of Abraham Walthour, p. 1, Liberty County, Georgia, SCC.

178. Testimony of John Stevens and William Gilmore in ibid., pp. 5–7. See also claim of Samuel Maxwell, supplemental testimony, Liberty County, Georgia, SCC.

179. Claim of Elvira Anderson, pp. 3–4, Warren County, Mississippi, SCC.

180. Testimony of Ellen Jenkins and of Sarah Ford in ibid., pp. 6–8.

181. Claim of William Cassels, p. 4, Liberty County, Georgia, SCC.

182. Claim of Harrison Woodcock, n.p., Hinds County, Mississippi, SCC; testimony of Mark Austin in claim of Toney Barnes, p. 17, ibid.; testimony of William Chase in claim of John Holdman, p. 7, Adams County, Mississippi, SCC; testimony of Richard Johnson in claim of Wiley Jackson, n.p., Escambia County, Florida, SCC.

183. Claim of Ellen Hampton, pp. 4–5, Cherokee County, Alabama, reel 2, WSCC. See also claim of Peter Winn, p. 4, Liberty County, Georgia, SCC.

184. Claim of Prince Stewart, p. 2, Liberty County, Georgia, SCC.

185. Claim of Toney Barnes, p. 12, Hinds County, Mississippi, SCC. Caroline Barnes, his wife, testified: "It was all my husbands. He and I made it" (testimony of Caroline Barnes in claim of Toney Barnes, p. 21, ibid.). For similar language in a postwar civil court, see *State v. John Griffin*, Jan. term 1877, CC, box 2, folder 9c, OCHM.

186. Testimony of Elijah Possroell in claim of Henry Brooker, n.p., Lexington County, South Carolina, SCC.

187. See Herbert G. Gutman, *The Black Family in Slavery and Freedom, 1750–1925* (New York, 1976), 270–77.

188. Claim of Susan Bennett, p. 2, Liberty County, Georgia, SCC.

189. Testimony of Nancy Hardeman in claim of William Hardeman, p. 12, Hinds County, Mississippi, SCC.

190. Claim of Jane Holmes, p. 2, Liberty County, Georgia, SCC.

191. Testimony of Martha Berry in claim of Albert Deval, n.p., Warren County, Mississippi, SCC.

192. Testimony of George Richardson in claim of Emily Frazier, p. 20, Limestone County, Alabama, SCC.

193. Testimony of Samson Bacon in claim of Prince Stevens, p. 11, Liberty County, Georgia, SCC.

194. Testimony of Brister Fleming in ibid., p. 18.

CHAPTER FOUR

1. Eric Foner, *Reconstruction: America's Unfinished Revolution, 1863–1877* (New York, 1988).

2. There is a rich literature on how ex-slaves carved out a presence in formal political processes through voluntary groups such as clubs, militias, parades, and washerwomen's informal networks. See Glenda Elizabeth Gilmore, *Gender and Jim Crow: Women and the Politics of White Supremacy in North Carolina, 1896–1920* (Chapel Hill, 1996); Julie Saville, *The Work of Reconstruction: From Slave to Wage Laborer in South Carolina, 1860–1870* (New York, 1994); Eric Foner, *Nothing but Freedom: Emancipation and Its Legacy* (Baton Rouge, 1983); and Tera W. Hunter, *To 'Joy My Freedom: Southern Black Women's Lives and Labors after the Civil War* (Cambridge, Mass., 1997).

3. On Africans' strategic use of formal institutions, see Michael J. Lowy, "A Good Name Is Worth More than Money: Strategies of Court Use in Urban Ghana," in *The Disputing Process—Law in Ten Societies*, ed. Laura Nader and Harry F. Todd Jr. (New York, 1978), 181–208; David William Cohen and E. S. Atieno Odhiambo, *Burying SM: The Politics of Knowledge and the Sociology of Power in Africa* (Portsmouth, N.H., 1992); Sara Berry, *No Condition Is Permanent: The Social Dynamics of Agrarian Change in Sub-Saharan Africa* (Madison, Wisc., 1993); Martin Chanock, "A Peculiar Sharpness: An Essay on Property in the History of Customary Law in Colonial Africa," *Journal of African History* 32, no. 1 (1991): 65–88; Richard Roberts and William Worger, "Law, Colonialism and Conflicts over Property in Sub-Saharan Africa," *African Eco-*

nomic History 25 (1997): 1–7; Roger Gocking, "Competing Systems of Inheritance before the British Courts of the Gold Coast Colony," *International Journal of African Historical Studies* 23, no. 4 (1990): 601–18.

4. Abraham Winfield and 10 others to O. O. Howard, Jan. 27, 1866, entry 15, Letters Received, Mar. 1865–June 1872, Correspondence, Records of the Commissioner, BRFAL, FSSP A-433.

5. Affidavit of Wm. S. Metzler in *State v. Alonzo Mitchell*, Oct. 24, 1877, CC, box 2, folder 15, OCHM. He made this threat even though both plaintiff and defendant were black.

6. Affidavit of Governor Manning, Aug. 17, 1867, in *United States v. Governor Manning*, Aug. 30, 1867, PCSum, box 4, PCNSC, RG 393, Part I. See also anonymous to Lt. F. L. Shoemaker, San Antonio, Texas, Nov. 19, 1869, box 1, entry 4851, Affidavits in Civil Affairs Cases, 1867–70, Dept. of Texas and 5th Military District (P), 1865–70, RG 393, Part I; and proceedings of a meeting of freedpeople at Newport Church, Liberty County, Georgia, Dec. 24, 1866, in Legislative Proceedings, 39th Congress, 2nd sess., Committee on Freedmen's Affairs, RG 233, FSSP D-16.

7. John Hope Franklin, ed., *Reminiscences of an Active Life: The Autobiography of John Roy Lynch* (Chicago, 1970), 61. Thanks to Christopher Waldrep for this reference. Beginning in 1863, a number of northern organizations sent teachers, many of them women, to parts of the South to set up schools for the freedpeople. See Willie Lee Rose, *Rehearsal for Reconstruction: The Port Royal Experiment* (London, 1964).

8. Testimony of Laura Towne, p. 69, File 3, AFIC. On Mississippi, see Franklin, ed., *Reminiscences of an Active Life*, 61–65.

9. Frank W. Klingberg, *The Southern Claims Commission* (Berkeley, 1955), 65–72, 76–84.

10. Ibid., 50–56.

11. Interrogatories prepared by the Commissioners for the use of the special commissioners, June 12, 1871, Vol. 1, Journal of the Commissioners, Mar. 16, 1871–Mar. 9, 1880, M87, roll 1, RRSCC. See also "First General Report," Dec. 14, 1871, in Journal of the Commissioners, ibid.

12. Final Report to the Secretary of War, pp. 165–66, AFIC; Edward L. Pierce, "Light on the Slavery Question: The Negroes in South Carolina," unmarked news clipping, n.p., Feb. 3, 1862, entry 574, BE 1861–64, Port Royal Correspondence Received by Sec. Treasury Chase, Nov. 25, 1861–Aug. 7, 1862, CWSAT; testimony of B. K. Lee Jr., p. 4, File 3, AFIC.

13. Testimony of Frederick A. Eustis, pp. 153–54, File 3, AFIC.

14. Testimony of Tennessee District witnesses, p. 45, File 7, AFIC.

15. Edward L. Pierce to Treas. Sec. Salmon P. Chase, June 2, 1862, entry 574, BE 1861–64, Port Royal Correspondence Received by Sec. Treasury Chase, CWSAT. On white northerners' views of blacks, see Foner, *Reconstruction*, and Saville, *Work of Reconstruction*.

16. Rose, *Rehearsal for Reconstruction.*

17. Testimony of Brig. Gen. Rufus Saxton (1863), in Philip D. Morgan, "Work and Culture: The Task System and the World of Lowcountry Blacks, 1700–1880," *William and Mary Quarterly* 39 (Oct. 1982): 593.

18. Testimony of Mr. Wm. E. Glover, p. 40, File 7, AFIC. See also testimony of Dr. T. S. Bell, p. 13, ibid.

19. Testimony of Capt. R. J. Hinton, p. 3, File 8, AFIC.

20. Ibid., p. 6.

21. Testimony of Hon. James Speed, pp. 23–24, File 7, AFIC. See also Pierce, "Light on the Slavery Question"; testimony of Harry McMillan, p. 120, File 3, AFIC; testimony of Alexander P. Ketchum, pp. 135–38, ibid.; and testimony of Frederick A. Eustis, pp. 151–52, 163, ibid.

22. Testimony of Brig. Gen. Rufus Saxton (1863) in Morgan, "Work and Culture," 593.

23. Testimony of Henry G. Judd (1863), in Morgan, "Work and Culture," 593. Well into the twentieth century, many observers assumed slaves could never hold property; the definitive work on the Southern Claims Commission states that only "[a] very small number of claims were filed by former slaves, for the obvious reason that during the war years they were virtually a propertyless class. Most of their claims, therefore, were disallowed for lack of a clear title, or for fraudulent transfer of title by former masters on the approach of the federal army" (Klingberg, *Southern Claims Commission*, 100).

24. Foner, *Reconstruction*, 143; Donald G. Nieman, *To Set the Law in Motion: The Freedmen's Bureau and the Legal Rights of Blacks, 1865–1868* (Millwood, N.Y., 1979), 9–10.

25. Testimony of Dudley J. Smith in claim of Henry Hall, n.p., Dallas County, Alabama, reel 6, WSCC.

26. *United States (Dinah Nelson) v. Anderson Sanders*, Sept. 9, 1867, PCSum, box 1, PCNSC, RG 393, Part I.

27. Testimony of Amelia in *United States v. Moses*, July 29, 1862, Beaufort, South Carolina, MM2734, entry 15, RG 153. On tactical use of courts in modern Ghana, see Lowy, "Good Name Is Worth More than Money," 181–208.

28. See Spl. Agt. Jno. R. Henry to Fisk, Knoxville, Tenn., May 29, 1866, Registered Letters Received, June 1865–Apr. 1869, Office of the Assistant Commissioner, Tennessee, entry 3379, BRFAL, FSSP A-6269; J. E. Eldredge to Sir, July 29, 1867, Bladenboro, North Carolina, reprinted in Ira Berlin, Steven F. Miller, and Leslie S. Rowland, "Afro-American Families in the Transition from Slavery to Freedom," *Radical History Review* 42 (1988): 98–99; and Laura F. Edwards, "Sexual Violence, Gender, Reconstruction, and the Extension of Patriarchy in Granville County, North Carolina," *North Carolina Historical Review* 68, no. 3 (1991): 253.

29. Katherine M. Franke, "Becoming a Citizen: Reconstruction Era Regulation of African American Marriages," *Yale Journal of Law & the Humanities* 11 (1999): 290–91.

30. Testimony of Warren Ramsay in *United States v. Anderson Sanders*, Sept. 9, 1867, PCSum, box 1, PCNSC, RG 393, Part I.

31. Testimony of Anderson Sanders in ibid.

32. Testimony of Wm. J. Minor, Apr. 25, 1865, reprinted in Ira Berlin, Steven F. Miller, Joseph P. Reidy, and Leslie S. Rowland, eds., *The Wartime Genesis of Free Labor: The Lower South*, ser. 1, vol. 3, *Freedom: A Documentary History of Emancipation, 1861–*

1867 (New York, 1990), 602; testimony of Charles in *United States v. Moses,* July 29, 1862, Beaufort, South Carolina, MM2734, RG 153; testimony of Robert Francis in *Richard Hamilton v. Robert Francis,* July 5, 1866, p. 43, entry 4352, Proceedings of Freedmen's Court, Dec. 1865–June 1867, Assistant Subassistant Commissioner, Yorktown, Virginia, BRFAL.

33. "Regular meeting of the church," Dec. 1, 1879, p. 131, First African Baptist Church (Richmond, Virginia) Minute Books, 1841–1930, Miscellaneous Microfilm Reel 494 (Accession 28255), Church Records, LV.

34. "Report of July 5, 1875," p. 7, ibid.

35. Minutes of First African Church, Oct. 1, 1888, p. 393, ibid.

36. Elizabeth Pleck, "Wife Beating in Nineteenth-Century America," *Victimology* 4, no. 1 (1979): 69.

37. Testimony of Sancho Richardson in *Lot Richardson v. January Richardson,* Apr. 24, 1868, Provost Court, Beaufort, South Carolina, box 2, PCNSC, RG 393, Part I; testimony of January Richardson in *Lot Richardson v. January Richardson,* ibid.

38. Affidavit of Margaret Clark, Dec. 1871, 037.326.5, CAP.

39. Mary Ames, *From a New England Woman's Diary in Dixie in 1865* (Springfield, Mass., 1906), 43–44; *Dolly Green v. Linda Allen,* June 18, 1868, PCB, Sept. 1865–June 1868, RG 393, Part IV.

40. Testimony of Maj. Samuel White in *United States v. Pvt. George Washington,* Oct. 9, 1865, Port Hudson, Louisiana, RG 153.

41. Provost Judge A. Hitchcock to L. Caziare, May 1, 1868, box 2, PCNSC, RG 393, Part I.

42. Some fortune-tellers were women. See the testimony of Dolly Green in *United States v. Linda Allen,* June 18, 1868, Provost Court, Beaufort, South Carolina, box 2, PCNSC, RG 393, Part I. On conjurers in Missouri, Virginia, and Louisiana, see H[enry] C[lay] Bruce, *The New Man. Twenty-Nine Years a Slave. Twenty-Nine Years a Free Man. Recollections of H. C. Bruce* (York, Pa., 1895), 52–59; for other states, see Harry Middleton Hyatt, *Hoodoo, Conjuration, Witchcraft, Rootwork,* 5 vols. (Cambridge, Md., 1970–74).

43. Testimony of Nat Pease in *State v. Alonzo Mitchell,* Oct. 24, 1877, CC, box 2, folder 15, OCHM. For an example of loud talking in a "contraband" camp, see testimony of John Collier, Negro contraband, in *United States v. Richard (Dick) Bell (Negro Contraband Teamster),* May 29, 1863, pp. 15–16, Murfreesboro, Tennessee, MM512, RG 153.

44. Elizabeth Ware Pearson, *Letters from Port Royal, 1862–1868* (Boston, 1906), 125–26.

45. Ibid., 241. Tera Hunter discusses similar verbal brawls among Atlanta washerwomen as "a method of airing grievances, seeking support, and obtaining resolution, with the sanction of the larger community." See Hunter, *To 'Joy My Freedom,* 63.

46. This interpretation draws from studies of oral history and performance in Africa. See, for example, Karin Barber, *I Could Speak until Tomorrow: Oriki, Women, and the Past in a Yoruba Town* (Washington, D.C., 1991).

47. Charles William Day, *Five Years' Residence in the West Indies* (London, 1852), 2:111–12.

48. *Joanah Henry v. Lucinda Underwood,* Oct. 25, 1881, Davis Bend Magistrate's Book, OCHM.

49. *Rose Joyce v. Clementine Green,* June 3, 1876, ibid.

50. *Florida Hulett v. Hunt Green Jr.,* Sept. 14, 1880, ibid.

51. *Quint Branch v. Jacob Jones,* Sept. 26, 1868, 037.326.4, CAP; testimony of Sampson Brown in *Sampson Brown v. Samuel Gardner,* Jan. 19, 1867, Provost Court, Sea Islands, Rockville, South Carolina, box A, PCNSC, RG 393, Part I.

52. Testimony of David Drayton in *United States v. David Drayton,* Nov. 1, 1866, Provost Court, Sea Islands, South Carolina, box A, PCNSC, RG 393, Part I.

53. On loud talking as a preface to fighting, see testimony of Nelson Wells in *State v. Alonzo Mitchell,* Oct. 24, 1877, CC, box 2, folder 15, OCHM; testimony of Iceum Marshall in *State v. Alonzo Mitchell,* ibid.; testimony of Thomas Brooks in *Delia Youngblood v. Margaret Lowe,* Sept. 13, 1867, PCA, vol. 1, RG 393, Part IV; and testimony of Jordan Perkins in *State (Jordan Perkins) v. John Wire and Plato Perkins,* Mar. 26, 1870, Boston, Texas, entry 4852, Statements of Charges, Proceedings of Trials, and Letters Received Relating to Civil Cases, 1868–70, Dept. of Texas and 5th Military District (P), 1865–70, RG 393, Part I.

54. Testimony of Phoebe Parson in *United States (Frances Ross and others) v. William Ross,* Dec. 12, 1867, PCBarn, box 2, PCNSC, RG 393, Part I. See also *United States v. Matt Spann,* Sept. 2, 1867, PCSum, box 4, ibid.

55. Testimony of Abraham Brown in *United States v. Charles Frazier,* Sept. 6, 1867, PCBerk, RG 393, Part IV. See also affidavit of Phill Castor in *State v. Daniel Brown,* Sept. 25, 1877, CC, box 2, folder 10, OCHM.

56. Testimony of Peter Johnson in *State v. Jacob Cooper,* July term 1872, CC, box 1, folders 16–17, OCHM.

57. Testimony of Charlotte Simms in ibid.

58. Testimony of John F. Knight in *State v. John F. Knight,* Nov. 7, 1871, 037.326.5, CAP. Comically, Knight was "somewhat deaf" and had to ask a black man what Jennie was yelling at him (testimony of Mack Jones in *State v. John F. Knight,* ibid.).

59. Testimony of George Mitchell in *State v. B. D. Armstrong,* Jan. 14, 1870, 037.326.4, CAP. The testimony does not show what the argument was about. See also testimony of Booker Piatt in *State v. Collins T. Cross,* Feb. 26, 1870, ibid.

60. Testimony of J. B. Droughon in *State v. B. D. Armstrong,* Jan. 14, 1870, ibid.; and affidavit of Willie Mitchell in *State v. Wm. Duggan,* Feb. 17, 1869, ibid.

61. Franke, "Becoming a Citizen," 303. Although black people lodged some of these complaints, state officials probably lodged many more, and may have used sex-crime laws to supply businesses with convicted chain gang labor.

62. Lt. Ben F. Cheney to Lt. Stuart Eldridge, Apr. 21, 1865, reprinted in Berlin et al., eds., *Wartime Genesis of Free Labor: The Lower South,* 886; *State v. William Johnson,* Dec. 23, 1872, CC, box 1, folder 21, OCHM.

63. Pearson, *Letters from Port Royal,* 70. Ex-slaves and local army officers also kept an unofficial, ad hoc court on the Frogmore plantation "to decide cases & disputes bet[ween] parties." See testimony of W. H. Alden in *Abram Huguenin v. Lymas Middleton,* Nov. 8, 1866, PCB, Sept. 1865–June 1868, RG 393, Part IV.

64. On black women's allegations of sexual violence, see Edwards, "Sexual Vio-

lence"; affidavit of Sukey Mayo in *State v. Allen Lyon*, Dec. 21, 1874, 037.326.6, CAP; *U.S. (Rosina Pinckney) v. Prince Chaplin*, Proceedings of a Military Commission at Hilton Head Island, South Carolina, Oct. 24, 1864, box 767, LL2665, RG 153; and affidavit of Ebby Ann, July 19, 1866, Anderson Dist., South Carolina, entry 3075, BRFAL.

65. In one eighteen-month period the provost courts in South Carolina prosecuted twice as many whites as blacks. See Report of Maj. Gen. E. R. S. Canby for Jan. 1, 1867–June 30, 1868, in Max L. Heyman Jr., *Prudent Soldier: A Biography of Major General E. R. S. Canby, 1817–1873* (Glendale, Calif., 1959), 316.

66. Testimony of Libby Hammond in *United States v. Stephen Moyer*, July 16, 1867, PCA, vol. 1, RG 393, Part IV.

67. Claude Elliott, "The Freedmen's Bureau in Texas," *Southwestern Historical Quarterly* 56 (July 1952): 6, quoted in Foner, *Reconstruction*, 120.

68. Testimony of Henry G. Judd, p. 81, File 3, AFIC.

69. See *Cuffee Days v. Wm. E. Towne*, Mar. 10, 1866, PCB, Sept. 1865–June 1868, RG 393, Part IV; *Edmund Vaughan v. William Wright*, Oct. 21, 1867, PCSum, box 4, PCNSC, RG 393, Part I; *United States v. John Jones*, May 16, 1867, Provost Court, Edgefield District, South Carolina, box 2, PCNSC, RG 393, Part I; deposition of William Mitchell at Beaufort, South Carolina, May 28, 1864, entry 578, Corresp. Received by Supervising Special Agent Browne, 1863–66, CWSAT; testimony of Isaac Robinson, June 25, 1866, Affidavits and Papers Relating to Complaints, 1865–67, Subassistant Commissioner for Savannah District, Georgia, BRFAL; testimony of William Boisfeuillet, Nov. 16, 1865, ibid.; testimony of Dennis Mitchell, Nov. 16, 1865, ibid.; testimony of Georgia Boisfeuillet, Nov. 16, 1865, ibid.

70. See, for example, charges against Tempy (colored), July 30, 1864, vol. 8, n.p., PMG; charges against Triton (colored) and others, Sept. 5, 1864, ibid.; *Freed-girl Jane v. her father Isaac Jackson*, Mar. 9, 1867, p. 92, entry 3191, BRFAL; affidavit of Caroline Currie, Nov. 5, 1867, entry 1594, Provost Court, 1867–68, Fayetteville, North Carolina, Towns and Posts, RG 393, Part IV; *Doc. Allston v. Anderson Walden and S. W. Seawell*, Mar. 9, 1868, ibid.; *Frank Cook v. John Taylor*, Jan. 9, 1866, p. 10, entry 4352, Proceedings of Freedmen's Court, Dec. 1865–June 1867, Assistant Subassistant Commissioner, Yorktown, Virginia, BRFAL.

71. Testimony of Henry G. Judd, pp. 80–81, File 3, AFIC.

72. Complaint of Virginia Barber, "List of Complaints," June 24, 1865, vol. 4, p. 76, PMG, RG 393, Part IV; complaint of Asa Webster, ibid.; complaint of Elijah Sears, ibid.

73. *United States v. James Allen Harris*, Nov. 14, 1867, Proceedings of a Military Commission at Little Rock, Ark., OO2704, RG 153.

74. Franklin, ed., *Reminiscences of an Active Life*, 59–65; Davis Bend Magistrate's Book, OCHM.

75. Harry August Volz III, "The Administration of Justice by the Freedmen's Bureau in Kentucky, South Carolina, and Virginia" (M.A. thesis, University of Virginia, 1975), 62–63. These courts heard cases that involved ex-slaves, either as defendants or plaintiffs or both. They did not try white-on-white crimes.

76. Volz, "Administration of Justice," 62–63. Larceny cases, in which blacks made

up 96 percent of the defendants, must be treated with skepticism. As Albert Colbey Smith shows, southern whites after emancipation thought of stealing as a "black" crime. See Albert Colbey Smith, "Down Freedom's Road: The Contours of Race, Class, and Property Crime in Black-Belt Georgia, 1866–1910" (Ph.D. diss., University of Georgia, 1982), 173, 175–79.

77. Volz, "Administration of Justice," 26. According to Donald Nieman, whose study includes other southern states, many of the ex-slaves' lawsuits before the bureau were against other blacks and concerned the "ownership of property, debts, and marital relations." See Nieman, *To Set the Law in Motion*, 11.

78. See, for example, *Clayborne Holmes v. Robert Ruffin*, July 25, 1866, pp. 28–29, Proceedings of Freedmen's Court, Dec. 1865–June 1867, Yorktown, Virginia, entry 4352, BRFAL; *Henry Miner v. Charles Collins*, Aug. 1, 1866, ibid.

79. Gilles Vandal, "'Bloody Caddo': White Violence against Blacks in a Louisiana Parish, 1865–1876," *Journal of Social History* 25 (Winter 1991): 376.

80. Gilles Vandal, "Black Violence in Post–Civil War Louisiana," *Journal of Interdisciplinary History* 25 (Summer 1994): 53.

81. Barry A. Crouch, "A Spirit of Lawlessness: White Violence; Texas Blacks, 1865–1868," *Journal of Social History* 18 (Winter 1984): 220.

82. Vandal, "'Bloody Caddo,'" 376.

83. Vandal, "Black Violence in Post–Civil War Louisiana," 49–54.

84. Heyman, *Prudent Soldier*, 316. Some Union officers in Mississippi also refused to give blacks a hearing. See Christopher Waldrep, *Roots of Disorder: Race and Criminal Justice in the American South, 1817–80* (Urbana, 1998), 101–2.

85. Franke, "Becoming a Citizen," 305–7; Reva B. Siegel, "'The Rule of Love': Wife Beating as Prerogative and Privacy," *Yale Law Journal* 105 (1996): 2134–41.

86. Affidavit of John Picksley, Nov. 8, 1865, entry 2945, Affidavits, Sept. 1865–June 1868, Office of the Assistant Commissioner, South Carolina, BRFAL.

87. Nieman, *To Set the Law in Motion*, 11; Barry A. Crouch, "The 'Chords of Love': Legalizing Black Marital and Family Rights in Postwar Texas," *Journal of Negro History* 79 (Fall 1994): 343–46.

88. Testimony of Henry G. Judd, pp. 80–81, File 3, AFIC.

89. Crouch, "'Chords of Love,'" 342–43.

90. For children and clothing, see complaint of Lucy Hill against Bob Hill, July 5, 1876, Davis Bend Magistrate's Book, OCHM; for poultry and kitchenware, see Elizabeth Hyde Botume, *First Days amongst the Contrabands* (Boston, 1893), 159–60; for melons, see testimony of Louisa Thigpen in *State v. Gray Thigpen*, Sept. 6, 1869, 037.326.4, CAP. See also *State v. Roland Rand*, Oct. 15, 1880, Davis Bend Magistrate's Book, OCHM; and statement of J. H. Wilson in complaint of Eliza Wilson, Dec. 7, 1867, entry 3035, Miscellaneous Records Relating to Complaints, May 1866–May 1868, Agent, Abbeville Court House, Subordinate Field Offices, South Carolina, BRFAL.

91. Botume, *First Days amongst the Contrabands*, 264–66.

92. Testimony of W. H. Burgess in *Dick Henderson v. Pompey Burgess*, Sept. 4, 1867, box 1, PCNSC, RG 393, Part I.

93. Testimony of Charles in *United States v. Moses*, July 29, 1862, MM2734, RG 153.

94. Testimony of Robert Francis in *Richard Hamilton v. Robert Francis*, July 5, 1866, p. 43, entry 4352, Proceedings of Freedmen's Court, Dec. 1865–June 1867, Yorktown, Virginia, BRFAL.

95. Jno. R. Henry, Spl. Agt., to Fisk, Knoxville, Tenn., May 29, 1866, Registered Letters Received, June 1865–Apr. 1869, Office of the Assistant Commissioner, Tennessee, entry 3379, BRFAL, FSSP A-6269.

96. Testimony of Edmund Brown in *State v. Gentry Bradford*, Aug. 13, 1867, PCSum, box 4, PCNSC, RG 393, Part I.

97. See, for example, *United States v. Richard Lewis and Nathan Clark*, Jan. 25, 1868, Provost Court, Aiken, South Carolina, box 1, PCNSC, RG 393, Part I; and testimony of Thomas Johnson in *Thomas Johnson v. Cato Foxworth*, Sept. 18, 1867, PCSum, box 1, ibid. Michael Lowy ("A Good Name Is Worth More than Money," 181–208) argues that Akan urbanites use courts as one of several forums for dispute.

98. Testimony of Charles Adams in *State v. John Griffin*, Jan. term 1877, CC, box 2, folder 9c, OCHM.

99. Testimony of James Wilson in *James Wilson v. Martin Dixon*, Nov. 22, 1866, Provost Court, Sea Islands, South Carolina, box A, PCNSC, RG 393, Part I. The fact that these cases wound up in court suggests that their extralegal settlements eventually broke down. Other extralegal settlements, presumably, held strong and therefore would not appear in court records.

100. Testimony of Garrett in *United States v. James A. Pack and others*, Aug. 12, 1867, PCSum, box 4, PCNSC, RG 393, Part I.

101. Testimony of John Johnson in *John Townsend v. Mathias Johnson*, Jan. 24, 1867, Provost Court, Sea Islands, South Carolina, box A, PCNSC, RG 393, Part I; "Exhibit A," July 18, 1866, in ibid., and "Exhibit B," Aug. 5, 1865, in ibid. For a similar case, see *E. M. Anderson v. Horace Cann*, Oct. 25, 1865, PCB, Sept. 1865–June 1868, RG 393, Part IV.

102. See, for example, testimony of Christopher Gillian in *Leander Dingle v. Thomas S. Waring*, Dec. 10, 1867, PCBerk, RG 393, Part IV.

103. Testimony of Peter H. Varner in *Thomas Matthews v. James Clarke*, Dec. 21, 1867, ibid.

104. Receipt between Michael Cain and George Morgan, Aug. 3, 1865, entry 3288, Miscellaneous Records, 1865–68, Subassistant Commissioner, Moncks Corner, South Carolina, BRFAL.

105. Receipt between Sorrow Gray and Warren Campbell, Mar. 15, 1866, ibid.

106. J. T. Trowbridge, *The South* (1866; reprint, New York, 1969), 344.

107. Charles Frederick Benjamin, *Memoir of James Allen Hardie, Inspector-General, United States Army* (Washington, D.C., 1877), 48–49. Benjamin served as clerk to the commission for most of its term.

108. Enclosure, State Department to Commissioners of Claims, Apr. 25, 1871, entry 325, Letters Received by the Commission, 1871–80, M87, roll 2, RRSCC; testimony of Judge A. D. Smith, Chairman, Board of U.S. Direct Tax Commissioners for South Carolina, pp. 1–3, File 3, AFIC.

109. Testimony of Judge A. D. Smith, pp. 3–4, File 3, AFIC.

110. Special Agent Robert B. Avery to Commissioner Orange Ferriss, June 4, 1878,

entry 326, Letters Received from Special Agents of the Commission, 1871–80, M87, roll 10, RRSCC. Emphasis is in original.

111. Special Agent John D. Edwards to Charles F. Benjamin, clerk, Office of Commissioners of Claims, Mar. 20, 1875, entry 326, Letters Received from Special Agents of the Commission, 1871–80, M87, roll 11, RRSCC.

112. Weekly Report of Special Agent Robert B. Avery, May 25, 1878, and June 22, 1878, entry 326, Letters Received from Special Agents of the Commission, 1871–80, M87, roll 10, RRSCC.

113. General Order, Postmaster General J. W. Marshall, June 10, 1871, entry 325, Letters Received by the Commission, 1871–80, M87, roll 2, RRSCC; Weekly Report of Special Agent Robert B. Avery, May 24, 1879, entry 326, Letters Received from Special Agents of the Commission, 1871–80, M87, roll 10, RRSCC.

114. News clipping from "Weekly Planet," May 1, 1875, enclosed in Weekly Report of Special Agent John D. Edwards, May 1, 1875, entry 326, Letters Received from Special Agents of the Commission, 1871–80, M87, roll 11, RRSCC.

115. Weekly Report of Special Agent Robert B. Avery, May 25, 1878, entry 326, Letters Received from Special Agents of the Commission, 1871–80, M87, roll 10, RRSCC. Claims agents were sometimes mistaken for "revenue men," out to arrest bootleg liquor-makers. See ibid., Aug. 24, 1878.

116. Special Commissioner M. F. Pleasants to Asa Owen Aldis, Commissioner of Claims, May 29, 1872, entry 325, Letters Received by the Commission, 1871–80, M87, roll 2, RRSCC.

117. Special Commissioner Virgil Hillyer to Commissioner Asa Owen Aldis, Feb. 25, 1874, entry 325, Letters Received by the Commission, 1871–80, M87, roll 4, RRSCC.

118. C. W. Dudley to Commissioners of Claims, June 3, 1874, entry 325, Letters Received by the Commission, 1871–80, M87, roll 4, RRSCC.

119. Special Agent R. B. Avery to Commissioner Orange Ferriss, Aug. 4, 1878, entry 329, Miscellaneous Papers, 1864–1900, M87, roll 9, RRSCC. See also Weekly Report of Special Agent Robert B. Avery, Dec. 7, 1878, entry 326, Letters Received from Special Agents of the Commission, 1871–80, M87, roll 10, RRSCC.

120. Testimony of Phoebe Ann Norman in claim of Lucy McIver, p. 3, Liberty County, Georgia, SCC. On plantation size and its impact on slave communities, see Robert William Fogel, *Without Consent or Contract: The Rise and Fall of American Slavery* (New York, 1989), 178–79.

121. Claim of William Cassels, ibid.

122. Spl. Cmr. Solon Moore to Commissioners of Claims, "Last page," claim of Louisa Pinson, Cherokee County, Alabama, reel 3, WSCC.

123. Testimony of Hon. Amos M. Elliott in claim of Edmund Moss, n.p., Shelby County, Alabama, reel 31, WSCC.

124. Testimony of James L. Coman in claim of Spencer Harris, p. 21, Limestone County, Alabama, SCC.

125. Special Agent W. W. Paine to Commissioners of Claims, July 18, 1876, in claim of Pompey Bacon, Liberty County, Georgia, SCC.

126. Testimony of William A. Fleming in claim of Tony Axon, supplemental testimony, ibid.

127. Special Commissioner Jos. B. Bates to Commissioners of Claims in claim of Spencer Harris, "Last page," Limestone County, Alabama, reel 22, WSCC.

128. Testimony of William A. Fleming in claim of Tony Axon, supplemental testimony, Liberty County, Georgia, SCC.

129. See the testimony of Gideon Jackson in claim of Prince Maxwell, p. 6, ibid.

130. Weekly Report of Special Agent Robert B. Avery, Nov. 16, 1878, entry 326, Letters Received from Special Agents of the Commission, 1871–80, M87, roll 10, RRSCC. See also ibid., Mar. 9, 1879.

131. Special Agent Enos Richmond to Commissioners of Claims, Mar. 11, 1874, entry 325, Letters Received by the Commission, 1871–80, M87, roll 4, RRSCC; Judge A. Garrignes, Special Commissioner at Opelousas, Louisiana, to Commissioner Asa Owen Aldis, Feb. 28, 1876, entry 325, Letters Received by the Commission, 1871–80, M87, roll 7, RRSCC.

132. Special Agent Robert B. Avery to Orange Ferriss, Commissioner of Claims, June 4, 1878, entry 326, Letters Received from Special Agents of the Commission, 1871–80, M87, roll 10, RRSCC.

133. Testimony of William Winn in claim of David Stevens, Liberty County, Georgia, SCC.

CHAPTER FIVE

1. On "usage," see *Thomas Waddill v. Charlotte D. Martin*, 38 N.C. 562 (1845).

2. Morton J. Horwitz, *The Transformation of American Law, 1780–1860* (Cambridge, Mass., 1977); Gregory S. Alexander, *Commodity and Propriety: Competing Visions of Property in American Legal Thought, 1776–1970* (Chicago, 1997); Thomas D. Morris, *Southern Slavery and the Law, 1619–1860* (Chapel Hill, 1996), 81–84. Of course, as Alexander points out, legal writers often disagreed on *how* to promote economic prosperity and about what a prosperous nation should look like. Different visions of the "proper" society shaped different conceptions of property, and vice versa. Overall, however, the "liberal," Blackstonian, or "classical" conceptions of property reigned triumphant through the 1910s, when legal Progressives and Realists began to reconceptualize property as a "bundle of rights." The South's postwar laws on crop liens were also part of this trend and are discussed below. See Harold D. Woodman, *New South—New Law: The Legal Foundations of Credit and Labor Relations in the Postbellum Agricultural South* (Baton Rouge, 1995).

3. Thomas D. Morris, *Southern Slavery and the Law*, 122.

4. Hugh Henry Brackenridge (1814), quoted in Alexander, *Commodity and Propriety*, 116.

5. Alexander, *Commodity and Propriety*, 190.

6. Ibid., 288–89.

7. Pres. Abraham Lincoln to [Maj. Gen.] Ulysses S. Grant (1862), in James M. McPherson, *Ordeal by Fire: The Civil War and Reconstruction* (New York, 1982), 254.

8. E. D. Townsend, Asst. Adj. Gen. to Maj. Gen. W. T. Sherman, Apr. 30, 1864, FSSP C-2305.

9. Roger L. Ransom and Richard Sutch, *One Kind of Freedom: The Economic Consequences of Emancipation* (New York, 1977), 53.

10. The government's handling of a famous Kentucky racehorse illustrates this concern. See Quartermaster General M. C. Meigs to Hon. S. P. Chase, July 25, 1863, box 11, entry 840, CWSAT; W. S. Rosecrans to M. C. Meigs, July 24, 1863, ibid.; and *United States v. Alexander*, United States Supreme Court No. 360, Dec. term 1864, vol. 1, entry 361, CWSAT.

11. Testimony of Judge A. D. Smith, Chairman, Board of U.S. Direct Tax Commissioners for South Carolina, pp. 1–3, File 3, AFIC.

12. McPherson, *Ordeal by Fire*, 271.

13. "Additional General Instructions," pp. 115–17, S. P. Chase to Benj. F. Flanders, Sup'g Sp. Agt. at New Orleans, May 25, 1863, entry 831, Office Record of General Instructions to Agents, n.d., CWSAT.

14. Affidavit of Mark L. DeMasse, Apr. 22, 1869, enclosed in Deputy Quartermaster Gen. James A. Plum to Bvt. Maj. Gen. M. C. Meigs, Quartermaster Gen., entry 329, Miscellaneous Papers, 1864–1900, M87, roll 9, RRSCC; "Instructions to Wm. P. Mellen, Supervising Spl. Agent, from S. P. Chase," pp. 5–10, Apr. 4, 1863, entry 831, Office Record of General Instructions to Agents, n.d., CWSAT.

15. "Explicit Instructions to keep accurate and detailed accounts: A circular letter," pp. 151–52, S. P. Chase to Wm. P. Mellen, Agent at Cincinnati, Ohio, June 15, 1863, entry 831, Office Record of General Instructions to Agents, n.d., CWSAT.

16. National Archives finding aid, Records of the Third Special Agency, CWSAT.

17. "Records of a Military Commission Appointed to Investigate Titles to Real Estate in the Lafourche District," Nov. 13, 1863, vol. 4, n.p., PMG, RG 393, Part IV.

18. See, for example, Records Relating to Real and Personal Property, Claims Records, 1863–64, entry 493, CWSAT.

19. See, for example, George Gage, Spl. Agt. at Beaufort, South Carolina, to J. S. Severance, Esq., n.d., Miscellaneous Office Papers, Fifth Agency, 1863–65, entry 579, CWSAT.

20. After the Civil War, northern states enacted laws that enshrined "liberty of contract" between independent agents as the basis for labor negotiation. See Amy Dru Stanley, "Beggars Can't Be Choosers: Compulsion and Contract in Postbellum America," *Journal of American History* 78 (Mar. 1992): 1265–93, and Charles Sellers, *The Market Revolution: Jacksonian America, 1815–1846* (New York, 1991), 33–34, 100–105.

21. Testimony of Nick Donald in claim of Caroline Friend, p. 25, Limestone County, Alabama, reel 21, WSCC.

22. Report of John D. Edwards (1874), in Frank W. Klingberg, *The Southern Claims Commission* (Berkeley, 1955), 84–85.

23. Spl. Agt. John D. Edwards to [Charles F.] Benjamin, May 2, 1874, entry 325, Letters Received by the Commission, 1871–80, M87, roll 4, RRSCC.

24. S. R. Harrington, Attorney, Little Rock, Ark., to Charles F. Benjamin, Clerk, Mar. 5, 1874, entry 325, Letters Received by the Commission, 1871–80, M87, roll 4, RRSCC.

25. S. R. Harrington, Attorney, Little Rock, Ark., to Charles F. Benjamin, Clerk, Feb. 22, 1874, entry 325, Letters Received by the Commission, 1871–80, M87, roll 4, RRSCC.

26. Special Commissioner Virgil Hillyer to J. B. Howell, Commissioner of Claims, Mar. 22, 1873, entry 325, Letters Received by the Commission, 1871–80, M87, roll 3, RRSCC.

27. See, for example, Special Commissioner M. F. Pleasants to Hon. A. O. Aldis, Nov. 3, 1871, entry 325, Letters Received by the Commission, 1871–80, M87, roll 2, RRSCC.

28. Testimony of Ceasar Jones in claim of Joseph James, p. 11, Liberty County, SCC.

29. Testimony of Linda Roberts in claim of William Golding, pp. 3, 7, ibid. See also testimony of William Golding in claim of Linda Roberts, p. 10, ibid.

30. Philip D. Morgan, "The Ownership of Property by Slaves in the Mid-Nineteenth-Century Low Country," *Journal of Southern History* 49, no. 3 (1983): 409–10; Edward Magdol, *A Right to the Land: Essays on the Freedmen's Community* (Westport, Conn., 1977).

31. Testimony of Joseph James in claim of Linda Jones, p. 6, Liberty County, Georgia, SCC. By the 1900s, as problematic properties like oil and trademarks caused physicalist and absolutist conceptions of property to decline, judges were more likely to recognize multiple interests in property. But in the 1870s these changes in legal thought were just beginning. See Kenneth J. Vandevelde, "The New Property of the Nineteenth Century: The Development of the Modern Conception of Property," *Buffalo Law Review* 29 (1980): 325–67.

32. Special Agent Robert B. Avery to Orange Ferriss, Commissioner of Claims, June 4, 1878, entry 326, Letters Received from Special Agents of the Commission, 1871–80, M87, roll 10, RRSCC.

33. See, for example, claim of Sam Harris, p. 4, Liberty County, Georgia, SCC.

34. Ibid.

35. Claim of Jacob Dryer, supplemental testimony, Liberty County, Georgia, SCC.

36. C. W. Dudley to Commissioners of Claims, June 3, 1874, entry 325, Letters Received by the Commission, 1871–80, M87, roll 4, RRSCC.

37. Gilmore & Richards [illegible], attorneys, to Commissioners of Claims, Sept. 5, 1878, in claim of Jacob Dryer, Liberty County, Georgia, SCC.

38. C. W. Dudley to Commissioners of Claims, June 3, 1874, entry 325, Letters Received by the Commission, 1871–80, M87, roll 4, RRSCC. See also Raymond Cay Jr. to Commissioner Asa Owen Aldis, Mar. 2, 1874, ibid.

39. Robert B. Avery to Charles F. Benjamin, June 1, 1878, entry 326, Letters Received from Special Agents of the Commission, 1871–80, M87, roll 10, RRSCC.

40. Claim of Benjamin Lettuce, supplemental testimony, June 6, 1877, Lauderdale County, Alabama, reel 18, WSCC. Avery was unmoved. In his comments, he wrote: "The old man . . . cant tell a story and repeat it again the same way five minutes afterwards" (Avery to Commissioners of Claims, June 6, 1877, ibid.). Another claimant had to prove that she could "count 100 with rapidity and readily add numbers up as large as 13+14" (testimony of Malinda Ward in claim of Maria Smith, n.p., Warren County, Mississippi, SCC).

41. Spl. Cmr. Geo. H. Patrick to Commissioners of Claims, Oct. 25, 1873, enclosed in claim of Edmund Moss, Shelby County, Alabama, reel 31, WSCC.

42. See, for example, Special Agent Enos Richmond to Commissioners of Claims, Mar. 11, 1874, entry 325, Letters Received by the Commission, 1871–80, M87, roll 4, RRSCC.

43. Special Commissioner Virgil Hillyer to Commissioner Asa Owen Aldis, Feb. 21, 1874, entry 325, Letters Received by the Commission, 1871–80, M87, roll 4, RRSCC.

44. Special Agent Enos Richmond to Commissioners of Claims, Mar. 11, 1874, entry 325, Letters Received by the Commission, 1871–80, M87, roll 3, RRSCC; Special Commissioner Virgil Hillyer to Commissioner Asa Owen Aldis, Feb. 21, 1874, ibid.; Special Commissioner Virgil Hillyer to J. B. Howell, Commissioner of Claims, Mar. 22, 1873, ibid.

45. Claim of James Mifflin, judgment, Liberty County, Georgia, SCC.

46. Special Agent Robert B. Avery to Orange Ferriss, Commissioner of Claims, June 4, 1878, entry 326, Letters Received from Special Agents of the Commission, 1871–80, M87, roll 10, RRSCC.

47. Claim of William Cassels, p. 1, Liberty County, Georgia, SCC.

48. On treatment of drivers, see, for example, claim of John Crawford, judgment, ibid. For a perceptive analysis of the links among law, free-labor ideology, and postwar developments in the South, see Stanley, "Beggars Can't Be Choosers," 1265–93.

49. Circular, May 20, 1872, vol. 1, Journal of the Commissioners, M87, roll 1, RRSCC.

50. Claim of John Bacon, judgment, Liberty County, Georgia, SCC. On the recognition of ownership, see enclosure, Charles F. Benjamin to Commissioners of Claims, Sept. 17, 1877, entry 325, Letters Received by the Commission, 1871–80, M87, roll 8, RRSCC, and claim of Edmund Bacon, judgment, Liberty County, Georgia, SCC. The commissioners also recognized inheritance among slaves. See claim of Nancy Bacon, ibid.

51. I have not been able to find any discussion of this change, even though just a year before there was ferocious debate over establishing the commission itself. The "Revised Questions," with the "special questions for female [and] colored claimants," are inserted without comment into the commissioners' Second General Report to Congress. See 2nd General Report, 1872, 42nd Cong., 3rd sess., vol. 1, Misc. Doc. No. 12, #1571, pp. 51–57.

52. Robert P. Brooks (1914), quoted in Eric Foner, *Reconstruction: America's Unfinished Revolution, 1863–1877* (New York, 1988), 135.

53. Robert V. Richardson (1865), quoted in Eric Foner, *Nothing but Freedom: Emancipation and Its Legacy* (Baton Rouge, 1983), 6.

54. Foner, *Reconstruction*, 170–74; Julie Saville, *The Work of Reconstruction: From Slave to Wage Laborer in South Carolina, 1860–1870* (New York, 1994), 110–13. Ex-masters in northern Nigeria also tried to control ex-slaves by manipulating property rights. See Jan Hogendorn and Paul Lovejoy, *Slow Death for Slavery: The Course of Abolition in Northern Nigeria, 1897–1936* (Cambridge, Eng., 1993).

55. Brig. Gen. John P. Hawkins to Gerritt Smith, Oct. 21, 1863, pp. 92–93, File 5, AFIC.

56. Testimony of Wm. Slade, p. 19, File 1, AFIC.

57. Rev. John Jones to Mrs. Mary Jones, Aug. 21, 1865, in Robert Manson Myers,

ed., *The Children of Pride: A True Story of Georgia and the Civil War* (New Haven, 1972), 1291–93. See also ibid., 1281–83. Eric Foner and Julie Saville have cogently explored the struggles over labor contracts and landownership that followed emancipation in the Low Country. See Foner, *Nothing but Freedom*, and Saville, *Work of Reconstruction*. See also letter of protest from Wm. Golden [Golding], Gabriel Andrews, & Toney Axon to Col. H. F. Sickles (1865), quoted in Magdol, *Right to the Land*, 273.

58. Claim of Prince Maxwell, p. 2, Liberty County, Georgia, SCC.

59. Steven Hahn, *The Roots of Southern Populism: Yeoman Farmers and the Transformation of the Georgia Upcountry, 1850–1890* (New York, 1983), 240–44; Shawn Everett Kantor, *Politics and Property Rights: The Closing of the Open Range in the Postbellum South* (Chicago, 1998), 123–24.

60. *Mr. Brewer & Wife v. John Jackson*, n.d., Provost Court, 1867–68, Fayetteville, North Carolina, Towns and Posts, RG 393, Part IV; Nancy Dunlap Bercaw, "Politics of Household during the Transition from Slavery to Freedom in the Yazoo-Mississippi Delta, 1861–1876" (Ph.D. diss., University of Pennsylvania, 1996), 204, 220–23; Saville, *Work of Reconstruction*, 131–32; *Frederick and Grace Wright v. William E. Stoney*, Dec. 2, 1867, PCBerk, RG 393, Part IV; J. T. Trowbridge, *The South* (1866; reprint, New York, 1969), 366.

61. Sara Rapport, "The Freedmen's Bureau as a Legal Agent for Black Men and Women in Georgia, 1865–1868," *Georgia Historical Quarterly* 73, no. 1 (Spring 1989): 29–39; Leslie A. Schwalm, *A Hard Fight for We: Women's Transition from Slavery to Freedom in South Carolina* (Urbana, 1997), 155–235; Foner, *Reconstruction*, 150–53.

62. Saville, *Work of Reconstruction*, 16–19.

63. Loren Schweninger, *Black Property Owners in the South, 1790–1915* (Urbana, 1990), 160.

64. On "dual tenure" in North Carolina, see Sharon Ann Holt, *Making Freedom Pay: North Carolina Freedpeople Working for Themselves, 1865–1900* (Athens, Ga., 2000), 84–94.

65. W. E. B. Du Bois, "The Negro Landholder of Georgia," *United States Bureau of Labor Bulletin* 6, no. 35 (1901): 671.

66. Schweninger, *Black Property Owners in the South*, 148–49; Foner, *Reconstruction*, 404.

67. On black migration into southern towns, see Foner, *Reconstruction*, 81–82.

68. Elsa Barkley Brown and Gregg D. Kimball, "Mapping the Terrain of Black Richmond," *Journal of Urban History* 21, no. 3 (1995): 314–15.

69. On black militias in the South, see ibid., 305–8; Rebecca J. Scott, "'Stubborn and Disposed to Stand their Ground': Black Militia, Sugar Workers, and the Dynamics of Collective Action in the Louisiana Sugar Bowl, 1863–87," *Slavery and Abolition* 20, no. 1 (1999); Saville, *Work of Reconstruction*, 143–51; and Foner, *Reconstruction*, 283–84.

70. Testimony of Sgt. Chas. F. Roberts in *United States (Frederick Sutton) v. George Certillion*, Jan. 3, 1866, Camp Hamilton, Virginia, MM3640, RG 153.

71. Lt. Col. J. H. Wilson to Lt. Col. Robert Macfeely, Aug. 12, 1863, reprinted in Ira Berlin et al., eds., *The Wartime Genesis of Free Labor: The Lower South*, ser. 1, vol. 3, *Freedom: A Documentary History of Emancipation, 1861–1867* (New York, 1990), 718.

72. On blacks selling things in Washington and Annapolis, see Paul R. Mullins, "Race and the Genteel Consumer: Class and African-American Consumption, 1850–1930," *Historical Archaeology* 33, no. 1 (1999): 31–32; on Wilmington and New Bern, see *United States v. Archer Newell*, June 7, 1865, Proceedings of a General Court-Martial, Wilmington, North Carolina, MM2269, RG 153, and R. Edward Earle, "Part XII: North Carolina and Its Fisheries," in *The Fish and Fishery Industries of the United States*, ed. George B. Goode (Washington, D.C., Senate Misc. Documents, 1884–87), 510; on Lynchburg, see John Richard Dennett, *The South as It Is: 1865–1866*, ed. Henry M. Christman (New York, 1965), 35; on Richmond, see Trowbridge, *South*, 178–79.

73. Dennett, *South as It Is*, 36. On black women marketing in Alabama rail stations, see Robert Somers, *The Southern States since the War, 1870–71* (1871; reprint, University, Ala., 1965), 166. Demand in the black community for gar, catfish, and eels reshaped the retail fish trade of New Berne, North Carolina (Earle, "Part XII: North Carolina and Its Fisheries," 485). Blacks in "certain parts of" Virginia "almost monopolized" the oyster trade (M. McDonald, "Part XI: Virginia and Its Fisheries," in *Fish and Fishery Industries of the United States*, 464).

74. Testimony of Peter Johnson in *State v. Jacob Cooper*, July term 1872, CC, box 1, folder 16–17, OCHM.

75. Brown and Kimball, "Mapping the Terrain of Black Richmond," 305.

76. Affidavit of C. C. Swears, Robt. Church, and John Gains, Feb. 17, 1866, Provost Marshal, Memphis, Tennessee, entry 3545, BRFAL; affidavit of Mayor John Park, Feb. 22, 1866, ibid. Only a few months before, whites in Vicksburg massacred blacks who ignored a demand to stop holding parties. See Privt. Calvin Holly to Maj. Gen. O. O. Howard, Dec. 16, 1865, reprinted in Ira Berlin, Joseph P. Reidy, and Leslie S. Rowland, eds., *The Black Military Experience*, ser. 2, *Freedom: A Documentary History of Emancipation, 1861–1867* (New York, 1982), 755.

77. "Wm. Hunter, Late Lieut. Col., 32 U.S. Infty to Major Reeves, Freedmans Dept.," Sept. 5, 1865, Provost Marshal, Memphis, Tennessee, entry 3545, BRFAL.

78. Capt. T. A. Walker to Capt. W. W. Deane, July 21, 1865, ibid.

79. Charles E. Orser Jr. and Annette M. Nekola, "Plantation Settlement from Slavery to Tenancy: An Example from a Piedmont Plantation in South Carolina," in *The Archaeology of Slavery and Plantation Life*, ed. Theresa A. Singleton (Orlando, 1985), 72. To give a sense of this plantation's scale, an acre is roughly as big as a football field.

80. Elizabeth Ware Pearson, *Letters from Port Royal, 1862–1868* (Boston, 1906), 330. See also T. J. Woofter Jr., *Black Yeomanry: Life on St. Helena Island* (New York, 1930), 213–14. These were only the latest in a series of changes in the architecture of Low Country plantations since the 1700s. See Thomas R. Wheaton and Patrick H. Garrow, "Acculturation and the Archaeological Record in the Carolina Lowcountry," in Singleton, ed., *Archaeology of Slavery and Plantation Life*, 244–48.

81. On the squad system, see J. William Harris, "Plantations and Power: Emancipation on the David Barrow Plantations," in *Toward a New South? Studies in Post–Civil War Southern Communities*, ed. Orville Vernon Burton and Robert C. McMath Jr. (Westport, 1982), 253–55, and Ralph Shlomowitz, "The Squad System on Postbellum

Cotton Plantations," in ibid., 264–73. On settlement patterns, see Orser and Nekola, "Plantation Settlement," 69–71, 77–79, and Richard Affleck, "Plantation Spatial Organization and Slave Settlement Pattern in the South Carolina Lowcountry: Toward a Dynamic View," *Annual Papers of the Univ. of South Carolina Anthropology Students Association* 4 (1989).

82. Somers, *Southern States since the War*, 120. Black children near Hillsboro, North Carolina, left school for weeks at a time to help their parents "in clearing off woody land & building houses for themselves," which the families could keep for two years (Robert George Fitzgerald Diary, Mar. 5, 1868, acc. no. 4177, Fitzgerald Family Papers, SHC).

83. Ransom and Sutch, *One Kind of Freedom*, 68–80. Southern Louisiana was an important exception. Sugar workers stayed on in clustered quarters for decades, possibly because planters succeeded in reimposing gang labor there. See John B. Rehder, *Delta Sugar: Louisiana's Vanishing Plantation Landscape* (Baltimore, 1999), 100. More work is needed to compare the geography of different postemancipation societies. Ex-slave *moradores* dispersed the centralized quarters of northeastern Brazil's sugar plantations, but Barry Higman cautions that some Jamaican plantations actually became more nucleated after emancipation in 1838, and he attributes these differences to "the nature of the productive process and the character of social relations." See Rebecca J. Scott, "Defining the Boundaries of Freedom in the World of Cane: Cuba, Brazil, and Louisiana after Emancipation," *American Historical Review* 99 (Feb. 1994): 96, and B. W. Higman, "The Spatial Economy of Jamaican Sugar Plantations: Cartographic Evidence from the Eighteenth and Nineteenth Centuries," *Journal of Historical Geography* 13, no. 1 (1987): 37–38. See also Charles E. Orser Jr., *The Material Basis of the Postbellum Tenant Plantation: Historical Archaeology in the South Carolina Piedmont* (Athens, Ga., 1988).

84. Frances B. Leigh, *Ten Years on a Georgia Plantation since the War* (1883; reprint, New York, 1969), 276.

85. David C. Barrow Jr., "A Georgia Plantation," *The Century Illustrated Monthly Magazine* 21 (1881): 832–33.

86. Georgia Writers' Project, Savannah Unit, Works Progress Administration, *Drums and Shadows: Survival Studies among the Georgia Coastal Negroes* (1940; reprint, Athens, Ga., 1986), 133. For cabins raised from the ground, see the testimony of Ann Bland, Sept. 11, 1867, in *United States v. Stephen Marshall*, Provost Court, Edgefield District, South Carolina, box 2, PCNSC, RG 393, Part I; and *United States v. Sophronia Brown*, Oct. 14, 1867, PCSum, box 4, ibid.

87. Barbara J. Heath and Amber Bennet, "'The Little Spots Allow'd Them': The Archaeological Study of African-American Yards," *Historical Archaeology* 34, no. 2 (2000): 43–44, 48–50. African Americans continued these practices into the 1940s; they socialized and performed domestic chores in yards that were dirt rather than grass and that were carefully swept with bundled sticks each day (Mary Baskerville, telephone interviews by author, Nov. 15, 1994, and Apr. 23, 1995, notes [in author's possession]). See also Patricia Samford, "The Archaeology of African-American Slavery and Material Culture," *William and Mary Quarterly* 53 (Jan. 1996): 92, 94; Richard Noble Westmacott, *African-American Gardens and Yards in the Rural South* (Knoxville,

1992); Sidney W. Mintz, *Caribbean Transformations* (1974; reprint, New York, 1989), 239–49; Kate Porter Young, *Notes on Sisterhood, Kinship, and Marriage in an African-American South Carolina Sea Island Community* (Memphis, Tenn., 1992), 8–10; and Lydia Mihelic Pulsipher and LaVerne Wells-Bowie, "The Domestic Spaces of Daufuskie and Monserrat: A Cross-Cultural Comparison," in *Cross-Cultural Studies of Traditional Dwellings*, ed. Nezar AlSayyad and Jean-Paul Bourdier (Berkeley, 1989), 1–24.

88. See, for example, *United States v. Marshall*; and testimony of Willis Stansell in *United States v. Sam Brown*, Dec. 12, 1867, box 2, ibid.

89. E. A. Rawlins to editor, Sept. 1866, *The Farmer* 1 (Nov. 1866): 421.

90. General Orders No. 23, Headquarters Dept. of the Gulf, Mar. 11, 1865, reprinted in Berlin et al., eds., *Wartime Genesis of Free Labor: The Lower South*, 593; testimony of Tobias Gibson, Apr. 25, 1865, reprinted in ibid., 608; Col. H. N. Frisbie to Thomas W. Conway, Oct. 2, 1865, reprinted in Berlin et al., eds., *Black Military Experience*, 701; affidavit of Mackey Woods, [Memphis, Tenn.], Dec. 12, 1865, reprinted in Ira Berlin, Barbara J. Fields, Thavolia Glymph, Joseph P. Reidy, and Leslie S. Rowland, eds., *The Destruction of Slavery*, ser. 1, vol. 1, *Freedom: A Documentary History of Emancipation, 1861–1867* (New York, 1985), 327. On the persistence of garden plots and other "privileges" in postemancipation labor agreements in Virginia, see Dennett, *South as It Is*, 14, 51.

91. *Frederick and Grace Wright v. William E. Stoney*.

92. *Joseph Bennett v. John F. Poppenheim*, Dec. 30, 1867, ibid.

93. Testimony of Calvin Usum in *Green Gardner v. David Boyd*, Mar. 26, 1870, Boston, Texas, entry 4852, Statements of Charges, Proceedings of Trials, and Letters Received Relating to Civil Cases, 1868–70, Dept. of Texas and the 5th Military District (P), 1865–70, RG 393, Part I.

94. Testimony of Caroline Hamlet in *State v. Green Edwards*, Oct. 17, 1877, CC, box 2, folder 18, OCHM; testimony of Isaac Allen in ibid.

95. Sub-Asst. Cmr. F. W. Liedtke to Bvt. Maj. A. M. L. Crawford, Sept. 10, 1866, in *Leander Dingle v. Thomas S. Waring*, PCBerk, RG 393, Part IV.

96. Testimony of John Waldrop in *United States v. John Hanson*, July 12, 1865, Proceedings of Military Commission, Louisa County, Virginia, MM2665, RG 153. See also testimony of John Sheehan in *State v. Gus Brown*, Apr. 17, 1877, CC, box 2, folder 10, OCHM, and testimony of George Elfe in *United States v. Carolina (freedman)*, Nov. 1, 1865, Proceedings of Military Commission, Charleston, South Carolina, MM3298, RG 153. At least one former slave won back property based on testimony about his "mark." See testimony of Casey Nesbit in *Casey Nesbit v. John Donnelly Sr.*, Dec. 14, 1867, PCBerk, RG 393, Part IV.

97. Testimony of Thos. H. Massy in *Jno Hart Trustee of Rebecca Haywood v. Saml Turner*, Nov. 1867 (n.d.), entry 1594, Provost Court, 1867–68, Fayetteville, North Carolina, Towns and Posts, RG 393, Part IV.

98. Atty. John A. Corley to Mil. Cmr. James Davidson, n.d., entry 4852, Statements of Charges, Proceedings of Trials, and Letters Received Relating to Civil Cases, 1868–70, Dept. of Texas and 5th Military District (P), 1865–70, RG 393, Part I.

99. Testimony of James Duke and testimony of Samuel Hall, both in *James Collier v. A. J. Wooten*, Mar. 28, 1870, Proceedings of Military Commission, Clarksville, Texas, State-

ments of Charges, Proceedings of Trials, and Letters Received Relating to Civil Cases, 1868–70, Dept. of Texas and 5th Military District (P), 1865–70, RG 393, Part I.

100. Affidavit of W. N. Whiteside, Dec. 27, 1869, Clarksville, Texas, box 1, entry 4851, Affidavits in Civil Affairs Cases, 1867–70, Dept. of Texas and 5th Military District (P), 1865–70, RG 393, Part I.

101. Testimony of Warren Ofeald in *United States v. William Green alias Douglass*, Jan. 28, 1865, Proceedings of Military Commission, Baton Rouge, La., MM1855, RG 153. For other property cases where "private marks" and other local knowledge influenced verdicts, see testimony of N. M. Grimes in *State v. Geo. Slaton*, Mar. 17, 1873, 037.326.5, CAP; testimony of T. W. Robinson in ibid.; *State v. Hyman Coffield*, n.d., 037.326.4, CAP; testimony of "Com modore young freed man" in *State v. Harry Pace*, June 16, 1866, 044.928.20, Criminal Action Papers Concerning Slaves and Free Persons of Color, 1864–76, Granville County, North Carolina, NCSA; and *State v. Addison McAdden and Burton Ellison*, Sept. 1873, 044.928.20, ibid.

102. Foner, *Reconstruction*, 150, 165–68.

103. Testimony of Carolina Trotti in *Carolina Trotti v. O. R. Parker*, Aug. 24, 1867, PCA, vol. 1, RG 393, Part IV.

104. Lt. Charles C. Jones Jr. to Rev. C. C. Jones (1862), in Myers, ed., *Children of Pride*, 987.

105. Harold D. Woodman, *New South—New Law: The Legal Foundations of Credit and Labor Relations in the Postbellum Agricultural South* (Baton Rouge, 1995), 13–52.

106. For examples from Mississippi, see Somers, *Southern States since the War*, 243, and Trowbridge, *South*, 342–43. The Georgia Supreme Court acknowledged this tendency in an 1888 opinion: "Landlords generally are on or near the rented premises, and have better opportunities to look after their rights and interests than purchasers would ordinarily have" (quoted in Woodman, *New South—New Law*, 41).

107. Testimony of August Macbeth in *August Macbeth v. civil magistrate P. M. C. Earnest*, July 1, 1868, PCBerk, RG 393, Part IV.

108. Arrest warrant for Owen Horne, Dec. 4, 1867, 037.326.3, CAP.

109. See, for example, testimony of Davis Weatherbee in *United States (Ned Ashley) v. Ben Busch and Davis Weatherbee*, Feb. 19, 1868, PCA, vol. 3, RG 393, Part IV.

110. Testimony of Paul Anderson in *Frederick and Grace Wright v. William E. Stoney*.

111. Suspicion fell heaviest on unbaled, small loads of cotton, the kind that all poor farmers brought to market. See Mary Ellen Curtin, "'Negro Thieves' or Enterprising Farmers? Markets, the Law, and African American Community Regulation in Alabama, 1866–1877," *Agricultural History* 74, no. 1 (2000): 29–31; and *State v. Isaac Weaver, Adkinson Weaver, James Hardin, Marcellus Evans, and Harry*, Jan. 11, 1866, 044.928.20, Criminal Action Papers Concerning Slaves and Free Persons of Color, 1864–76, Granville County, North Carolina, NCSA.

112. Testimony of York Mikell in *United States v. York Mikell*, Nov. 26, 1866, Provost Court, Sea Islands, South Carolina, box A, PCNSC, RG 393, Part I.

113. Testimony of Booker Piatt in *State v. Collins T. Cross*, Feb. 26, 1870, 037.326.4, CAP.

114. Christopher Waldrep, *Roots of Disorder: Race and Criminal Justice in the American South, 1817–80* (Urbana, 1998), 103.

115. "South Carolina Morals" (1877), quoted in Edward L. Ayers, *Vengeance and Justice: Crime and Punishment in the 19th-Century American South* (New York, 1984), 176. On white fears of a black crime wave, see Dennett, *South as It Is*, 42, and Trowbridge, *South*, 118–19.

116. Waldrep, *Roots of Disorder*, 98–99, 176.

117. Albert Colbcy Smith, "Down Freedom's Road: The Contours of Race, Class, and Property Crime in Black-Belt Georgia, 1866–1910" (Ph.D. diss., University of Georgia, 1982), 173–75. As black newspaper editors pointed out, it is very unlikely that these prosecutions reflected actual crime rates. More likely, thousands of white criminals roamed free while innocent black people went to the chain gangs. See *Savannah Tribune* (1893 and 1894) in Ayers, *Vengeance and Justice*, 228–29.

118. Foner, *Reconstruction*, 594.

119. The children taught by Elizabeth Hyde Botume in the Sea Islands were able to identify and distinguish even machine-standardized items such as primer books. See Elizabeth Hyde Botume, *First Days amongst the Contrabands* (Boston, 1893), 45–49.

120. Testimony of Peter Burton in *United States v. Frank Curry*, June 21, 1867, PCA, vol. 1, RG 393, Part IV.

121. State Attorney N. C. Read, "Statement of Facts," in *State of Texas v. Madison Wilson*, n.d., entry 4852, Statements of Charges, Proceedings of Trials, and Letters Received Relating to Civil Cases, 1868–70, Dept. of Texas and 5th Military District (P), 1865–70, RG 393, Part I.

122. Confederate money, which blacks had used during the war despite their skepticism, became worthless in 1865. Even worse, it took at least two years for federal money to circulate freely in the South (Ransom and Sutch, *One Kind of Freedom*, 60). See also Dennett, *South as It Is*, 9, 46–47, 99.

123. Testimony of Shady Lewis in *Shady Lewis v. James Brennan*, Oct. 19, 1867, box 4, PCNSC, RG 393, Part I.

124. Testimony of Ned Byerson in *Samuel Dobson v. Ned Byerson*, Dec. 22, 1866, PCB, Sept. 1865–June 1868, RG 393, Part IV. See also testimony of Robert Gwinnin in *Thomas Johnson v. Cato Foxworth*, Sept. 18, 1867, PCSum, box 1, PCNSC, RG 393, Part I.

125. Curtin, "'Negro Thieves,'" 19–38.

126. On cooperative societies in Memphis, see Armstead Robinson, "Plans Dat Comed from God: Institution Building and the Emergence of Black Leadership in Reconstruction Memphis," in Burton and McMath, eds., *Toward a New South*, 87. On a "Society meeting" and "feast" in Portsmouth, Virginia, see testimony of Philip Randall in *United States v. William Bailey*, Mar. 1, 1866, Fortress Monroe, Virginia, MM3684, RG 153.

127. Testimony of Winfred Nowlin in *United States v. William Jennings*, Jan. 2, 1866, Proceedings of a Military Commission at Lynchburg, Virginia, MM3420, RG 153.

128. Testimony of Cornelia Simmons in *United States v. Isaac Simmons*, Apr. 28, 1868, Provost Court, Beaufort, South Carolina, box 2, PCNSC, RG 393, Part I. On burial societies in Memphis, see Robinson, "Plans Dat Comed from God," 87.

129. Testimony of Henry Ruth in *Rachel Bostwick v. Toney Davis*, Dec. 8, 1866, PCB, Sept. 1865–June 1868, RG 393, Part IV.

130. Testimony of Bess Milligan in *Bess Milligan v. Joseph Burnam*, Feb. 11, 1867, Provost Court, Sea Islands, James Island, South Carolina, box A, PCNSC, RG 393, Part I.

131. R. E. Windham to Capt. Liedtke, Sept. 13, 1867, box 4, ibid.

132. Testimony of Pvt. Hope Montgomery in *United States v. Cpl. George Campbell*, Dec. 14, 1865, DeValls Bluff, Ark., MM3796, RG 153.

133. Testimony of Pvt. Nathan Dixon in ibid.

134. *Louis Willis v. Flanders Dickey Sr.*, Nov. 8–10, 1882, Davis Bend Magistrate's Book, OCHM; *Abram Huguenin v. Lymas Middleton*, Nov. 8, 1866, PCB, Sept. 1865–June 1868, RG 393, Part IV.

135. Testimony of Rose Duggins in *Macbeth v. Earnest*, July 1, 1868.

136. Decree, in *Robert Willis v. R. H. Daily*, Apr. 21, 1866, PCB, Sept. 1865–June 1868, RG 393, Part IV.

137. Testimony of Miss Laura M. Town[e], pp. 69–70, File 3, AFIC.

138. John W. De Forest, *A Union Officer in the Reconstruction* (New Haven, 1948), 98–99.

139. Ibid., 99. Other northerners spoke more carefully about "thoughtless" and "thoughtful" gift-giving. See Philena Carkin, "Reminiscences of My Life and Work among the Freedmen of Charlottesville Virginia From Mar. 1st 1866 to July 1st 1875. Vol. 1," 90–92, Philena Carkin Papers (no. 11123), UVA.

140. Laura M. Towne, *Letters and Diary of Laura M. Towne; Written from the Sea Islands of South Carolina, 1862–1884*, ed. Rupert Sargent Holland (1912; reprint, New York, 1969), 23.

141. Martha Schofield, Diary, pp. 43–44, 67, typescript copy, no. 999-z, SHC; Pearson, *Letters from Port Royal*, 21.

142. Holt, *Making Freedom Pay*, 113.

143. Carkin, "Reminiscences of My Life and Work," 90–92.

144. Towne, *Letters and Diary*, 23.

145. Ibid., 123.

146. Ibid., 133–34.

147. In the emerging business of credit reporting, agencies such as R. G. Dun evaluated reputation and personal character alongside tangible assets in assessing borrowers' worthiness for credit. On parallel processes in East Africa, see Sally Falk Moore, "From Giving and Lending to Selling: Property Transactions Reflecting Historical Changes on Kilimanjaro," 108–27, in *Law in Colonial Africa*, ed. Kristin Mann and Richard Roberts (Portsmouth, N.H., 1991).

148. Pierce, "Light on the Slavery Question," entry 574, BE 1861–64, Port Royal Correspondence Received by Sec. Treasury Chase, Nov. 25, 1861–Aug. 7, 1862, CWSAT.

149. Testimony of H. Styles [Stiles] before Smith-Brady Commission, Feb. 3, 1865, reprinted in Berlin et al., *Wartime Genesis of Free Labor: The Lower South*, 585. See also Col. Saml. Thomas to Brig. Genl. L. Thomas, June 15, 1864, reprinted in ibid., 838. Observant witnesses such as Charles Nordhoff noted (with less exaggeration than Styles) that this "same strong local attachment" had also been "characteristic of the black freedmen in the British West Indies." See Charles Nordhoff, *The Freedmen of*

South Carolina: Some Account of their Appearances, Character, Conditions, and Peculiar Customs (New York, 1863), 11.

150. Saville, *Work of Reconstruction*, 18. See also Pearson, *Letters from Port Royal*, 234.

151. Mark R. Schultz, "The Dream Realized? African American Landownership in Central Georgia between Reconstruction and World War II," *Agricultural History* 72, no. 2 (1998): 303–4.

152. Foner, *Reconstruction*, 105.

153. J. M. Simms to "General," enclosure in Tillson to "General," Letters Sent, Correspondence, Office of the Assistant Commissioner, Georgia, entry 626, BRFAL, FSSP A-5161.

154. E. A. Kozlay to H. W. Smith, Dec. [n.d.], 1865, Orangeburg, South Carolina, Reports of Conditions and Operations, July 1865–Dec. 1868, Reports, Office of the Assistant Commissioner, South Carolina, entry 2929, BRFAL, FSSP A-7014.

155. Samuel Boles to Bvt. Maj. Gen. Birge, June 16, 1865, entry 1022, Records of the Assistant Adjutant General Relating to the Restoration of Property in the Savannah Area, Mar. 1865–Feb. 1866, Subassistant Commissioner, Savannah, Georgia, Subordinate Field Offices, BRFAL, FSSP A-5863.

156. Akans today continue to make claims to land based on long ago "first settlers." See Kwame Arhin, "Rank and Class among the Asante and Fante in the Nineteenth Century," *Africa* 53, no. 1 (1983).

157. Cheryll Ann Cody, "Kin and Community among the Good Hope People after Emancipation," *Ethnohistory* 41, no. 1 (1994); Shepard Krech III, "Black Family Organization in the Nineteenth Century: An Ethnological Perspective," *Journal of Interdisciplinary History* 12, no. 3 (1982); Sydney Nathans, "Fortress without Walls: A Black Community after Slavery," in *Holding on to the Land and the Lord: Kinship, Ritual, Land Tenure, and Social Policy in the Rural South*, ed. Robert L. Hall and Carol B. Stack (Athens, Ga., 1982), 55–65.

158. E. A. Rawlins to editor, Sept. 1866, *The Farmer* 1 (Nov. 1866): 421.

159. Cody, "Kin and Community," 33–37.

160. Krech, "Black Family Organization," 442; Cody, "Kin and Community," 43–44; Schultz, "Dream Realized?" Cooperation between brothers figures strongly in the histories of all three places. See also R. S. Bennett, Intendant of Beaufort to A. Pleasanton, May 16, 1871, entry 99, General Correspondence, South Carolina, Records of or Relating to Direct Tax Commissions in Southern States and to Direct Taxes in Other States, Records of the Internal Revenue Service, Record Group 58, National Archives, Washington, D.C., FSSP Z-31.

161. Shaw's immediate reference is to a boll weevil infestation, but his narrative is rich with testimony about kinship and property. See Theodore Rosengarten, *All God's Dangers: The Life of Nate Shaw* (New York, 1989), 223.

CHAPTER SIX

1. Testimony of Sarah Waite in *United States v. Hester Scott*, Jan. 29, 1867, Provost Court, Sea Islands, South Carolina, box A, PCNSC, RG 393, Part I.

2. Hendrik Hartog, *Man and Wife in America: A History* (Cambridge, 2000), 63–92.

3. Ira Berlin, Steven F. Miller, and Leslie S. Rowland, "Afro-American Families in the Transition from Slavery to Freedom," *Radical History Review* 42 (1988): 89–121.

4. This chapter builds on recent work by Noralee Frankel, Leslie Schwalm, and Nancy Bercaw but focuses primarily on black-black rather than white-black relations. See Noralee Frankel, *Freedom's Women: Black Women and Families in Civil War Era Mississippi* (Bloomington, Ind., 1999); Leslie A. Schwalm, *A Hard Fight for We: Women's Transition from Slavery to Freedom in South Carolina* (Urbana, 1997); and Nancy Dunlap Bercaw, "Politics of Household during the Transition from Slavery to Freedom in the Yazoo-Mississippi Delta, 1861–1876" (Ph.D. diss., University of Pennsylvania, 1996). Emancipation sent many other identities into flux, as well. Frederick Cooper argues that ex-slaves in coastal Kenya, Zanzibar, and Pemba adopted and manipulated "ethnic" identities (such as "Arab" and "Swahili") in the wake of emancipation there. See Frederick Cooper, *From Slaves to Squatters: Plantation Labor and Agriculture in Zanzibar and Coastal Kenya, 1890–1925* (New Haven, 1980), 163–72, 288.

5. Elizabeth Hyde Botume, *First Days amongst the Contrabands* (Boston, 1893), 234.

6. Interview of Minksie Walker in George P. Rawick, ed., *The American Slave: A Composite Autobiography* (Westport, Conn., 1972), vol. 11, Arkansas Narratives, part 7, and Missouri Narratives, 369. See also Theodore Rosengarten, *All God's Dangers: The Life of Nate Shaw* (New York, 1989), for Ned Cobb's memories of his father.

7. On the Gordonsville, Virginia, station, see Philena Carkin, "Reminiscences of my Life and Work among the Freedmen of Charlottesville Virginia From Mar. 1st 1866 to July 1st 1875. Vol. 1," Philena Carkin Papers (no. 11123), UVA; on the Warrenton, North Carolina station, see Margaret Newbold Thorpe (1869), quoted in "A 'Yankee Teacher' in North Carolina, edited by Richard Morton," *North Carolina Historical Review* 30 (Oct. 1953 [1869]): 569.

8. Testimony of Peter Anchrum in *John Lance v. Peter Anchrum, alias Cord*, Jan. 23, 1867, Provost Court, Sea Islands, South Carolina, box A, PCNSC, RG 393, Part I. A good horse cost as much as $100 in 1867, about as much as a black man would earn in ten months of wage work (Roger L. Ransom and Richard Sutch, *One Kind of Freedom: The Economic Consequences of Emancipation* [New York, 1977], 49, 65).

9. Testimony of Lewis Green in *United States v. W. H. Garland, Jr.*, Aug. 29, 1867, PCSum, box 4, PCNSC, RG 393, Part I. On children's fishing in South Carolina, see Elizabeth Ware Pearson, ed., *Letters from Port Royal, 1862–1868* (Boston, 1906), 156–57, and Eliza Ann Summers, *"Dear Sister": Letters Written on Hilton Head Island, 1867* (Beaufort, 1977), 15. On children and hunting in North Carolina, see Sharon Ann Holt, *Making Freedom Pay: North Carolina Freedpeople Working for Themselves, 1865–1900* (Athens, Ga., 2000), 7.

10. Claim of Robert Brandon, p. 16, Madison County, Alabama, SCC.

11. Pearson, *Letters from Port Royal*, 191–92.

12. Testimony of Jack Washington in *United States v. Jack Washington*, Dec. 5, 1866, Provost Court, Sea Islands, South Carolina, box 2, entry 1524, RG 393, Part IV.

13. On children's work in North Carolina, see Holt, *Making Freedom Pay*, 7; on Texas and Arkansas, see Cheryll Ann Cody, "Kin and Community among the Good Hope People after Emancipation," *Ethnohistory* 41, no. 1 (1994): 39.

14. Claim of Horace Hillman, p. 13, DeSoto County, Mississippi, SCC.

15. William F. Allen, typescript diary, p. 200, May 28, 1864 (microfilm, [reel 33/ roll 157]), State Historical Society of Wisconsin, Madison.

16. Testimony of Wilson Titus in *United States (Bester, dec'd) v. Fitzgerald*, Sept. 30, 1867, p. 49, Proceedings of a Military Commission at Vicksburg, Mississippi, OO2701, RG 153.

17. Testimony of Amelia in *United States v. Eliza E. Lewis*, Aug. 4, 1865, Jacksonville, Florida, MM2682, RG 153.

18. Lucy Chase to My Dear Friends, July 1, 1864, reprinted in Henry L. Swint, ed., *Dear Ones at Home: Letters from Contraband Camps* (Nashville, 1966), 123.

19. Testimony of James Pack in *Nero Tindall v. John Hodges*, Sept. 5, 1867, PCSum, box 1, PCNSC, RG 393, Part I; testimony of Isaiah DuBose in ibid.

20. Testimony of James Pack in ibid.

21. Agent D. A. Newman to Col. E. M. L. Ehlers, Subassistant Commissioner, Sept. 30, 1867, entry 1057, Miscellaneous Papers, 1867–68, Agent, Warrenton-Woodville, Georgia, Subordinate Field Offices, BRFAL.

22. Lt. James DeGrey (1867), quoted in Berlin, Miller, and Rowland, "Afro-American Families in the Transition," 116.

23. Testimony of James Reavis in *Thomas Hardy v. Bevins Brandon*, Nov. 24, 1865, 044.928.21, Miscellaneous Records of Slaves and Free Persons of Color, undated, 1755–1871, Granville County, North Carolina, NCSA.

24. *State v. John Taylor and Jim Knight*, Fall term 1866, 037.311.3, Superior Court, Edgecombe County, North Carolina, Minutes, vol. 1, 1862, 1866–72, NCSA.

25. Testimony of Serena Blizer in *Serena Blizer v. W. S. Kennedy*, Sept. 2, 1867, PCSum, box 1, PCNSC, RG 393, Part I. See also testimony of John Jones in *United States v. Anderson Sanders*, Sept. 9, 1867, ibid.

26. Julie Saville, *The Work of Reconstruction: From Slave to Wage Laborer in South Carolina, 1860–1870* (New York, 1994), 53–56.

27. William F. Mugleston, "The Freedmen's Bureau and Reconstruction in Virginia: The Diary of Marcus Sterling Hopkins, a Union Officer," *Virginia Magazine of History and Biography* 86, no. 1 (1978): 55. For a similar view, see Enclosure, J. M. Gachy to Capt. E. Pickett, May 27, 1867, entry 1057, Miscellaneous Papers, 1867–68, Agent, Warrenton-Woodville, Georgia, Subordinate Field Offices, BRFAL.

28. A. E. Niles to H. W. Smith (1866), quoted in Saville, *Work of Reconstruction*, 103.

29. Berlin, Miller, and Rowland, "Afro-American Families in the Transition," 108.

30. Affidavit of Jesse Wall, f.m.c., Apr. 22, 1870, Marion County, Texas, box 1, entry 4851, Affidavits in Civil Affairs Cases, 1868–70, Dept. of Texas and 5th Military District (P), 1865–70, RG 393, Part I. A white unionist in Maryland explained freedpeople's beliefs in similar terms. See Joseph Hall to Maj. Gen. Howard, Aug. 20, 1865, reprinted in Ira Berlin et al., eds., *The Wartime Genesis of Free Labor: The Upper South*, ser. 1, vol. 2, *Freedom: A Documentary History of Emancipation, 1861–1867* (New York, 1993), 542–43.

31. Some of the freedpeople who fought their old masters for custody of their children hired those same children out (James Murray to Maj. Gen. Lew. Wallace, Dec. 5, 1864, reprinted in Berlin et al., eds., *Wartime Genesis of Free Labor: The Upper South*,

524–25; Joseph Hall to General Howard, Sept. 14, 1865, in ibid., 544–45; and affidavit of Derrinda Smothers, Sept. 18, 1865, ibid., 546).

32. Affidavit of Peter Williams, Jan. 10, 1868, entry 3272, Statements Relating to Complaints, Subassistant Commissioner, Marion, South Carolina, BRFAL. For a similar complaint in Alabama, see Katherine M. Franke, "Becoming a Citizen: Reconstruction Era Regulation of African American Marriages," *Yale Journal of Law & the Humanities* 11 (1999): 285.

33. Frankel, *Freedom's Women*, 137–38. See also *Freedman Dick v. Wife*, Mar. 9, 1867, p. 44, entry 3191, Journal of Complaints ("Memorandum Book"), May 1866–Dec. 1867, Acting Assistant Commissioner, Darlington, South Carolina, BRFAL.

34. Capt. Chas. Enllorse to Cmdg. Officer of Brenham Post, Nov. 25, 1869, entry 4852, Statements of Charges, Proceedings of Trials, and Letters Received Relating to Civil Cases, 1868–70, Dept. of Texas and 5th Military District (P), 1865–70, RG 393, Part I.

35. *Mr. Brewer & Wife v. John Jackson*, n.d., entry 1594, Provost Court, 1867–68, Fayetteville, North Carolina, Towns and Posts, RG 393, Part IV.

36. Lt. & S.A. Commissioner to Capt. Eugene Pickett, A.A.A. Gen., Feb. 4, 1867, entry 1057, Miscellaneous Papers, 1867–68, Agent, Waynesboro, Georgia, Subordinate Field Offices, BRFAL.

37. Testimony of Charles Stewart [Jr.] in *Charles Stewart [Sr.] v. John M. Plowden*, Oct. 14, 1867, PCSum, box 1, PCNSC, RG 393, Part I.

38. Testimony of James Tindall in *Tindall v. Hodges*, Sept. 5, 1867, PCSum, box 1, PCNSC, RG 393, Part I.

39. Sister [illegible] to Dear Sister and Brothers, Apr. 29, 1889, Neal Family Papers, no. 4370, SHC; affidavit of E. P. Jackson in *State v. John Howell*, Apr. 30, 1870, 037.326.5, CAP; affidavit of Fanny Wells in ibid.

40. J. T. Trowbridge, *The South* (1866; reprint, New York, 1969), 221–22.

41. Testimony of William Collier in claim of Henry Slaughter, pp. 5–6, Morgan County, Alabama, reel 30, WSCC. On a "family partnership" among ex-slaves in Hale County, Alabama, see Sydney Nathans, "Fortress without Walls: A Black Community after Slavery," in *Holding on to the Land and the Lord: Kinship, Ritual, Land Tenure, and Social Policy in the Rural South*, ed. Robert L. Hall and Carol B. Stack (Athens, Ga., 1982), 56.

42. Testimony of Winfred Nowlin in *United States v. William Jennings*, Jan. 2, 1866, Proceedings of a Military Commission at Lynchburg, Virginia, MM3420, RG 153. For an example from Macon, Georgia, see Sidney Andrews, *The South since the War* (1866; reprint, New York, 1969), 350–51.

43. Testimony of Lydia Taylor in *State v. Taylor and Knight*.

44. Trowbridge, *South*, 221–22.

45. Testimony of Col. Geo. H. Hanks, 15th Reg't., Corps d'Afrique, Feb. 6, 1864, p. 37, File 11, Louisiana, AFIC.

46. On at least one Mississippi plantation, the Union army required blacks to form "labor companies." See "Rules and Regulations . . . for the Government of the Freedmen at Davis Bend. Miss." (early 1865?), reprinted in Ira Berlin et al., eds., *The Wartime Genesis of Free Labor: The Lower South*, ser. 1, vol. 3, *Freedom*, 868.

47. See the testimony of August Ward in *Thomas Archer v. Marcus Chisholm*, Apr. 2, 1866, PCB, Sept. 1865–June 1868, RG 393, Part IV. Black sugar workers in Louisiana went on strike for the right to form "sub-associations." See Paul K. Eiss, "A Share in the Land: Freedpeople and the Government of Labour in Southern Louisiana, 1862–65," *Slavery and Abolition* 19, no. 1 (1998).

48. Laura Towne, Manuscript Diary and Letters, 1862–64, pp. 126–27, typescript, Penn School Papers, SHC (permission granted by Penn Center, Inc., St. Helena Island, S.C.). See also the testimony of Morris Corley in *Thornton Corley v. Mark Etheridge*, July 19, 1867, PCA, vol. 1, RG 393, Part IV. For kinship language in Virginia, see John Richard Dennett, *The South as It Is: 1865–1866*, ed. Henry M. Christman (New York, 1965), 74.

49. Testimony of Mrs. J. Landry, p. 9, in "Workers, Laborers, and Wages," vol. 5, entry 1758, Miscellaneous Records of District and Parish Provost Marshals, 1862–66, Subordinate Provost Marshals in the Department of the Gulf, RG 393, Part IV.

50. Testimony of Miss Lucy Chase, p. 24, File 2, AFIC.

51. [W. F. Allen] "Marcel," "The Negro Dialect" in *The Negro and His Folklore in Nineteenth-Century Periodicals*, ed. Bruce Jackson (Austin, 1967), 76; Andrews, *South since the War*, 229; testimony of Laura M. Towne, p. 66, File 3, AFIC.

52. Testimony of Robert Smalls, p. 105, File 3, AFIC. And northerners began to follow Smalls's lead. See the testimony of Capt. E. W. Hooper, p. 226, File 3, AFIC. At times, white witnesses before the American Freedmen's Inquiry Commission of 1863 testified about black families in language that presaged the "culture of poverty" arguments of 1960s social science: "I think there is a large distinction between the respect [children pay] to the father and the mother." Because the father "oftentimes deserts the mother," the children "fail to respect him. The tendency seems to be universally to disregard him" (testimony of Henry G. Judd, p. 86, File 3, AFIC).

53. Robert Somers, *The Southern States since the War, 1870–71* (1872; reprint, University, Ala., 1965), 120–21. See also E. A. Rawlins to editor, Sept. 1866, *The Farmer* 1 (Nov. 1866): 421.

54. Botume, *First Days amongst the Contrabands*, 67. Archaeological evidence from Glynn County, Georgia, suggests that conditions worsened in the first few months after emancipation for the people living in the Low Country. See Theresa A. Singleton, "Archaeological Implications for Changing Labor Conditions," in *The Archaeology of Slavery and Plantation Life*, ed. Theresa A. Singleton (Orlando, 1985), 303.

55. Brig. Gen. Davis Tillson to Maj. Gen. O. O. Howard, Feb. 12, 1866, entry 15, Letters Received, Mar. 1865–June 1872, Correspondence, Records of the Commissioner, BRFAL, FSSP A-5810.

56. *Prince Herron v. John Herron*, n.d., Provost Marshal, Memphis, Tennessee, entry 3545, BRFAL.

57. Edward F. O'Brien, Sub-Asst. Cmr. at Mount Pleasant, South Carolina, to Bureau Adjutant A. M. L. Crawford, Oct. 11, 1866, BRFAL, FSSP A-7096.

58. Samuel Boles to Bvt. Maj. Gen. Birge, June 16, 1865, entry 626, Letters Sent, Correspondence, Office of the Assistant Commissioner, Georgia, BRFAL, FSSP A-5863.

59. Samuel Boles to Bvt. Maj. Gen. Birge, June 16, 1865, entry 1022, Records of

the Assistant Adjutant General Relating to the Restoration of Property in the Savannah Area, Mar. 1865–Feb. 1866, Subassistant Commissioner, Savannah, Georgia, Subordinate Field Offices, BRFAL, FSSP A-5863. See also Charles Joyner, *Down by the Riverside: A South Carolina Slave Community* (Urbana, 1984), 42–43.

60. Botume, *First Days amongst the Contrabands*, 120–21.

61. Ibid., 66.

62. Testimony of Henry Mack in *United States v. David Drayton*, Nov. 1, 1866, Provost Court, Sea Islands, South Carolina, box A, PCNSC, RG 393, Part I. The girl who answered the door was living with the Draytons but seems not to have been a relative by blood or marriage. Black-black conflict should not be overstated: the biggest and most violent expression of identity in Memphis came from members of the city's Irish working class, who on April 30, 1866, killed fifty-four blacks and burned down every black church and school in the city. See Armstead Robinson, "Plans Dat Comed from God: Institution Building and the Emergence of Black Leadership in Reconstruction Memphis," in *Toward a New South? Studies in Post–Civil War Southern Communities*, ed. Orville Vernon Burton and Robert C. McMath Jr. (Westport, Conn., 1982), 79–81.

63. Herbert G. Gutman, "Persistent Myths about the Afro-American Family," *Journal of Interdisciplinary History* 6 (Autumn 1975): 198–99.

64. Robinson, "Plans Dat Comed from God," 79–81.

65. Henry Rowntree to Esteemed Friends (1864), quoted in Berlin et al., eds., *Wartime Genesis of Free Labor: The Lower South*, 824.

66. Louisiana Free Men of Color to the Commander of the Department of the Gulf (1864), reprinted in Berlin et al., eds., *Wartime Genesis of Free Labor: The Upper South*, 570–71. See also Baton Rouge Free Blacks to the Provost Marshal of Baton Rouge [Nov. 1863], reprinted in Ira Berlin, Joseph P. Reidy, and Leslie S. Rowland, eds., *The Black Military Experience*, ser. 2, *Freedom* (1982), 159–60.

67. "Account of visits to contraband camp and hospital and to color'd schools in St. Louis by the American Freedmen's Inquiry Commission [Dec. 3, 1863]," reprinted in Berlin et al., eds., *Wartime Genesis of Free Labor: The Upper South*, 585.

68. Testimony of Lewis Parker in *State v. Jacob Cooper*, July term 1872, CC, box 1, folders 16–17, OCHM.

69. Testimony of Harmen N[illegible], July 9, 1866, entry 2660, Records Relating to Court Cases, Feb. 1865–Dec. 1868, Subassistant Commissioner, Greensboro, North Carolina, Subordinate Field Offices, BRFAL.

70. Testimony of Lorena Neely in claim of Edmund Moss, p. 13, Shelby County, Alabama, reel 31, WSCC.

71. Testimony of Pvt. Reuben Phinney in *United States (Columbus Friarson, dec'd) v. Pvt. Robinson C. Banks*, Nov. 20, 1865, Chattanooga, Tennessee, MM3675, entry 15, RG 153.

72. Testimony of Eliza Long in *United States (Phillis Wadkins, dec'd) v. Eliza Long*, Nov. 20, 1865, MM3192, RG 153. Phillis's former master called her "tyrannical and quarrelsome"; another white witness thought she was "very troublesome, frequently creating some difficulty with the other Negroes." But, clearly, she had the ears of many of the freedpeople around her upcountry Georgia home (testimony of Jonathan Wadkins, ibid.; testimony of John Kidd, ibid.).

73. Testimony of Gillem Fitzgerald (freedman) in *United States (Bester, dec'd) v. Fitzgerald*, Sept. 30, 1867, p. 64, Proceedings of a Military Commission at Vicksburg, Mississippi, OO2701, RG 153. Fitzgerald killed Bester. See also testimony of Harry McMillan, p. 128, File 3, AFIC.

74. A'Lelia Bundles, *On Her Own Ground: The Life and Times of Madam C. J. Walker* (New York, 2001), 35–40.

75. Towne, *Letters and Diary*, 190–94. Towne wrote perceptively about a nine-year-old orphan named Pompey who was taken in, put to work, and beaten by an older man. Although "the neighbors interfere[d]," Towne recalled, "everyone's hand is against him, because . . . [unlike Pompey] that man has relatives and influence" (ibid., 190–94). Towne also wrote of a woman who died "utterly neglected" because she "has no 'parents'" (Towne, Manuscript Diary and Letters, 133). See also *Brown v. Wilson*, Nov. 29, 1866, Provost Court, Sea Islands, South Carolina, box A, PCNSC, RG 393, Part I. In at least a few cases, children were sexually abused in their new homes. See Statement of Adelade Rose (col'd), Apr. 6, 1866, Provost Marshal, Memphis, Tennessee, entry 3545, BRFAL; affidavit of Alfred and Martha Pelham, Apr. 5, 1868, Statements of Charges, Proceedings of Trials, and Letters Received Relating to Civil Cases, 1868–70, Dept. of Texas and the 5th Military District (P), 1865–70, RG 393, Part I; and *State (Mattie) v. Ned Washington*, Oct. 8, 1868, ibid.

76. Testimony of March Haynes in *United States (Gallant Morris, dec'd) v. Amos Vandross*, Jan. 17, 1865, Proceedings of a Military Commission at Hilton Head, South Carolina, MM1606, box 1030, RG 153.

77. Testimony of Ellen Simkins in *Delia Youngblood v. Margaret Lowe*, Sept. 13, 1867, PCA, no vol., RG 393, Part IV. See also testimony of John Lewis in *United States (Jacob Allen) v. John Lewis*, May 1, 1866, Proceedings of a Military Commission, Charleston, South Carolina, MM3934, RG 153.

78. A. W. Eddins, "The State Industrial School Boys' Slang," *Publications of the Texas Folk-Lore Society* 1 (1916): 45. In the 1770s the Jamaican slaveowner Edward Long thought that "the greatest affront that can possibly be offered a Creole Negroe, is to curse his father, mother, or any of his progenitors" (Edward Long, *The History of Jamaica, or General Survey of the Antient and Modern State of That Island* [1774; reprint, London, 1970], 2:416). The history of the dozens may go back even further. According to T. C. McCaskie (*State and Society in Pre-Colonial Asante* [Cambridge, Eng., 1995], 216–18), during the nineteenth century, state officials in Asante (today part of Ghana) publicly paraded the severed skulls of enemies defeated in war. These officials "stopped . . . repeatedly 'to identify each skull' [with] a formulaic 'preamble' insult *wo ɔse, wo ne*! ('your father, your mother!') with the imprecative and dismissive sense of 'who were they?' . . . then to recite [each skull's] history . . . its crimes against Asante" and how exactly it was severed from its owner.

79. Testimony of March Haynes in *United States v. Vandross*, Jan. 17, 1865.

80. Testimony of Dr. Dorland in ibid. Vandross was a newcomer from the mainland himself: "Nobody knows him but me," said a man who had come over with him (testimony of Caesar Peat in ibid.).

81. Typical examples from the 1860s include testimony of Benjamin Kribs in *State (Wm. H. Taylor Sr.) v. Wm. Taylor Jr.*, Feb. 15, 1869, Jacksboro, Texas, box 1, entry 4851,

Affidavits in Civil Affairs Cases, 1867–70, Dept. of Texas and 5th Military District (P), 1865–70, RG 393, Part I; charges against Edward Donahue, citizen, June 4, 1864, Court Issue Docket Book [Provost Marshal, Vicksburg, MS, Apr. 11, 1864–Aug. 22, 1865], OCHM; and charges against Donald McDonald, citizen, Aug. 3, 1864, ibid. On the legal history of domestic violence, see, inter alia, Reva B. Siegel, "'The Rule of Love': Wife Beating as Prerogative and Privacy," *Yale Law Journal* 105 (1996): 2117–2207; and Hartog, *Man and Wife in America*, 40–62.

82. On black women workers in Atlanta, see Tera W. Hunter, *To 'Joy My Freedom: Southern Black Women's Lives and Labors after the Civil War* (Cambridge, Mass., 1997).

83. Barbara J. Heath and Amber Bennet, "'The Little Spots Allow'd Them': The Archaeological Study of African-American Yards," *Historical Archaeology* 34, no. 2 (2000): 44; David Colin Crass and Mark J. Brooks, eds., "Cotton and Black Draught: Consumer Behavior on a Postbellum Farm" (Columbia, S.C., 1995), 65–66, 170–71; testimony of Olivia Goodloe in claim of Washington Patterson, n.p., Morgan County, Alabama, reel 30, WSCC; Lewis to My darling Mother, May 8, 1865, Blackford Family Papers, no. 1912, SHC.

84. Testimony of Fred Maxfield in *State v. Boise Huff, alias Frederick Maxfield*, Dec. 17, 1867, PCBerk, box A, PCNSC, RG 393, Part I.

85. Testimony of Tom Bowles in *United States v. Alex, Jack, and others*, May 23, 1867, Provost Court, Edgefield District, South Carolina, box 1, PCNSC, RG 393, Part I.

86. *George Thompson v. Charles Howard*, Nov. 23, 1877, Davis Bend Magistrate's Book, OCHM. On men usurping their wives' property in courtroom testimony, see testimony of Charles Adams in *State v. John Griffin*, Jan. term 1877, CC, box 2, folder 9c, OCHM.

87. Botume, *First Days amongst the Contrabands*, 221, 273. See also Pearson, *Letters from Port Royal*, 55.

88. Herbert G. Gutman, *The Black Family in Slavery and Freedom, 1750–1925* (New York, 1976), 166–67.

89. Testimony of Rebecca Clegg in *United States v. Maria Brooks*, Nov. 8, 1867, Provost Court Edgefield, South Carolina, box 2, RG 393, Part I. See also the testimony of David Peter in *United States v. Maria Brooks* and *United States v. Edward Coleman*, June 29, 1867, PCA, no vol., RG 393, Part IV.

90. Testimony of David Peter in *United States v. Maria Brooks*.

91. Cody, "Kin and Community," 39.

92. Testimony of Lydia Taylor in *State v. Taylor and Knight*.

93. Testimony of Tena Sinclair in *United States v. Lucy Deas*, Nov. 10, 1866, PCB, Sept. 1865–June 1868, RG 393, Part IV; testimony of Lucy Deas, in ibid.

94. Affidavit of Redding Em, freedman, before Agent Charles F. Sawyer, Feb. 15, 1867, entry 1024, Register of Letters Received and Endorsements Sent and Received, Dec. 1866–Apr. 1868, vol. 346, Agent, Savannah, Georgia, Subordinate Field Offices, BRFAL. Emphasis is in original.

95. Affidavit of Harry Williams, Apr. 10, 1866, entry 3075, Miscellaneous Records Relating to Affidavits, Charges and Specifications, and Proceedings of Provost Courts, Sept. 1866–Aug. 1867, Acting Subassistant Commissioner, Anderson District, Anderson Court House, South Carolina, BRFAL.

96. *State v. Roland Rand,* Oct. 15, 1880, Davis Bend Magistrate's Book, OCHM.

97. Statement of J. H. Wilson in complaint of Eliza Wilson, Dec. 7, 1867, entry 3035, Miscellaneous Records Relating to Complaints, May 1866–May 1868, Agent, Abbeville Court House, Subordinate Field Offices, South Carolina, BRFAL.

98. Testimony of Dessica Bliging in *United States v. August Bliging,* Nov. 8, 1866, Provost Court, Sea Islands, South Carolina, box A, PCNSC, RG 393, Part I.

99. Testimony of Moll Scott in ibid.

100. Testimony of Dessica Bliging in ibid.

101. Frankel, *Freedom's Women,* 106.

102. George C. Corliss to Acting Asst. Adj. Gen. Stuart Eldridge (1866), Friars Point, Mississippi, quoted in Bercaw, "Politics of Household," 241.

103. Testimony of Prince Kennedy in *United States v. Prince Kennedy,* Oct. 3, 1867, PCSum, box 4, PCNSC, RG 393, Part I. January Boyd, Jane Boyd's father, made the original complaint to the Sumter magistrate on Sept. 14, 1867.

104. Testimony of J. S. Shaffer in *United States v. Matt Spann,* Sept. 27, 1867, PCSum, box 4, PCNSC, RG 393, Part I.

105. Testimony of George Robinson in *United States v. George Robinson (alias Spears),* Aug. 10, 1867, PCSum, box 4, PCNSC, RG 393, Part I.

106. Ibid.

107. Testimony of Paul Frierson in *United States v. Robinson,* Aug. 10, 1867.

108. Testimony of Prince Simons in ibid. For violent threats by a husband in Louisiana, see the testimony of Elizabeth Young in *United States (Sally Repp) v. Charles Repp,* Mar. 25, 1865, Proceedings of Military Commission, Baton Rouge, La., MM1818, RG 153. Sally Repp "used to quarrel" with her husband over his illegal business of smuggling horses out of Union lines, "and he said, 'Sally—you attend to your business, and let me alone, if you dont . . . I will Kill you some of these days sure.' "

109. Writing of white-on-black rape, Angela Y. Davis argues that rape was both an expression and a foundation of economic domination. See Angela Y. Davis, *Women, Race, and Class* (New York, 1981), 175. The same seems to be the case with violence in ex-slave couples. On domestic violence among Mississippi freedpeople, see Frankel, *Freedom's Women,* 106–7, and Bercaw, "Politics of Household," 240–44. On domestic violence among North Carolina freedpeople, see Laura F. Edwards, *Gendered Strife and Confusion: The Political Culture of Reconstruction* (Urbana, 1997), 63, 178–82.

110. Schwalm, *Hard Fight for We,* 261ff; Edwards, *Gendered Strife,* 181–82.

111. Decree in *Nancy Bacon v. Titus Bacon,* Mar. 31, 1868, Provost Court, Beaufort, South Carolina, box 2, PCNSC, RG 393, Part I.

112. *State v. Bob Hill,* July 5, 1876, Davis Bend Magistrate's Book, OCHM.

113. Testimony of Rev. William Stewart in *Sarah Robinson v. Andrew Robinson,* Apr. 23, 1867, PCB, Sept. 1865–June 1868, RG 393, Part IV.

114. See indictments ("true bills") in *State v. Philip Brozile & Eliza Ann Clark,* Oct. term 1877, CC, box 2, folder 17, OCHM; and *State v. Harrison [Brooks], a slave,* 1862–66, box 1, folder 13, Warren County, Mississippi, Court Papers, Criminal Court, OCHM.

115. Virginia Ingraham Burr, ed., *The Secret Eye: The Journal of Ella Gertrude Clanton Thomas, 1848–1889* (Chapel Hill, 1990), 282; *State v. Taylor and Knight.* One elderly

woman asked the Freedmen's Bureau agent at Darlington, South Carolina, to compel her husband "to marry her after the Yankees way" (affidavit of Judy, May 31, 1866, entry 3191, BRFAL).

116. Affidavit of Rosa Freeman before Capt. A. S. A. Comer, July 24, 1866, entry 1017, Affidavits and Papers Relating to Complaints, Savannah, Georgia, Subordinate Field Offices, BRFAL.

117. *Richmond Planet*, Apr. 9, 1890, and *Savannah Colored Tribune*, Apr. 22, 1876, both quoted in Elizabeth Pleck, "Wife Beating in Nineteenth-Century America," *Victimology* 4, no. 1 (1979): 65–66; Holland Thompson (1867), quoted in Eric Foner, *Reconstruction: America's Unfinished Revolution, 1863–1877* (New York, 1988), 88.

118. Siegel, "'Rule of Love,'" 2134–41, 2153; Franke, "Becoming a Citizen," 251–309. As Franke points out, southern courts often used domestic violence as a cheap excuse to put black men on chain gangs.

119. Frankel, *Freedom's Women*, 106.

120. Testimony of George R. Dudley in *State v. Mary Ward*, n.d., 037.326.6, CAP. See also testimony of Alonzo Porter in *State v. Gray Thigpen*, Sept. 6, 1869, 037.326.4, CAP, and indictment in *State v. Jane Dupree*, fall term 1868, 037.326.4, CAP.

121. Statement of Andy Rawlins, Oct. 16, 1865, Provost Marshal, Memphis, Tennessee, entry 3545, BRFAL.

122. Capt. M. Mitchell to Major [A. T. Reeve], Dec. 20, 1865, reprinted in Berlin, Reidy, and Rowland, eds., *Black Military Experience*, 671.

123. Testimony of George Robinson in *United States v. Robinson*. When Jane Anderson's husband threatened her in an argument over food, her mother intervened, saying that "rather than have [to see her daughter] killed . . . she would . . . pay for the provisions and offered five dollars." See testimony of Jane Anderson in *United States (Jane Anderson) v. James Anderson*, Apr. 7, 1868, Provost Court Beaufort, South Carolina, box 2, PCNSC, RG 393, Part I.

124. Laura F. Edwards, "Sexual Violence, Gender, Reconstruction, and the Extension of Patriarchy in Granville County, North Carolina," *North Carolina Historical Review* 68, no. 3 (1991); testimony of George Robinson in *United States v. Robinson*; Provost Judge A. S. Hitchcock to Lt. Louis V. Caziare, Acting Asst. Adjt. Gen., Apr. 21, 1868, box 2, PCNSC, RG 393, Part I; *United States v. Matt Spann*, Sept. 2, 1867.

125. William Forbes's mother tried repeatedly to convince one of the older men at her son's Tallahassee workplace to "drop this fuss with William." See testimony of Warren Fisher in *United States (Ben Saunders) v. William Forbes*, Mar. 15, 1866, Proceedings of a Military Commission at Tallahassee, Florida, MM3726, RG 153.

126. Testimony of Frances Ross in *United States (Frances Ross and others) v. William Ross*, Dec. 12, 1867, PCBarn, box 2, PCNSC, RG 393, Part I.

127. Testimony of Charles Reddick in *United States v. Ross*. For a similar case, see Frankel, *Freedom's Women*, 106.

128. Testimony of Jackson Black in *United States v. Alexander Black, alias Cheek*, Provost Court, Clarksville, Tennessee, MM1030, RG 153.

129. Alexander Black to Brig. Gen. L. Thomas, Dec. 27, 1864, in *United States v. Black*.

130. Ibid.

131. Testimony of Alonzo Porter in *State v. Thigpen.*

132. Testimony of Tony Bowles in *United States v. Tony Bowles,* Feb. 20, 1867, Provost Court, Sea Islands, South Carolina, box A, PCNSC, RG 393, Part I. Harold Courlander observed similar patterns in Haiti in the 1930s. "It is not uncommon to see a woman standing alone before her house or walking up a trail narrating loudly, for all possible hearers, the details of a transaction in which she believes herself to have been badly treated. . . . Songs are a formalized outlet for outraged sensibilities." See his "Profane Songs of the Haitian People," *Journal of Negro History* 27 (July 1942): 322–23.

133. Testimony of Tony Bowles in *United States v. Bowles.*

134. Testimony of Lucy Bryan in ibid. Julius Monroe heard her say to Bowles: "You go[t] all our money now and you cant have the flat[boat], for we go[t] to live off that" (testimony of Julius Monroe in ibid.).

135. Testimony of Julius Monroe in ibid.

136. William F. Allen diary, May 28, 1864, p. 200. In the 1960s, Akans used courts in part to project "ideas of correct behavior . . . to teach them [the defendants] sense," or to make them "know themselves" (Michael J. Lowy, "A Good Name Is Worth More than Money: Strategies of Court Use in Urban Ghana," in *The Disputing Process—Law in Ten Societies,* ed. Laura Nader and Harry F. Todd Jr. [New York, 1978], 182, 204).

137. Kate Porter Young, *Notes on Sisterhood, Kinship, and Marriage in an African-American South Carolina Sea Island Community* (Memphis, Tenn., 1992), 10–15; Patricia Guthrie, *Catching Sense: African American Communities on a South Carolina Sea Island* (Westport, Conn., 1996), 32–34, 111–12. In the 1780s, well-to-do people in Gold Coast sent children to Europe both to be educated and "to learn sense and get a good head." This usage adds another dimension to the meaning of "sense." See Emmanuel Akyeampong, "Africans in the Diaspora: The Diaspora and Africa," *African Affairs* 99 (2000): 192.

138. Testimony of E. B. Willis in *State v. Nathan Gibson,* July 13, 1871, CC, box 1, folder 9, OCHM.

139. Testimony of Elsie Nelson in *United States v. Sanders.* On the "price of paternalistic protection" for North Carolina freedwomen, see Edwards, "Sexual Violence," 255–56.

140. Some historians argue that social relations among enslaved African Americans were "egalitarian," largely because they could not own property. See Deborah Gray White, *Ar'n't I a Woman? Female Slaves in the Plantation South* (New York, 1985), 153, 158; Philip D. Morgan, *Slave Counterpoint: Black Culture in the Eighteenth-Century Chesapeake and Lowcountry* (Chapel Hill, 1998), 533; and Davis, *Women, Race, and Class,* 18–19. On black-black conflict as a reflection or "manifestation" of white oppression, see Brenda Stevenson, "Distress and Discord in Virginia Slave Families, 1830–1860," in *In Joy and in Sorrow: Women, Family, and Marriage in the Victorian South, 1830–1900,* ed. Carol Bleser (New York, 1991), 103–24; Ann Patton Malone, *Sweet Chariot: Slave Family and Household Structure in Nineteenth-Century Louisiana* (Chapel Hill, 1992), 228–29; Lawrence McDonnell, "Money Knows No Master: Market Relations and the American Slave Community," in *Developing Dixie: Modernization in a Tradi-*

tional Society, ed. Winfred B. Moore Jr., Joseph F. Tripp, and Lyon G. Tyler Jr. (Westport, Conn., 1988), 38; introduction to Ira Berlin and Philip D. Morgan, eds., *Cultivation and Culture: Labor and the Shaping of Slave Life in the Americas* (Charlottesville, 1993), 38–39; and Ira Berlin, *Many Thousands Gone: The First Two Centuries of Slavery in North America* (Cambridge, Mass., 1998), 138. William Dusinberre extends this argument even further and attributes nearly all evidence of conflict among slaves to their master's strategy of "divide and conquer." See William Dusinberre, *Them Dark Days: Slavery in the American Rice Swamps* (New York, 1996), 177.

CONCLUSION

1. Zora Neale Hurston, "My People, My People!" in *Dust Tracks on a Road* (1942; reprint, New York, 1991), 215–18.

2. Evelyn Brooks Higginbotham, "African-American Women's History and the Metalanguage of Race," in *Feminism and History*, ed. Joan W. Scott (New York, 1992), 183–208.

3. As much as one-third of the black-owned land in the South was "heirs' property" by the 1970s (C. Scott Graber, "A Blight Hits Black Farmers," *Civil Rights Digest* 10, no. 3 [1978]: 21–22).

4. William C. Saunders, "Growing up on Johns Island: The Sea Islands Then and Now," in *Sea Island Roots: African Presence in the Carolinas and Georgia*, ed. Mary A. Twining and Keith E. Baird (Trenton, 1992), 125. On the problems of credit, tax sales, and partition sales, see Graber, "Blight Hits Black Farmers," 20–29, and Thomas W. Mitchell, "From Reconstruction to Deconstruction: Undermining Black Landownership, Political Independence, and Community through Partition Sales of Tenancies in Common," Paper presented at the Land Tenure Center, Research Paper no. 132, Madison, Wisc., 2000. For a positive view of heirs property, see Kay Young Day, "Kinship in a Changing Economy: A View from the Sea Islands," in *Holding on to the Land and the Lord: Kinship, Ritual, Land Tenure, and Social Policy in the Rural South*, ed. Robert L. Hall and Carol B. Stack (Athens, Ga., 1982), 11–24.

5. This is an ongoing problem. The main legal weapon has been "partition sales," where developers convince one of the heirs to sell his or her fractional interest, then ask a court to "partition" that interest from the tract. If the court decides the land cannot be subdivided equitably, it orders the entire tract sold and divides the proceeds. Unscrupulous developers can approach any of the heirs, who sometimes number in the hundreds, live far away, and may not know their rural relatives. Early casualties included lands north of Mobile, Alabama (which turned out to contain oil deposits), and Sea Islands, South Carolina (where several posh golf resorts were built). The Farmers Home Administration may have colluded in these forced sales by refusing to make loans unless black farmers could prove absolutely clear land titles, contrary to the language in its congressional mandate. The Emergency Land Fund and other nonprofit groups have defended hundreds of black-owned farms from partition sales (Graber, "Blight Hits Black Farmers," 20–29; Mitchell, "From Reconstruction to Deconstruction," 3).

6. Sydney Nathans, "Fortress without Walls: A Black Community after Slavery," in Hall and Stack, eds., *Holding on to the Land*, 62; Graber, "Blight Hits Black Farmers," 26. This dilemma also appears in Hurston's autobiography, *Dust Tracks on a Road*, 61.

7. On Billie Holiday's childhood, see Robert O'Meally, *Lady Day: The Many Faces of Billie Holiday* (New York, 1991). Lyrics from "God Bless the Child," by Billie Holiday and Arthur Herzog Jr. (© 1941 by Edward B. Marks Music Company, copyright renewed, used by permission), courtesy of Carlin America, Inc.

8. On the paradoxical message of racial "uplift," see Higginbotham, "African-American Women's History," 199.

9. Orlando Patterson, *Rituals of Blood: Consequences of Slavery in Two American Centuries* (Washington, D.C., 1998), 3–7, 25–42; U.S. Department of Labor, Office of Policy Planning and Research, [Daniel Patrick Moynihan and Nathan Glazer], "The Negro Family: The Case for National Action," Washington, D.C., Mar. 1965. Dinesh D'Souza (*The End of Racism: Principles for a Multiracial Society* [New York, 1995], 97) thinks slavery did not destroy "the two-parent black family unit," but that it did foster "a culture of self-defeating and irresponsible attitudes and behavior among black Americans."

10. Writing of colonialism in Africa, Frederick Cooper points out that interpreting social institutions as acts of resistance flattens "the texture of people's lives" and tends to reduce very "complex strategies of coping . . . with forces inside and outside the community . . . into a single framework." "Significant as resistance might be," Cooper suggests, "Resistance is a concept that may narrow our understanding of African history rather than expand it." See Frederick Cooper, "Conflict and Connection: Rethinking Colonial African History," *American Historical Review* 99, no. 5 (Dec. 1994): 1532–33. For good examples of how Africanists treat intra-African relations within the context of white-run colonialism, see Frederick Cooper, *Plantation Slavery on the East Coast of Africa* (New Haven, 1977), and Michael J. Watts, "Idioms of Land and Labor: Producing Politics and Rice in Senegambia," in *Land in African Agrarian Systems*, ed. Thomas J. Bassett and Donald E. Crummey (Madison, Wisc., 1993), 157–93.

11. Sara Berry, "Tomatoes, Land, and Hearsay: Property and History in Asante in the Time of Structural Adjustment," *World Development* 25, no. 8 (1997): 1233–34; Sara S. Berry, *Chiefs Know Their Boundaries: Essays on Property, Power, and the Past in Asante, 1896–1996* (Portsmouth, 2001); Gordon R. Woodman, *Customary Land Law in the Ghanaian Courts* (Accra, Ghana, 1996), 216–48; Mahir Saul, "Land Custom in Bare: Agnatic Corporation and Rural Capitalism in Western Burkina," in Bassett and Crummey, eds., *Land in African Agrarian Systems*, 80–81; Kwame Arhin, "Rank and Class among the Asante and Fante in the Nineteenth Century," *Africa* 53, no. 1 (1983); Thomas Holt, *The Problem of Freedom: Race, Labor, and Politics in Jamaica and Britain, 1832–1938* (Baltimore, 1992), 172; Jean Besson, "Land Tenure in the Free Villages of Trelawny, Jamaica: A Case Study in the Caribbean Peasant Response to Emancipation," *Slavery and Abolition* 5, no. 1 (1984): 5, 18; Sidney W. Mintz, *Caribbean Transformations* (1974; reprint, New York, 1989); and Lydia Pulsipher, "'He Won't Let She Stretch She Foot': Gender Relations in Traditional West Indian

Houseyards," in *Full Circles: Geographies of Women over the Life Course*, ed. Cindi Katz and Janice Monk (New York, 1993), 107–21.

12. Hendrik Hartog, "Pigs and Positivism," in *Folk Law: Essays in the Theory and Practice of Lex Non Scripta*, ed. Alison Dundes Renteln and Alan Dundes (Madison, Wisc., 1994), 711–50; Martin Chanock, "A Peculiar Sharpness: An Essay on Property in the History of Customary Law in Colonial Africa," *Journal of African History* 32, no. 1 (1991): 65–88; Carol M. Rose, *Property and Persuasion: Essays on the History, Theory, and Rhetoric of Ownership* (Boulder, 1994).

13. On the historiography of the family in Africa, see Shula Marks and Richard Rathbone, "The History of the Family in Africa: Introduction," *Journal of African History* 24 (1983): 145–61.

14. Michael Merrill, "Cash Is Good to Eat: Self-Sufficiency and Exchange in the Rural Economy of the United States," *Radical History Review* 4 (Winter 1977): 42–71; Steven Hahn, *The Roots of Southern Populism: Yeoman Farmers and the Transformation of the Georgia Upcountry, 1850–1890* (New York, 1983); Christopher Clark, *The Roots of Rural Capitalism: Western Massachusetts, 1780–1860* (Ithaca, 1990); deposition of Peter Perkins in *Sarah T. Thornton v. Lunsford A. Paschall*, May 31, 1862, 044.928.14, Granville County, Civil Action Papers Concerning Slaves and Free Persons of Color, 1846–75, NCSA.

15. See, for example, claim of Edward Middleton, Beaufort County, South Carolina, SCC; claim of John Thomson, Charleston County, South Carolina, SCC; claim of Joseph Freshley, Lexington County, South Carolina, SCC; and claim of Richard Taylor, Beaufort County, South Carolina, SCC.

16. Thomas D. Russell, "A New Image of the Slave Auction: An Empirical Look at the Role of Law in Slave Sales and a Conceptual Reevaluation of Slave Property," *Cardozo Law Review* 18 (Nov. 1996): 473–523.

17. John Niven, *Martin Van Buren: The Romantic Age of American Politics* (New York, 1983), 18, 151–52. Thanks to Robert Forbes for this reference.

18. Sara Berry, "Concentration without Privatization? Some Consequences of Changing Patterns of Rural Land Control in Africa," in *Land and Society in Contemporary Africa*, ed. R. E. Downs and S. P. Reyna (Hanover, N.H., 1988), 63–64; Watts, "Idioms of Land and Labor."

19. Richard Roberts, *Warriors, Merchants, and Slaves: The State and the Economy in the Middle Niger Valley, 1700–1914* (Stanford, Calif., 1987), 112–26; Richard Roberts, "Conflicts over Property in the Middle Niger Valley at the Beginning of the Twentieth Century," *African Economic History* 25 (1997): 91; Jan Hogendorn, "The Economics of Slave Use on Two 'Plantations' in the Zaria Emirate of the Sokoto Caliphate," *International Journal of African Historical Studies* 10, no. 3 (1977): 378; Orlando Patterson, *Slavery and Social Death: A Comparative Study* (Cambridge, Mass., 1982), 182–86; Gyan Prakash, *Bonded Histories: Genealogies of Labor Servitude in Colonial India* (Cambridge, Eng., 1990); Baas Terwiel, "Bondage and Slavery in Early Nineteenth-Century Siam," 118–37, in *Slavery, Bondage, and Dependency in Southeast Asia*, ed. Anthony Reid (New York, 1983); Ira Berlin and Philip D. Morgan, eds., *Cultivation and Culture: Labor and the Shaping of Slave Life in the Americas* (Charlottesville, 1993).

20. This may explain why white southerners railed so much louder about "miscegenation" than about the ownership of property by slaves. This is not to say that color lines were always clear in practice; they weren't. See Walter Johnson, "The Slave Trader, the White Slave, and the Politics of Racial Determination in the 1850s," *Journal of American History* 87 (June 2000): 13–38.

Bibliography

PRIMARY SOURCES

Manuscript Collections

Chapel Hill, N.C.
    Southern Historical Collection, Wilson Library, University of North Carolina
        Blackford Family Papers (no. 1912)
        Edward Ward Carmack Papers (no. 1414)
        Fitzgerald Family Papers (no. 4177)
        Neal Family Papers (no. 4370)
        Penn School Papers (no. 3615)
        Martha Schofield Papers (no. 999-z)
Charlottesville, Va.
    The Albert and Shirley Small Special Collections Library, University of Virginia
        Library
        Philena Carkin Papers (no. 11123)
        Gardner's Photographic Sketchbook of the American Civil War, 1861–1865, Washing-
          ton, Philip and Solomons, 1865
        Proceedings of Mayor's Court, Fredericksburg, Virginia (no. 4141)
College Park, Md.
    Records of the Freedmen and Southern Society Project, University of Maryland
        at College Park
Madison, Wisc.
    State Historical Society of Wisconsin
        William F. Allen, Manuscript Diary and Letters, 1863, Microfilm
New Haven, Conn.
    Manuscripts and Archives, Yale University Library
        African Postcard Collection
Raleigh, N.C.
    North Carolina State Archives

Edgecombe County Miscellaneous Records
Records of the North Carolina Supreme Court
Simpson and Biddle Family Papers
Richmond, Va.
  The Library of Virginia, Archives Research Services
    Auditor of Public Accounts (Record Group 48), Condemned Blacks Executed
      or Transported, 1781–1865 (APA 756), State Records
    Court of Oyer and Terminer, Essex County, Virginia, Order Book 45, 1823–
      26, Microfilm Reel 94, Local Records
    Martha Ann Carter Dettor Collection (Accession 34298), The History of Law-
      rence Creek, ca. 1834, Personal Papers Collection
    First African Baptist Church (Richmond, Virginia) Minute Books, 1841–1930,
      Miscellaneous Microfilm Reel 494 (Accession 28255), Church Records
Vicksburg, Miss.
  Old Court House Museum
    Davis Bend Magistrate's Book
    Court Issue Docket Book, Records of the Provost Marshal, 1864–65
    Warren County, Mississippi, Circuit Court Papers, Criminal Cases
    Warren County, Mississippi, Court Papers, Criminal Court

Government Manuscript Collections

Accra, Ghana
  National Archives
    Appeal from Native Tribunal of Anamabo, J. D. Taylor v. Kobina Kwansah
      (Case No. 29/1909), 1907, ADM 11/1/40
    Attuaboe Native Affairs, 1907, Case No. 489/1907, ADM 11/1/13
    Birim District Appeals from Decisions of Native Courts, Jan. 25, 1907–Oct. 12,
      1909, Case No. 409/1908, ADM 11/1/1440
    Cape Coast High Court, Aug. 19, 1868–Feb. 21, 1870, SCT 5/4/91
    Cape Coast High Court, Aug. 14, 1871–Jan. 19, 1872, SCT 5/4/96
    Cape Coast High Court, Mar. 2, 1874–Apr. 3, 1877, SCT 5/4/99[101]
    Cape Coast High Court, Mar. 18, 1874–June 9, 1874; Aug. 11, 1879–Aug. 18,
      1882, SCT 5/4/100
    Cape Coast High Court, Apr. 7, 1877–Aug. 7, 1879, SCT 5/4/102
    Cape Coast High Court, Aug. 19, 1882–Sept. 17, 1883, SCT 5/4/103
    Cape Coast Judicial Assessor's Court Record Book, Oct. 20, 1876–Apr. 18,
      1877; June 8, 1886–Feb. 4, 1887, SCT 5/4/19
    Elmina District Commissioner's Court, May 10, 1879–Jan. 27, 1885, SCT
      23/4/1
    Elmina District Commissioner's Court, Mar. 16, 1880–Jan. 13, 1885, SCT
      23/4/2
    J. C. de Graft Johnson v. C. S. de Graft Johnson, ADM 11/1/975
    Kumasi Regional Archives, File D234, 1908

Laws and Customs of Native Communities (Case No. 169/07) SNA Board 150
(Jan. 12, 1907–Nov. 8, 1910), 1907–10, ADM 11/1503

Native Customary Law of Succession to Property Other than Stool Property,
Case No. 22/1925, ADM 11/1/919

College Park, Md.

National Archives

Records of Civil War Special Agencies of the Treasury Department, Record
Group 366

Kew, England

Public Record Office

Colan, Staff Surgeon Second Class Thomas, Journal of Her Majesty's Corvette
"Rattlesnake," Cape of Good Hope and West Coast of Africa Station, Jan. 1,
1873–Dec. 31, 1873, ADM 101/141

Delmege, Surgeon A. G., Journal of Detachment of Royal Marines, Gold
Coast Station, June 9, 1873–July 28, 1873, ADM 101/142, Public Record
Office

London, England

Foreign and Commonwealth Office

Gold Coast General Views, 1887. Ghana 2

Gold Coast: Photographs of Scenery, Natives, Buildings and Industries, 1901. Ghana
7, Box 2

*Gold Coast Photographs, 1914–1930; Views of Public Works Projects Including
Gold Coast Hospital, and Photographs of the Legislative Council in 1919.*
Ghana 13

Photographs of Sir William Maxwell's Tour of the Hinterland of the Gold Coast, 1897.
Ghana 9

Washington, D.C.

National Archives

Case Files, Southern Claims Commission, Records of the Third Auditor, Allowed Case Files, Records of the U.S. General Accounting Office, Record
Group 217

Case Files, Southern Claims Commission, Records of the 3rd Auditor, Disallowed Case Files, Records of the U.S. General Accounting Office, Record
Group 217

Case Files, Southern Claims Commission, Alabama Allowed Case Files, Microfilm Publication 2062, held at Wallace State Community College

Court-Martial Case Files, 1809–1938, Court-Martial Records, Records of the
Office of the Judge Advocate General, 1808–1942, Record Group 153

Provost Marshal Field Organizations of the Civil War, Part IV, Records of Military Installations, Records of United States Army Continental Commands,
1821–1920, Record Group 393, Part IV

Records of Geographical Divisions and Departments and Military (Reconstruction) Districts, Part I, Records of United States Army Continental Commands, 1821–1920, Record Group 393, Part I

Records of or Relating to Direct Tax Commissions in Southern States and to Direct Taxes in Other States, Records of the Internal Revenue Service, Record Group 58

Records of the American Freedmen's Inquiry Commission, File O-328 (1863), Entry 12, Letters Received, 1805–89, Correspondence, 1800–1947, General Records of the Adjutant General's Office, Record Group 94

Records of the Bureau of Refugees, Freedmen, and Abandoned Lands, Record Group 105

Records of the Bureau of the Census, Record Group 29

Records Relating to the Southern Claims Commission, Letters Received, 1871–80, General Records of the Department of the Treasury, Record Group 56 (reproduced as National Archives Microfilm Publication M87, rolls 1–14)

Government Publications

Colonial Office. Despatches Addressed by the Earl of Canarvon to the Governor of the Gold Coast Respecting the Nature of the Queen's Jurisdiction in the Protectorate, and Domestic Slavery. Confidential. Sept. 1874, CO 879/6 no. 56, Public Record Office, Kew.

———. Gold Coast. Domestic Slavery. The Jurisdiction of the Judicial Assessor, and the Legal Character and Limitations of British Power Upon the Gold Coast, Mar. 1874, CO 879/6, no. 47, Public Record Office, Kew.

"Colonial Reports—Miscellaneous." Vol. 33. London: Foreign and Commonwealth Office.

Consolidated Index of Claims by the Commissioners of Claims to the House of Representatives from 1871–1880. Washington, D.C., 1892.

[Crowther, F. G.] "'The Epwe Speaking People,' by the Late F. G. Crowther, Sec. for Native Affairs, 1909 to 1917 (Dated 22nd October, 1912)." Gold Coast Review 3 (Jan.–June 1927).

[de Graft Johnson, J. C.] Memorandum on Vestiges of Slavery in Gold Coast, by J. C. de Graft Johnson, African Assistant Secretary for Native Affairs, Accra, Oct. 17, 1927, CO 323/1027/7, Public Record Office, Kew.

Royal Commission on Fugitive Slaves. 1876. HCA 30/1029. Report of the Commissioners. Minutes of the Evidence and Appendix, with General Index, of Minutes of Evidence and Appendix. Presented to both houses of Parliament by Command of her Majesty. Public Record Office, Kew.

U.S. Census Office. Agriculture of the United States in 1860; Compiled from the Original Returns of the Eighth Census. Washington, D.C., 1864.

———. Population of the United States in 1860; Compiled from the Original Returns of the Eighth Census. Washington, D.C., 1864.

U.S. Congress. Senate. Senate Misc. Documents. The Fish and Fishery Industries of the United States, Section II: A Geographical Review of the Fisheries Industries and Fishing Communities for the Year 1880. Edited by George B. Goode. Washington, D.C.: Government Printing Office, 1884–87.

U.S. Congress. 42nd Cong., 1872, 3rd Sess., Vol. I, Miscellaneous Documents.

U.S. Department of Agriculture. Division of Publications. *Outline Map of the United States*—scale [1:5,840,000]. 53 × 83 cm. Circa June 1, 1870. Washington, D.C., 1870.

U.S. Department of Justice. "Two Men Plead Guilty in Southwest Florida Slavery Ring," May 26, 1999. Washington, D.C.

U.S. Department of Labor, Office of Policy Planning and Research. [Moynihan, Daniel Patrick, and Nathan Glazer.] "The Negro Family: The Case for National Action." Washington, D.C., March 1965.

Welman, C. W., Sec. for Native Affairs, Accra. "Introductory," *Gold Coast Review* 1 (Aug. 1925). Foreign and Commonwealth Office, London.

Published Court Cases

Francois v. Lobrano, 10 Rob. 450 (1845)

Graves v. Allan, 52 Ky. 190 (1852)

Livaudais' Heirs v. Fon, 8 Mart. 161 (La. 1820)

Robert McNamara v. John Kerns et al., 24 N.C. 66 (1841)

Rice v. Cade et al., 10 La. 288, 1836 WL 746 (La.)

Richardson v. Broughton, 3 Strob. 1 (1848)

State v. John Davis, 24 N.C. 153 (1841)

Thomas Waddill v. Charlotte D. Martin, 38 N.C. 562 (1845)

Contemporary Publications

[Allen, W. F.] Marcel. "The Negro Dialect." In *The Negro and His Folklore in Nineteenth-Century Periodicals*, edited by Bruce Jackson, 74–81. Austin, 1967.

Ames, Mary. *From a New England Woman's Diary in Dixie in 1865*. Springfield, Mass., 1906.

Andrews, Sidney. *The South since the War*. 1866. Reprint, New York, 1969.

Ball, Charles. *Slavery in the United States: A Narrative of the Life and Adventures of Charles Ball*. Lewistown, Pa., 1836.

[Ball, James Presley.] *Ball's Splendid Mammoth Pictorial Tour of the United States, Comprising Views of the African Slave-Trade; of Northern and Southern Cities; of Cotton and Sugar Plantations; of the Mississippi, Ohio, and Susquehanna Rivers, Niagara Falls, &c. Compiled for the Panorama*. Cincinnati, 1855.

Barrow, David C., Jr. "A Georgia Plantation." *The Century Illustrated Monthly Magazine* 21 (1881): 830–36.

Benjamin, Charles Frederick. *Memoir of James Allen Hardie, Inspector-General, United States Army*. Washington, D.C., 1877.

Botume, Elizabeth Hyde. *First Days amongst the Contrabands*. Boston, 1893.

Brown, William Wells. *Narrative of William W. Brown, a Fugitive Slave. Written by Himself*. 1847. Reprint, Boston, 1848.

Bruce, H[enry] C[lay]. *The New Man. Twenty-Nine Years a Slave. Twenty-Nine Years a Free Man. Recollections of H. C. Bruce*. York, Pa., 1895.

Burke, Emily P. *Reminiscences of Georgia.* Oberlin, Ohio, 1850. Rare Book Collection, Huntington Library, San Marino, Calif.

Charleston City Gazette, Oct. 1, Nov. 9, Dec. 4, Dec. 9, Dec. 11, 1799.

Cobb, Thomas R. R. *An Inquiry into the Law of Negro Slavery in the United States of America.* 1858. Reprint, Athens, Ga., 1999.

Curry, James. "Narrative of James Curry, a Fugitive Slave." *The Liberator,* Jan. 10, 1840.

Day, Charles William. *Five Years' Residence in the West Indies.* 2 vols. London, 1852.

Deedes, Henry. *Sketches of the South and West.* Edinburgh, 1869.

Dennett, John Richard. *The South as It Is: 1865–1866.* Edited by Henry M. Christman. New York, 1965.

Douglass, Frederick. *Narrative of the Life of Frederick Douglass, an American Slave, Written by Himself.* Edited by David W. Blight. 1845. Reprint, Boston, 1993.

Duganne, A. J. H. *Twenty Months in the Department of the Gulf.* New York, 1865.

Eddins, A. W. "The State Industrial School Boys' Slang." *Publications of the Texas Folk-Lore Society* 1 (1916): 44–46.

Edwards, Bryan. *The History, Civil and Commercial, of the British West Indies.* 2 vols. London, 1793.

Fedric, Francis. *Slave Life in Virginia and Kentucky; or, Fifty Years of Slavery in the Southern States of America.* London, 1863.

First Annual Report of the Educational Commission for Freedmen. Boston, 1863.

Grandy, Moses. *Narrative of the Life of Moses Grandy, Formerly a Slave in the United States of America.* Boston, 1844.

Hall, James. *Letters from the West; Containing Sketches of Scenery, Manners, and Customs; and Anecdotes Connected with the First Settlements of the Western Sections of the United States.* London, 1828.

Henson, Josiah. "Autobiography of the Reverend Josiah Henson." In *Four Fugitive Slave Narratives,* edited by Robin W. Winks. Reading, Mass., 1969.

[Ingraham, J. H.]. *The South-West. By a Yankee.* 2 vols. New York, 1835. Rare Book Collection, Huntington Library, San Marino, Calif.

Kemble, Frances Anne. *Journal of a Residence on a Georgian Plantation in 1838–1839.* New York, 1961.

Leigh, Frances B. *Ten Years on a Georgia Plantation since the War.* 1883. Reprint, New York, 1969.

Long, Edward. *The History of Jamaica, or General Survey of the Antient and Modern State of That Island.* 3 vols. 1774. Reprint, London, 1970.

Lugard, Frederick D. *The Dual Mandate in British Tropical Africa.* London, 1922.

Lyell, Charles. *A Second Visit to the United States of North America.* 2 vols. New York, 1850.

Mallard, R. Q. *Plantation Life before Emancipation.* Richmond, Va., 1892.

Mugleston, William F. "The Freedmen's Bureau and Reconstruction in Virginia: The Diary of Marcus Sterling Hopkins, a Union Officer." *Virginia Magazine of History and Biography* 86, no. 1 (1978): 45–102.

Myers, Robert Manson, ed. *The Children of Pride: A True Story of Georgia and the Civil War.* New Haven, 1972.

Nordhoff, Charles. *The Freedmen of South Carolina: Some Account of Their Appearances, Character, Conditions, and Peculiar Customs.* New York, 1863. Rare Book Collection, Huntington Library, San Marino, Calif.

Northup, Solomon. *Twelve Years a Slave: Narrative of Solomon Northup, a Citizen of New-York, Kidnapped in Washington City in 1841, and Rescued in 1853.* Auburn, N.Y., 1853.

Olmsted, Frederick Law. *The Cotton Kingdom: A Traveller's Observations on Cotton and Slavery in the American Slave States, 1853–1861.* 1861. Reprint, New York, 1996.

———. *A Journey in the Seaboard Slave States.* New York, 1859.

Osofsky, Gilbert. *Puttin' on Ole Massa: The Slave Narratives of Henry Bibb, William Wells Brown, and Solomon Northup.* New York, 1969.

Parker, Allen. *Recollections of Slavery Times.* Worcester, Mass., 1895.

Pearson, Elizabeth Ware. *Letters from Port Royal, 1862–1868.* Boston, 1906.

"Preamble and Regulations of the Savannah River Anti-Slave-Traffick Association." 1846. Rare Book Collection, Huntington Library, San Marino, Calif.

Raymond, Charles A. "The Religious Life of the Negro Slave." *Harper's New Monthly Magazine* 27 (1863): 479–85, 676–82, 816–25.

Roles, John. *Inside Views of Slavery on Southern Plantations.* New York, 1864.

Roper, Moses. *A Narrative of the Adventures and Escape of Moses Roper, from American Slavery.* London, 1834.

Russell, William Howard. *My Diary North and South.* 1863. Reprint, Gloucester, Mass., 1969.

Sarbah, John Mensah. *Fanti Customary Laws.* 1897. Reprint, London, 1968.

Smith, Venture. *A Narrative of the Life and Adventures of Venture A Native of Africa, But Resident Above Sixty Years in the United States of America. Related by Himself.* 1798. Reprint, Middletown, Conn., 1897.

Somers, Robert. *The Southern States since the War, 1870–71.* 1871. Reprint, University, Ala., 1965.

Steward, Austin. "Twenty-Two Years a Slave and Forty Years a Freeman." In *Four Fugitive Slave Narratives,* edited by Robin W. Winks. Reading, Mass., 1969.

Stroyer, Jacob. *My Life in the South.* 1879. Reprint, Salem, Mass., 1898.

Summers, Eliza Ann. *"Dear Sister": Letters Written on Hilton Head Island, 1867.* Beaufort, 1977.

Swint, Henry L., ed. *Dear Ones at Home: Letters from Contraband Camps.* Nashville, 1966.

[Thomson, Mortimer]. *What Became of the Slaves on a Georgia Plantation? Great Auction Sale of Slaves at Savannah, Georgia, March 2d & 3d, 1859. A Sequel to Mrs. Kemble's Journal.* N.p., 1863.

Thorpe, Margaret Newbold. "A 'Yankee Teacher' in North Carolina." Edited by Richard Morton. *North Carolina Historical Review* 30 (Oct. 1953).

Thorpe, Thomas Bangs. "Sugar and the Sugar Region of Louisiana." *Harper's New Monthly Magazine* 7 (Oct. 1853): 746–67.

Towne, Laura M. *Letters and Diary of Laura M. Towne; Written from the Sea Islands of South Carolina, 1862–1884.* Edited by Rupert Sargent Holland. 1912. Reprint, New York, 1969.

Trowbridge, J. T. *The South.* 1866. Reprint, New York, 1969.

Interviews

Baskerville, Mary. Telephone interviews by the author, Nov. 15, 1994, Apr. 23, 1995.
Dove, Naa Kwaale. Interview by the author, Oct. 28, 1996.
Holcomb, Thomas. Interview by Craig Baskerville, Apr. 27, 1976. Audio recording in author's possession.
Odotei, Nana Dr. Irene. Interview by the author, Oct. 28, 1996.
Reaves, Osborne, Ltc. (ret.). Telephone interview by the author, Apr. 6, 1999.

SECONDARY SOURCES

Affleck, Richard. "Plantation Spatial Organization and Slave Settlement Pattern in the South Carolina Lowcountry: Toward a Dynamic View." In *Annual Papers of the Univ. of South Carolina Anthropology Students Association.* Vol. 4. 1989.
Akyeampong, Emmanuel. "Africans in the Diaspora: The Diaspora and Africa." *African Affairs* 99 (2000): 183–215.
Alexander, Gregory S. *Commodity and Propriety: Competing Visions of Property in American Legal Thought, 1776–1970.* Chicago, 1997.
Allott, A. N. "Native Tribunals in the Gold Coast, 1844–1927." *Journal of African Law* 1, no. 3 (1957): 163–71.
Alter, George, Claudia Goldin, and Elyce Rotella. "The Savings of Ordinary Americans: The Philadelphia Savings Fund Society in the Mid-Nineteenth Century." *Journal of Economic History* 54 (Dec. 1994): 735–67.
Amissah, A. N. "The Supreme Court, A Hundred Years Ago." In *Essays in Ghanaian Law, 1876–1976.* Legon, Ghana, 1976.
Arhin, Kwame. "Rank and Class among the Asante and Fante in the Nineteenth Century." *Africa* 53, no. 1 (1983): 2–22.
Austin, Gareth. "Human Pawning in Asante, 1800–1950: Markets and Coercion, Gender and Cocoa." In *Pawnship in Africa: Debt Bondage in Historical Perspective,* edited by Toyin Falola and Paul Lovejoy. Boulder, 1994.
———. "'No Elders Were Present': Commoners and Private Ownership in Asante, 1807–1896." *Journal of African History* 37, no. 1 (1996): 1–30.
Ayers, Edward L. *Vengeance and Justice: Crime and Punishment in the 19th-Century American South.* New York, 1984.
Barber, Karin. *I Could Speak until Tomorrow: Oriki, Women, and the Past in a Yoruba Town.* Washington, D.C., 1991.
Barton, Keith C. "'Good Cooks and Washers': Slave Hiring, Domestic Labor, and the Market in Bourbon County, Kentucky." *Journal of American History* 84 (Sept. 1997): 436–60.
Bauer, Raymond A., and Alice H. Bauer. "Day to Day Resistance to Slavery." *Journal of Negro History* 27 (Oct. 1942): 388–419.
Bercaw, Nancy Dunlap. "Politics of Household during the Transition from Slavery to Freedom in the Yazoo-Mississippi Delta, 1861–1876." Ph.D. diss., University of Pennsylvania, 1996.

Berlin, Ira. *Many Thousands Gone: The First Two Centuries of Slavery in North America.* Cambridge, Mass., 1998.

Berlin, Ira, Steven F. Miller, and Leslie S. Rowland. "Afro-American Families in the Transition from Slavery to Freedom." *Radical History Review* 42 (1988): 89–121.

Berlin, Ira, Barbara J. Fields, Thavolia Glymph, Joseph P. Reidy, and Leslie S. Rowland, eds. *The Destruction of Slavery.* Ser. 1, vol. 1, *Freedom: A Documentary History of Emancipation, 1861–1867.* New York, 1985.

Berlin, Ira, Thavolia Glymph, Steven F. Miller, Joseph P. Reidy, Leslie S. Rowland, and Julie Saville, eds. *The Wartime Genesis of Free Labor: The Lower South.* Ser. 1, vol. 3, *Freedom: A Documentary History of Emancipation, 1861–1867.* New York, 1990.

Berlin, Ira, Steven F. Miller, Joseph P. Reidy, and Leslie S. Rowland, eds. *The Wartime Genesis of Free Labor: The Upper South.* Ser. 1, vol. 2, *Freedom: A Documentary History of Emancipation, 1861–1867.* New York, 1993.

Berlin, Ira, and Philip D. Morgan, eds. *Cultivation and Culture: Labor and the Shaping of Slave Life in the Americas.* Charlottesville, 1993.

Berlin, Ira, and Philip D. Morgan, eds., *The Slaves' Economy: Independent Production by Slaves in the Americas.* Portland, Oreg., 1991.

Berlin, Ira, Joseph P. Reidy, and Leslie S. Rowland, eds. *The Black Military Experience.* Ser. 2, *Freedom: A Documentary History of Emancipation, 1861–1867.* New York, 1982.

Berry, Sara S. *Chiefs Know Their Boundaries: Essays on Property, Power, and the Past in Asante, 1896–1996.* Portsmouth, 2001.

———. "Concentration without Privatization? Some Consequences of Changing Patterns of Rural Land Control in Africa." In *Land and Society in Contemporary Africa,* edited by R. E. Downs and S. P. Reyna, 53–75. Hanover, N.H., 1988.

———. "Custom, Class, and the 'Informal Sector': Or Why Marginality Is Not Likely to Pay." Working Papers, African Studies Center, Boston University, n.s., no. 1 (1978): 1–22.

———. *No Condition Is Permanent: The Social Dynamics of Agrarian Change in Sub-Saharan Africa.* Madison, Wisc., 1993.

———. "Oil and the Disappearing Peasantry: Accumulation, Differentiation and Underdevelopment in Western Nigeria." In *State, Oil, and Agriculture in Nigeria,* edited by Michael Watts, 202–22. Berkeley, 1987.

———. "Tomatoes, Land, and Hearsay: Property and History in Asante in the Time of Structural Adjustment." *World Development* 25, no. 8 (1997): 1225–41.

Besson, Jean. "Land Tenure in the Free Villages of Trelawny, Jamaica: A Case Study in the Caribbean Peasant Response to Emancipation." *Slavery and Abolition* 5, no. 1 (1984): 3–23.

Bevin, H. J. "The Gold Coast Economy about 1880." *Transactions of the Gold Coast and Togoland Historical Society* 2 (1956): 73–88.

Bishir, Catherine W. "'Severe Survitude to House Building': The Construction of Hayes Plantation House, 1814–1817." *North Carolina Historical Review* 68, no. 4 (1991): 373–403.

Breeden, James O., ed. *Advice among Masters: The Ideal in Slave Management in the Old South.* Westport, Conn., 1980.

Brown, Carolyn A. "Testing the Boundaries of Marginality: Twentieth-Century Slavery and Emancipation Struggles in Nkanu, Northern Igboland, 1920–1929." *Journal of African History* 37, no. 1 (1996): 51–80.

Brown, Elsa Barkley, and Gregg D. Kimball. "Mapping the Terrain of Black Richmond." *Journal of Urban History* 21, no. 3 (1995): 296–346.

Brown, Kenneth L., and Doreen C. Cooper. "Structural Continuity in an African-American Slave and Tenant Community." *Historical Archaeology* 24, no. 4 (1990): 7–19.

Bundles, A'Lelia. *On Her Own Ground: The Life and Times of Madam C. J. Walker.* New York, 2001.

Burr, Virginia Ingraham, ed. *The Secret Eye: The Journal of Ella Gertrude Clanton Thomas, 1848–1889.* Chapel Hill, 1990.

Cade, John B. "Out of the Mouths of Ex-Slaves." *Journal of Negro History* 20 (July 1935): 294–337.

Campbell, John. "As 'A Kind of Freeman'?: Slaves' Market-Related Activities in the South Carolina Upcountry, 1800–1860." In *The Slaves' Economy: Independent Production by Slaves in the Americas,* edited by Ira Berlin and Philip D. Morgan, 131–69. London, 1991.

Cardoso, Ciro Flamarion S. "The Peasant Breach in the Slave System: New Developments in Brazil." *Luso-Brazilian Review* 25, no. 1 (1988): 49–57.

Cardoso, Ruth C. L. "Creating Kinship: The Fostering of Children in *Favela* Families in Brazil." In *Kinship Ideology and Practice in Latin America,* edited by Raymond T. Smith, 196–203. Chapel Hill, 1984.

Chanock, Martin. "A Peculiar Sharpness: An Essay on Property in the History of Customary Law in Colonial Africa." *Journal of African History* 32, no. 1 (1991): 65–88.

Clark, Christopher. *The Roots of Rural Capitalism: Western Massachusetts, 1780–1860.* Ithaca, 1990.

Clayton, Thomas H. *Close to the Land: The Way We Lived in North Carolina, 1820–1870.* Edited by Sydney Nathans. Chapel Hill, 1983.

Cody, Cheryll Ann. "Kin and Community among the Good Hope People after Emancipation." *Ethnohistory* 41, no. 1 (1994): 25–72.

Cohen, David William, and E. S. Atieno Odhiambo. *Burying SM: The Politics of Knowledge and the Sociology of Power in Africa.* Portsmouth, N.H., 1992.

Cooper, Barbara M. "Reflections on Slavery, Seclusion and Female Labor in the Maradi Region of Niger in the Nineteenth and Twentieth Centuries." *Journal of African History* 35, no. 1 (1994): 61–78.

Cooper, Frederick. "Conflict and Connection: Rethinking Colonial African History." *American Historical Review* 99, no. 5 (Dec. 1994): 1516–45.

———. *From Slaves to Squatters: Plantation Labor and Agriculture in Zanzibar and Coastal Kenya, 1890–1925.* New Haven, 1980.

———. "Review Article: The Problem of Slavery in African Studies." *Journal of African History* 20 (1979): 103–25.

Corten, Andre, and Isis Duarte. "Five Hundred Thousand Haitians in the Dominican Republic." *Latin American Perspectives* 22, no. 3 (1995): 94–110.

Courlander, Harold. "Profane Songs of the Haitian People." *Journal of Negro History* 27 (July 1942): 320–44.

Crass, David Colin, and Mark J. Brooks, eds. "Cotton and Black Draught: Consumer Behavior on a Postbellum Farm." South Carolina Institute of Archaeology
and Anthropology, University of South Carolina: Occasional Papers of the Savannah River Archaeological Research Program, 1995.

Creel, Margaret Washington. *"A Peculiar People": Slave Religion and Community-
Culture among the Gullahs.* New York, 1988.

Cronon, William. *Nature's Metropolis: Chicago and the Great West.* New York, 1991.

Crouch, Barry A. "The 'Chords of Love': Legalizing Black Marital and Family
Rights in Postwar Texas." *Journal of Negro History* 79 (Fall 1994): 334–51.

———. "A Spirit of Lawlessness: White Violence; Texas Blacks, 1865–1868." *Journal
of Social History* 18 (Winter 1984): 217–32.

Curtin, Mary Ellen. "'Negro Thieves' or Enterprising Farmers? Markets, the Law,
and African American Community Regulation in Alabama, 1866–1877." *Agricultural History* 74, no. 1 (2000): 19–38.

Davis, Angela Y. *Women, Race, and Class.* New York, 1981.

Dew, Charles. *Bond of Iron: Master and Slave at Buffalo Forge.* New York, 1994.

Diawara, Mamodou. "Women, Servitude, and History: The Oral Historical Traditions of Women of Servile Condition in the Kingdom of Jaara (Mali) from the
Fifteenth to the Mid-Nineteenth Centuries." In *Discourse and Its Disguises: The Interpretation of African Oral Texts,* edited by Karin Barber and P. F. de Moraes Farias,
109–37. Birmingham, Eng., 1989.

Diggins, John Patrick. *On Hallowed Ground: Abraham Lincoln and the Foundations of
American History.* New Haven, 2000.

D'Souza, Dinesh. *The End of Racism: Principles for a Multiracial Society.* New York, 1995.

Du Bois, W. E. B. "The Negro Landholder of Georgia." *United States Bureau of Labor
Bulletin* 6, no. 35 (1901): 647–77.

Dumett, Raymond, and Marion Johnson. "Britain and the Suppression of Slavery
in the Gold Coast Colony, Ashanti, and the Northern Territories." In *The End of
Slavery in Africa,* edited by Suzanne Miers and Richard Roberts, 71–116. Madison, Wisc., 1988.

Dupre, Daniel S. *Transforming the Cotton Frontier: Madison County, Alabama, 1800–
1840.* Baton Rouge, 1997.

Dusinberre, William. *Them Dark Days: Slavery in the American Rice Swamps.* New York,
1996.

Edwards, Laura F. *Gendered Strife and Confusion: The Political Culture of Reconstruction.*
Urbana, 1997.

———. "Sexual Violence, Gender, Reconstruction, and the Extension of Patriarchy in Granville County, North Carolina." *North Carolina Historical Review* 68,
no. 3 (1991): 237–60.

Egerton, Douglas R. *He Shall Go Out Free: The Lives of Denmark Vesey.* Madison, Wisc.,
1999.

Eiss, Paul K. "A Share in the Land: Freedpeople and the Government of Labour in
Southern Louisiana, 1862–65." *Slavery and Abolition* 19, no. 1 (1998): 46–89.

Falola, Toyin, and Paul Lovejoy, eds., *Pawnship in Africa: Debt Bondage in Historical
Perspective.* Boulder, 1994.

Flanders, Ralph B. "Two Plantations and a County of Ante-Bellum Georgia." *Georgia Historical Quarterly* 12 (Mar. 1928): 1–37.

Faust, Drew Gilpin. *James Henry Hammond and the Old South: A Design for Mastery.* Baton Rouge, 1982.

Fogel, Robert William. *Without Consent or Contract: The Rise and Fall of American Slavery.* New York, 1989.

Foner, Eric. *Nothing but Freedom: Emancipation and Its Legacy.* Baton Rouge, 1983.

———. *Reconstruction: America's Unfinished Revolution, 1863–1877.* New York, 1988.

Franke, Katherine M. "Becoming a Citizen: Reconstruction Era Regulation of African American Marriages." *Yale Journal of Law & the Humanities* 11 (1999): 251–309.

Frankel, Noralee. *Freedom's Women: Black Women and Families in Civil War Era Mississippi.* Bloomington, Ind., 1999.

Franklin, John Hope. *From Slavery to Freedom: A History of Negro Americans.* 3rd ed. New York, 1967.

———, ed. *Reminiscences of an Active Life: The Autobiography of John Roy Lynch.* Chicago, 1970.

French, Howard. "The Ritual Slaves of Ghana: Young and Female." *New York Times,* Jan. 20, 1997, pp. A1, A5.

Frey, Sylvia. *Water from the Rock: Black Resistance in a Revolutionary Age.* Princeton, 1991.

Genovese, Eugene D. *Roll, Jordan, Roll: The World the Slaves Made.* New York, 1972.

Georgia Writers' Project, Savannah Unit, Works Progress Administration. *Drums and Shadows: Survival Studies among the Georgia Coastal Negroes.* 1940. Reprint, Athens, Ga., 1986.

Getz, Trevor R. "The Case for Africans: The Role of Slaves and Masters in Emancipation on the Gold Coast, 1874–1900." *Slavery and Abolition* 21, no. 1 (2000): 128–45.

Gilbert, Michelle. "The Cracked Pot and the Missing Sheep." *American Ethnologist* 16 (May 1989): 213–29.

Gilmore, Glenda Elizabeth. *Gender and Jim Crow: Women and the Politics of White Supremacy in North Carolina, 1896–1920.* Chapel Hill, 1996.

Gocking, Roger. "British Justice and the Native Tribunals of the Southern Gold Coast Colony." *Journal of African History* 34, no. 1 (1993): 93–113.

———. "Competing Systems of Inheritance before the British Courts of the Gold Coast Colony." *International Journal of African Historical Studies* 23, no. 4 (1990): 601–18.

———. *Facing Two Ways: Ghana's Coastal Communities under Colonial Rule.* Lanham, Md., 1999.

———. "The Historic Akoto: A Social History of Cape Coast, Ghana, 1848–1948." Ph.D. diss., Stanford University, 1981.

Goldin, Claudia, and Robert A. Margo. "Wages, Prices, and Labor Markets before the Civil War." In *Strategic Factors in Nineteenth Century American Economic History,* edited by Claudia Goldin and Hugh Rockoff, 67–104. Chicago, 1992.

Graber, C. Scott. "A Blight Hits Black Farmers." *Civil Rights Digest* 10, no. 3 (1978): 20–29.

Grimsley, Mark. *The Hard Hand of War: Union Military Policy toward Southern Civilians, 1861–1865.* New York, 1996.

Gudeman, Stephen, and Stuart B. Schwartz. "Cleansing Original Sin: Godparenthood and the Baptism of Slaves in Eighteenth-Century Bahia." In *Kinship Ideology and Practice in Latin America,* edited by Raymond T. Smith, 35–58. Chapel Hill, 1984.

Guthrie, Patricia. *Catching Sense: African American Communities on a South Carolina Sea Island.* Westport, Conn., 1996.

Gutman, Herbert G. *The Black Family in Slavery and Freedom, 1750–1925.* New York, 1976.

———. "Persistent Myths about the Afro-American Family." *Journal of Interdisciplinary History* 6 (Autumn 1975): 181–210.

Guyer, Jane. "Wealth in People, Wealth in Things: Introduction." *Journal of African History* 36, no. 1 (1995): 83–90.

———. "Wealth in People as Wealth in Knowledge: Accumulation and Composition in Equatorial Africa." *Journal of African History* 36, no. 1 (1995): 91–120.

Haag, Pamela. "'The Ill-Use of a Wife': Patterns of Working-Class Violence in Domestic and Public New York City, 1860–1880." *Journal of Social History* 25 (Spring 1992): 447–77.

Hahn, Steven. *The Roots of Southern Populism: Yeoman Farmers and the Transformation of the Georgia Upcountry, 1850–1890.* New York, 1983.

Hailey, William Malcom Lord. *An African Survey: A Study of Problems Arising in Africa South of the Sahara.* London, 1957.

Hall, Gwendolyn Midlo. *Africans in Colonial Louisiana: The Development of Afro-Creole Culture in the Eighteenth Century.* Baton Rouge, 1992.

Harris, J. William. "Plantations and Power: Emancipation on the David Barrow Plantations." In *Toward a New South? Studies in Post–Civil War Southern Communities,* edited by Orville Vernon Burton and Robert C. McMath Jr., 246–64. Westport, Conn., 1982.

Hartog, Hendrik. *Man and Wife in America: A History.* Cambridge, 2000.

———. "Pigs and Positivism." In *Folk Law: Essays in the Theory and Practice of Lex Non Scripta,* edited by Alison Dundes Renteln and Alan Dundes, 711–50. Madison, Wisc., 1994.

Heath, Barbara J. *Hidden Lives: The Archaeology of Slave Life at Thomas Jefferson's Poplar Forest.* Charlottesville, 1999.

Heath, Barbara J., and Amber Bennet. "'The Little Spots Allow'd Them': The Archaeological Study of African-American Yards." *Historical Archaeology* 34, no. 2 (2000): 38–55.

Heyman, Max L., Jr. *Prudent Soldier: A Biography of Major General E. R. S. Canby, 1817–1873.* Glendale, Calif., 1959.

Higginbotham, Evelyn Brooks. "African-American Women's History and the Metalanguage of Race." In *Feminism and History,* edited by Joan W. Scott, 183–208. New York, 1992.

Higman, B. W. "The Spatial Economy of Jamaican Sugar Plantations: Cartographic Evidence from the Eighteenth and Nineteenth Centuries." *Journal of Historical Geography* 13, no. 1 (1987): 17–39.

Hine, Darlene Clark. "Rape and the Inner Lives of Black Women in the Middle West: Preliminary Thoughts on the Culture of Dissemblance." *Signs* 14 (Summer 1989): 912–20.

Hogendorn, Jan. "The Economics of Slave Use on Two 'Plantations' in the Zaria Emirate of the Sokoto Caliphate." *International Journal of African Historical Studies* 10, no. 3 (1977): 369–83.

Holt, Sharon Ann. *Making Freedom Pay: North Carolina Freedpeople Working for Themselves, 1865–1900.* Athens, Ga., 2000.

Holt, Thomas. *The Problem of Freedom: Race, Labor, and Politics in Jamaica and Britain, 1832–1938.* Baltimore, 1992.

Hopkins, A. G. *An Economic History of West Africa.* New York, 1973.

Hopkins, Antony. "Property Rights and Empire Building: Britain's Annexation of Lagos, 1861." *Journal of Economic History* 40 (Dec. 1980): 777–98.

Horwitz, Morton J. *The Transformation of American Law, 1780–1860.* Cambridge, Mass., 1977.

Hudson, Larry E., Jr. *To Have and to Hold: Slave Work and Family Life in Antebellum South Carolina.* Athens, Ga., 1997.

Hughes, Sarah S. "Slaves for Hire: The Allocation of Black Labor in Elizabeth City County, Virginia, 1782 to 1810." *William and Mary Quarterly* 35 (Apr. 1978): 260–86.

Hunter, Tera W. *To 'Joy My Freedom: Southern Black Women's Lives and Labors after the Civil War.* Cambridge, Mass., 1997.

Hurston, Zora Neale. *Dust Tracks on a Road.* 1942. Reprint, New York, 1991.

Hyatt, Harry Middleton. *Hoodoo, Conjuration, Witchcraft, Rootwork.* 5 vols. Hannibal, Mo., 1970–74.

Jackson, Bruce. *The Negro and His Folklore in Nineteenth-Century Periodicals.* Austin, 1967.

Johnson, Michael P. "Planters and Patriarchy: Charleston, 1800–1860." *Journal of Southern History* 46, no. 1 (1980): 45–72.

———. "Work, Culture, and the Slave Community: Slave Occupations in the Cotton Belt in 1860." *Labor History* 27 (Summer 1986): 325–55.

Johnson, Walter. "The Slave Trader, the White Slave, and the Politics of Racial Determination in the 1850s." *Journal of American History* 87 (June 2000): 13–38.

———. *Soul by Soul: Life inside the Antebellum Slave Market.* Cambridge, Mass., 1999.

Joyner, Charles. *Down by the Riverside: A South Carolina Slave Community.* Urbana, 1984.

Kantor, Shawn Everett. *Politics and Property Rights: The Closing of the Open Range in the Postbellum South.* Chicago, 1998.

Karasch, Mary. "Suppliers, Sellers, Servants, and Slaves." In *Cities and Society in Colonial Latin America,* edited by Louisa Schell Hoberman and Susan Migden Socolow, 251–83. Albuquerque, N.M., 1986.

Kelley, Robin D. G. *Yo' Mama's Disfunktional! Fighting the Culture Wars in Urban America.* Boston, 1997.

Klein, Anatole Norman. "Inequality in Asante: A Study of the Forms and Meanings of Slavery and Social Servitude in Pre- and Early-Colonial Akan-Asante Society and Culture." Ph.D. dissertation, University of Michigan, 1980.

Klein, Martin. *Slavery and Colonial Rule in French West Africa*. New York, 1998.

Klingberg, Frank W. *The Southern Claims Commission*. Berkeley, 1955.

Kludze, A. K. P. "A Century of Changes in the Law of Succession." In *Essays in Ghanaian Law*, edited by Gordon R. Woodman, 233–65. Legon, Ghana, 1976.

Kolchin, Peter. *American Slavery, 1619–1877*. New York, 1993.

———. "Reevaluating the Antebellum Slave Community: A Comparative Perspective." *Journal of American History* 70 (Dec. 1983): 579–601.

Kopytoff, Igor, and Suzanne Miers. "African 'Slavery' as an Institution of Marginality." In *Slavery in Africa: Historical and Anthropological Perspectives*, edited by Suzanne Miers and Igor Kopytoff, 3–81. Madison, Wisc., 1977.

Krech, Shepard, III. "Black Family Organization in the Nineteenth Century: An Ethnological Perspective." *Journal of Interdisciplinary History* 12, no. 3 (1982): 429–52.

Leavitt, Genevieve. "Slaves and Tenant Farmers at Shirley Plantation." In *The Archaeology of Shirley Plantation*, edited by Theodore R. Reinhart. Charlottesville, 1984.

Lewis, Ronald L. *Coal, Iron, and Slaves: Industrial Slavery in Maryland and Virginia, 1715–1865*. Westport, Conn., 1979.

Lichtenstein, Alex. "'That Disposition to Theft, with Which They Have Been Branded': Moral Economy, Slave Management, and the Law." *Journal of Social History* 21 (Spring 1988): 413–40.

Lovejoy, Paul E., and Jan S. Hogendorn. *Slow Death for Slavery: The Course of Abolition in Northern Nigeria, 1897–1936*. Cambridge, Eng., 1993.

Lowy, Michael J. "A Good Name Is Worth More than Money: Strategies of Court Use in Urban Ghana." In *The Disputing Process—Law in Ten Societies*, edited by Laura Nader and Harry F. Todd Jr., 181–208. New York, 1978.

Magdol, Edward. *A Right to the Land: Essays on the Freedmen's Community*. Westport, Conn., 1977.

Malone, Ann Patton. *Sweet Chariot: Slave Family and Household Structure in Nineteenth-Century Louisiana*. Chapel Hill, 1992.

Mann, Kristin. "Owners, Slaves, and the Struggle for Labor in the Commercial Transition at Lagos." In *From Slave Trade to Legitimate Commerce: The Commercial Transition in Nineteenth-Century West Africa*, edited by Robin Law, 144–71. New York, 1995.

Manning, Patrick. *Slavery and African Life: Occidental, Oriental, and African Slave Trades*. New York, 1990.

Marks, Shula, and Richard Rathbone. "The History of the Family in Africa: Introduction." *Journal of African History* 24 (1983): 145–61.

Marshall, Woodville K. "Provision Ground and Plantation Labor in Four Windward Islands: Competition for Resources during Slavery." In *Cultivation and Culture: Labor and the Shaping of Slave Life in the Americas*, edited by Ira Berlin and Philip D. Morgan, 203–20. Charlottesville, 1993.

McCaskie, T. C. *State and Society in Pre-Colonial Asante.* Cambridge, Eng., 1995.

McCurry, Stephanie. *Masters of Small Worlds: Yeoman Households, Gender Relations, and the Political Culture of the Antebellum South Carolina Low Country.* New York, 1995.

McCusker, John J. *How Much Is That in Real Money? A Historical Price Index for Use as a Deflator of Money Values in the Economy of the United States.* Worcester, 1992.

McDonald, Roderick A. *The Economy and Material Culture of Slaves: Goods and Chattels on the Sugar Plantations of Jamaica and Louisiana.* Baton Rouge, 1993.

McDonnell, Lawrence. "Money Knows No Master: Market Relations and the American Slave Community." In *Developing Dixie: Modernization in a Traditional Society,* edited by Winfred B. Moore, Joseph F. Tripp, and Lyon G. Tyler Jr. Westport, Conn., 1988.

McKee, Larry. "The Ideals and Realities behind the Design and Use of 19th Century Virginia Slave Cabins." In *The Art and Mystery of Historical Archaeology: Essays in Honor of James Deetz,* edited by Anne Elizabeth Yentsch and Mary C. Beaudry. Boca Raton, 1992.

McPherson, James M. *Ordeal by Fire: The Civil War and Reconstruction.* New York, 1982.

McSheffrey, Gerald M. "Slavery, Indentured Servitude, Legitimate Trade and the Impact of Abolition in the Gold Coast, 1874–1901." *Journal of African History* 24, no. 3 (1983): 349–68.

Merrill, Michael. "Cash Is Good to Eat: Self-Sufficiency and Exchange in the Rural Economy of the United States." *Radical History Review* 4 (Winter 1977): 42–71.

Metcalfe, G. E., ed. *Great Britain and Ghana: Documents of Ghana History, 1807–1957.* London, 1964.

Miller, Joseph C. *Way of Death: Merchant Capitalism and the Angolan Slave Trade, 1730–1830.* Madison, Wisc., 1988.

Miller, Steven F. "Plantation Labor Organization and Slave Life on the Cotton Frontier: The Alabama-Mississippi Black Belt, 1815–1840." In *Cultivation and Culture: Labor and the Shaping of Slave Life in the Americas,* edited by Ira Berlin and Philip D. Morgan, 155–69. Charlottesville, 1993.

Miller, T. Michael, ed. *Pen Portraits of Alexandria, Virginia, 1739–1900.* Bowie, Md., 1987.

Mills, Gary B. *Civil War Claims in the South: An Index of Civil War Damage Claims Filed before the Southern Claims Commission, 1871–1880.* Laguna Hills, Calif., 1980.

———. *Southern Loyalists in the Civil War: The Southern Claims Commission.* Baltimore, 1994.

Mintz, Sidney W. *Caribbean Transformations.* 1974. Reprint, New York, 1989.

Mitchell, Thomas W. "From Reconstruction to Deconstruction: Undermining Black Landownership, Political Independence, and Community through Partition Sales of Tenancies in Common." Paper presented at the Land Tenure Center, Research Paper no. 132, Madison, Wisc., 2000.

Mohr, Clarence L. *On the Threshold of Freedom: Masters and Slaves in Civil War Georgia.* Athens, Ga., 1986.

Moore, John Hebron. *The Emergence of the Cotton Kingdom in the Old Southwest: Mississippi, 1770–1860*. Baton Rouge, 1988.

Moore, Sally Falk. "From Giving and Lending to Selling: Property Transactions
Reflecting Historical Changes on Kilimanjaro." In *Law in Colonial Africa*, edited
by Kristin Mann and Richard Roberts, 108–27. Portsmouth, N.H., 1991.

———. *Social Facts and Fabrications: "Customary" Law on Kilimanjaro, 1880–1980*.
Cambridge, Eng., 1986.

Morgan, Philip D. "The Ownership of Property by Slaves in the Mid-Nineteenth-
Century Low Country." *Journal of Southern History* 49, no. 3 (Aug. 1983): 399–420.

———. *Slave Counterpoint: Black Culture in the Eighteenth-Century Chesapeake and Lowcountry*. Chapel Hill, 1998.

———. "Task and Gang Systems: The Organization of Labor on New World Plantations." In *Work and Labor in Early America*, edited by Stephen Innes, 189–220.
Chapel Hill, 1988.

———. "Work and Culture: The Task System and the World of Lowcountry Blacks,
1700–1880." *William and Mary Quarterly* 39 (Oct. 1982): 563–99.

Morris, Christopher. "The Articulation of Two Worlds: The Master-Slave Relationship Reconsidered." *Journal of American History* 85 (Dec. 1998): 982–1007.

Morris, Thomas D. *Southern Slavery and the Law, 1619–1860*. Chapel Hill, 1996.

Mullins, Paul R. "Race and the Genteel Consumer: Class and African-American
Consumption, 1850–1930." *Historical Archaeology* 33, no. 1 (1999): 22–38.

Nathans, Sydney. "Fortress without Walls: A Black Community after Slavery." In
*Holding on to the Land and the Lord: Kinship, Ritual, Land Tenure, and Social Policy
in the Rural South*, edited by Robert L. Hall and Carol B. Stack, 55–65. Athens,
Ga., 1982.

Nieman, Donald G. *To Set the Law in Motion: The Freedmen's Bureau and the Legal
Rights of Blacks, 1865–1868*. Millwood, N.Y., 1979.

Niven, John. *Martin Van Buren: The Romantic Age of American Politics*. New York,
1983.

Ollennu, N. A. *The Law of Succession in Ghana*. Accra and Kumasi, Ghana, 1960.

Olwell, Robert. "'Loose, Idle and Disorderly': Slave Women in the Eighteenth-
Century Charleston Marketplace." In *More Than Chattel: Black Women and Slavery
in the Americas*, edited by David Barry Gaspar and Darlene Clark Hine, 97–110.
Bloomington, Ind., 1996.

O'Meally, Robert. *Lady Day: The Many Faces of Billie Holiday*. New York, 1991.

Orser, Charles E., Jr., and Annette M. Nekola. "Plantation Settlement from Slavery
to Tenancy: An Example from a Piedmont Plantation in South Carolina." In *The
Archaeology of Slavery and Plantation Life*, edited by Theresa A. Singleton, 67–94.
Orlando, 1985.

Painter, Nell Irvin. "Soul Murder and Slavery: Toward a Fully Loaded Cost Accounting." In *U.S. History as Women's History*, edited by Linda Kerber, Alice
Kessler-Harris, and Kathryn Kish Sklar, 125–46. Chapel Hill, 1995.

Patterson, Orlando. *Rituals of Blood: Consequences of Slavery in Two American Centuries*. Washington, D.C., 1998.

————. *Slavery and Social Death: A Comparative Study.* Cambridge, Mass., 1982.

Penningroth, Dylan. "Claiming Kin and Property: African American Life before and after Emancipation." Ph.D. diss., Johns Hopkins University, 1999.

Perbi, Akosua. "Domestic Slavery in Asante, 1800–1920." M.A. thesis, University of Ghana at Legon, 1978.

————. "The Legacy of Slavery in Contemporary Ghana." Unpublished paper presented at University of Ghana at Legon, n.d.

Phillips, Ulrich B. *Life and Labor in the Old South.* Boston, 1929.

Pleck, Elizabeth. "Wife Beating in Nineteenth-Century America." *Victimology* 4, no. 1 (1979): 60–74.

Poku, K. "Traditional Roles and People of Slave Origin in Modern Ashanti: A Few Impressions." *Ghana Journal of Sociology* 5 (Feb. 1969): 34–38.

Powell, Mary G. *The History of Old Alexandria, Virginia, from July 13, 1749 to May 24, 1861.* Richmond, 1928.

Prakash, Gyan. *Bonded Histories: Genealogies of Labor Servitude in Colonial India.* Cambridge, Eng., 1990.

Pulsipher, Lydia Mihelic. "'He Won't Let She Stretch She Foot': Gender Relations in Traditional West Indian Houseyards." In *Full Circles: Geographies of Women over the Life Course,* edited by Cindi Katz and Janice Monk, 107–21. New York, 1993.

Pulsipher, Lydia Mihelic, and LaVerne Wells-Bowie. "The Domestic Spaces of Daufuskie and Monserrat: A Cross-Cultural Comparison." In *Cross-Cultural Studies of Traditional Dwellings,* edited by Nezar AlSayyad and Jean-Paul Bourdier, 1–28. Berkeley, 1989.

Ranger, Terence. "The Invention of Tradition in Colonial Africa." In *The Invention of Tradition,* edited by Eric Hobsbawm and Terence Ranger, 211–62. Cambridge, Eng., 1983.

Ransom, Roger L., and Richard Sutch. *One Kind of Freedom: The Economic Consequences of Emancipation.* New York, 1977.

Rapport, Sara. "The Freedmen's Bureau as a Legal Agent for Black Men and Women in Georgia, 1865–1868." *Georgia Historical Quarterly* 73, no. 1 (Spring 1989): 26–53.

Rathbone, Richard. *Murder and Politics in Colonial Ghana.* New Haven, 1993.

Rawick, George P., ed. *The American Slave: A Composite Autobiography.* 19 vols. Westport, Conn., 1972.

Rehder, John B. *Delta Sugar: Louisiana's Vanishing Plantation Landscape.* Baltimore, 1999.

Reidy, Joseph. *From Slavery to Agrarian Capitalism in the Cotton Plantation South: Central Georgia, 1800–1880.* Chapel Hill, 1992.

Reis, João José. *Slave Rebellion in Brazil: The Muslim Uprising of 1835 in Bahia.* Translated by Arthur Brakel. 1986. Reprint, Baltimore, 1993.

Reitz, Elizabeth J., Tyson Gibbs, and Ted A. Rathbun. "Archaeological Evidence for Subsistence on Coastal Plantations." In *The Archaeology of Slavery and Plantation Life,* edited by Theresa A. Singleton, 163–91. Orlando, 1985.

Roberts, Richard. "Conflicts over Property in the Middle Niger Valley at the Beginning of the Twentieth Century." *African Economic History* 25 (1997): 79–96.

————. *Warriors, Merchants, and Slaves: The State and the Economy in the Middle Niger Valley, 1700–1914*. Stanford, Calif., 1987.

Roberts, Richard, and Suzanne Miers. "The End of Slavery in Africa." In *The End of Slavery in Africa*, edited by Suzanne Miers and Richard Roberts, 3–68. Madison, Wisc., 1988.

Roberts, Richard, and William Worger. "Law, Colonialism and Conflicts over Property in Sub-Saharan Africa." *African Economic History* 25 (1997): 1–7.

Robertson, Claire C. "Post-Proclamation Slavery in Accra: A Female Affair?" In *Women and Slavery in Africa*, edited by Claire C. Robertson and Martin A. Klein, 220–45. Madison, Wisc., 1983.

Robertson, Claire C., and Martin A. Klein. "Women's Importance in African Slave Systems." In *Women and Slavery in Africa*, edited by Claire C. Robertson and Martin A. Klein, 3–25. Madison, Wisc., 1983.

Robinson, Armstead L. "Beyond the Realm of Social Consensus: New Meanings of Reconstruction for American History." *Journal of American History* 68 (Sept. 1981): 276–97.

————. "Plans Dat Comed from God: Institution Building and the Emergence of Black Leadership in Reconstruction Memphis." In *Toward a New South? Studies in Post–Civil War Southern Communities*, edited by Orville Vernon Burton and Robert C. McMath Jr., 71–102. Westport, Conn., 1982.

Robinson, Robert B., and James D. Hardy Jr. "An *Actio de Peculio* in Ante-Bellum Alabama." *Journal of Legal History* 11, no. 3 (1990): 364–71.

Rose, Carol M. *Property and Persuasion: Essays on the History, Theory, and Rhetoric of Ownership*. Boulder, 1994.

Rose, Willie Lee. *Rehearsal for Reconstruction: The Port Royal Experiment*. London, 1964.

Rosengarten, Theodore. *All God's Dangers: The Life of Nate Shaw*. New York, 1989.

Russell, Thomas D. "A New Image of the Slave Auction: An Empirical Look at the Role of Law in Slave Sales and a Conceptual Reevaluation of Slave Property." *Cardozo Law Review* 18 (Nov. 1996): 473–523.

Samford, Patricia. "The Archaeology of African-American Slavery and Material Culture." *William and Mary Quarterly* 53 (Jan. 1996): 87–114.

Sanford, Douglas W. "The Archaeology of Plantation Slavery in Piedmont Virginia: Context and Process." In *Historical Archaeology of the Chesapeake*, edited by Paul A. Shackel and Barbara J. Little, 115–30. Washington, D.C., 1994.

Sarudy, Barbara Wells. *Gardens and Gardening in the Chesapeake, 1700–1805*. Baltimore, 1998.

Saul, Mahir. "Land Custom in Bare: Agnatic Corporation and Rural Capitalism in Western Burkina." In *Land in African Agrarian Systems*, edited by Thomas J. Bassett and Donald Crummey, 75–100. Madison, Wisc., 1993.

Saunders, William C. "Growing Up on Johns Island: The Sea Islands Then and Now." In *Sea Island Roots: African Presence in the Carolinas and Georgia*, edited by Mary A. Twining and Keith E. Baird, 119–27. Trenton, 1992.

Saville, Julie. *The Work of Reconstruction: From Slave to Wage Laborer in South Carolina, 1860–1870*. New York, 1994.

Scarpino, Philip V. "Slavery in Callaway County, Missouri: 1845–1855." *Missouri Historical Review* 71, no. 3 (1977): 22–43.

Schulman, Gayle M. "Site of Slave Block?" *Magazine of Albemarle County History* 58 (2000): 64–86.

Schultz, Mark R. "The Dream Realized? African American Landownership in Central Georgia between Reconstruction and World War II." *Agricultural History* 72, no. 2 (1998).

Schwaab, Eugene L. *Travels in the Old South: Selected from the Periodicals of the Times.* Lexington, Ky., 1973.

Schwalm, Leslie A. *A Hard Fight for We: Women's Transition from Slavery to Freedom in South Carolina.* Urbana, 1997.

Schwartz, Stuart B. *Slaves, Peasants, and Rebels: Reconsidering Brazilian Slavery.* Urbana, 1992.

Schweninger, Loren. *Black Property Owners in the South, 1790–1915.* Urbana, 1990.

———. "A Negro Sojourner in Antebellum New Orleans." *Louisiana History* 20 (Summer 1979): 305–14.

Scott, James C. *Weapons of the Weak: Everyday Forms of Peasant Resistance.* New Haven, 1987.

Scott, Rebecca J. "Defining the Boundaries of Freedom in the World of Cane: Cuba, Brazil, and Louisiana after Emancipation." *American Historical Review* 99 (Feb. 1994): 70–102.

———. "'Stubborn and Disposed to Stand their Ground': Black Militia, Sugar Workers, and the Dynamics of Collective Action in the Louisiana Sugar Bowl, 1863–87." *Slavery and Abolition* 20, no. 1 (1999): 103–26.

Sellers, Charles. *The Market Revolution: Jacksonian America, 1815–1846.* New York, 1991.

Sellers, James Benson. *Slavery in Alabama.* 1950. Reprint, Tuscaloosa, 1994.

Sensbach, Jon F. *A Separate Canaan: The Making of an Afro-Moravian World in North Carolina, 1763–1840.* Chapel Hill, 1998.

Shifflett, Crandall A. "The Household Composition of Rural Black Families: Louisa County, Virginia, 1880." *Journal of Interdisciplinary History* 6 (Autumn 1975): 235–60.

Shlomowitz, Ralph. "The Squad System on Postbellum Cotton Plantations." In *Toward a New South? Studies in Post–Civil War Southern Communities*, edited by Orville Vernon Burton Jr. and Robert C. McMath, 265–80. Westport, Conn., 1982.

Siegel, Reva B. "'The Rule of Love': Wife Beating as Prerogative and Privacy." *Yale Law Journal* 105 (1996): 2117–2207.

Singleton, Theresa A. "Archaeological Implications for Changing Labor Conditions." In *The Archaeology of Slavery and Plantation Life*, edited by Theresa A. Singleton. Orlando, 1985.

Slaughter, James B. *Settlers, Southerners, Americans: The History of Essex County, Virginia, 1608–1984.* Salem, W.Va., 1985.

Smith, Albert Colbey. "Down Freedom's Road: The Contours of Race, Class, and Property Crime in Black-Belt Georgia, 1866–1910." Ph.D. dissertation, University of Georgia, 1982.

Smith, Julia Floyd. *Slavery and Rice Culture in Low Country Georgia, 1750–1860*. Knoxville, 1985.

Southall, Eugene Portlette. "The Attitude of the Methodist Episcopal Church, South, toward the Negro from 1844 to 1870." *Journal of Negro History* 16, no. 4 (1931): 359–70.

Sprinkle, John H., Jr. "The Contents of Charles Cox's Mill House Chest." *Historical Archaeology* 25, no. 3 (1991): 91–93.

Stampp, Kenneth. *The Peculiar Institution: Slavery in the Ante-Bellum South*. 1956. Reprint, New York, 1975.

Stanley, Amy Dru. "Beggars Can't Be Choosers: Compulsion and Contract in Post-bellum America." *Journal of American History* 78 (Mar. 1992): 1265–93.

Stansell, Christine. *City of Women: Sex and Class in New York, 1789–1860*. Urbana, 1987.

Stevenson, Brenda. "Distress and Discord in Virginia Slave Families, 1830–1860." In *In Joy and in Sorrow: Women, Family, and Marriage in the Victorian South, 1830–1900*, edited by Carol Bleser, 103–24. New York, 1991.

Sutton, Inez. "Law, Chieftaincy and Conflict in Colonial Ghana: The Ada Case." *African Affairs* 83, no. 330 (1984): 41–62.

Sydnor, Charles Sackett. *Slavery in Mississippi*. New York, 1933.

Taylor, Joe Gray. *Negro Slavery in Louisiana*. Baton Rouge, 1963.

Terwiel, Baas. "Bondage and Slavery in Early Nineteenth-Century Siam." In *Slavery, Bondage, and Dependency in Southeast Asia*, edited by Anthony Reid, 118–37. New York, 1983.

Thomas, Brian W. "Power and Community: The Archaeology of Slavery at the Hermitage Plantation." *American Antiquity* 63, no. 4 (1998): 531–51.

Thompson, Mary V. "'Better . . . Fed than Negroes Generally Are': The Diet of the Mount Vernon Slaves." Unpublished paper presented at Montpelier Mansion, Laurel, Maryland, May 19, 1999.

———. "'They Appear to Live Comfortable Together': Private Life of the Mount Vernon Slaves." Unpublished paper dated Jan. 20, 1999.

Vandal, Gilles. "Black Violence in Post–Civil War Louisiana." *Journal of Interdisciplinary History* 25 (Summer 1994): 45–64.

———. "'Bloody Caddo': White Violence against Blacks in a Louisiana Parish, 1865–1876." *Journal of Social History* 25 (Winter 1991): 373–88.

Vandevelde, Kenneth J. "The New Property of the Nineteenth Century: The Development of the Modern Conception of Property." *Buffalo Law Review* 29 (1980): 325–67.

Vaughan, Megan. "Which Family? Problems in the Reconstruction of the History of Family as an Economic and Cultural Unit." *Journal of African History* 24, no. 2 (1983): 275–83.

Volz, Harry August, III. "The Administration of Justice by the Freedmen's Bureau in Kentucky, South Carolina, and Virginia." M.A. thesis, University of Virginia, 1975.

Waldrep, Christopher. *Roots of Disorder: Race and Criminal Justice in the American South, 1817–80*. Urbana, 1998.

Ward, W. E. F. *A History of Ghana*. New York, 1963.

Watts, Michael J. "Idioms of Land and Labor: Producing Politics and Rice in

Senegambia." In *Land in African Agrarian Systems*, edited by Thomas J. Bassett and Donald E. Crummey, 157–93. Madison, Wisc., 1993.

Westmacott, Richard Noble. *African-American Gardens and Yards in the Rural South.* Knoxville, 1992.

Wheaton, Thomas R., and Patrick H. Garrow. "Acculturation and the Archaeological Record in the Carolina Lowcountry." In *The Archaeology of Slavery and Plantation Life*, edited by Theresa A. Singleton. Orlando, 1985.

Wheeler, Linda. "Excavation Reveals Slaves as Entrepreneurs." *Washington Post*, Oct. 13, 1998, B3.

White, Deborah Gray. *Ar'n't I a Woman? Female Slaves in the Plantation South.* New York, 1985.

White, Landeg. *Magomero: Portrait of an African Village.* Cambridge, Eng., 1987.

White, Luise. "Bodily Fluids and Usufruct: Controlling Property in Nairobi, 1917–1939." *Canadian Journal of African Studies* 24, no. 3 (1990): 418–38.

Wilks, Ivor. *Asante in the Nineteenth Century: The Structure and Evolution of a Political Order.* 1975. Reprint, New York, 1989.

———. "Land, Labor, Capital and the Forest Kingdom of Asante: A Model of Early Change." In *The Evolution of Social Systems*, edited by J. Friedman and M. J. Rowlands, 487–534. London, 1977.

Willis, Justin, and Suzanne Miers. "Becoming a Child of the House: Incorporation, Authority and Resistance in Giryama Society." *Journal of African History* 38, no. 3 (1997): 479–95.

Wood, Betty. *Women's Work, Men's Work: The Informal Slave Economies of Lowcountry Georgia.* Athens, Ga., 1995.

Woodman, Gordon R. *Customary Land Law in the Ghanaian Courts.* Accra, Ghana, 1996.

Woodman, Harold D. *New South—New Law: The Legal Foundations of Credit and Labor Relations in the Postbellum Agricultural South.* Baton Rouge, 1995.

Woofter, T. J., Jr. *Black Yeomanry: Life on St. Helena Island.* New York, 1930.

Wright, Marcia. *Strategies of Slaves and Women: Life-Stories from East/Central Africa.* New York, 1993.

Yarak, Larry W. "Murder and Theft in Early Nineteenth-Century Elmina." In *Banditry, Rebellion, and Social Protest in Africa*, edited by Donald Crummey, 33–47. Portsmouth, N.H., 1986.

———. "West African Coastal Slavery in the Nineteenth Century: The Case of the Afro-European Slaveowners of Elmina." *Ethnohistory* 36 (Winter 1989): 44–60.

Young, Amy L. "Task and Gang Labor: Work Patterns at a Kentucky Plantation." *North American Archaeologist* 18, no. 1 (1997): 41–66.

Young, Kate Porter. *Notes on Sisterhood, Kinship, and Marriage in an African-American South Carolina Sea Island Community.* Memphis, Tenn., 1992.

Zelizer, Viviana A. *The Social Meaning of Money: Pin Money, Paychecks, Poor Relief, and Other Currencies.* Princeton, 1997.

Acknowledgments

I feel incredibly fortunate to have been able to work with Michael Johnson and Sara Berry during the last seven years. From the very beginning, Michael Johnson has shaped this project in countless ways. His encouragement and advice gave me the confidence to build ideas and see where they would lead. Sara Berry not only guided me toward the background in African Studies I needed to conduct research in Africa but also has helped me think through the issues involved in relating that research to North American history. Always with warmth, they devoted enormous care, effort, and time to advising this project. Their example has taught me a great deal about what it means to be a teacher and scholar. I am deeply grateful to them.

My training and research from 1994 to 1998 were supported by fellowships from the Johns Hopkins University History Department and a Dean's Graduate Fellowship from the Johns Hopkins University. The Smithsonian's National Museum of American History provided a graduate fellowship during the summer of 1996. A travel grant from the Institute for Global Studies in Culture, Power, and History at Johns Hopkins University permitted me to do research in Ghana. An anonymous benefactor funded a Southern History Research Fellowship at Johns Hopkins, which made possible my research during the summer of 1997. The Mellon Foundation's Sawyer Seminar Fellowship provided additional support during 1997–98. The W. M. Keck Foundation and Andrew W. Mellon Foundation provided fellowships for research at the Huntington Library in San Marino, California, during the summer of 1998. Thanks also to the Organization of American Historians and the Society of American Historians for recognizing and supporting this project early on. I am grateful to the Carter G. Woodson Institute for Afro-American and African Studies at the University of Virginia for a predoctoral fellowship during the last year of writing my dissertation.

Many, many thanks are due the staff of the National Archives of the United States. Without their expert and generous assistance, this project could not have been completed. I am especially grateful to Bill Creech, Wayne DeCesar, Robert Ellis, Candra Flanagan, David Foreman, Brenda French, Michael Meier, Michael Musick, Marc Rivera, Jody Scott, Aloha South, and Reginald Washington. Many thanks are due to

John White, Dick Schraeder, Mike Martin, and Susan Ballinger of Manuscripts, Wilson Library, UNC-CH, for sharing their knowledge of the University of North Carolina collections and for welcoming an old friend back to Chapel Hill. I must also acknowledge the excellent staff at the Alderman Library of the University of Virginia, especially Marie-Louise Kragh, Mike Plunkett, Regina Rush, and Rey Antonio. Tom and Betty Lowry, of the Index Project, shared their knowledge of Record Group 153. Leslie Rowland and Susan O'Donovan generously made available the resources of the Freedmen and Southern Society Project at the University of Maryland and guided me through this unique collection. Rachel DeLue, Jennifer Watts, and Jennifer Tucker helped me think through the historical dimensions of photographs and American art. Ruth Mitchell of the Maryland Historical Society patiently tracked down an obscure map despite a collectionwide reorganization. I had great conversations about archival resources with Gregg Kimball and John Kneebone at the Virginia State Library, and with Earl Ijames at the North Carolina State Archives. At the Old Court House Museum in Vicksburg I was lucky to be able to draw on the experience of Gordon Cotton, Jeff Giambrone, and (from afar) Chris Waldrep. Thanks are due to Ceil Hodges, who knew where to look in Hurston's writings, and to Gayle Schulman, who straightened out the tangled history of Charlottesville's slave auction block.

Research staff at the Smithsonian's National Museum of American History, especially Michael Harris and Ray Kondratas, generously shared their knowledge of the collections. Theresa Singleton of the Museum of Natural History helped me think through the implications of archaeology for historical writing. Pete Daniel has been a wonderful mentor, adviser, and friend long after my time at the Smithsonian. Thanks to Stephen Paczolt of the Geography and Map Division, Library of Congress, for locating several hard-to-find county maps. I found the photographs of southern Ghana on the suggestion of Erin Haney, who is preparing a study of the history of Akan photographers. Caroline Branney and Amanda Green graciously accommodated my research at the library of the Foreign and Commonwealth Office, London, as did Rebecca Engsberg, Ann DeVeaux, and Michael Hughes at the Quinnipiac University Law Library.

I am grateful to Philip D. Morgan, Joseph C. Miller, David Thelen, and three anonymous reviewers for the *Journal of American History* for their comments, which were extremely helpful in developing this work. The staff of the University of North Carolina Press has made the publication process truly enjoyable. I would especially like to thank Charles Grench, Kate Torrey, Amanda McMillan, and Mary Caviness. Helpful comments on earlier versions of Chapter 1 were given by Sara Berry, Philip D. Curtin, Michael Johnson, Bryan Callahan, Michel-Rolph Trouillot, Paul Trawick, and members of the Institute for Global Studies Seminar at Johns Hopkins. My research in Ghana would not have been possible without the help of the staff of the Ghana National Archives, especially Judith Botchway, Joseph Anim-Asante, Frank Abloh, and the director, C. K. Gadzekpo. My research on the history of Ghana was greatly enriched by conversations with Emmanuel Akyeampong, Nana Dr. Abiyie Boaten, Dr. Akosua Perbi, Nana Dr. Irene Odotei, Alistair Chisholm, Kelly Tucker, and Jemima Ritch-Adjei. As I wrote my dissertation, Simone Ameskamp, Herman Bennett, Reginald Butler, Max Edelson, Shelly Eversley, Jack P. Greene, Dirk Hartog, Marjoleine Kars, Anthony Kaye, John McKiernan-Gonzalez, Marya McQuirter, Zachary Morgan, Bill O'Donnell, Nell Painter, Judd Stitziel, Linda Tucker, Ron Walters, and the members of the seminars on nineteenth-century America and the American South at Johns Hopkins provided many helpful discussions and much-needed words of encouragement. My efforts to transform my dissertation into a book owe much to comments by David Brion Davis and Robert C. Forbes, Chris Brown, Hubert Ngatcha Njila, Maurie McInnis, Peter Onuf, Richard Roberts, Rebecca Scott, Paul Halliday, Reginald Butler, and contributions at a History Department workshop at the University of Virginia. Cindy Aron, Ed Ayers, Eugene Genovese, Grace Hale, Nancy McLean, Elizabeth Meyer, Michael Johnson, Sara Berry, Steven Hahn, Elizabeth Regosin, and an anonymous reader for the UNC Press read the whole manuscript with care and thoughtfulness. Some of them did it more than once! At critical moments late in the process, Ira Berlin and Walter Johnson gave unique comments about the "big picture." And I will never forget the stream of newspaper clippings that Penelope Baskerville, my mother, mailed to me over the past eight years: articles that sparked my thinking on swept yards, kinship, and many other topics.

A special thanks to Markus Goldstein, Erin Haney, Samuel Kattah Jr., Fred Knight, Earl Nkrumah Hadley, Natasha Gray, Peter Angong-Manu, Jemima Ritch-Adjei, and Chris and Barbara Udry for making my time in Ghana such a positive, unforgettable experience. My stay in California was richer for having gotten to know Bill Deverell, Jennifer Watts, David and Cindy Igler, Sharon Block, Cynthia VanZandt, Miriam Feldblum, Amy and Jack Meyers, Mark Wild, Clark Davis, and Cheryl Koos. I owe a lot to Paul Bertoni, Crystal Feimster, Suchi Gururaj, Will Jones, Elvis Lewis III, Ken Mack, Nandini Mani, Jason Plaks, Valerie Smith, Judd, Simone, Shelly, Marya, and Fred Wherry, and John McKiernan-Gonzalez for being so constantly thoughtful and understanding. Crystal kindly let me share her office at Yale's Department of African American Studies. I can't forget the late-night rap sessions, workshops, and the occasional road trip I shared with the incredible group at the University of Virginia's Woodson Institute during 1999–2002, including Reginald and Scot, Joseph Hellweg, Rosanne Adderley, Rolland and Cynthia Murray, Wende Marshall, Hanan Sabea, Scott Saul, and especially Wallace Best and Adrian Gaskins. I have treasured Reginald as a friend and mentor for four years now. Jennifer Tucker provided key comments at critical moments as this project took shape, and she has been a true friend through it all.

"Don't thank me," Uncle Ozzie always tells me, "thank your mother and father!" I know, I know. . . . But I also know why I am writing about family: it's all those times at 210 Birch and 166 Witherspoon, Wappingers Falls and Newport News, Ithaca and Iowa City, Newark, Paterson, and Woodbridge—times that showed me what family is all about and why it matters. So, my greatest thanks go to my family—Ailey, Mom (Penelope Baskerville) and Dad (Stephen Penningroth), Judy, Uncle Ozzie, Karen, Greg, Beth, Mike, Sharon, Steven, Michelle, Uncle Edwin, Jordan, Joshua, Mia, Alisha, Stephany, Danielle, Renee, Jackie, Mark, Jackie, Reggie, Martine, Jeff, Johnnie

Mae and Obie Mason, Grandma Mary and Grandma Charlotte, Aunt Ann, Uncle Phil, Petschie, Brigitte, Søren, Agneta, Robin, Lindsay, Rachel, Chris, Bob, and Susan—for the love, advice, and help they have given me all my life. And my greatest inspiration comes from those who have gone before—Nana and Uncle Tom, Pop-Pop, Grandma Yolanda, Aunt Jackie, and especially Uncle Craig—thank you.

Index

and, 32; genealogies and, 160; kinship-based power and, 176

Farmers: in Africa, 17, 20; "heirs' property" of, 20, 188, 266 (nn. 3, 5); trading by slaves with, 66; as sharecroppers, 144, 148, 151; tenant, 148, 152–53; crop disputes by, 150–54, 252 (nn. 106, 111), 253 (n. 117). *See also* Garden patches, slave

Farmers Home Administration, 266 (n. 5)

Feme covert, 180

Fences. *See* Open-range laws

Ferry services, 65, 67

"Fictive kinship," 86, 87

First African Church of Richmond, 101, 117–18

Fishermen, 17, 20, 65, 249 (n. 73)

Fitzgerald, Richard, 175

Fitzsimmons, Judy, 121

Florida, 46

Foraging, 1, 10, 74, 133 (*see also* Property: Civil War seizures of)

Forts, African, 17, 20, 23, 25

Fortune-tellers, 118, 238 (n. 42)

France, 17, 207 (n. 99)

Francis, Robert, 124

Frazier, Charles, 119

Frazier, Emily, 81, 85

Fredericksburg, Va., 82, 100–101

Freedmen's Bureau, 109–17, 121–24, 132, 151, 240 (n. 75), 241 (n. 77); marriage-related cases, 123, 181; child custody petitions, 167–68, 257–58 (n. 31); domestic violence cases, 180

Freedom, 4, 78, 191, 192; African slaves' view of, 13, 24, 27, 40, 43; American view of, 13, 43, 78; slaves' buying of, 45, 54–55. *See also* Emancipation

Freedpeople, 20, 78, 85, 90, 103; contraband camps and, 4–5; in Africa, 28–41, 203–4 (n. 44); legal constraints on, 55; property ownership by, 55, 144, 148, 185–86; claims com-

mission filings by, 70, 220 (n. 200); church's role for, 102–3; post–Civil War legal system and, 109, 111–30, 142, 143–44, 150–52, 181–82; schools for, 115, 157, 236 (n. 7); contracts and, 142–43, 151, 169, 171–72, 245 (n. 20); postemancipation informal economy and, 155–58; trading by, 155–58; land's importance to, 158–61; postemancipation family concerns of, 163–86

Freehold rights, 41

Freeman, David, 182

Freeman, Rosa, 181–82

Friarson, Columbus, 174

Frierson, Paul, 180

Frogmore plantation, 239 (n. 63)

Fugitive slaves, 10, 28, 57

Fuller, Samuel, 97

Funerals, 34–35, 155, 206 (n. 77)

Ga, 17, 203 (n. 42)

Gandu, 209 (n. 17)

Gang labor system, 46, 47, 51, 52, 53, 59, 250 (n. 83)

Garden patches, slave, 47–51, 53, 56, 59, 77; family members' tending of, 83, 84, 146–49, 165–66, 224 (n. 24); postemancipation changes in, 143, 146, 150

Gender issues, 53–54, 63–64, 164, 198 (nn. 32, 33). *See also* Loud talking; Men; Women

Genealogies, 31–33, 41, 42, 136, 160

Georgia, 59, 66, 133, 149, 153, 158, 252 (n. 106); Union army in, 1–3; slaves' informal economy in, 7, 60, 68; claims commission filings in, 10, 70, 73–74, 76; post–Civil War land set aside in, 144. *See also* Low Country

Ghana (formerly Gold Coast), 9, 10, 11, 13–44; court system, 23–24, 25; funerals, 34, 206 (n. 77); emancipation, 41–44; customary law, 207 (n. 100). *See also* Gold Coast Colony

(n. 54); slaves' informal economy, 7,
46–48, 49, 59, 63, 68; claims com-
mission filings, 74, 220 (n. 202)
Lowe, Clarinda, 95
Lyell, Charles, 65
Lynch, John Roy, 114
Lynchings, 69

Macbeth, August, 153, 156
Mack, Henry, 119, 173
Mallard, Robert Quarterman, 103
Mallard, Thomas, 1, 84
Malnutrition, 56
Mansah, Abinabah, 32
Maples, Francis, 229 (n. 94)
Maria (slave), 98, 117
Marketing: by slaves, 61–69; by freedpeople, 145, 146, 153, 155, 157, 166
Marks, property, 32, 94–95, 151, 189,
251 (n. 96)
Marriage: emancipation and, 9, 164,
176–83, 263–64 (n. 115); to enslaved women, 20; between people
of different nations, 23, 25, 269
(n. 20); between Christians and non-
Christians, 24; spousal work contributions, 82–83, 104, 176–80; property
issues and, 83, 103–7, 163, 176, 179–
82; misconceptions about blacks and,
114–15; extralegal processes and,
117, 182–84; legal system and, 123,
181–82. See also Domestic violence
Maryland, 59, 65, 160
Masters, 10, 42, 94–95, 103; slaves' relationship with, 6, 7–8, 10, 43, 79–
80, 200–201 (n. 5); slave informal
economy and, 7, 47–61, 66, 69, 78,
108, 139–40, 192; in Africa, 22, 24,
27–31, 33–36, 40, 247 (n. 54); views
on inheritance by slaves, 24, 43, 89–
90; paternalism and, 43; views on
kinship with blacks, 43, 108; slave
property and, 45, 80, 91, 137, 139,
141, 208 (n. 3); slave hiring out by,

53–54, 81, 83; brutality of, 57, 58,
78, 79; plantation layout and, 91–92,
96, 107; post–Civil war expectations
of, 142–43, 185. See also Plantations:
owners of
Matrilineal inheritance, 203 (n. 42),
207 (n. 94)
Matthews, Thomas, 229 (n. 100)
Maxwell, Prince, 143
McCaskell, Julia Ann, 98
McConnell, John, 48
McIntosh, Matilda, 85, 225 (n. 41)
McIver, William, 51
McLaughlin, Henrietta, 96
McQueen, James, 73
McShane, Burwell, 88
Memphis, Tenn., 145, 146, 260 (n. 62)
Men, 20, 164, 198 (n. 33); marriage
and property and, 83, 103–7, 176–
77, 179–82; domestic violence and,
180, 182–83, 263 (nn. 108, 109),
264 (n. 118)
Mensah, Abinabah, 32, 34
Methodist churches, 102, 233 (n. 157)
Middle Passage, 6, 7, 131, 190
Middleton, Simon, 85
Migration, 59, 145–46, 173–75, 190
Mikell, York, 153
Military courts. See Provost courts
Militias, 69, 145
Miller, James, 100
Miller, Lewis, 56
Millwood plantation (S.C.), 146, 148
"Miscegenation," 269 (n. 20)
Missionaries, 17, 115
Mississippi, 59, 68, 120, 122, 133, 241
(n. 84); claims commission filings,
10, 70, 72, 74
Missouri, 48
Mitchell, Joshua, 178
Money: Civil War and, 4–5, 61, 253
(n. 122); slave earnings and, 51–
54, 56, 60, 65–66, 81, 97–98, 208
(n. 3), 212 (n. 55); loans from family,

84, 166; protection of, 97–98; con-
jure and, 101–2; black church contri-
butions, 102–3; misconceptions
about blacks and, 115, 140; out-of-
court settlements and, 125
Monroe, Clarissa, 195 (n. 4)
Monroe, Crawford, 224 (n. 37)
Monroe, John, 224 (n. 37)
Monroe, Julius, 184, 265 (n. 134)
Moradores, 250 (n. 83)
Morgan, George, 126
Morris, Gallant, 175–76
Moses (slave), 85, 117, 225 (n. 43)
Moss, Edmund, 68–69, 129
Murray, William, 213 (n. 88)
Muslims, 17
Mutual aid societies, 102–3, 161

Natchez, Miss., 62, 63, 66–67, 122
National Association of Colored
Women, 188
Native Americans, 220 (n. 201), 221
(n. 204)
Native assessors, 23–24, 31, 37–38
Neal, Sim, 68
Nelson, Dinah, 117
Netherlands, 17
Newell, Joshua, 185
New Orleans, La., 62, 63
Nichols, D. B., 4–5
Nigeria, 25, 247 (n. 54)
"Nigger house," 96
North Carolina, 50, 59, 117; court rul-
ings, 48, 94, 95, 214 (n. 91), 219
(n. 182)
Northrup, Solomon, 51, 56

Odd Fellows' Lodge, 117
Olmsted, Frederick Law, 52, 53, 54, 57,
58, 59, 61, 63, 65–66
Omanhene. *See* Chiefs, Akan
Open-range laws, 143
Orphans, 175–76, 261 (n. 75)
Osgood, Rachel, 95–96

Osgood, Samuel, 95
Overseers, 58, 59, 66, 92, 218 (n. 166)
Overwork, 51, 52–53, 56, 84. *See also*
Time, economy of

Pack, Alfred, 125
Page, Horace, 55, 208 (n. 6), 213
(n. 88)
Parker, Allen, 213 (n. 89)
Parson, Phoebe, 119
Partition sales, 266 (n. 5)
Partnerships, 85, 121–22
Patents, 69
Paternalism, 43, 129
Patriarchy, 168. *See also* Gender issues
Patrilineal inheritance, 203 (n. 42)
Patton, Martha, 48, 83, 104
Pawns, 22–23, 202 (nn. 24, 25); inher-
itance by, 24; British outlawing of,
25–26; kinship and, 30, 41; testi-
mony by, 33; burial practices and,
35–36
Pearson, Elizabeth Ware, 118, 148
Perbi, Akosua, 39, 40
Perkins, Maria, 79, 80
Peter, David, 178
Philadelphia Savings Fund Society, 78
Picksley, John, 123
Pierce, Edward, 5
Pigs, 1, 2, 4, 6, 61, 81, 82, 83, 86, 87,
90, 93–96, 105–6, 115, 123, 125,
127, 151
Piggins, 51
Plantations: Civil War seizures of, 1–3,
133–36; owners of, 3–4, 43, 142–
43 (*see also* Masters); labor systems,
7, 46–47, 50–53, 59, 80, 84, 250
(n. 83); slaves' access to land and,
47–49, 59–60; harvest season, 51–
52, 56; slaves' economic contribution
to, 55–57, 191; layout of, 91–92, 96,
107, 128, 146, 148–50, 161, 250
(n. 83); crop disputes and, 150–54
Plantation stores, 56–57

Poor funds, 103
Porters, 19, 65, 201 (n. 12)
Portugal, 17
"Private crops," 49, 150
Property, 79–109, 188–92; loss compensation (*see* Southern Claims Commission); Civil War seizures of, 1–5, 73–74, 121, 133–36, 138–39, 196 (n. 10), 229 (n. 94); slaves' ownership of, 3–7, 9–12, 45–47, 50–51, 53–60, 67–70, 72, 76–80, 108–9, 115–16, 136–41, 191–92, 208 (n. 3); slaves as, 6, 8, 14, 22, 23, 45, 132, 133–34, 136, 142, 191; emancipation and issues of, 9, 11, 26–27, 30–31, 33–34, 36, 40, 42, 133–34, 185–86; claims cases, 10–11, 14, 69, 199–200 (n. 39), 208 (n. 3), 219 (n. 182), 225 (n. 43); legal theories on, 11, 24, 132, 161, 244 (n. 2); African perspectives on, 14, 15, 20–21, 27–38, 40, 189; kinship and, 15, 21–22, 24–25, 28–36, 39, 41, 42, 85–89, 108–9, 158–61, 185–86, 190, 192; social relationships and, 15, 42, 44, 80, 82, 86, 103, 108–9, 129, 136–38, 154–58, 161, 185–86, 189–92; laws on, 22, 23, 41, 45, 55, 68–69, 131–33, 136, 219 (n. 182); disputes over, 26–36, 42, 107–8, 150, 163; freehold rights and, 41; multiple claims on, 41, 246 (n. 31); U.S.–Gold Coast comparisons, 41–44; animals owned as, 47, 93–95, 97, 105, 125, 140, 151; freedpeople's ownership of, 55, 144, 148, 185–86; master-slave relationship and, 79, 80, 91; family and, 82–85, 89, 103–9, 137–38, 163; marriage and, 83, 103–7, 176–77, 179–82; work traded for, 85; inheritance of, 89–91, 105, 107; display and acknowledgment of, 91–97, 99–100, 107, 108, 116, 125, 128, 136, 137, 146, 148, 149–51, 154–55, 161, 189; storage of, 96–97; black church and, 99–

103; post–Civil War legal system and, 111–16, 121, 123–30, 142, 143–44, 150–52; misconceptions about blacks and, 114–15, 129–30, 137, 237 (n. 23); receipts for, 125–26, 135–36; post–Civil War reconceptualization of, 131–61. *See also* Cotton; Land
Provost courts, 109, 111–13, 116, 120–25, 132, 151, 181
Provost marshals, 112, 116, 121
Public argument, 99, 111, 116, 118–20, 124, 238 (n. 45)
Public language, 63–64

Quarterman, Jacob, 47, 97
Quotah, Quow, 24
Qwacoe, Eccra, 32, 205 (n. 69)

Race, 43, 129–30, 192. *See also* Stealing; Violence: white-on-black; White supremacy
Rape, 43, 120
Raymond, Charles, 98, 102
Reconstruction, 78, 109, 111–30, 142–44, 150–52
Reddick, Charles, 183
"Redeemer" laws, 152
Republican Leagues, 116
Resistance, 7, 8, 189, 200–201 (n. 5), 267 (n. 10)
Rhodes, Danger, 81
Rice, 46, 48
Richardson, Thomas, 87
Richmond, Va., 68, 101, 145
Rifle corps, 69
Rivers, informal economy and, 64–67
Rivers, Prince, 102–3
Roberts, Linda, 138
Robinson, George, 180
Robinson, Lavinia, 180
Robinson, Sarah, 181
Roper, Moses, 57
Ross, Frances, 119, 183
Ross, William, 119, 183

Ruffin, Edmund, 52–53
Rum, 34–35

Saccoom, Cobbina, 35
Salt, 61, 216 (n. 137)
Sam, Quamin, 35
Sam, Quamina, 30
Sanders, Anderson, 117
Sarbah, John Mensah, 23, 37
Savannah, Ga., 46, 63, 67
Saville, Julie, 158
Saxton, Rufus, 114
Schools, 17, 115, 157, 236 (n. 7)
Scott, Hester, 163
Scott, William, 34
Sea Islands, 120, 177, 266 (n. 5)
Self-hired slaves, 53, 54, 81
"Sense," importance of, 184, 265
    (n. 137)
Sex-crime laws, 239 (n. 61)
Sexual abuse, 261 (n. 75). See also Rape
Sexual relations, slave-master, 43
Sharecroppers, 144, 148, 151
Shaw, Nate, 161
Sherman, William T., 1, 5, 74, 144
Shoes, 100, 232 (n. 142)
Simmons, Isaac, 155
Simons, Prince, 180
Slaughter, Henry, 229 (n. 94)
Slave drivers, 80, 222 (n. 3)
Slaveowners. See Masters
Slavery: abolition in Africa of, 13, 14,
    25–27, 37, 40, 42, 43, 164, 185–86,
    256 (n. 4); property laws and, 22, 23;
    pawnship vs., 22–23, 202 (n. 25);
    body markings of, 32; customary law
    and, 37; U.S.–Gold Coast compar-
    isons, 41–44; customs related to,
    59–60, 69. See also Masters
Slaves: garden patches of (see Garden
    patches, slave); property ownership
    by (see Property: slaves' ownership
    of); Civil War and, 1–5, 57, 61, 73–
    74, 170, 258 (n. 46); property seized
    from, 1–5, 73–74, 121, 138–39, 196

(n. 10), 229 (n. 94); household property of, 2, 4, 103–7, 176–77; freedom's importance to, 4, 78; contraband camps and, 4–5; in South
America, 6, 7; in Caribbean region,
6, 7, 20, 43, 118–19, 211 (n. 33);
masters' relationship with, 6, 7–8,
10, 79–80, 200–201 (n. 5); informal
economy of, 6–7, 46–69, 77, 78,
103, 108, 139–40, 142, 192; as property, 6, 8, 14, 22, 23, 45, 132, 133–
34, 136, 142, 191; marketing and
trading by, 6, 46, 47, 60–69, 78, 85;
entrepreneurship by, 6, 51; in Africa,
8–9, 13–44; as fugitives, 10, 28, 57;
kinship and, 11, 13–14, 15, 21–22,
24–25, 27–36, 39, 41–43, 85–89,
108–9, 185; ancestry and, 14, 31–36,
39–42, 205–6 (n. 71), 208 (n. 105);
as porters, 19, 65, 201 (n. 12); inheritance by, 24, 30, 43, 89–91, 105, 107,
247 (n. 50); property disputes and,
26–36, 42, 107–8; native vs. imported, 31, 204–5 (n. 58); burial
practices of, 35–36; paternalist ideology and, 43, 129; insurrections by,
45; buying of freedom by, 45, 54–55;
Sunday labor and, 47, 51, 52, 57, 208
(n. 3); animal ownership by, 47, 93–
95, 97, 105, 125, 140, 151; access to
land and, 47–49, 59–60; time's avail-
ability to, 49–54, 57–60, 77, 211
(n. 33); skilled work and, 51, 77;
money earned by, 51–54, 56, 60, 65,
97–98, 208 (n. 3), 212 (n. 55); coal
mining and, 52–53; factory work by,
52–53; overwork by, 52–53, 56, 84;
hired work by, 53–54, 80–82, 103;
separation of families of, 54, 57, 79,
88, 188, 267 (n. 9); guardians for,
55; stealing by, 56, 57, 67, 68, 91,
214 (n. 104), 219–20 (n. 187), 227
(n. 78), 229 (n. 96); clothing of, 56,
57, 100, 232 (nn. 138, 142); whipping of, 57, 58, 78; forced migration

Taxes, land, 134
Taylor, J. D., 30–31, 33–34
Taylor, John, 179
Teachers, 113, 115, 157–58, 236 (n. 7)
Tenant farmers, 148, 152–53
Tennessee, 70, 117, 145, 146, 260 (n. 62)
Texas, 70, 122, 168, 220 (n. 199)
Theft. *See* Stealing
Thigpen, Louisa, 184
Thompson, Charlotte, 87
Thornton, Taylor, 73
Time, economy of, 49–54, 57–60, 77, 211 (n. 33)
Tindall, James, 169
Tobacco, 48, 52, 53
Towne, Laura, 114, 157, 261 (n. 75)
Trade: by slaves, 6, 20, 46, 47, 60–69, 78; Fante states and, 17, 19, 25; women and, 20, 63–64; slave exchange networks and, 85; post–Civil War, 155–58. *See also* "Legitimate commerce"; Slave trade
Transportation, 64
Traynor, Richard, 97
Treasury Department, U.S., 135–36
"Tribes": customary law and, 14, 38
Truck patches. *See* Garden patches
Turner, Benjamin Sterling, 5, 55, 81, 208 (n. 6)

Union army, 43, 65, 74, 118, 126; property seizure by, 1–5, 73–74, 121, 133–36, 138–39, 196 (n. 10), 229 (n. 94); contraband camps and, 4–5; freedpeople and, 142–43; labor companies and, 258 (n. 46). *See also* Provost courts
Urban League, 188
Urban migration, 145–46

Van Buren, Martin, 191
Vandross, Amos, 175–76, 261 (n. 80)
Verkins, Sarah, 105
Verkins, William, 105

Vesey, Denmark, 45–46
Vested rights, 132–33
Vicksburg, Miss., 74, 145, 249 (n. 76)
"Vigilance Committees," 69
Violence, 122–23; brutality of masters', 57, 58, 78, 79; white-on-black, 120–21, 122, 146–48, 249 (n. 76), 260 (n. 62), 263 (n. 109); black-on-black, 122, 260 (n. 62). *See also* Domestic violence
Virginia, 53, 55, 59, 66, 145; claims commission filings, 70; Freedmen's Bureau courts, 122
Voting rights, 111

Wadkins, Phillis, 174, 260 (n. 72)
Wagons, 5, 47, 64, 97, 107, 139
Waite, Paul, 163, 164
Waite, Sarah, 163, 164
Walker, Caroline, 86–87
Walker, Madam C. J. (Sarah Breedlove), 175
Walker, Minksie, 164
Waller, Tom, 146
Walthour, Abraham, 105
War Claims Commission, 221 (n. 204)
Ward, Malinda, 230 (n. 108)
Ward, Mary, 182
Warren County, Miss., 74, 153
Washington, Jack, 166
Watts, Samuel, 33
Weddings, 106, 107
West Virginia, 70, 220 (n. 199)
Wharton, Mary, 33
Whipping of slaves, 57, 58, 78
White supremacy, 12, 121, 182
Williams, Lewis, 54
Williams, Sam, 76
Williamson, Charles, 90
Wilson, James, 125
Wilson, John, 87
Winn, William, 130
Witchcraft, 37. *See also* Conjure
Women, 8, 20, 53; as market traders, 20, 63–64; slave ancestry knowledge

of, 33, 205–6 (n. 71); rape of, 43,
120; loud talking and, 63–64, 183–
84; marriage and property and, 82–
83, 103–7, 176–77, 179–82, 263–
64 (n. 115); work contributions by,
82–83, 104, 176–80; property ownership by, 104–5, 181, 220 (n. 201);
postemancipation gender relations
and, 164, 176–77. *See also* Domestic
violence

Work, 9, 13, 85, 192; hiring out for, 53–
54, 81, 83, 103, 164, 257–58 (n. 31);
by family, 82–84, 104, 164–69, 176–
80, 224 (n. 29), 250 (n. 82)
Wyat, Bayly, 158

Yaboah, Quessi, 35
Young, Amanda, 85
Young, John, 82